MARINUS ANTHONY VAN DER SLUIJS

TRADITIONAL COSMOLOGY

THE GLOBAL MYTHOLOGY OF COSMIC CREATION AND DESTRUCTION

Volume Six

Miscellaneous Themes

All-Round Publications
Vancouver, 2018

copyright © Marinus Anthony van der Sluijs 2018

published 2018 by All-Round Publications

All rights reserved. No part of this publication may be reproduced or transmitted in any form or by any means, electronic or mechanical, including photocopying, recording, or by information storage and retrieval system, without the prior written permission of the publisher, except in the case of brief quotations embodied in critical articles and reviews.

first edition

ISBN 978-1-9994383-1-9

contents

editorial notes		III
acknowledgments		VIII

PART VI: MISCELLANEOUS THEMES

33*, 38*	giant or malevolent beings	1
34*	union and shared language with animals	3
300*	collapse of the sky	5
312*	flood, fire, a dragon and battle	9
332*	the column disrupted amid earthquakes	12
339*	disruption of the column as separation	13
343*	celestial arc	14
359*	altered motion of stars and planets	19
369*	dismembered body parts as miscellaneous entities	26
372*	inversion of the earth	27
407*	abundant vegetation	30
448	absence of regular seasons	33
449	cold period	38
450	the morning or evening star as a comet	50
451	hot flood	72
452	humans placed above other animals	75
453	a long object, flood and fire	78
454	a comet, flood and fire	78
455	cosmic impact	83
456	rock art produced by mythical beings	99
457	inversion of sky and earth	110
458	rain of flammable materials	117
459	fossils as mythical beings	121
	Europe	121
	Asia	123
	Australia	124
	America	127
460	volcanic eruption	131
461	abstract concepts acquired in containers	136
462	drowned land	139
	Europe	139
	Asia	141
	Australia	142

	Africa	144
	South America	144
463	anthropomorphic creator or culture hero	146
464	edible sky	146
465	ugly male	148
466	appearance of the sun, light or heat at elevation or dissipation of low or collapsed sky	149

quotations in other languages 153

bibliography 162

index 185

editorial notes

The 447 themes identified in the previous 5 volumes of *Traditional Cosmology* (2011; 2018) are referred to in the form "§ ...", where volume 1 covers §§1-69, volume 2 §§70-177, volume 3 §§178-299, volume 4 §§300-425 and volume 5 §§426-447. The present volume offers a miscellany of additional mythological sources.

Much of the material presented here illustrates new motifs (§§448-466). Themes marked by an asterisk, such as §34*, were already introduced in the earlier volumes, but are supplemented with new examples, both in this volume and in volume 5. In contrast to §§1-425, there is no suggestion of an internal chronological order in the arrangement of the new themes; although for creation myths and in combination with §§1-425 such an order very likely exists, it largely remains to be determined. Suggestions to this end as also regarding the origin of these traditions are offered in forthcoming volumes entitled *On the Origin of Myth*.

In line with a current trend, relatively small ethnic groups are identified by their endonyms instead of exonyms which may be more familiar, but are often derogatory or antiquated:

ENDONYM:	EXONYM:	ENDONYM:	EXONYM:
			Indians
		Nuxalk	Bella Coola
Diné	Navajo or Navaho	Romani	Gypsies
Haudenosaunee	Iroquois	Sahtú	North Slavey,
Huni Kuin	Kaxinawá or Cashinauá	Sakha	Hare or Hareskin Yakut
Inuit	Eskimo	Selk'nam	Ona
Khanty	Ostyak	T'atsaot'ine	Yellowknives
Mansi	Vogul	Tohono O'odham	Papago
Mapuche	Araucanians	Ukomno'm	Yuki
Nanai	Gold(i)	Yámana	Yaghan or Yahgan
Niimíipu	Nez Percés		
Nlaka'pamux	Thompson River		

No use is made of titles granted by religious, monarchic or other political authorities which imply social or moral superiority of the glorified individual, such as 'Rabbi', 'Saint', 'Reverend', 'Father', *'Reverendus Pater'* ('R. P.'), 'Brother', 'Sir', 'Major', 'Justice', 'Lord' and 'Don' (Spanish). The sole exception is when the title is indispensable for identification of the person in question, such as 'Rabbi Isaac'.

British orthography is followed. Unless antiquated spellings such as 'praesent', 'phaenomenon', 'aera', 'saecular', 'poenal', 'musaeum', 'primaeval', 'mediaeval', 'coelestial', 'sphaere', 'aequal', 'aequation' and 'paediatric' are restored, consistency demands that Greek *archaeo-* and *palaeo-* as the first member of a composite noun are spelled *archeo-* and *paleo-*, respectively. An exception is granted for these two cases, based on convention and the sensitivity of the issue in the archaeological world. The unfortunate result is eyesores of the type 'palaeosecular'. In archaic ethnonyms such as 'Aegyptians', 'Aethiopians', 'Chaldaeans', 'Sabaeans', 'Mycenaeans', 'Aramaeans' and 'Judaeans', the diphthong is not spelled, but in Latin names of individuals it is: 'Bar-Hebraeus', 'Linnaeus'.

In neoclassical composite nouns, the final vowel of the first member – which grammarians lacking a historical-linguistic background often treat as a meaningless 'connecting vowel' – ought to be dropped if the second member begins with a vowel; just like 'arthro-' + '-itis' becomes 'arthritis' (not 'arthroitis') and 'leuko-' + '-haemia' becomes 'leukaemia' (not 'leukohaemia'), so 'Mesoamerica' should be 'Mesamerica', 'archaeoastronomy' 'archaeastronomy', 'psychoanalysis' 'psychanalysis' and 'psychoelectric' 'psychelectric'. Eschewing pedantry, the conventional forms, however repugnant to a classically trained ear, have nevertheless been maintained.

In dates, an italicised *c* before a date stands for "*circa*".

Geographic coordinates are notated in degrees and minutes rounded off to whole numbers. The four cardinal directions are abbreviated to 'N', 'E', 'S' and 'W'.

Throughout this work, double quotation marks ("...") are reserved for literal quotations. Single quotation marks ('...') serve the same purpose inside quotations, but are also used to signal special terminology or non-standard usage of words. In quotations, all text in italics, underlined or bold style are faithful to the original, except where noted otherwise in the accompanying footnote. Square brackets ([...]) mark interpolations reproduced from the original or my own interpolation of the conventional interjection "*sic*". To improve legibility, it is not noted when adjustments are made to the division of a quoted texts into paragraphs.

Sources composed in foreign languages are quoted in English translation. Existing English translations are cited wherever they were available, reliable and reasonably up-to-date; when marked by the symbol (•), the original wording is supplied in an appendix. In other cases, indicated by the symbol (•), a new translation is provided, framed by single quotation marks – except when the quotation is indented – and with the original wording relegated to the same appendix.

Untranslated words in a foreign language, other than proper nouns, are only given in the main text where they illuminate the discussion; they are offered without quotation marks in italicised transcription, not in the original writing system.

For each language, transcriptions are phonemic, not allophonic. For example, as the fricative [f] was an allophone of [p] during the Biblical stage of the Hebrew language, the Hebrew letter פ (*pē*) is always rendered as *p*. Accordingly, the Hebrew word for 'book, scroll' (ספר) is rendered as *sēpɛr*, not *sēphɛr*. This preference is not obvious, as the Masoretic system of punctuation – which arose centuries afterwards – marked allophones. The polytonic orthography notating ancient Greek is carried over into transcriptions as it was employed since the 3rd century BCE. By contrast, accents and length marks are not given for Latin words, as they never were by native speakers themselves. For the sake of consistency, I have deliberately digressed from the common practice in Assyriology to reproduce Sumerian text in non-italic type. Following convention, the glottal stop [ʔ] or *alif* in Arabic words, normally transliterated as ', is not spelled in prevocalic positions at the beginning of words: *abū*, not *'abū* ('father'). By contrast, the corresponding Hebrew *'ālɛp* is always spelled: *'ɛrɛṣ* ('earth').

Proper nouns denoting well-known ancient Egyptian, Hebrew or classical individuals or places are spelled conventionally, not according to their original forms:

CONVENTIONAL:	AUTHENTIC:
Ra	Rʿ(.w)
Abraham	ʾAbrāhām
Enoch	Ḥănōk
Isaiah	Yəšaʿyāhū
Joshua ben Levi	Yəhōšūaʿ bɛn Lēvī
Judah bar Ezekiel	Yəhūdā bar Yəḥɛzqēl
Noah	Noaḥ
Yahweh	Yahwẹ

Aphrodite	Aphrodítē
Herakles	Heraklḗs
Hesperos	Hésperos
Kronos	Krónos
Ogyges	Ōgýgēs
Pandora	Pandṓra
Phaethon	Phaéthōn
Plato	Plátōn
Prometheus	Promētheús
Strabo	Strábōn
Pliny	Plinius

For less familiar classical names, Latinised forms take precedence over Greek ones: 'Theo', not 'Theōn'. In the case of a post-medieval Western author publishing under a Latinised name, his ordinary name in the native language – or hers, as the case may perhaps be – is used in the main text and the references, while the Latin name is added between square brackets ([...]) behind the native name in the respective entry in the bibliography.

Ancient authors from most cultures, including Jewish, Arabic and Indian ones, are generally identified by their full names, because they are relatively unknown to a wider public. Because the full names of Arabic authors are often long, they are only given upon the first mention of the author in a chapter, after which the best known abbreviated form of the name is used. For classical authors, the surname usually suffices: 'Cicero', not 'Marcus Tullius Cicero'. When an actual surname is not known, qualifiers such as geographic designations are only used where confusion might arise, as between Philo of Byblus and Philo of Alexandria, or when the writer is relatively unknown, like Theopompus of Chios; Herodotus of Halicarnassus is famous, hence simply 'Herodotus'.

Titles of older written works mentioned in the text or notes are consistently spelled in italic type. This includes books with a clear author, such as *De Civitate Dei* or *Pharsalia*, and other literary compositions and compilations, such as the *Book of the Dead* or the *Iliad*. For the benefit of a wider audience, titles of older foreign texts are given in the original language, followed between brackets by a translation into English: *De Rerum Natura* (*On the Nature of Things*). In cases of ancient works for which the English title is composed of words cognate with the ones found in the original title, only the English title is given: *Theogony*, not *Theogonia* (*Theogony*). The titles of works written in Greek or Latin are supplied even if no other works of the same author are known or extant, contrary to classicist convention: thus 'Strabo, *Geography*' instead of just 'Strabo'. Nor are these titles abbreviated, as classicists ordinarily prefer, but they are cited in full: *Meteorology* rather than *Met.*. For books of the Hebrew and Christian Bible only the standard English titles, usually based on Latin or Latinised Greek ones, are used: *Genesis*, not *Bərēšīt* (*In the Beginning*). Author's names are omitted in the case of some spurious traditional attributions of works to often legendary individuals:

TITLE:	TRADITIONAL AUTHOR:
1 *Enoch* (*Ethiopic Enoch*) (Hebrew)	Enoch (3rd to 1st century BCE)
Genesis to *Deuteronomy* (Hebrew)	Moses (Mošē; mid-15th century BCE)
Mahābhārata (Hindū)	Vyāsa (2nd millennium BCE?)
Revelation of John (Greek)	John the Apostle or the Evangelist (1st century CE)
Songs of Dzitbalché (Maya)	Ah Bam (c1440 CE)

A few common Latin terms are italicised and abbreviated: *et al.* (*et alii*), *cf.* (*confer*), *e. g.* (*exempli gratia*), *viz.* (*videlicet*), *i. e.* (*id est*), *fl.* (*floruit*), *s. v.* (*sub voce*) and *vs.* (*versus*). 'In' is always used instead of *apud*. The Latin imperative *confer* ('*cf.*'), literally 'bring together', recommends the perusal of another work in the implicit meanings of both 'see' and 'compare'. Accordingly, it is used in both senses. The abbreviation '*et al.*' is reserved for publications with a minimum of 3 contributors.

In cases where a work was written, presented or published – perhaps in a different language – in an earlier year than the year of the cited publication, the original year is for clarification sometimes added between brackets after the cited year: "Muck 1978 (1956)".

Date ranges given for the recording of traditional information – for example "recorded 1810-1814" – mean that the recording either lasted throughout that period or occurred at some unspecified time within it. Dates provided for 'personal communication' may vary by a day in each direction, due to differences in time zones between myself and the correspondent, between myself at the time of contact and at the time of citing, or both.

Finally, in the bibliography no distinction is made in titles between italic and normal script, except in the case of botanical or zoological names following Linnaean taxonomy, names of sea-going vessels, foreign words and titles embedded in titles. When of a series only one volume without a separate title is cited, its number is placed inside the brackets. An elevated number following the year of publication, as in "1986^2", refers to the specific edition that was consulted. And because it is customary in eastern Asia to place one's family name before one's personal name at all times, no comma is placed between the surname and the personal name in citations with Chinese, Korean or Japanese authors, while the personal name is spelled in full to help identify the author in publications where the first name was mistakenly treated as the surname.

acknowledgments

Without the continuous magnanimous support of the Mainwaring Archive Foundation, much of the material presented in these volumes would still be languishing on dusty library shelves, physical or digital, while the concept of a global template for traditional cosmologies, comprising scores of counterintuitive motifs, would remain embryonic and poorly substantiated. I offer my heartfelt thanks to this enlightened organisation.

The University of Pennsylvania Museum of Archaeology and Anthropology (Philadelphia, Pennsylvania, United States of America) graciously continued to acknowledge my research in the position of a Consulting Scholar.

In addition, I am deeply indebted to my comrade Ev Cochrane for eagle-eyed proofreading, providing astute comments with an admirable degree of patience and years of discussion and note-sharing. My late friend and compatriot Dr. Johan B. Kloosterman, too, generously shared sources and interpretations with me, including the Mbuti traditions of earth inversion. As I later found out from the research notes which he bequeathed to me, he had also been aware of the Huni Kuin myth of the inversion of sky and earth, provided in a 19th-century Portuguese source with tricky wording which his daughter Jessica and Dr. Els Lagrou helped me decipher.

Others generously shared of their knowledge and time. Dr. Peter Bisschop offered an improved translation of a sentence in the *Matsya Purāṇa*. Thor Conway supplied background information about his field work among the Ojibwe. Alfred H. Qöyawayma discussed the unreliability of Frank Waters' *Book of the Hopi*. Art Wolfe clarified the source of the Udege myth on the two suns. And Dr. Yu Yohan and Dr. James Grayson advised on editions of the Korean shamanic myth.

Just as essential as these diverse intellectual contributions was the practical support of my wife, Seong Hee Jo, who designed the covers of this series and helped me to realise the dream of being a 'travelling scholar'.

PART VI

MISCELLANEOUS THEMES

33*, 38*
giant or malevolent beings

THE BELIEF in an extinct race of *giant and often malevolent beings* – composed of humans, other animals or a combination of both – was practically universal. A sizeable subset of traditions in which such creatures are linked with fossils is treated under a separate heading (§459).

Legends involving the former existence of giant kangaroos circulated in various parts of Australia, for example among the Nawu people (around Port Lincoln, South Australia).[1] So did stories about giant birds. A native group in western Victoria, quite likely the Djabwurung, recalled a time "long ago, when the volcanic hills were in a state of eruption" (§460) and "some very large birds, which were incapable of flight, and resembled emus" still roamed the land:

> They lived long ago, when the volcanic hills were in a state of eruption. The native name for them is 'meeheeruung parrinmall' – 'big emu', and they are described, hyperbolically, as so large that their 'heads were as high as the hills', and so formidable that a kick from one of them would kill a man. … The last specimen of this extinct bird was seen near the site of Hamilton. In all probability, skeletons will be some day found …[2]

The demise of these ancient beings was often believed to have been collective and violent, involving one or more of a range of natural disasters such as earthquakes, hurricanes, sustained darkness, flood, fire and lightning (§§300-313). In an account from the Diné (Four Corners Region), a pair of heroes sets about cleansing the world of "great giants" and other monsters, marking the fifth destruction of the world:

> Naiyenesgony and Tobaidischinni went over the earth slaying all enemies. … they said, '… There are people around the world eating our

---

[1] Cawthorne 1880s: preface. Towards the end of the story, the twin heroes transform into mammals. The myth reads like an Australian version of the common theme of 'twin heroes slaying monsters', of which the feats of Xbalanque and Hunahpu, related by the Quiché Maya (Guatemala; §§444, 460), provide another example. For a tradition from the Wiradjuri involving giant kangaroos, see van der Sluijs 2011a: 140-141.

[2] recorded 1840-1900, in Dawson 1881: 92-93. On the volcanism, compare §460. Hamilton is in southwestern Victoria.

people (the Navajo). Some of these people are great giants and some are as small as flies; we wish to kill them with lightning.' The sun ... gave them lightning with which to destroy all enemies, and a great stone knife. They then went over the world. Naiyenesgony killed with the lightning arrows and Tobaidischinni scalped with his knife.[3]

In some instances, indigenous speakers familiar with prehistoric species recognised by palaeontologists featured these in their expression of traditional stories. Although this will at times have been a fanciful addition, the more common motivation will have been their belief that the scientific reconstruction of such extinct animals corresponded to the characteristics assigned to the pertinent creatures in native lore. An example is a tradition from the Potawatomi (central North America) according to which mastodons and mammoths were annihilated by the culture hero before he retreated from the affairs of humans:

> During his different excursions over the surface of the earth, Nanaboojoo killed all such animals as were hurtful to us, as the mastodon, the mammoth, etc.[4]

Caution is urged in contexts where the meaning of the word 'mammoth' is ambiguous. For example, a chief of the Tuscarora (between North Carolina and New York) supplied some Haudenosaunee accounts of the "age of monsters", one of which "they called Oyahguaharh, supposed to be some great mammoth", who was "at length killed, after a long and severe contest", while a "great horned serpent ... was compelled to retire in the deeps of the lake by thunder bolts".[5] Although there is every possibility that these mythical creatures – like countless others worldwide – bore some relationship to extinct fauna, the chief typically used the

---

[3] recorded 1885, in Stevenson 1891: 279-280. Arnold Clifford (b. c1967), botanist and tradition keeper of the Tahchiini clan of the Diné, confirmed the narrative in a conversation with me on 23 March 2014 in Albuquerque (New Mexico). On serial epoch-ending catastrophes, see §§411-413. Compare van der Sluijs 2011d: 30-31 for a Zuñi myth of twin heroes wiping out a race of monsters by various methods, including lightning.

[4] Potogojecs, Potawatomi chief, on 18 or 19 November 1846 at Council Bluffs (Iowa), to Pierre-Jean de Smet (1801-1873), in a letter by de Smet dated 10 January 1847, in de Smet 1847: 352. To related Algonquian nations, Nanaboojoo was known under the slightly different names 'Nanabush' (§454) and 'Manabozho' (van der Sluijs 2011d: 142). See §§376-406 on the retreat of the creator or culture hero.

[5] Tawennaki ('Two Things of Equal Value') *alias* Yutana Nire ('Lone Pine Tree') *alias* Elias Johnson (1837-1913), chief of the Tuscarora, in Johnson 1881: 42. Johnson related the elimination of these monsters in the same breath as the mass death caused by the fall of a "blazing star" (§455), but did not causally connect the two.

word "mammoth" in the generic sense of 'giant',[6] so the perceived zoological identity of this animal remains conjectural.

34*
union and shared language with animals

A universal trait in accounts of a former 'golden age' or 'age of myth' is that of *perfect interspecies communication* as 'people were still animals', 'animals were people' or all living beings 'spoke the same language'. Often, the interaction between all forms of life at that time is characterised as harmonious (compare §407). A speaker in one of Plato's dialogues dwelled on the verbal communication between humans and other animals during the fabulous 'age of Kronos':

> Well, then, if the foster children of Cronus, having all this leisure and the ability to converse not only with human beings but also with beasts, made full use of all these opportunities with a view to philosophy, talking with the animals and with one another and learning from every creature that, through possession of some peculiar power he may have had in any respect beyond his fellows perceptions tending towards an increase of wisdom, it would be easy to decide that the people of those old times were immeasurably happier than those of our epoch. Or if they merely ate and drank till they were full and gossiped with each other and the animals, telling such stories as are even now told about them, in that case, too, it would, in my opinion, be very easy to reach a decision.[7]

The T'atsaot'ine (north of Great Slave Lake, Northwest Territories, Canada) spoke of 'all the animals which then dwelled and conversed with man', during the time of primordial darkness.[8] Another, vivid example is this statement from the Tohono O'odham (southwestern Arizona) concerning the time when "the sun was nearer to the earth than now, the seasons were equal, and there was no necessity for clothing to guard against the inclemency of the weather" (§§34*, 430, 448):

> In these primeval days all men and animals lived in harmony, and spoke a common language. The howl of the wolf, the growl of the

---

[6] *e. g.*, Johnson 1881: 42, 57.
[7] Eleatic Stranger, in Plato, *Politicus* (*Statesman*), 16 (272B-D), tr. Fowler 1925: 60-61.
[8] Julien Ttsinnayinén, a T'atsaot'ine, recorded September 1862 at Great Slave Lake, in Petitot 1886: 373 (•); *cf.* 1887: 359.

bear, the voice of the mountain cat, the bark of the coyote, and the song of the forest birds, were alike mediums of intelligible communication to the human race.[9]

And the Cherokee (eastern and southeastern United States of America) offered a poignant account of mankind's growing departure from nature, perhaps even more relevant today than when it was first recorded:

> In the old days quadrupeds, birds, fishes, and insects could all talk, and they and the human race lived together in peace and friendship. But as time went on the people increased so rapidly that their settlements spread over the whole earth and the poor animals found themselves beginning to be cramped for room. This was bad enough, but to add to their misfortunes man invented bows, knives, blowguns, spears, and hooks, and began to slaughter the larger animals, birds and fishes for the sake of their flesh or their skins, while the smaller creatures, such as the frogs and worms, were crushed and trodden upon without mercy, out of pure carelessness or contempt.[10]

false positives

Frank Waters (1902-1995) claimed that the Hopi (northeastern Arizona) did not attribute a single language to "the First People", but something akin to telepathy:

> Although they were of different colors and spoke different languages, they felt as one and understood one another without talking. It was the same with the birds and animals. ... they all felt as one, people and animals. ... they were so close together in spirit they could see and talk to each other from the center on top of the head.[11]

However, Waters' information regarding the Hopi traditions about creation cannot be relied upon. Hopi elders themselves dismissed it and an American scholar had no doubt that "the first 36 pages of *Book of the Hopi* are completely the fantasy of Otto Pentiwa, Oswald White Bear Fredericks, and Frank Waters with a piece here and there from a variety

---

[9] José María Ochoa *alias* Con Quien ('the Gambler'), chief of the central Tohono O'odham, tr. Phyllena Wallace Tonge (1827-1912) of Cahuabi (Pima County), in Davidson 1865: 131.
[10] A'yûñ´inĭ ('Swimmer'; c1835-1899), an East Cherokee tradition keeper;Ităgû´năhĭ *alias* John Ax (c1800-after 1900), an East Cherokee; and Tsuskwănûñ´năwa´tă ('Worn-out-Blanket') *alias* James D. Wafford (1806-c1896), a West Cherokee; recorded before 1887, in Mooney 1891: 319. In a later edition (1900: 250), Mooney added "plants" to the list of beings capable of speech.
[11] purportedly recorded before 1963 by Oswald 'White Bear' Fredericks (1906-1996), a Hopi, in Waters 1978: 12, 15.

of narrators. In other words, the account which is the ideological starting point for the whole book is an artificial construction. Waters admits this himself: 'It stands for itself as a synthesis of intuitive, symbolic belief given utterance for the first time' (1963: xxiii)."[12] Despite Waters' listing of his informants,[13] the contamination is so severe that this material is best ignored altogether.[14] A promising way to salvage its authentic elements would be for someone conversant with the Hopi language to revisit the collection of Oswald Fredericks' original correspondence, notes and interviews.[15]

300*
collapse of the sky

Collapse of the sky was often associated with other disasters such as fire (§§302, 304-305, 309-312, 335, 396) and sudden darkness (§§333, 354). For example, the Barasana (concentrated in southeastern Colombia) shared the following tale:

> In the beginning the world was made entirely of rock and there was no life. *Romi Kumu*, Woman Shaman, took some clay and made a cassava griddle. She made three pot-supports and rested the griddle upon them. The supports were mountains holding up the griddle, the sky. She lived on top of the griddle. She lit a fire under the griddle. The heat from the fire was so intense that the supports cracked and the griddle fell down on the earth below, displacing it downwards so that it became the Underworld; the griddle became this earth. (Variant: the griddle fell through the earth below and became the Underworld.) She then made another griddle which is the layer above this earth, the sky.[16]

---

[12] Geertz 1983: 553-554.
[13] Waters 1978: XII-XIII.
[14] Alfred H. Qöyawayma (personal communication, 31 December 2016), a cousin of Oswald 'White Bear' Fredericks, makes the same point. My original note of caution (van der Sluijs 2011d: 164 note 494) was too weakly worded. I rescind all of my earlier citations from Waters' version of Hopi creation mythology.
[15] Of special interest will be the contents of box-folder 4. 78 labelled "The Four Worlds" and dated 25 October 1959, in the White Bear Fredericks Collection 1953-1965, NAU.MS.316, held at the Special Collections and Archives Department of Cline Library, Northern Arizona University, Flagstaff (Arizona).
[16] Bosco, the brothers Pau and Pasico, and Maximilliano, recorded September 1968 - December 1970 at Caño Colorado (Pirá-paraná region), in Hugh-Jones 1979: 263.

The variant in which the old sky becomes the present earth implies that the current race of humans originally came down from – or rather with – the sky; the variant in which it fell through the earth does not, but leaves one wondering how people could have survived such an event. Other significant elements in the story are the apparent solidity of the former sky (§§279, 281) and the collapse of the three "pot-supports", which represent *axes mundi* in their function as props of the sky (§§236, 269, 337). The story continues with an account of the deluge followed by a second conflagration brought on by solar heating, which again caused the sky to collapse (§429). The suspicion arises that this part of the story has been duplicated.

In a myth from the Nivaclé (Paraguay and northwest Argentina), an unexpectedly prolonged day and night follow the caving in of the sky, at a time when the sun and moon do not yet exist (§436):

> The sky had collapsed. ... They did not know what night was anymore, because after it had been daytime for four days, they thought that it was not going to get dark anymore. At Fitsakajich's request the people looked toward the east, and saw that nighttime was approaching. When it got dark there was no moon and no sun, only the stars. Then the same thing happened with nights as had happened with days; now it did not dawn but remained dark. The Nivaklé spent four continuous nights in darkness, just as previously they had spent four continuous days.[17]

On another occasion, the same informant attributed the fall of the sky to the collapse of one of the two sky pillars (§§268, 338):

> The sky had two tree trunks that supported it. One was 'The Old Trunk', and it was old and hard; the other, 'The New Trunk', was new and soft. Fitsakajich saw Tsiché, the invisible one, preparing to cut down the old trunk with his axe, because he well knew that if he managed to topple it, the new trunk that had not hardened yet would fall, too. Fitsakajich thought: 'What will happen to us? Tsiché is on one side of that tree, and if he manages to cut it, what will happen to the earth? It will cease to exist; the sky will fall down.' When he saw that very little remained of the old trunk he said: 'I'll go down below to see that Tsiché. Why is he doing this to us?' They did not know what was going to happen, but Fitsakajich could see from above what was occurring down below. He told them: 'There is very little left of

---

[17] As·etí *alias* Comisario (b. c1912), of the Jotoy Ihavós ('grassland people'; around the Santa Teresita mission, near Mariscal Estigarribia), recorded 1980, in Wilbert & Simoneau 1987: 40-41. Subsequently, the sun and the moon arrived and the proper day and night were instituted.

> the trunk of the sky because Tsiché is cutting it down. What will happen is that those people who live up there in the sky will fall on top of us. Nothing will happen to them; we are the ones who are in danger.'[18]

Another tree, the only one to survive, provides shelter from the oppressive sky – suggestive of an *axis mundi* (§§75, 140):

> When the people found out that the sky was going to fall, they were very fearful, but Fitsakajich told them: 'I'll find a tree that can support the sky. If the day comes when I need to have strength, we'll be safe, but I am going to look for a tree that can withstand that weight.' ... Then Fitsakajich went to Pepper Tree and asked him if he could withstand the weight of the sky that was going to fall, and the tree answered: 'I can.' Fitsakajich went back to the people and told them that he had found a tree that could support the weight of the sky. 'Let's all go to the pepper tree.' They all went and then suddenly Fitsakajich told them: 'Tsiché has finished cutting down the trunk of the sky.' They looked up and saw that the sky was falling. It was going to fall on top of them. Then it fell on them. They were under Pepper Tree and, although the sky broke all its branches, it did not break its trunk. [19]

Omitting the prolonged day, the narrator again dwelled on the extended darkness following the sky's breakdown:

> Fitsakajich said: 'The other Nivaklé will not survive this as you have. My brothers, my fathers, and mothers, what will we eat now?' They could not see anything because there was total darkness. They were covered by the sky, and it was completely dark there underneath the tree. During the time that they were there by the trunk of the tree, Fitsakajich had some logs, and each time he made fire he used only a single one. Still, they had nothing to eat, and after spending two or three days covered by the sky they decided to eat the leather they had ... the sky was hard as a rock ...[20]

Eventually, the light is restored by cutting through the thick sky (§466).[21] A third version provided by a different raconteur agrees in the basic outline:

---

[18] As·etí, as above, in Wilbert & Simoneau 1987: 97-98.
[19] As·etí, as above, in Wilbert & Simoneau 1987: 98. This pepper tree is *Schinus molle*.
[20] As·etí, as above, in Wilbert & Simoneau 1987: 98-99.
[21] Compare also the version told by As·etí as given in Wilbert & Simoneau 1987: 104.

> ... the sky, *vôôs*, fell, in those times. It started raining long, until it began to fall. The men were very afraid. They asked the shamans to order the rain to stop. But not even those who sang to the rain knew anything to do. The next day they saw how the clouds fell. – The terrible moment has arrived. – they say the men said. *Vôôs* crushed the huts, killing all those who had taken refuge inside. It was very heavy.[22]

People survive the catastrophe under several specimens of what is apparently the same arboreal species:

> Among the men there was one who admonished the others to look for a *molle* tree, *ôtjayuc*, to take refuge. Because the sky would topple all other trees. Only *ôtjayuc* would resist it. It could not crush or overturn it. All the men who were positioned under other trees would be smashed. Only *otjayuc* could put up with the weight of *vôôs*. The men left running towards the forest and found some *otjayuc* trees to guard themselves against *vôôs* which was falling; taking their women, their children and a few sheep which they allowed themselves to herd quickly. A very intense darkness covered them. They could not see each other anymore. They were disoriented. They did not know what to do. ... They did not know what to do because they were very afraid. It was not like daytime. They could not see, since it was darker than during the night.
>
> – Are you still alive? – asked some.
>
> – Yes, I am alive. – answered the others. ...
>
> Many years we hear that the ancients said that the sky was going to fall and so it happened. All those died who took refuge under the white quebracho, the red quebracho and the other trees. All were knocked down by the sky. Only the *ôtjayuc* trees resisted it, saving those who protected themselves beneath them. ... The people of all the villages died.[23]

As before, the solution was for the people to cut through the solid collapsed sky (§466): 'Only those who stayed near the man who had the

---

[22] Chajanaj, of the Tovok Ihavós of the Pilcomayo, recorded mid-1971 - mid-1972, in Chase-Sardi 1981: 93 (•); *cf.* Wilbert & Simoneau 1987: 101.

[23] Chajanaj, as above, in Chase-Sardi 1981: 93-95 (•). The indigenous name of the tree is variously spelled as *otjayuc* and *ôtjayuc*. Wilbert & Simoneau (1987: 101-102, 112 note 1) translated it as "*molle* tree" and identified it as *Lithraea molleoides*, but it may well be *Schinus molle*, another member of the *Anacardiaceae* or cashew family. The white quebracho is *Aspidosperma quebracho-blanco*, the red one *Schinopsis lorentzii*.

Majôctsi teeth were saved. All those years he guarded them. Those were the only ones who were saved. ... But since then the sky has not fallen anymore.'[24]

312*
flood, fire, a dragon and battle

false positives

In a Chinese tale set in the period 676-679 CE, Qiántáng, the younger brother of the "Dragon Lord" of Dòngtíng Lake (northeast Húnán, south-central China), is revealed to have caused the flood associated with the legendary emperor Yáo (*c*2356-2255 BCE):

> The Dragon Lord said, 'He is my beloved younger brother. ... In the past, [the Sage Ruler] Yao 堯 suffered from nine years of flooding; this was because of one of this fellow's rages. ... Still, he has been fettered and tied up here. Thus, Qiantang's people wait for him day after day.' He had not yet finished speaking when
>
> A loud sound suddenly burst forth;
> The heavens split; the ground cracked;
> The palace and hall rocked and bucked;
> Clouds and mist rolled in.
>
> A moment later, there was a crimson dragon, more than one-thousand *chi* long.
>
> With flashing eyes and bloodied tongue;
> Vermilion scales and fiery mane.
> Its neck was fastened with a metal lock;
> The lock dragged a jade pillar.
> One-thousand thunder claps and ten-thousand lightning bolts
> Violently whirled about its body.

---

[24] Chajanaj, as above, in Chase-Sardi 1981: 95 (•); *cf.* Wilbert & Simoneau 1987: 102, who translated "*Majôctsi*" as "tuco-tuco", a rodent of the genus *Ctenomys*. Other versions include: one told in 1986 by the shaman Leguán (b. *c*1916) and translated by Pascual Benítez (b. early 1960s), of Laguna Escalante, in 1987: 105, in which "a very hard tree" protects nine people when the "very low" sky falls (§§457, 466); and one related in 1986 by Asejetáx *alias* Angel Capa, of the middle Pilcomayo Nivaclé, and translated by Clemente Calderón (b. early 1960s), half Nivaclé and half Argentine Criollo, of San Leonardo de Escalante, in 1987: 108.

> Sleet, snow, rain, and hail
> All came down at once.
>
> Then it broke through the azure sky and flew away.²⁵

This episode must be treated with caution, however, because the story is a work of fiction. Although it is possible that its author reworked a genuine tradition about Qiántáng into his narrative, this cannot simply be assumed. Certainly, an authentic source includes the appearance of a dragon at Dòngtíng Lake among the tumultuous events of Yáo's reign,²⁶ but this appears to have been an earth-bound monster and was not directly linked with the flood.

In a liturgical text from the Maya of Chumayel (Yucatán), a rain of fire and a deluge of water both ensue when the "9 who are Gods" (*bolon ti ku*), of the underworld, attack the "13 who are Gods" (*Oxlahun ti ku*), of the sky:

> The dawning of the land
> ... And then there were finished
> The 13 who are Gods
> By the 9 who are Gods.
> They then brought down fire;
> ...
> And then were finished
> The 13 who are Gods.
> And so then their heads were beaten,
> And then their faces were flattened,
> And then they were forgotten,
> And then they were also carted away.
> And then were planted the four changers
> Together with the Soot Heads.
> ...

---

²⁵ Lǐ Cháowēi (c766-c820 CE), *Dòngtíng Líng Yīn Zhuàn* (*The Tale of the Supernatural Marriage at Dòngtíng*), tr. Cai 2016: 6-7. The *chǐ* measures about 0.33 m. According to Cai (2016: 31), the earliest extant appearances of the story are in Chén Hàn (ed.), *Yìwén Jí* (*Collection of Strange Reports*; c840 CE), in Lǐ Fǎng (ed.), *Tàipíng Guǎngjì* (*Extensive Records of the Tàipíng Era*; 978 CE), 419, and Zēng Zào (ed.), *Lèishuō* (*Categorised Tales*; 1136 CE), 28.

²⁶ "Coming down to the time of Yao, the ten suns [once] came out together. They scorched the standing grain and the sheaves and killed herbs and trees, so that the people had nothing to eat. [Moreover,] Chayu, Nine Gullet, Typhoon, Mound Pig, Chisel Tusk, and Long Snake all were causing the people harm. Yao therefore commanded Yi [the Archer] ... upward to shoot the ten suns and downward to kill Chayu, to chop Long Snake in two at Dongting Lake", Líu Ān (ed.), *Huáinánzǐ* (*Master of Huainan*; 139 BCE), 8. 6, tr. J. S. Major, in trs. Major *et al.* 2010: 275-276. On the shooting of the ten suns, see §§443-444.

A deluge of water,
A storm of water
Then reached the hearts
Of the four changers,
Who radiated in heaven
And radiated also on the land.
Said the 4 who are Gods,
The 4 who are Fathers of the Land,
'This water shows them
To their faces.
Then let us finish
The flattening of the lands. ...'[27]

The word translated in this passage as "the four changers" is *cangel*, also spelled as *canhel*. An early lexicographer understood this to mean "*dragon*".[28] The idea being that of a sceptre decorated with the head of a snake, a Spanish translation of the same text rendered *colabi u cangel* ("then were planted the four changers") as 'And his Serpent of Life was stolen' and *uchic ol / Cangelil i* ("the hearts / Of the four changers") as 'the Great Serpent was stolen';[29] the theft of this 'serpent' supposedly coincided with the fall of the sky. Although they did not identify their source, this reading apparently inspired some catastrophists to conclude that the myth involves the fall of a dragon or serpent from the sky.[30] Yet this interpretation is untenable. Because the word seems to have lost the reptilian connotation over time, it would be unsafe to allocate a mean-

---

[27] Juan Josef Hoíl, *Book of Chilam Balam of Chumayel* (1782 CE), 29. 3-4, 7 (42-43; 3036-3098), tr. Edmonson 1986: 154-156; *cf.* van der Sluijs 2011d: 13, 76 note 223. The text describes the rituals performed in 1618 CE on occasion of the end of the calendrical *baktun* cycle, which recurs about every 400 years, Edmonson 1986: 24-25, 44. That some of the rites reenacted myths of cosmic catastrophes is likely. For "The dawning of the land", Bolio (1941: 62) translated 'It was the moment when the earth had just awakened' (•), Roys (1967: 99) "This was after the creation of the world had been completed" and Luxton (1995: 76-77, at 17. 3 [1686]) "when the realization of the world was completed". Instead of "The flattening of the lands" (compare Bolio 1941: 53: 'the levelling' [•]), Luxton (1995: 76-78-79, at 17. 15 [1730]) translated "the flooding of the world". Edmonson (1986: 155 note on 3064; *contra* Roys 1967: 99 note 3) rejected the conception that 'Oxlahun ti ku' and 'Bolon ti ku' were two single deities representing the collective deities of respectively the sky and the underworld; Luxton (1995: 76-77, at 17. 1-14 [1681-1713]) puzzlingly had "the Oxlahuntiku" and "the Bolontiku", but also "Oxlahuntiku" and "his head", "his face" and so on. The story goes on to tell of the erection of five trees – representative of *axes mundi* – at the cardinal points and the centre, *cf.* van der Sluijs 2011a: 208; 2011b: 97, 136; 2011c: 128, 131, 186, 226, 234 note 940.
[28] Beltran 1746: 177 *s. v.* 'Dragon'.
[29] Juan Josef Hoíl, *Book of Chilam Balam of Chumayel*, tr. Bolio 1941: 62-63 (••).
[30] *e. g.*, Muck 1978 (1956): 169, followed, with the wrong page number, by LaViolette 1997: 268.

ingful rôle to the animal – hence the alternative translation "insignia".³¹ The more recent translator quoted above is probably right that *cangel* refers to "the four changers" – the supporters of the sky at the cardinal points (compare §236) who also function as the 'year-bearers' marking "the 4 days out of the sacred 20 that could begin the 365-day year" – and no despoliation is involved at all.³² The Mesoamerican myth of the lifting of the sky by these custodians of the cardinal directions before or after the flood is well known.³³

332*
the column disrupted amid earthquakes

The mythology of the Yali (Baliem Valley, Papua, Indonesia) centred on the repeated felling of a creative cosmic tree called Yeli, turned into a pig, whose scattered fragments were planted in the earth (compare §368) and thereby terminated a period of catastrophic earthquakes:

> The beginning is that Yeli was felled. A Hûl tree kangaroo chopped from one side and a Hîsalî tree kangaroo from the other side. They threw the splinters behind them, so that they flew in all directions. These are the sacral stones. The tree stood in Konowî, on the Saruk River.
>
> When it was felled, it raised itself again far to the east in the direction of Koropun in the place Masamlu. But Hûl and Hîsalî followed it and felled it again. Then it raised itself on the Pasin Pass and passed the mountain. Again they followed it and felled it, and when it fell down the one branch splintered completely. The splinters flew all around. The other branch made itself independent and went the northern way in the direction of the villages Npsan, Serekasi and Mîmbanam. ...
>
> From there, Yeli went to Tanggusene (near Sanggalpunu) and fell down there (sahûng-tîbag). That happened with such a tremendous earthquake that the Limlim people all perished. From there he went to Luruk and fell down (sahûng-tîbag). All the rivers carried its blood. From there he went over Waniyok and Piliyam over the Îlît mountain

---

³¹ Thus, Roys (1967: 99, *cf.* 67 note 5) rendered the two phrases above as respectively "he was despoiled of his insignia" and "the theft of the insignia"; compare Edmonson 1986: 156 note on 3089.
³² *Cf.* Edmonson 1986: 5-6, 25, 156 note on 3089. Luxton (1995: 76-77, at 17. 9, 15 [1699, 1724]) translated "the Yearbearer" on the first occasion, but "the Yearbearers" on the second.
³³ *e. g.*, van der Sluijs 2011c: 146-147 (after: Aztec); 2011d: 76 (before: Maya).

to Sîyelma, at the Ferawe mountain. The mountain is said to be a splinter of Yeli.

The people ... carried the splinters of Yeli with them and put them into the earth to steady and fix the earth, because the earth had become mud, Yeli had turned it to mud. On the mountains, too, they laid the splinters of Yeli, and so the mountains got their names.[34]

339*
disruption of the column as separation

The Yali maintained that the felling of the 'pig-tree' Yeli, apart from stabilising the earth (§332*), coincided with the elevation of the sky to its present height:

> There was a tree, which stood in Koropun. The top was fused with the sky. The people from Koropun and from Turam tried to fell it, but failed to do so. Then they brought in the Sama man Kuwilahun. The latter brought the teeth of the Hûl and of the Hîsalî tree kangaroo.
>
> When he came to the tree, he began to hack. He put the first splinter which broke loose away for himself and said: 'With that I will build my sacral men's house'. Then they continued hacking, the Hûl on the back side, the Hîsalî on the front side. The tree fell over. When they also chopped off the top, which was fused with the sky, the celestial vault lifted. When the tree fell over, it became a pig. It became Yeli, the Yeli pig. The pig came hither and, in doing so, made noises like an aeroplane.[35]

Or according to another version:

> Yeli, who created everything, was in the beginning in a place called Korupun. He was there in the form of a pig. The pig was also called Songgûwa. There a man called Kabî-ngil-ngilibungî found him. He shot him with a bamboo arrow, but the pig pulled the arrow out and

---

[34] Pabîjon = Pabîon *alias* Stepanus (b. c1935), from Pasikni and of the Sama tribe, and Mahasu, from Angguruk, recorded 1972, in Zöllner 1977: 463-464 #1d (•). Compare 1977: 10, 57-58, 60, 158, 316, 337, 341, 364, 366-369, 417 note 22, 439 note 29, 462, 465-470, 549-578, 598, tr. 1988: 2, 17-19, 25-26, 104-107, 170-172; note that the English version of the book (1988) translates only a small portion of the original text and does so imprecisely. Tree kangaroos are marsupials of the genus *Dendrolagus*. For the tree's repeated reappearance in different places, compare §§341, 345.
[35] Lîbahon, from Nisikni, recorded 1975, in Zöllner 1977: 466 #1g (•). The tree top's organic merger with the sky is a special case of the tree's reaching to the sky (§73).

walked away. The blood of the Yeli pig gathered and turned into the Purumdal pond. The pig continued on its way and walked to the place Kasin, where a man called Kasin-pit-piribungî lived. Here it stood straight up and with its tongue licked the sky, which was still close to the earth. The sky dome rose up only when the pig was dead.[36]

343*
celestial arc

The *axis mundi* was sometimes presented in *bent form*, even as a semicircle or arch (§343).[37] Both extremities may come down to form the image of a curved bridge or two juxtaposed columns joined at the top. In some traditions, the curvature was related to the symbolism of the rainbow, the Milky Way, the ecliptic band or the zodiacal light, but this cannot be demonstrated for all.

One instance is a myth from the Nivaclé (Paraguay and northwest Argentina) concerning "the two trunks of the sky" which "grew and became firm" to stabilise "Sky and Earth" after the inversion of the latter (§457):

> When Rainbow came down to earth, the sky did not have its supports yet, but it received them as soon as the rainbow's two ends had reached the earth and sunk into it.[38]

The Dusun (Tempassuk district, west coast of Sabah) viewed the rainbow as an *axis mundi* in its conductive aspect (§§157-177): "Long ago the rainbow was a path for men. Those who lived up country used the rainbow as a bridge when they wished to go down country in search of wives. ... they made the rainbow as a bridge and you can see the floor and hand rail of the bridge in the rainbow to the present day."[39]

In several cases, the arc is combined with a vertical cylinder reminiscent of a more typical *axis mundi*. For example, the standard creation myth of Japan attributes the formation of the first land to a pair of twin deities plunging down a spear from a heavenly bridge:

---

[36] Kornelis (b. c1945), from Waniyok and of the Mûhî tribe, recorded 1975, in Zöllner 1988: 174 #5c.
[37] *e. g.*, van der Sluijs 2011a: 202; 2011b: 5 note 20, 196-197; 2011d: 93, 109.
[38] As·etí *alias* Comisario (b. c1912), of the Jotoy Ihavós ('grassland people'; around the Santa Teresita mission, near Mariscal Estigarribia), recorded 1980, in Wilbert & Simoneau 1987: 104.
[39] Sirinan, a Low-Country Dusun, of Kampong Piasau, in 1910 or 1911, in Evans 1913: 425-426.

> Izanagi no Mikoto and Izanami no Mikoto stood on the floating bridge of Heaven, and held counsel together, saying: 'Is there not a country beneath?' Thereupon they thrust down the jewel-spear of Heaven, and groping about therewith found the ocean.[40]

And the Winikina subtribe of the Warao (central Orinoco Delta, Venezuela) based their custom of smoke-induced shamanic trance on the example of a mythical child-ancestor who – in ecstatic flight – traced a path of solidified smoke from the centre of the earth towards the zenith and thence towards the "House of Tobacco Smoke" forged in the east by "Creator Bird of the Dawn" (*Domu Hokonamana Ariawara*), which was "a round, white house made of tobacco smoke" that "looked like a cloud":

> The House of Smoke is situated to the East, halfway between the junction of earth and sky and the zenith of the cosmic vault. It came about long before there lived any Warao. Then one day there appeared in the center of the earth a man and a woman. ... they had a four-year-old son who was very intelligent. ... 'There must be something in the East as well', reasoned the boy, 'something light and colorful.' He decided to go and explore the universe.
>
> Now, although the young boy's body was relatively light, it was far too heavy for flight. The boy thought much about this until one day he asked his father to pile up firewood under his hammock. For four days he abstained from food and drink. In the evening of the fifth day he lit the wood with virgin fire and went to sleep. Then with the surging heat and smoke of the new fire the boy's spirit ascended to the zenith.
>
> Someone spoke to him, saying, 'Follow me. I will show you the bridge to the House of Smoke in the East.' Soon the boy found himself on a bridge made of thick white ropes of tobacco smoke. He followed the invisible spirit guide until, a short distance from the center of the celestial dome, he reached a point where marvelous flowers began meandering alongside the bridge in a rainbow of brilliant colors – a row of red and a row of yellow flowers on the left, and lines of blue and green flowers on the right. A gentle breeze wafted them back and forth. Like the bridge they adorned, the flowers were made of solidified tobacco smoke. Everything was bright and tranquil. The invisible guide ushered the boy toward the House of Smoke. ... The bridge led right to the door of the House of Smoke in the East.

---

[40] Toneri Shinnō & Ō no Yasumaro (eds.), *Nihongi* (*Japanese Chronicles*; 720 CE), 1. 1. 5, tr. Aston 1896: 10-11, *cf.* 1. 1. 7-9. The "jewel-spear of Heaven" (*nu-boko* or *tama-boko*) is a form of *axis mundi*, *cf.* 1896: 11 note 1.

> ... the boy awakened from his ecstatic trance. ... The smoke of his cigars formed a path from the center of the earth to the zenith, where the bridge commences that leads to the House of Smoke in the East. ... Much time elapsed, and when many people appeared in the center of the earth, they knew nothing about *bahana* and the bridge that reached from their village to the House of Tobacco Smoke. ... Finally many Warao appeared in the center of the earth. Again the young *bahanarotu*, who was himself a Warao, shot the same pair of *bahana* spirits down to earth from the House of Smoke. The young man who received them survived and learned how to travel the bridge of tobacco smoke in the sky. ... That is why *bahana* continued on earth to the present day. It is not so perfect or so powerful as it was long ago, when the first *bahanarotu* received four spirit helpers. Nevertheless, *bahana* prevails.[41]

In a subsequent, more succinct paraphrase, the round dwelling is revealed to be an egg:

> The soul of the light-shaman ascends to the top of the sky to rendezvous with the invisible psychopomp who resides to the east of the zenith. After resting there for several days and being provided with a final cigar, he follows the soul-guide to a bridge made of thick ropes of solidified tobacco smoke, which commences a short distance from the center of the world. Beautiful flowers border the bridge: a row of red and a row of yellow flowers on the left and lines of blue and green flowers on the right. At the end of the bridge is a white ovular house, also made of tobacco smoke. It is the residence of *Kanobo* Mawari, the patron deity of light-shamans. In primordial times this birthplace of light-shamanism originated through the will of the Creator-Bird of the Dawn.[42]

The palette of colours represented by the combination of the smoke and the flowers cannot fail to remind one of the rainbow, while smoke cross-culturally is a common expression of an *axis mundi* (§150).[43] In later summaries of the above account, the zenith is treated as the upper end of

---

[41] recorded March and July 1970 by Johannes Wilbert (b. 1927), probably from Antonio Lorenzano Pacheco (1914-1996), of the Sohoburoho band of the Winikina, tradition keeper and chief of the village of Morichito, in Wilbert 1972: 65-70 (*cf.* 59, 62-63, 72, 77), abbreviated in 1993: 122-123. Warao shamanism is known as *bahana*, a 'light' shaman as a *bahanarotu*.

[42] first recorded as above, in Wilbert 1993 (1975): 96. The *kanobo* are the supreme gods, located at the cardinal points.

[43] *e. g.*, van der Sluijs 2011b: 107-108, 164, 168, 170, 230; 2011c: 37, 69, 221, 225, 238; 2011d: 9, 19 note 56, 218 note 694.

the smoke column in its capacity as an *axis mundi* (compare §129);[44] as seen from Venezuela, the zenith is far from the celestial pole, but corresponds approximately with the maximum altitude of the summer sun. Also, the "House of Tobacco Smoke" is then pictured as "a large cosmic egg, a creation of the bird-spirit, Mawári", positioned not due east, but to the "Northeast of the world axis and on the plain near the top of the sky"; leading from its "western portal" was "a suspension bridge of ropes of tobacco smoke which connects the egg with the zenith and the world axis."[45] Compare:

> A rope bridge of tobacco smoke spans the celestial abyss and connects the threshold of Mawári's house with the top of the axis mundi.[46]

> Through the power of his thought, Mawari created an egg-shaped house northeast of the zenith. Made of tobacco smoke this 'Cosmic Egg' looks like a cloud. The house is attached to the world by means of a rope-bridge of tobacco smoke, decorated with two rows of red and yellow flowers along the left side and two rows of blue and green flowers along the right side ... The peculiarity of the flowers alongside the celestial bridge between the zenith and the egg is that they consist only of the stems and the florescences of tobacco plants.[47]

A similar bridge – though serpentine rather than smoky – was imagined to join the zenith to a mountain in the southeast, which was one of the cosmic mountains of the cardinal and intercardinal directions (compare §225); thus, a smoking ritual in the initiation of a canoe-maker "elevates the neophyte in a trance-like dream to the zenith":

> Here he is met by a black psychopomp who leads him to the head of a celestial bridge that spans the gap from the center of the sky to the world mountain in the southeast. The bridge, however, is an enormous serpent, rigid and stretched out above the abyss. Its wide-open mouth hisses when the soul of the novice approaches. The monster has eight horns, two pairs in front and two in the rear. The two pairs

---

[44] *e. g.*, Wilbert 1973-1974: 93 = 1993: 140, 143; 1993 (1975): 87, 91-92; 1979: 139 = 1993: 14; 1981: 38-39, 45, 48, 50, 52 = 1993: 184, 194-195, 198, 200; 1985: 165 = 1993: 165.
[45] first recorded as above, perhaps with additions by Lorenzano, Jaime Zapata (1909 - before 2007), a Winikina rain shaman of Ahakanoko, or others, in Wilbert 1981: 40 = 1993: 185-186.
[46] first recorded as above, in Wilbert 1981: 53 (*cf.* 61) = 1993: 200 (*cf.* 209), with very minor orthographic differences.
[47] first recorded as above, in Wilbert 1985: 147-148, 158 = 1993: 148, 159. The reprinted edition (1993: 148) reads differently: "The house is attached to the earth by rows of red and yellow flowers on the left side and two rows of blue and green flowers on the right side."

on the right side of the body are red and green and those on the left side are yellow and blue. Flowers of the same color decorate each horn ...[48]

As for the central vertical component of the *axis mundi*, "The Warao do not think of the world axis as a solid column, but rather as a bundle of conduits, each one specific to its destination. ... the world axis of the Warao universe represents a dynamic bundle of pathways, one of which leads to the anchor point of the rope-bridge that conducts *bahana* shamans from the top of the sky to the House of Tobacco Smoke."[49] Some conduits are now "destroyed".

false positives

The famous French anthropologist Marcel Griaule (1898-1956) published much material on the creation mythology of the Dogon (Mali). According to this, the first "light in the universe" arrived with "a gigantic arch" which descended after the separation of "an enormous egg" (*aduno tal*) into two placentas, the upper one forming the sky and the lower one the original earth:

> Seeing this, Amma decided to send to earth the Nommo of the other half of the egg, creators of the sky and the stars. They came down to earth on a gigantic arch, at the centre of which stood the two Nommo of the sky, who had assumed the guise of blacksmiths. ... The arch constituted a new, undefiled earth; its descent coincided with the appearance of light in the universe, which till then had been in darkness.[50]

The "arch of Nommo" was associated with the quotidian movement of the sun: "The advent of the arch of Nommo denotes not only the delimitation of space but also the measurement of times and seasons: the year was linked to the apparent movement of the sun, avatar of the other portion of the placenta of Yurugu".[51] The language suggests that the arch

---

[48] recorded 1954-1977 by Wilbert, probably from Lorenzano, in Wilbert 1977: 25. Additional details are in 1993 (1975): 99-100.
[49] Wilbert 1985: 165 = 1993: 166, with very minor orthographic differences. For more on the pathways branching out from the zenith, see 1972: 62-64, 73-74 (revised in 1993: 118-119, 125-126); 1993 (1975): 89 Fig. 3. 1, 91-92, 97.
[50] Griaule & Dieterlen 1954: 86. The Nommo were sons of God, two in each placenta.
[51] Griaule & Dieterlen 1954: 86-87. Yurugu was the male Nommo in the lower placenta, of which he tore a portion which became the old earth.

related to the ecliptic band, which is the apparent path of the sun, moon and planets, but this would conflict with its alleged identity as "a new, undefiled earth".

This contradiction is probably part of a much wider problem with the reliability of Griaule's results, many of which seem to have been more his own invention or the creative thinking of his main informants than actual tradition.[52] Although it would be rash to dismiss all of Griaule's alleged Dogon mythology as complete fabrication and hence 'false positives' for the present study, the difficulty in separating authentic tradition from layers of interpretation – which is, to some extent, inherent in all ethnological fieldwork – means that Griaule's findings should only be used with great caution, certainly not as evidence to build a theory on.[53]

359*
altered motion of stars and planets

Disturbances in the regular motions of the fixed stars and the planets are frequently encountered in cosmological traditions.[54] They can be divided into relatively orderly changes, in which the relative positions between the stars are preserved, and disorderly ones, in which one or more stars seem to be 'unpinned' relative to each other or move helter-skelter. The former group includes inversions of the apparent direction of movement and rotation around a different pole, the latter chaotic trajectories, sudden displacements and falls of a single body or multiple ones. For orderly interventions, some texts are specific enough to indicate whether the change was permanent or temporary. Disorderly interruptions are necessarily ephemeral, but the renewed order arising from them may differ from the original state. In all cases, the anomaly may be presented as a past, future or merely hypothetical event.

The following discussion of examples is not structured according to the above classification, however, because the sources often lack the precision required to unambiguously classify them or appear to combine multiple categories. Falls of stars, planets or comets onto the earth are

---

[52] van Beek 1991.
[53] By extension, this warning applies to all citations of Griaule's work in van der Sluijs 2011a; 2011c.
[54] Compare the stars' confusion about their locations upon what appears to be their first appearance in the sky, according to Icelandic myth (§436).

treated in §455. Analogous themes in the mythology of solar and lunar anomalies are suns or moons on a different path (§436), reversed suns (§§373, 373*) and fallen suns or moons (§437).

Alterations in the courses of planets constitute a group of traditions in the disorderly category. In a Talmūdic discussion on whether astrology applies to the Jews, God assures Abraham that he could move Ṣédeq to the opposite part of the sky at will:

> '... What is thy calculation? Because Zedek stands in the West? I will turn it back and place it in the East.' And thus it is written, *Who hath raised up Zedek from the east? He hath summoned it for his sake.*[55]

In this very same chapter in the *Talmūd*, Ṣédeq is equated with the planet Jupiter.[56]

A few sources allege that Venus or the morning or evening star on one occasion strayed from its usual course. Some appear to have dated this event to historical times, others to a mythical epoch. A Chinese text reported:

> Once T'ai-Pai [Venus] suddenly ran into Lang-Hsing [Wolf Star, Sirius], though it is more than 40 degrees south of the Yellow Road. Once, moreover, Venus was visible in full daylight and, while moving across the sky, rivaled the sun in brightness.[57]

And the Yolngu (eastern Arnhem Land) remembered an occasion when Barnumbir, the morning star held on a string controlled by one or two custodians in the spirit world (§450), escaped:

> Yangoor talks: 'I want to send this my morning-star to another country. I must send him a very long way.' He pulls a lot of string out of

---

[55] Rab *alias* 'Abbā 'Arīkā (175-247 CE), to Judah bar Ezekiel (220-299 CE), in *Babylonian Talmūd*: *Šabbāt*, 24 (156a-b), tr. Freedman 1938: 800, from which the bracketed apposition "[Jupiter]", inserted by the translator for clarification, is omitted. The Aramaic original of the sentences "Because Zedek stands in the West? I will turn it back and place it in the East" is: "*dq'y ṣdq bm'rb mhrrn' wmwqmyn' lyh bmzrh*", ed. 1972: 156b. 'Zedek' is an alternative transliteration to 'Ṣédeq'. The compulsory Biblical 'proof passage' is *Isaiah*, 41. 2.

[56] Compare Stieglitz 1981: 135.

[57] cited in Huáng Cháng, *Sūzhōu Shíkè Tiānwéntú* (*Sūzhōu Astronomical Chart*; 1193 CE), trs. Rufus & Tien 1945: 5. *Tàibái* is the modern spelling of T'ai-pai, *Lángxīng* for 'wolf star'. The 'Yellow Road' is the sun's path along the ecliptic. The original Mandarin text will have to be consulted in order to determine whether Venus' "moving across the sky" is to be taken literally, as an extreme aberration of its ordinary course, or merely refers to its normal location in the vicinity of the sun. For the increased brightness, see §450.

the dilly-bag. 'I must send this morning-star a long way', he says. He pulls all the string out of the bag. He throws the morning-star and the star climbs up the pandanus and goes out into the dark sky and does not come back because all the string has gone out of the dilly-bag.[58]

Several traditions associate erratic behaviour of stars or planets with other dramatic events, such as eclipses, a flood (§§303-305, 308, 310-313, 336, 356, 397), battle (§§311-313, 329, 358-361) and demise of an *axis mundi* (§§318-345). As far as the planet Venus is concerned, the Greek grammarian Castor of Rhodes (1st century BCE) is on record with the statement that it once "changed its colour, size, shape and course, a thing which has never happened before or since."[59] According to the otherwise unknown mathematicians Adrastus of Cyzicus and Dio of Naples, the portent "happened in the reign of Ogygus", that is to say, concomitant with the famous legendary flood of Ogyges, which the ancients generally regarded as a historical event postdating the creation of the world by centuries.

The Sakha (northeast Siberia), too, seem to have believed in the possibility of Venus – known as Čolbon and formerly in possession of a tail (§450) – deviating towards the earth, with grave consequences:

> If it approaches the earth, it means destruction, storm and frost, even in the summer; 'Saint Leontius, however, blessed her and thus her tail disappeared'.[60]

The combination of disasters and unsettled movement of other planets is attested in this Chinese historical entry for *c*142 BCE:

---

[58] Manuwa Wongupali (1917-1979), of the Djambarrpuyŋu clan of the Yolngu, recorded 1954-1956 at Milingimbi, in Robinson 1956: 50; *cf.* van der Sluijs 2011d: 245-246. In Pittingngor, where it lands, Durikiyoo "paints the tuft of feathers with red ochre" and "Durikiyoo throws the morning-star and the star climbs up the milkwood tree and goes into the sky." The spirits of the dead then arrange that those at "Joorningor, which is Elcho Island", can "have the red morning-star", while those at Pittingngor "have the white one". Durikiyoo then supplies Naikala, the true guardian of the original morning star, with "another morning-star", Robinson 1956: 50-51. Although the myth is somewhat hard to follow, it is safe to conclude that it deals with the origin of the respective colours and trajectories of morning stars, such as Venus' and Jupiter's shift from red to white with higher altitudes or Mars' occasional appearance as a red morning star – see further van der Sluijs 2009b; van der Sluijs & James 2013: 299-301.
[59] Castor of Rhodes, in Varro, *De Gente Populi Romani* (*On the Race of the Roman People*), in Augustine, *De Civitate Dei* (*On the City of God*), 21. 8, tr. Green 1972: 48-51.
[60] recorded 1877 in Namsky District (Sakha Republic), in Seroshevskiy 1896: 668, tr. Mándoki 1968: 489. This was not recorded in 1866 and it is, of course, incorrect to say that the planet Venus "is visible twice a day", both *contra* 1968: 487.

> In ... the tenth month, both the sun and the moon were eclipsed and appeared red for five days. On the last day of the twelfth month it thundered. The sun turned purple; the five planets turned back in their courses and remained in the constellation of the Great Secret; the moon passed through the constellation of the Heavenly Court.[61]

Perhaps it was this record which inspired the following roughly contemporary but more general passage addressing a ruler who violates nature:

> ... the sun and moon [suffer] partial eclipses;
> the five planets lose their proper orbits;
> the four seasons overstep one another.
> In the day it is dark and at night it is light;
> mountains crumble and rivers flood ...[62]

The same corpus acknowledges deviations from the usual order for the sun, moon and planets, accompanied by catastrophes (compare §436), as a general type of event:

> When sun and moon err in their periodic motions, fireflies have no light, wind and rain are not appropriate to the season, and destruction occurs and disasters arise. When the five asterisms err in their periodic movements, provinces and states meet with calamity.[63]

Elsewhere, additional catastrophes accompany a collective shift of stars instead of irregular planetary motions. For example, Jewish lore links the deluge with a curious change in the movement of one specific group of stars:

> That day was the seventeenth of Iyar, a day on which the star group *Kimah* sets in the day, and the fountains become depleted. But because they altered their practices, the Holy One, blessed be He, altered upon

---

[61] Sīmǎ Qiān, *Shǐjì* (*Scribe's Records*) = *Tàishǐgōng Shū* (*Records of the Grand Historian*; c109-91 BCE), 11 (*Xiàojǐng Běnjì* [*Imperial Annals of Xiàojǐng*]), tr. Watson 1971: 373. It is, of course, impossible for the sun and the moon to be eclipsed at the same time, so some other obscuration of both must be intended. It is not clear which constellations correspond to the "Great Secret" and the "Heavenly Court".

[62] Líu Ān (ed.), *Huáinánzǐ* (*Master of Huainan*; 139 BCE), 20. 3, trs. S. A. Queen & J. S. Major, in Major et al. 2010: 797. Cf. *Zhúshū Jìnián* (*Bamboo Annals*; 3rd century BCE), 3. 17. 4-5, tr. Legge 1865: 125-126.

[63] Líu Ān (ed.), *Huáinánzǐ*, 7. 55. 7-16, tr. H. D. Roth, in Major et al. 2010: 243. De Harlez (1891: 201) accidentally translated 'the sun and the earth' instead of "sun and moon" and 'the five planets' instead of "the five asterisms" (••). The Mandarin reads rìyuè ("sun and moon") and wǔxīng ('the five planets') respectively (Harold Roth, personal communication, 10 November 2015).

them the works of creation. And he brought the star group *Kimah* up in the day. And he took two stars from *Kimah* and brought a flood to the world.[64]

Insofar as Kīmā is understood to be a star group, most likely the Pleiades, it is inconceivable that the inversion was limited to it alone; certainly, the text allows that the change affected all stars, but Kīmā was the most prominent or significant one. The text also leaves it unclear whether Kīmā subsequently resumed its original rising pattern or not.

In a Babylonian myth, the god Marduk reflects on the time of the deluge, when "the control of heaven and earth was undone" (*ši-piṭ šamê^e u erṣetim^{tim} up-ta-aṭ-ṭir*), the "very heavens" (*šamê^{[e]}*) were "made to tremble" (*uš-tar-i-bu*) and "the positions of the stars of heaven changed, and I did not return them to their places." ([*ka*]*kkabāni^{meš} šá-ma-mi man-za-as-su-nu iš-ni-ma ul ú-tir áš-ru-uš-šu-un*)[65] The same occasion saw the disappearance of "the *mēsu*-tree",[66] a likely reference to the collapse of an *axis mundi*.[67]

Chinese tradition similarly combines a lasting displacement of all heavenly bodies with the deluge and collapsing world pillars – sky-supporting mountains (§§75, 236) in this case:

> In ancient times Gong Gong and Zhuan Xu fought, each seeking to become the thearch. Enraged, they crashed against Mount Buzhou;
> Heaven's pillars broke;
> the cords of Earth snapped.
> Heaven tilted in the northwest, and thus the sun and moon, stars and planets shifted in that direction.

---

[64] Joshua ben Levi (3rd century CE), in *Babylonian Talmūd: Rōš ha-Šānā* (New Year), 1 (11b), tr. adapted from Schorr & Malinowitz 1999: 11b. Instead of "at daybreak" (Simon 1938: 43), translating *bayyōm* as 'in the day' is more accurate from a linguistic point of view. The month 'Iyyar falls in the spring. *Mazzal* is best translated as 'star group' instead of "constellation" (Schorr & Malinowitz 1999: 11b), because it is inclusive of constellations as well as asterisms. *Kīmā*, here spelled '*Kimah*', most likely corresponds to the Pleiades, though disagreement exists. For the two dislodged stars, see §455.

[65] Kabti-ilāni-Marduk, *Erra and Išum*, 1. 133-134, ed. Cagni 1969: 72, tr. Dalley 2000: 290. Compare van der Sluijs 2011d: 16-17, 72, 85-86, 116. Reiner et al. (1992: 91 s. v. '**šipṭu**') give "judgment, verdict" as the main meaning of *šipṭu*; Cagni (1969: 73) translated 'government' (•). *Uš-tar-i-bu* is a form of the verb *ra'ābu* meaning "to be overcome by trembling, to be set in violent motion", Reiner & Roth 1999: 2-3 s. v. '**ra'ābu**'. *Manzāzu* is the word used for "station, position", Oppenheim & Reiner 1977: 234, 237 s. v. '**manzāzu**'.

[66] Kabti-ilāni-Marduk, *Erra and Išum*, 1. 148, 150.

[67] van der Sluijs 2011d: 72, 85-86, *cf.* 2011b: 14, 131.

Earth became unfull in the southeast, and thus the watery floods and mounding soils subsided in that direction.[68]

The "northwest" was the direction towards which the ancient Chinese situated Mount Bùzhōu. A parallel account in the same work mentions the partial damage to the sky, but omits the disruption among the celestial bodies:

> Going back to more ancient times,
> the four pillars were broken;
> the nine provinces were in tatters.
> Heaven did not completely cover [the earth];
> Earth did not hold up [Heaven] all the way around [its circumference].
> Fires blazed out of control and could not be extinguished;
> water flooded in great expanses and would not recede.
> Ferocious animals ate blameless people;
> predatory birds snatched the elderly and the weak.
> Thereupon, Nüwa
> Smelted together five-colored stones in order to patch up the azure sky,
> cut off the legs of the great turtle to set them up as the four pillars,
> killed the black dragon to provide relief for Ji Province,
> and piled up reeds and cinders to stop the surging waters.
> The azure sky was patched;
> the four pillars were set up;
> the surging waters were drained; ...[69]

Further, a little-known Hindū myth links celestial upheaval, together with colossal earthquakes, tsunamis and hurricanes, with the sun's initiation of rotatory movement while it was still on its lathe – a possible *axis mundi* – at the time of creation (§§435, 447):

> Thereupon, the sun-god said to Tvaṣṭṛ 'So be it'. Permitted by the sun-god Viśvakarmā mounted him on his lathe in the Śākadvīpa and began to whet the disc that had been originally circular and rough. When the sun, the central pivot of the worlds, began to rotate, the Earth along with the oceans, mountains and forests rose up into the sky. ... the entire firmament including the moon, planets and stars came tumbling as if pulled down and agitated. Waters of ocean

---

[68] Líu Ān (ed.), *Huáinánzǐ*, 3. 1, tr. J. S. Major, in trs. Major *et al.* 2010: 115, *cf.* note 4. Modern spellings for the respective proper nouns are 'Gònggōng', 'Zhuānxū' and 'Bùzhōu'. A 'thearch' is literally a divine ruler.
[69] Líu Ān (ed.), *Huáinánzǐ*, 6. 7, tr. J. S. Major, in trs. Major *et al.* 2010: 224–225. With tonal signs, 'Nüwa' is spelled 'Nǚwā'. On the four pillars, see §§221-241, 260, 337.

splashed up. The great mountains crumbled down with their rows of ridges broken up and scattered. The abodes having Dhruva the Pole Star for their support came down ..., as the cords of rays that held them together, snapped. Thousands of huge clouds were tossed up by gusts of wind as they fell and whirled about with great velocity. They rumbled terribly as they were shattered to pieces.

... with the Earth, sky and nether regions whirling about along with the rotating Sungod the entire cosmos became excessively agitated at that time. On seeing the three worlds thus whirled about, the celestial sages and Devas eulogised the sun-god along with Brahmā.[70]

Dislodgement of the pole star (*Dhruvaḥ*), as implied in the citation given above, is also included in the *Mahābhārata* among the omens foreboding the great war on which this epic centres:

The Polar star is shining intensely and moving to the right.[71]

For some societies, commotion of the celestial bodies signalled the coming end of the world, often among a host of other signs. Thus the apocalyptic tradition of Judaism:

The moon will change its order
and will not appear at its (normal) time.
At that time it will appear in the sky
and will arrive at ... at the edge of the great chariot in the west
and will shine very much more (brightly) than its normal light.
Many heads of the stars will stray from the command and will change their ways and actions
and will not appear at the times prescribed for them.[72]

The Pitahawirata band of the Pawnee (Nebraska) expected replacement of the North Star by the South Star at the termination of the cosmic era:

---

[70] 'Brahmā', in *Brahmā Purāṇa*, 30. 80-88, tr. Shastri 1985: 167-168. Tvaṣṭṛ is the divine smith, Viśvakarmā ('all-maker') the creator. Śākadvīpa was a mythical landscape. For the sun as "the central pivot of the worlds", see the note in §435. On the sky, earth and underworld as "three worlds", see §§79-80.

[71] Vyāsa, in *Mahābhārata*, 6 (*Bhīṣma Parva* [*Book of Bhīṣma*]): 1 (*Jambūkhaṇḍa-Nirmāṇa Parva*): 3. 17, tr. Cherniak 2008: 24-25. Narahari Achar (2003: 20) argued that this merely referred to a comet of a type called *dhruvaketu* ('pole star comet'); see the discussion in §450.

[72] 1 *Enoch* (*Ethiopic Enoch*; 3rd to 1st century BCE), 80. 4-6, trs. Nickelsburg & VanderKam 2012: 110; *cf.* Knibb 1984: 269-270. Compare §§429, 391*.

The Morning-Star said further that in the beginning of all things they placed the North Star in the north, so that it should not move; it was to watch over the other stars and over the people. The North Star is the one which is to end all things. The Morning-Star told the people that the North Star stood in the north and to its left was a pathway which led from north to south; that when a person died they were taken by the North Star and they were placed upon the pathway which led to the Star of Death – the land of the spirits – the South Star.

The Morning-Star also said that in the beginning of all things they gave power to the South Star for it to move up close, once in a while, to look at the North Star to see if it were still standing in the north. If it were still standing there it was to move back to its place. ... The North Star continued to tell the people that whenever the South Star came up from the south it would come up higher; that when the time approached for the world to end the South Star would come higher ... The North Star would then disappear and move away and the South Star would take possession of the earth and of the people.

... some of the signs have come to pass ... but the Morning-Star is still good to us, for we continue to live. ... The North Star and the South Star will end all things.[73]

369*
dismembered body parts as miscellaneous entities

A widespread theme is the *formation of defining aspects of the landscape from the dispersed body parts of a dismembered being,* in some cases explicitly described as composed of stones or flames (§§364-369).[74] For example, the Potawatomi (central North America) related that a "great manitou came on earth and chose a wife among the children of men", with whom he begot four sons, including Nanaboojoo, who was "the friend of the human race, the mediator between man and the Great Spirit", and Chakekenapok, "the man of flint, or fire-stone". The latter was chopped up by the former for matricide:

---

[73] a woman to her grandson Ari-Wa-Kis *alias* Young Bull *alias* Captain Jim (c1835-1916), shaman of the Pitahawirata band of the Pawnee (Nebraska), recorded 1896-1906, in Dorsey 1906: 135-136, *cf.* 490-491.
[74] Compare the fragmentation of sun or moon, §447.

In coming into the world he caused the death of his mother. Nanaboojoo, having arrived at the age of manhood, resolved to avenge the death of his mother, (for among us revenge is considered honorable); he pursued Chakekenapok all over the globe. Whenever he could come within reach of his brother, he fractured some member of his body, and after several rencontres [sic], finally destroyed him by tearing out his entrails. All fragments broken from the body of this man of stone then grew up into large rocks; his entrails were changed into vines of every species, and took deep root in all the forests; the flintstones scattered around the earth indicate where the different combats took place.[75]

372*
inversion of the earth

A sudden movement in which *the earth goes topsy-turvy* is a common motif.[76] At the outset, it is important to remember that traditional societies widely perceived the earth – in its overturning as in many other mythological settings – as a more or less flat disc or plane, not a sphere, comprising either the known landmass or the sum of all landmasses and seas.[77]

In several traditions, toppling of the earth is linked together with other disasters, such as the deluge, collapse of the sky (§§300, 300*, 353, 466) or an inversion of the sky and either the earth or the netherworld (§457). For example, a shaman of the Kalaallit (western Greenland) asserted that the flood had coincided with an inversion of the earth: '... before the great flood inundated the land; but because the earth turned itself over, that which previously was up came down.'[78] Upon perceiving a comet, peasants in Menen (West Flanders) would exclaim: '... the sky is going to fall, the earth turns!'[79] And a shaman of the Zulu (southern Africa) recounted the following dire occasion:

---

[75] Potogojecs, Potawatomi chief, on 18 or 19 November 1846 at Council Bluffs (Iowa), to Pierre-Jean de Smet (1801-1873) in a letter by de Smet dated 10 January 1847, in de Smet 1847: 347-348. See the note in §§33*, 38* on the name 'Nanaboojoo'.

[76] *e. g.*, van der Sluijs 2011d: 165 (Kiribati).

[77] Compare van der Sluijs 2011a: 7, 18, 53, 104, 214, 216-219; 2011b: 41-42, 62-65, 76, 93, 103, 125; 2011c: 101, 105, 143, 171, 214 note 846, 223; 2011d: 19 note 56.

[78] recorded 7 November 1738 by Poul Hansen Egede (1708-1789), in Egede 1740: 96, tr. (to German) 1790: 182 (•); *cf.* Cranz 1765: 262, 266.

[79] Harou 1902: 571 (•).

> ... the earth turned upside down and what had become the sky became down, and what was the heavens became up. The whole world was turned upside down. The sun rose in the south and set in the north. Then came drops of burning black stuff, like molten tar, which burned every living thing on earth that could not escape. After that came a terrible deluge of water accompanied by winds so great that they blew whole mountaintops away. And after that came huge chunks of ice bigger than any mountain and the whole world was covered with ice for many generations.[80]

The first sentence is utterly incoherent and almost certainly garbled; a clearer meaning is obtained by reading "what had been the sky" instead of "what had become the sky". It looks as if the narrator envisioned the earth and the sky as a single structure consisting of two layers which turned over as a whole, so that the earth's trading places with the sky necessarily implied inversion of its top and bottom.

Some cultures associated the earth's overturning with its 'separation from the sky' (§§39, 46-47, 56-57, 77-80, 212, 240, 267, 294, 339, 339*, 350, 374, 404, 408). The Māori (New Zealand) provide an example in case:

> ... after the Sky-father and Earth-mother had been separated, the face [front] of their mother had been overturned so that she faced Hades.[81]

At this time, the "family of gods ... still dwelt in [a faint light] like the moonlight of this earth, because neither stars, the moon, nor the sun had been placed in position." And a member of the Kalaallit viewed the lifting of the sky from its former limit at the mountain peaks to its present height as the consequence of the flood: '... that the sky, before this, rested on the tops of the mountains, but after the great flood, which inundated the whole earth, it was raised up to the height which it has now.'[82] If this belief was consistent with the Kalaallit opinion cited above that the flood was coeval with an inversion of the earth, it follows that – in the cosmogonic system of this nation – the overturning of the earth,

---

[80] Vusamazulu Credo Mutwa (b. 1921), a Zulu shaman of the Msimango tribe, on 2 October 1999, in anonymous 2000: 11. See §457 on the inversion of sky and earth, §436 on the disturbance in the sun's course, §458 on the molten tar, and §449 on the ice. See also the note of caution regarding Mutwa's credibility in §§436, 440.

[81] Nepia Te Ika Pohuhu (c1802-1882), priest of the Ngāti Hinepare subtribe of the Ngāti Kahungunu tribe (around Napier, North Island), recorded spring 1863 by Hoani Te Whatahoro Jury (1841-1923), tr. Smith 1913: 135.

[82] recorded 12 July 1738 by Poul Hansen Egede (1708-1789), in Egede 1740: 89, tr. (to German) 1790: 166-167 (•).

the elevation of the sky and the flood were joint aspects of the same complex reality.

There may be a correlation between 'sun shooting' (§444) and a capsizing earth. A suggestive example is an account given by the Udege (southeastern Siberia) of an archer's shooting of a troublesome second sun (§§443-444):

> With a shrill whistle, the arrow sped straight to its mark and vanished into the burning soul of one of the suns. A great rumbling was to be heard as if the earth were turning over; and the wounded sun turned a deathly pale.[83]

Traditional expectations for a coming end of the world often parallel traditions about past events (§§359*, 373*, 415-421, 429, 434, 436, 439, 443, 454-455). A relevant example in the present context is the belief expressed in the Mahāyāna branch of Buddhism that the earth will turn over in the distant future, just after multiple concurrent suns have burned up the world (§443):

> First, two suns appear in the sky, then four, then sixteen and because of the heat everything will burn up. These consequences will even make themselves felt to the Altan melekei (the golden frog), who represents the image of Uran Mandsu-shirin, as located below the mountain Sumber, encompassing the entire earth. As this animal realises that the humidity required for its life diminishes, it has to change its position and turn upside-down and with this revolution the entire world will turn over, too.[84]

Turning of the earth may also be envisioned on the horizontal plane instead of vertically. If the shift is large enough for eastern landscapes to become western in relation to the celestial bodies and *vice versa*, the experience on the ground is similar to that of a reversed sun (§§373, 373*). For example, the K'ahsho Got'ine, a subgroup of the Sahtú (around Fort Good Hope and Colville Lake, Northwest Territories, Canada), related a tale entitled 'the earth turns back on itself':

> At first, the Courtesans dwelled where the sun rises (in the east). The Kollouches used to be dogs, but later they became people. The Dènè (people), then, dwelled towards the west, we, being the people. …

---

[83] recorded before 1977, in autumn 1977 or in spring 1981, in Riordan 1989: 184.
[84] an unidentified text, in Bastian 1871: 585 (•). 'Sumber' denotes the cosmic mountain Sumeru, whilst 'Mandsu-shirin' surely stands for 'Mañjuśrī'.

> Then, suddenly, the earth did thus: from one side to the other it turned itself back, it pirouetted, it is like that; and since then, at the same moment, the Kollouches dwelled in the west, turning towards the other side of the Bighorns mountains, and we came to be on this side here. At the very beginning we used to live beside the great sea and there was no one on this earth here. … Before that, one used to live in the west. It was not very long ago.[85]

Apparently, the narrator related the inversion of east and west to the earth – or rather the North American continent – rotating in relation to the sea, with the Rocky Mountains – here called the 'Bighorns' – as a pivot.

407*
abundant vegetation

One of the principal determinants of a former 'golden age' is an *abundance of vegetation*, providing easy access to food.[86] Australia furnishes examples of the theme, according to which the central desert was a delightful place to live in. For instance, the Wangkangurru (northeast of Lake Eyre, South Australia) recalled an age of verdancy ended by a catastrophic blaze: "Tradition has it that before the white man came, many years ago, upon the Warburton and Diamantina, there was a most wonderfully luxuriant season. Following this a terrible fire came sweeping

---

[85] recorded 1862-1881, in Petitot 1887: 229-230 (••). Compare the paraphrase: 'In the beginning, the Phantoms lived in the east. These Phantoms were at first dogs which metamorphosed into men. So we, the People (*Dènè*), we were living in the west (*Tahan*) … Then suddenly the earth did thus: it turned on itself by inverting the cardinal points. It was as if it had pirouetted on its heel. Since then, the Phantoms have lived to the west of the Rocky Mountains; while we came to the east of these same mountains. So, at the very beginning, we lived on the shore of the great western sea, while to the east of the Mackenzie there was still no inhabitant; because we are the inhabitants of the plateaux of the high mountains. We did not yet know the *Nakotsia-kotchô* (the Mackenzie) and we lived in the middle of the Rocky Mountains.' 1886: 230-231 (•). 'Harlots' and 'dogs' are denigrating references to the Kollouches – nations on the west coast, such as the Haida. The Mackenzie River flows through Canada's Northwest Territories, just east of the Rocky Mountains. In the original account, the story continues with the sighting of a curious 'flaming star' (*lléré kollé*; •) in the south and the discovery of metals in the rotated earth; this sequel is presented as a separate story in 1886: 232-234 and was interpreted by Petitot (1887: 229) as a 'recent memory of a volcanic eruption to the west' (•). The translation provided in 1976: 57 is too misleading to be used.

[86] Compare van der Sluijs 2011d: 255-260 (Romani; Australia; Ifugao; Zoroastrians; Romans; Solomon Islands; Makiritare).

almost down to Lake Eyre. Many of the blacks were burnt to death."[87] According to the Dieri and other nations, "the deserts of Central Australia were once fertile, well-watered plains":

> The rich soil of the country, watered by abundant rain, supported a luxuriant vegetation, which spread from the lake-shores and the river-banks far out across the plains. The trunks of lofty gum-trees rose through the dense undergrowth, and upheld a canopy of vegetation, that protected the country beneath from the direct rays of the sun.[88]

The Scottish physician, naturalist and anthropologist William Ramsay Smith (1859-1937) published an account of an unprovenanced legend describing how the land, long ago, emerged from glacial conditions (compare §449):

> ... the frozen water, like a pavement of solid crystal covering portions of the earth, began to melt and to flow in liquid state. Then the earth staggered and rolled and trembled as if in dreadful agony. Rocks rose and formed mountains, hills, and valleys, and the silvery liquid rolled between as rivers, streams, and lakes.[89]

A halcyon age ensued, in which the earth was blanketed by lush plant life and teeming with forms of life no longer seen today:

> ... a mist had risen from the ocean, rivers, lakes, and valleys, and had covered the earth like a shroud. Nothing was visible. Then the mist slowly melted away. ... the face of the barren earth had changed, and was covered with vegetation that was very beautiful to behold. The air was filled with sweet and reviving fragrance that was shed by flowers of every form and colour. Some of the trees rose to heights of many hundreds of feet, and their trunks at the ground were from thirty to forty feet thick. Vegetation reigned supreme. ... The sun was concentrating her rays upon the water within the earth, and was bringing forth life in forms most strange to behold. ... mythical beings that are now known to us only in legends.[90]

---

[87] recorded 1903-1923 in Mungeranie (South Australia), in Horne & Aiston 1924: 9. The Warburton and Diamantina are rivers flowing northeast of Lake Eyre. This "terrible fire" may well be related to the fire which escaped from a celestial "long staff" in a tradition from the Wurundjeri (Melbourne, Victoria; §§449, 454).
[88] Gregory 1906: 3-4.
[89] Smith 1930: 179.
[90] Smith 1930: 180-181. These conditions came to an end when the waters of the ocean rose.

Smith combined this report with a portrait of the Nullarbor Plain (South Australia), now arid, as a "Land of Perfect Bliss":

> On the Plain of Nullarbor there existed a wonderful and beautiful country. ... Many shrubs and ferns grew on the hillsides, and in the valley and on the plain there were large gum-trees and plants with beautiful flowers. The ground was covered with a soft carpet of green grass. The flowers and the grass had the ordered appearance of a well-laid-out garden. ... Thus in the Land of Perfection there was no need for one creature to prey upon another in order to live. Neither the bird nor the fish needed to hunt the insect. So all lived in happiness and harmony.[91]

Similar traditions obtained among the northern Arrernte (central Australia):

> The totemic ancestors, however, live in an environment infinitely superior to that in which the present-day native has to battle for his existence. The great sire and his horde of sons live under ideal conditions, in a land of natural riches and plenty. Their easy toil is rewarded by an abundance of food. ... In the myths a highly idealized picture is given of the Burt Plain and the bordering northern MacDonnell ridges. Every creek and rill contains water. The plain is green with herbs and grasses; the mountains are decked brightly with a multicoloured covering of wildflowers. The air is heavy with the scent of eucalypt and acacia buds. Clustering swarms of native bees hum around the pale yellow blossoms of the bloodwood trees, eager to collect the sweet honey. The rocky caves are filled with nimble wallabies; and in the burrows on the plains the sharp-nosed bandicoots are sporting carelessly.[92]

A shaman from an Ojibwe band in Ontario testified to the stability of the food supply prior to a comet's wrecking of the world (§454): "Before the comet came, life on the earth was easy for the Indians. ... There were no

---

[91] Smith 1930: 174-175. Although the bulk of Smith's material was purchased or plagiarised from the Ngarrindjeri preacher, inventor and writer David Unaipon = Ngunaitponi (1872-1967), this legend was not in Unaipon's manuscript (1924-1925). It must be treated with the greatest of caution (*contra* Campbell 1967: 478), because, besides appearing to be much embellished, it inextricably blends impressions of former geological realities as reconstructed by scientists with the portrayal of the Nullarbor Plain as a vast quadrangular city, possibly based on *axis mundi* lore, and the visionary experience of another world by the soul of a "sick man", reminiscent of a near-death experience and illustrative of the afterlife believed in by the natives.
[92] Strehlow 1947: 35-36.

cycles of more food and less food."[93] And the Huni Kuin (Acre, northwestern Brazil, and adjacent area in Peru) had this to say regarding the time when it was always day (§435), before a deluge of rain came, the sky fell and it changed places with the earth (§457):

> The Caxinauás are living, made houses, live in very beautiful villages, lots of vegetables abound [sic].
>
> The Caxinauás do not think about anything (they fear nothing), they are very happy, they live, far from the mighty river on the border they live.[94]

448
absence of regular seasons

Stories of the sun and moon formerly and habitually moving at different speeds (§§432-433) or along different paths (§436) imply that a diurnal and seasonal cycle of some sort prevailed, but with different variables than current cycles. Several cultures specifically recalled a time – generally an 'age of creation', a 'golden age' or the period immediately following it – when *the seasons did not yet alternate in a predictable cycle* at all, which is almost tantamount to claiming that no seasons existed; either an unvarying condition obtained (compare §§3, 435, 440) or weather and climate were highly unstable.[95] For example, adherents of the Bön religion (Tibet) spoke of the "original god of the world ... *Yang dag rgyal po*" as "a *deus otiosus*, who existed when there was neither sun nor moon, nor time, nor the seasons, but only pure potentiality."[96]

---

[93] Wabmaymay ('Dawn Pileated Woodpecker'), a storyteller of the Ketegaunseebee (Garden River) band, prior to 1910, to Sah-kah-odjew-wahg-sahor ('Sun Rising over the Mountain') *alias* Fred Pine (b. 1897), of the same band, recorded 1980-1985 at the Garden River reservation (near Sault Ste. Marie, Ontario), in Conway 1992: 243.
[94] Bô-rô *alias* Vicente Penna Sombra, a Huni Kuin, recorded c1908, in Capistrano de Abreu 1914: 481 (•), with addition of capital letters. When the same narrator later stated that 'there were no vegetables' (1914: 484 [•]), he was obviously referring to cultivated plants, as he went on to relate the onset of agriculture. See the note in §440 on the reliability of the translation of Koch-Grünberg (1927: 229-230).
[95] This theme was not explored in depth in van der Sluijs 2011a-d, but see 2011d: 258 note 827, where "ecliptic plane" should be read instead of "equator". On the problematic use of *Genesis 8.* 22 as evidence for the introduction of the seasonal and diurnal cycles after the deluge, see §435.
[96] Tucci 1980: 214. Tucci's source has not yet been identified. On the otiose deity, compare §375.

One common expression of the belief in a time preceding the alternation of seasons is that of a uniform condition or 'season' of pleasant climate, traditionally viewed as one of the main characteristics of the 'golden age' and, logically, a direct cause of the lush vegetation (§§407, 407*). Some sources provide sufficient detail to show that this 'eternal spring' (*ver perpetuum*), in addition to its temporal uniformity, was also thought to have prevailed worldwide, but other traditions restrict the paradisiacal climate to a particular geographic region only. The Wangkangurru qualification of a past age of splendid verdancy in the Central Australian outback as "most wonderfully luxuriant season" (§407*) suggests that only a single season prevailed. Similarly, the Ojibwe in unambiguous terms attributed the stable provision of food before the coming of a comet (§§407*, 454) to the delectable climate of the time:

> Before the comet came, life on the earth was easy for the Indians. The moon never died [waxed and waned] at that time. There were no cycles of more food and less food. No seasons, until that comet burnt up the country.[97]

> That comet made a different world. After that, survival was hard work. The weather was colder than before.[98]

Within the classical world, the Roman poet Ovid – writing in 8 CE – appears to have been the first to explicitly mention introduction of the seasons, in association with the banishment of Saturn and the end of his glorious rule:

> Golden was that first age, which, with no one to compel, without a law, of its own will, kept faith and did the right. ... The earth herself, without compulsion, untouched by hoe or plowshare, of herself gave all things needful. And men, content with food which came with no one's seeking, gathered the arbute fruit, strawberries from the mountain-sides, cornel-cherries, berries hanging thick upon the prickly bramble, and acorns fallen from the spreading tree of Jove. Then spring was everlasting, and gentle zephyrs with warm breath played with the flowers that sprang unplanted. Anon the earth, untilled, brought forth her stores of grain, and the fields, though unfallowed, grew white with the heavy, bearded wheat. Streams of milk and

---

[97] Wabmaymay to Sah-kah-odjew-wahg-sahor, as above, in Conway 1992: 243. The statement regarding the former absence of lunar phases is puzzling – is the implication that the sun did not yet move (§435)?
[98] Wabmaymay to Sah-kah-odjew-wahg-sahor, as above, in Conway 1985: 99.

streams of sweet nectar flowed, and yellow honey was distilled from the verdant oak.

After Saturn had been banished to the dark land of death, and the world was under the sway of Jove, the silver race came in, lower in the scale than gold, but of greater worth than yellow brass. Jove now shortened the bounds of the old-time spring, and through winter, summer, variable autumn, and brief spring completed the year in four seasons. Then first the parched air glared white with burning heat, and icicles hung down congealed by freezing winds.[99]

The Tohono O'odham (southwestern Arizona) preserved the memory of a single equable season:

> At that time the sun was nearer to the earth than now, the seasons were equal, and there was no necessity for clothing to guard against the inclemency of the weather.[100]

And the Selk'nam (northeastern Tierra del Fuego, southern Chile and Argentina) described the earliest epoch they could recall as "the days when all the forest was evergreen, before *Kerrhprrh* the parakeet painted the autumn leaves red with the colour from his breast, before the giants *Kwonyipe* and *Chashkilchesh* wandered through the woods with their heads above the tree-tops; in the days when *Krren* (the sun) and *Kreeh* (the moon) walked the earth as man and wife, and many of the great sleeping mountains were human beings".[101] Another version reveals that deciduous trees existed elsewhere, to the north, while evergreens dominated the homeland of the Selk'nam:

> In ancient times, however, it was not like that, but all the trees always had green leaves.

---

[99] Ovid, *Metamorphoses*, 1. 89-90, 101-120, tr. Miller 1977: 8-11; *cf.* van der Sluijs 2011d: 258. Macrobius (*Saturnalia Convivia* [*Saturnalian Dinner Parties*], 1. 8. 7, tr. Kaster 2011: 88-89) wrote that "when chaos existed, time did not" (*cum chaos esset, tempora non fuisse*), but because in the context his "time" represents the god Kronos, it is not warranted to translate *tempora* as "times and seasons", as Davies (1969: 64) had done, even though this is probably correct conceptually.

[100] José María Ochoa *alias* Con Quien ('the Gambler'), chief of the central Tohono O'odham, tr. Phyllena Wallace Tonge (1827-1912) of Cahuabi (Pima County), in Davidson 1865: 131. On the low sun, compare §430.

[101] recorded 1902-1907, probably from Aneki ('Awkward' or 'Left-Handed'; b. 1870s), in Bridges 1948: 412. See §§428, 430 for the original presence of Sun and Moon on Earth, while a former, powerful and low sun was in the sky.

> And it came to pass that a young man named Camschoat went to the far, far north, where it is warmer and returned, saying that in those countries many great trees had green leaves in summer and red ones in autumn. The Onas did not want to give him credence, so that the young man, indignant, set off again for the north and later returned in the form of the *cotorra* (a small parrot of Tierra del Fuego, all green except the chest which is red) loaded with red leaves to show to the incredulous. Having arrived, he alighted on the trees, of which the leaves in his vicinity became red. ... Cotorra is the Spanish name while the indigenous Ona is *Kerrk-perrk*.[102]

This latter source adds that the introduction of deciduous trees in Selk'nam territory occurred in the sixth of eight cosmic epochs, following the ascent of the sun and moon into the sky in the fourth (§430) and the sun's first settings below the horizon in the fifth (§436); the eighth era is the present one.[103]

Not all societies looked back with fondness or even a neutral attitude on the time without regular seasons. Some groups lamented that the weather was persistently unpleasant throughout this period. Thus, the Hopi of Oraibi (Arizona) believed that the world was dark and cold and the firmament low (§3) before "*Matcito* appointed times and seasons and ways for the heavenly bodies".[104] And the Buna (a loose grouping of castes and tribes in Central and Eastern Bengal), who are accustomed to a monsoon climate, passed on a negative memory of a different time:

> ... in the beginning there was no rain and the change of season was difficult. One day a man of their group went to the god of rain, whom also they call Sing-Bhonga, and prayed for rain to have a clearance of one season from the other. The great god granted his prayer and henceforth the rain occurs at the change of every season.[105]

Elsewhere, the complaint was that the weather in some distant past was changeable, perhaps even felicitous at times, but unpredictable. Ojibwe informants other than the shaman cited above reported on the instability of the seasons in the period immediately following the golden age (compare §440, 449):

---

[102] Cojazzi 1911: 143 (•), *cf.* 145. 'Ona' is an old designation of the Selk'nam. In Spanish, *cotorra* appears to be a general South American word for any species of the Psittacid family. The species referred to here must be the austral parakeet (*Enicognathus ferrugineus*). 'Kerrk-perrk' is another spelling of 'Kerrhprrh'.
[103] Cojazzi 1911: 145.
[104] recorded 1869-1879, in Powell 1881: 25; *cf.* 1879: 800.
[105] recorded by Minendranatha Vasu (b. 1911), in Basu 1939: 86.

> Life was very different from that time on: the seasons were unbalanced, the days unsettled ...
>
> ... just as there is the daily rise and set of Sun giving day and night, so is there the annual change of season giving summer and winter, periods of growth and decline. It was not always so. Both Beboon (Winter) and Neebin (Summer), coveting the year, made war upon each other for primacy over and possession of the entire year. The Anishinaubaeg endured so much misery during the struggle that the enemies were finally persuaded to a truce by which the year was partitioned equally between them ...
>
> But before the division of the year into summer and winter was settled once and for all, Beboon took Neebin and locked him up somewhere in the northern sky. It was the Fisher who, learning of the act and where Neebin was concealed, set out to free the prisoner.[106]

The Niimíipu nation (Columbia River Plateau, Pacific northwest) dated the settling of the seasons to the end of a glacial period, which saw "the enmity between Youn, the Cold, and Lo-ki-ye-wah, the Heat", "just before the people came":

> When the clouds from the Northeast met the clouds from the Southwest, they mingled as if fighting. ... The coyote, boss of all, appeared upon the scene and cut the throat of Lokiyewah, saying, 'From this time onward it shall not always be cold, neither shall it be always warm. Part of the time it shall be warm and part of the time cold.' So the seasons were settled.[107]

And according to the Ute (primarily Utah and Colorado), it was before the gods "established the days and the nights, the seasons and the years, with the length thereof", that Tä-vi, the fickle "sun-god", had the unpleasant habit of shining either too fiercely from a position close to Earth or not at all (§§430, 436, 440).[108]

---

[106] Johnston 2005: 147-148. 'Anishinaubaeg' is an alternative name for 'Ojibwe'. Competition between a 'winter king' and a 'summer king' was a common element of European folklore. Scholars usually interpret it in terms of the regular seasonal alternation, but unstable seasonality of the type illustrated in the Ojibwe myth makes better sense.

[107] probably recorded 1873-1907 by Susan Law <Sue> McBeth (1830-1893) or her sister Kate Christine McBeth (1832-1915), in McBeth 1908: 263-264.

[108] recorded as above, in Powell 1881: 24-25; cf. 1879: 799. In the version given in 1881: 54-56, the sun's name is spelled as 'Ta´-vï'.

449
cold period

Various traditions recall a period of *unusual and insufferable cold weather or climate*, often in connection with ice and snow and responsible for mass deaths.[109]

Frequently, such a condition characterises the very earliest remembered time. As a persistent predicament, it amounts to a seasonless time negatively perceived (§448). A myth from the Shuswap (Kamloops area, British Columbia) opens as follows: "At that time the earth was very cold, for the Cold People of the north ruled the elements, and delighted in having cold winds blow over the Indian country all the time. Thus people suffered much, and constantly shivered."[110] The Niimíipu expatiated on the icy backdrop to "the enmity between Youn, the Cold, and Lo-ki-ye-wah, the Heat", when the seasons had not yet been settled (§448):

> The children of Lo-ki-ye-wah were all killed but one daughter. She was with child. ... When that son grew up, he came as far north as the eastern side of The Dalles. ... There was a frozen sea there then. They fought on ice. ... They still fought although the ice was crushing under them. ... This battle was fought just before the people came.[111]

In a story from the Ojibwe (§440), the land sighs under a prolonged cold at a time when access to the sky – where heat is holed up – is hermetically sealed:

> The hunter's name was Ojeeg, or the Fisher ... As hunting formed his constant occupation, his son began early to emulate his father in the same employment, and would take his bow and arrows, and exert his skill in trying to kill birds and squirrels. The greatest impediment he met with, was the coldness and severity of the climate. He often returned home, his little fingers benumbed with cold, and crying with vexation at his disappointment. Days, and months, and years passed away, but still the same perpetual depth of snow was seen, covering

---

[109] Krüger (2013: 78-83, 150-151) discussed early 19th-century awareness among local peasants of the formerly much larger extent of glaciers in the Alps and the South American Andes. However, rather than folk tradition these cases appear to have been inferences drawn from careful observations of erratic boulders and scratches, possibly of relatively recent date.
[110] Sixwi'lexken, a Shuswap born near Big Bar (British Columbia), recorded 1900, in Teit 1909: 624.
[111] probably recorded 1873-1907 by the McBeth sisters, in McBeth 1908: 264.

all the country as with a white cloak. ... Ojeeg told the Otter to make the first attempt to try and make a hole in the sky.[112]

And informants from the Cherokee, who should be quite accustomed to climatic extremes, claimed that the first fire was confined to a special tree on an inaccessible island at a time of lasting cold:

> In the beginning there was no fire, and the world was cold, until the Thunders (Aní'-Hyûñ'tĭkwălâ'skĭ), who lived up in Gălûñ'lătĭ, sent their lightning and put fire into the bottom of a hollow sycamore tree which grew on an island. ... This was a long time ago. ... still there was no fire, and the world was cold ...[113]

Such tales are hardly surprising for higher latitudes, but recollections of an exceptionally cold or icy primeval condition are attested at lower parallels as well. The Efé branch of the Mbuti (northern Ituri Forest, northeastern Congo) looked back on the time before fire was discovered as an age of cold, which is somewhat surprising considering the equatorial latitude at which its members live: 'In the beginning, the Pygmies did not have fire, so they had to eat everything raw; they sat in front of their huts with outstretched legs and froze.'[114]

Memories of an original cold period are also found in the southern hemisphere. One instance hails from the Bibbulmun people (southwestern tip of Australia).[115] Another Australian legend, otherwise unprovenanced (§407*), has it that the land was, long ago, covered by "frozen water, like a pavement of solid crystal covering portions of the earth".[116]

---

[112] recorded 1822-1839, in Schoolcraft 1839: 57-58, 62. Vine Deloria (1995: 99) mentioned "a Chippewa creation story, which says that God tried four times to create the present world but the first three efforts were doomed to failure because there was too much ice." While this account does not look suspicious, it should not be used until its source, which was not named by Deloria, has been discovered. The "Chippewa" most likely are the Ojibwe, as opposed to the Denésoliné, who are also known as 'Chipewyans'. The four attempts call to mind the cross-cultural motif of serial aeons (§§410-413).

[113] A'yûñ'inĭ ('Swimmer'; c1835-1899), an East Cherokee tradition keeper; and Ităgû'năhĭ alias John Ax (c1800-after 1900), an East Cherokee; recorded 1887-1890, in Mooney 1900: 240-241. Gălûñ'lătĭ was "the world above", where spiritual beings dwell, 1900: 231. Compare §§150, 168 for the retrieval of fire from or via an *axis mundi*.

[114] recorded 1934-1935, in Schebesta 1936: 133 (•). The introduction of fire corresponded with that of death (1936: 133-134, *cf.* 130), ending an 'age of myth'. The Mbuti used to be categorised as 'Pygmies'.

[115] van der Sluijs 2011a: 76-77; 2011d: 168.

[116] Smith 1930: 179. See the earlier note of caution (§407*) regarding the reliability of this passage.

The coolness is perhaps a natural consequence of the primordial darkness universally attested in myth (§§6-7), a connection which is again found at diverse latitudes on both hemispheres. In their description of the time preceding that of two suns (§443), the Samogitians (western Lithuania) combined primeval cold with darkness:

> In the beginning God inhabited the sky alone, then he created angels, who should serve him in the sky, and humans, who should worship him on the earth, which was previously uninhabited. But there was darkness and cold everywhere, and the angels and humans complained to God that they could not bear the great cold and the dense darkness.[117]

An unidentified branch of the Miao from southeastern Yúnnán (China) linked low temperatures with the absence of celestial luminaries:

> In ancient times, there was neither sun nor moon in the sky. Darkness covered the earth and it was freezing cold all year round.[118]

The Wurundjeri (Melbourne, Victoria) related that, at the time of creation, "it was 'plenty dark'": "For a long time after the creation, in the winter they were very cold, for they had no fire ..."[119] And the Hopi of Oraibi stated that the world was dark and cold and the firmament low (§3) before Matcito regulated the seasons (§448) and celestial bodies.[120]

In other traditions, a cold episode does not precede or equal, but follow the age of 'creation' by a considerable time.[121] This incident can also be regarded as a type of irregular and disagreeable 'season' (§448).

---

[117] recorded 1878-1882, in Veckenstedt 1883: 237 (•).

[118] Táo Yǒnghuá, a Miao, recorded before 1982 in Wénshān Zhuàng and Miáo Autonomous Prefecture (Yúnnán), tr. Miller 1994: 85.

[119] recorded April 1840 - 1844, in Howitt 1845: 191. The tradition allows that the summer temperatures were bearable. Bear further in mind that winters in Victoria can be cold even on the present climate. The Wiradjuri (New South Wales) remembered a time when the original, anthropomorphic sun vanished and the "semi-darkness that ensued was bewildering and ... struck terror into everyone" (2011d: 207; compare §§431, 439). This tradition may or may not relate to the same period.

[120] recorded 1869-1879, in Powell 1881: 25; cf. 1879: 800.

[121] The Mah Meri (Melaka, Malaysia) claimed that their ancestors, following the age of the seven suns and moons and the eastern giant guarding the sky pillars (§443, compare §120), passed through the land "Padang Berimbun (= P. Běrambun, 'the plain of dew'), where the surface of the earth was covered with deep dew, which was bitterly cold." – a young Jakun informant, recorded 1891-1906 by Walter William Skeat (1866-1953), in Skeat & Blagden 1906: 318. Taking the tropical habitat of the Mah Meri into account, this could very well be a memory of snow. If climate change had occurred, the land in question need not be so cold today.

The Zoroastrian tradition knew of a 'golden age' presided over by the early king Yima (§§398, 409), which came to an end with the arrival of a devastating long-lasting 'winter'. The god Ahura Mazdā thus announced this to Yima:

> Upon the material world the fatal winters are going to fall, that shall bring the fierce, foul frost; upon the material world the fatal winters are going to fall, that shall make snow-flakes fall thick, even an aredvî deep on the highest tops of mountains. And all the three sorts of beasts shall perish, those that live in the wilderness, and those that live on the tops of the mountains, and those that live in the bosom of the dale, under the shelter of stables. Before that winter, those fields would bear plenty of grass for cattle: now with floods that stream, with snows that melt, it will seem a happy land in the world ...[122]

Apart from the feats of Ojeeg touched on above, the mythological repertoire of the Ojibwe included the episode of the strife between Beboon ('Winter') and Neebin ('Summer') just after the golden age, when the seasonal cycle had not yet been regulated (§§440, 448). In the course of this, Winter achieved dominion for a time by imprisoning Summer:

> Life was very different from that time on: the seasons were unbalanced, the days unsettled ... But before the division of the year into summer and winter was settled once and for all, Beboon took Neebin and locked him up somewhere in the northern sky.[123]

The Aymará of Bolivia, too, appear to have had a tradition regarding a mass death caused by sudden freezing: "Ages & ages ago, the Snow God

---

[122] *Avesta: Vendīdād* (*Given against the Daevas*; before the 8th century BCE), 2. 2. 22-24 (46-60), tr. Darmesteter 1880: 15-16. An *aredvī* apparently corresponds to 14 'fingers'. This Persian tradition of an 'ice age' may have originated outside Iran, perhaps in the homeland of Indo-European or even earlier ancestors. The lasting cold is structurally analogous to the deluge of other traditions. In a twist that suggests contact with the Hebrew myth of Noah's flood, Yima is instructed to build an enclosure (*vara*) within which all seeds and living beings survive the cataclysm. However, unlike the ark, this structure was a quadrangular city located at a place from which Yima did not return, where "the stars, the moon, and the sun are only once (a year) seen to rise and set, and a year seems only as a day" (2. 2. 25-40 [61-132], tr. 1880: 16-20). This mysterious place doubled as a type of paradise and, judging by the description, was located at the geographical north pole – not unlike the land of the Hyperboreans in Greek myth (van der Sluijs 2011b: 124). The statement about the apparent movement of the celestial bodies as seen from this location must have been based on either travellers' reports or a sophisticated astronomical understanding of the earth's rotational properties; in the latter case, the passage must postdate the 6th century BCE, probably by centuries – see the discussion in 2011a: 6-13. A recent study of the *vara* is Vidale 2017.
[123] Johnston 2005: 147-148.

'Kun' destroyed all life on earth, and only the ill-tempered 'supaya' (devils) lived to roam the highlands of Bolivia. The 'Pacha-Camaj' (Gods of Fertility) then sent down their own sons, the 'Paka-Jakes' (Eagle Men), to create a new race of their beloved Aymara people, all of whom had been snowed under by Kun. The Paka-Jakes settled on the land around holy Lake Titicaca, recreated the Aymaras, and named the province Pacajes after themselves."[124] And in a tale from the Yámana (southern Tierra del Fuego, South America), a condition of 'general darkness with much snow and ice' is brought on and subsequently removed by the character Héšpul ('sparrow'), but few further details are supplied (§439).[125] Another Yámana account of instant glaciation is the following:

> It was in the old time. Spring approached once more. ... But Léxuwa is very sensitive and irritable, she wants to be treated especially genteelly. Now when those men, women and children screamed so loudly and so long, she heard this noise and was very displeased about that.
>
> Deeply offended, she suddenly in her anger called forth a thick snowstorm, accompanied by strong frost and much ice. From then on, snow and ever more snow fell for months on end. Snow fell continuously and the entire earth became covered with ice; because there was also a very grievous cold. The water froze in all the waterways. Many, many people died; for they could not board their canoes and travel out to look for food. They could not even leave the living huts to gather firewood; because everywhere lay very much snow. Ever more people died.
>
> At long, long last, the snowfall finally ceased. ... the whole earth was covered with that until high above the mountain tops. ... so thick was the ice cover which had settled over the whole earth at that time. An extraordinarily strong frost then held sway and a fearsome mass of snow had fallen. All this had been caused by Léxuwakīpa, she is a very delicate, sensitive woman. Since that time, the Yamana treat every bandurria with the highest reverence.[126]

The following short account was probably based on the same recording:

---

[124] anonymous 1943. The story must be treated with caution, as its provenance is not stated.
[125] Alfredo (b. 1850s), recorded early 1920; and Hálupens *alias* William (b. c1867), recorded 1923, in Gusinde 1937: 1271-1272 (•). Gusinde identified the species of the protagonist as *Taeniptera pyrope*. Presumably, he meant *Xolmis pyrope*, the fire-eyed diucon.
[126] Gusinde 1937: 1232-1233 (•); *cf.* 1951: 349-350. Léxuwakīpa corresponds to the black-faced ibis (*Theristicus melanopis*), locally known as the *bandurria*, 1937: 1155 note 84, 1232 note 174.

> The very touchy Lə́xuwakīpa felt offended by the people. In revenge she caused a great deal of snow to fall. A huge mass of ice finally covered the whole earth. ... That woman planned to destroy the whole world and all the people.[127]

Often, the cold interval long after the creation of the world is combined with other catastrophes, such as flood, fire, cosmic combat or revolution and contact with a comet. In the worldview of the Yámana, the global freezing coincided with a mighty social conflict: "The glaciation occurred just at the time of the universal revolution in Yáiaašága, when the men were carrying on their battle with the women and gained control of the kína."[128] In a legend from the Veluwe (central-eastern Netherlands), an age of bitter cold ensues after the thunder god and the ancient race of 'winter giants' (*Winterreuzen*) engage in a mighty clash, the heavens burn and are torn apart, the world is dislodged, the thunder god and a giant monster snake which assists the giants crash onto the earth and the earth sinks into the sea:

> Now the iceberg fleet of the white winter giants came floating from the north ... Many sad times passed, during which the formidable winter giant reigned supreme.[129]

Other examples are two Inuit accounts of glaciers forming in the wake of the deluge. A tribe of the Central Inuit of Cumberland Sound or Davis Strait (northeast Canada), either the Oqomiut or the Akudnirmiut, told: "A long time ago the ocean suddenly began to rise, until it covered the whole land. The water even rose to the top of the mountains and the ice drifted over them. When the flood had subsided the ice stranded and ever since forms an ice cap on the top of the mountains."[130] And the Inuit of Tasiilaq (southeast Greenland) reported:

---

[127] Alfredo, Uškëšlánen *alias* Charlin = Charley (b. c1867) and Šepišáalawayénčis *alias* Richard Black (b. c1874), recorded January 1920, in Gusinde 1937: 1155, tr. adapted from 1961: 1115-1116 (•). In 1922, the shaman Mašémikens *alias* Pedro (c1862-1923) confirmed this tradition, 1937: 1156-1157.

[128] Alfredo, Uškëšlánen and Šepišáalawayénčis, as above, in Gusinde 1937: 1155, tr. adapted from 1961: 1116 (•).

[129] an old lady merchant, heard between 1882 and 1892 by Gustaaf van de Wall Perné (1877-1911), in van de Wall Perné 1911: 23 (•). After the earth had dried up again, the places where the serpent and the thunder god had fallen remained as two lakes, the Uddelermeer and the Bleeke Meer. Although elements of the myth were borrowed from Icelandic lore, as the author admitted, the general outline as provided here seems to be authentic.

[130] recorded 1883-1884, in Boas 1888: 637-638.

> ... the water poured over everything. When the earth reappeared, it was entirely covered by a glacier. Little by little this decreased, and two human beings fell down from heaven, by whom the earth was peopled. One can see every year that the glacier is shrinking.[131]

The reverse was intimated by the T'atsaot'ine (north of Great Slave Lake, Northwest Territories, Canada), who shared the memory of an episode of intense snowfall, even by north Canadian standards, in the time of primordial darkness:

> In the beginning, one lived on this earth just like today; for what has always been, what is done has always been done. Man has always been a pilgrim on the earth, he has always hunted and fished to obtain sustenance, he has always drunk, eaten and slept, he has always slept with his wife and begotten children. Now during one winter, something happened which had not always been: so much snow fell that the earth was as if buried by it and the top of the highest firs alone appeared. This was not tenable. So all the animals which then dwelled and conversed with man departed for the sky in search of heat; because on this earth, converted into a glacier, one died of cold and need. ... it was gloomy and cold on the earth.[132]

Eventually, the bursting of one of at least seven celestial bags causes an outburst of heat, which melts the ice and thereby gives rise to a deluge (§440). The tradition of the Ojibwe of Ontario concerning a comet which burned the earth (§454) reflects as follows on the fallout of that event: "That comet made a different world. After that, survival was hard work. The weather was colder than before."[133] At tropical latitudes, the Quiché Maya (Guatemala) recounted that their first ancestors – long expectant

---

[131] recorded 1883-1885, in Holm 1888: 144, tr. (to German and English) Nansen 1893: 260 (•). On the notion of human ancestors descending from the sky, see van der Sluijs 2011a: 113-114 and §§157, 160, 286.

[132] Julien Ttsinnayinén, a T'atsaot'ine, recorded September 1862 at Great Slave Lake, in Petitot 1886: 373 (•). A year later, Petitot (1887: 358-360) published a word-for-word translation of the original recording, which reveals that the words 'and begotten children' as well as 'for the sky' were secondary additions (cf. tr. 1976: 5), the former perhaps inspired by the missionary's opinion that sexual congress ought not to be indulged in for pleasure alone and the latter to assist comprehension. A shorter version (1876: 74) was: 'At the beginning of time ... a deluge of snow took place in the month of September. ... the snow which covered it until the top of the tallest firs ...' (•) Compare §34* for the common language of humans and other animals.

[133] Wabmaymay ('Dawn Pileated Woodpecker'), a storyteller of the Ketegaunseebee (Garden River) band, prior to 1910, to Sah-kah-odjew-wahg-sahor ('Sun Rising over the Mountain') alias Fred Pine (b. 1897), of the same band, recorded 1980-1985 at the Garden River reservation (near Sault Ste. Marie, Ontario), in Conway 1985: 99 = 1992: 244.

of the first sunrise – were overcome by circumstances most peculiar for Central America:

> After that a great downpour began, which cut short the fire of the tribes. And hail fell thickly on all the tribes, and their fires were put out by the hail. Their fires didn't start up again. ... Then he started a fire. ... And so again the tribes arrived, again done in by the cold. Thick were the white hail, the blackening storm, and the white crystals. The cold was incalculable. They were simply overwhelmed. Because of the cold all the tribes were going along doubled over, groping along ...[134]

And in the southern hemisphere, the Wurundjeri tradition quoted above continues with an account of a deity's "long staff" – a comet? – responsible for the near-extinction of monsters and the temporary availability of fire, after which the cold of primordial times returns (compare §453):

> ... to add to their misery, the whole land was full of deadly snakes and guanos; but good Karackarock, their truly womanly divinity, did not forget or forsake them. ... Karackarock, a native divinity of the true feminine sort, a worker, came a long way armed with a long staff – native women carry such – and with this she went over the whole land killing the reptiles; but just before she had killed them all the staff broke, and the kind did not all perish.
>
> Misery there was in the breaking of that weapon, but there was also mercy, for Karackarock had so warmed it as well as herself with such a great slaughter, that when the staff snapped there came out of it fire. Fire they now had to warm themselves, and to cook with. Their condition was much improved, but did not long continue so, for Wang, the crow, a mysterious bird, ... watched his opportunity and flew away with it. For a long time they were again in a most sad and fireless condition ...[135]

The administration of heat to the earth is, of course, inseparably tied to the sun, while some groups – on less rational grounds – attributed a cooling effect to the moon. In myths already cited from the Ute (§§436, 447), the Kogi (§436), the Atayal (§433), Korea (§443), the Lisu (§443), the Shasta and Klamath (§443), the Nivaclé (§391*), the Chamba Leko and the

---

[134] *Popol Vuh* (*Book of the People*), 4, tr. Tedlock 1996: 153-154. The disasters were not entirely concurrent, as a short interval in which fires were rekindled occurred between the first hailstorm and the second one.
[135] recorded April 1840 - 1844, in Howitt 1845: 191-192. By "guanos" the author probably meant goannas or monitor lizards (*Varanus*).

Daka (§391*), terrestrial cooling is effected by anomalous solar or lunar characteristics such as one or more intolerably long nights, excess moons, a contest between the sun and moon and wounding of the sun.

Other traditions relate an unexpected cold period to the first rising of the sun or moon into the sky (§430). For example, the Quiché dated the various cold disasters mentioned earlier to the period directly preceding the first sunrise, while the Yámana association of the sudden global glaciation with a social revolution, noted above, similarly connects this story to that of the concomitant ascent of the former sun, who had burned the world, and his son (§§430, 443). The Nivaclé (Paraguay and northwest Argentina) well remembered "that period of freezing cold".[136] One account blames it on Jive'cla, the moon, who had just risen from Earth into the sky (§430):

> ... when the time came for the south wind to blow, it brought the vapour of *Jive'cla*'s cold and the next day there was a great frost at this height (indicates with the hand). It came from *Jive'cla*.[137]

The motif of a period of cold also shades into that of the weak, invisible, withdrawn or enclosed sun (§§439-440), on the logic that the extinction of sunlight caused by the sun's waning, shielding or withdrawal from the sky promotes cooling. Although most mythical reports of the sun's former weakening or confinement emphasise the ensuing darkness more than the meteorological ramifications, some dwell on the latter. It has been claimed that the Seneca branch of the Haudenosaunee Confederacy (New York State) possessed a tradition of seven successive worlds – separated by episodes of cleansing necessitated by the people's corruption – of which the second and fourth one ended in freezing conditions, brought about by diminution of sunlight:

> *Swen-i-o* ordered the Sun to withdraw its warmth from the face of Mother Earth, leaving only the Moon to exert his power upon Nature Land. The lesser light of the Moon was unable to warm Mother Earth. A state of cold settled upon Nature Land. This caused the devastation of the Second World. ...
>
> The cleansing of the Fourth World was exerted by the combined efforts of the Sun, the Moon, and Water upon Mother Earth.[138]

---

[136] Tanté, in Wilbert & Simoneau 1987: 35.
[137] Tanuuj, of the Tovok Ihavós of the Pilcomayo, recorded mid-1971 - mid-1972, in Chase-Sardi 1981: 54 (•).

Of the fifth world, too, "The cleansing was exerted by the powers of the Sun and Moon".[139] The Ojibwe myth cited above concerning Winter's locking up of Summer in the northern part of the sky can be seen as equivalent to the motif of the sun's temporary imprisonment (compare §440). And a story from the Zulu (southern Africa) tells how – "in those faraway days when creation was young" – incessant quarrelling between the sun and the earth caused by the moon (§391*) impelled the sun to withdraw into his hut (§440), thus causing a deadly 'ice age':

> In fact the Sun's condition appeared to deteriorate even more. In fact his illness grew worse as the days became months and the months became years. And the Earth herself began to stiffen from the intense cold. There was now frost in her hair and icicles dangled brightly from her eyelashes. She began to tremble as she fought with all means within her reach to bring the Sun back to life again. ...

> The Earth began to freeze. The Moon began to tremble with cold and there was misery in the heavens and misery upon the Earth itself. The Sun no longer rose in the heavens; only the Moon – a dull and darkened orb – still showed her stolen light briefly and occasionally in the skies. The forests were dark, brittle and frozen. The plains were covered under a thick blanket of rock-hard snow. The streams and the rivers no longer flowed, being held captive. Under great snarling boulders of merciless ice, the waves of the ocean were frozen and the sand of the coasts was hard, cold, and cruel with ice. ... The animals no longer grazed upon the plains of the Earth but starved in caves and in caverns deep under the ground. ...

> After many, many years, a sickly Sun, now recovered from his pretended illness, showed his face over the mountains of the East, and the world was somewhat warmed by the returning Lord of Day. But it was still cold, for a long time still ...[140]

---

[138] Twylah Hurd Nitsch (1913-2007), self-proclaimed Seneca tradition keeper, recorded 1923-1975, in Steiger 1978: 165-166. See the note in §429 regarding the question of Nitsch's reliability and compare again §§410-413 for a succession of ages.

[139] Twylah Hurd Nitsch, as above, in Steiger 1978: 167.

[140] Vusamazulu Credo Mutwa (b. 1921), a Zulu shaman of the Msimango tribe, in Mutwa 1996: 78, 81-82, 94. The earth's trembling obviously refers to earthquakes. According to the story, the pair of human ancestors – Kintu and Mamaravi – managed to survive these hardships by the theft of fire from the realm of the gods atop a "mountain of Crystal", familiar motifs in the mythology of *axes mundi* (§§150, 154-155, 168). See §§436, 440 for a word of warning regarding Mutwa's credibility as a conduit of authentic tradition.

Another Zulu tale, which may be a variation on the one cited above, correlates a past perversion of the sun's course, overturning of the earth and inversion of sky and earth to a series of other disasters (§§372*, 436, 457), the last one of which delivered fresh water to the land: "And after that came huge chunks of ice bigger than any mountain and the whole world was covered with ice for many generations."[141]

false positives

In Aztec myth, one of the cosmic eras or 'suns' – variously counted as the second or the fourth – is ended by catastrophic winds.[142] The retelling by the American journalist and historian Carleton Beals (1893-1979) adds that the tempests induced a sort of 'ice age': "Whirlwinds and cyclones swept over the world, picking up sand, stones, rocks, waters and finally trees, houses and human beings. The snowy capes of the mountain peaks were whisked away, converting the whole world with an immense white sheet."[143] Beals did not identify his source, but was clearly relying on a discussion of the past extinctions of humanity in the *Codex Ríos* (c1566 CE) by the Mexican archaeologist and politician Alfredo Chavero (1841-1906): '… the *Ehecatonatiuh* in which it was finished by snows and hurricanes … In the *Ehecatonatiuh*, four heads of *Ehécatl*, the god of the winds, blow hurricanes in all directions, and *Quetzalcoatl* makes a rain of snow fall from the heavens which concludes with humanity saving itself, only another couple, in a grotto.'[144] However, the image in the *Codex Ríos* which Chavero was concerned with does not convincingly show snow or ice and the accompanying commentary[145] does not refer to these elements either. Accordingly, this facet of the story must have been a figment of Chavero's imagination.

The Lower Umpqua (southwest Oregon) provided the following testimony: "(When in former days the) ground was covered with ice, much snow (lay) on the ground, and it became very cold, then the people had no way of drinking (water freely). From one well only could they drink, and all people drank from it. Although many were the people, still they

---

[141] Vusamazulu Credo Mutwa, on 2 October 1999, in anonymous 2000: 11.
[142] van der Sluijs 2011d: 265-267.
[143] Beals 1970: 33, cited in LaViolette 1997: 152.
[144] Chavero 1880: 65 (•), *cf.* 29.
[145] '… the second age, which they say lasted 4010 years, in which they say the world subsequently came to an end by a surge of very strong winds', Pedro de los Ríos and others, *Codex Ríos* = *Codex Vaticanus A* (MS. Vaticanus 3738), pl. VIII, ed. Kingsborough 1831: 166 (•).

all drank there. (And when) ice began to appear on the water (of the rivers), then all inhabitants could not go anywhere. They were forced to go along the surface of the ice. Then (at such times there would always be some) old man who knew that (ancient) custom of the people of long ago. (He would then tell it to his people.) ... Then at last it would rain."[146] From the wording, it seems clear that this is not a myth, but a memory of how the ancestors would historically respond to severe winters.

According to Frank Waters, finally, the Hopi (northeastern Arizona) contended that Tokpa, the second era of the world, came to an end by the earth's overturning, which ushered in a period of intense freezing:

> ... Sótuknang called on the Ant People to open up their underground world for the chosen people. When they were safely underground, Sótuknang commanded the twins, Pöqánghoya and Palöngawhoya, to leave their posts at the north and south ends of the world's axis, where they were stationed to keep the earth properly rotating. The twins had hardly abandoned their stations when the world, with no one to control it, teetered off balance, spun around crazily, then rolled over twice. Mountains plunged into seas with a great splash, seas and lakes sloshed over the land; and as the world spun through cold and lifeless space it froze into solid ice. This was the end of Tokpa, the Second World. For many years all the elements that had comprised the Second World were frozen into a motionless and lifeless lump of ice. But the people were happy and warm with the Ant People in their underground world. ...
>
> Eventually Sótuknang ordered Pöqánghoya and Palöngawhoya back to their stations at the poles of the world axis. With a great shudder and a splintering of ice the planet began rotating again. When it was revolving smoothly about its own axis and stately moving in its universal orbit, the ice began to melt and the world began to warm to life.[147]

As noted above (§34*), Waters' version of the Hopi traditions of creation must be dismissed as watered down, inauthentic and overly fanciful. In the quotation considered here, the implication that the Hopi were traditionally aware of the earth's sphericity and axial rotation beggars belief. It might still emerge that they possessed an authentic memory of refrigeration of the world associated with intense shaking (§32) and perhaps

---

[146] William Smith, an Alsea, and his wife Louisa, a Lower Umpqua, recorded March-April 1911 at the Siletz reservation (northwestern Oregon), in Frachtenberg 1922: 629, cf. 627-628; 1914: 76-79.
[147] purportedly recorded before 1963 by Oswald 'White Bear' Fredericks (1906-1996), a Hopi, in Waters 1978: 16. Compare van der Sluijs 2011d: 164, 264.

the abandonment of the twin extremities of a cosmic column by its guardians, but this cannot simply be assumed.

450
the morning or evening star as a comet

Some traditions endow *the morning or evening star, often specified as the planet Venus, with cometary or meteoric properties*, be it in its present or a former state and in direct or indirect, more ambiguous language (compare §§165, 398, 405-406). The majority of cases suggest no awareness of the physical identity of Venus or other planets as both morning and evening star.[148]

Explicit association of the morning or evening star with a comet or meteor is rare.[149] The Aztecs contended that, following the immolation of the legendary king Quetzalcōātl on a pyre, his heart or soul rose into the sky in the shape of a *quetzal* bird (*Pharomachrus* sp.). Seemingly conflicting traditions variously identify this catasterised form of the god as the morning star – identified as Venus – and a comet.[150] As an example of the

---

[148] As it can be cumbersome to repeat the wordy phrase 'morning or evening star', it might be useful to introduce a comprehensive term such as 'twilight star'. The inner planets Mercury and Venus are full-time twilight stars, the outer planets part-time ones.

[149] Compare van der Sluijs 2009b: 459, 472-474; 2011d: 244-245. Some possible examples lack satisfactory proof. In Mesopotamia, the goddess Inanna (Sumerian) *alias* Ištar (Akkadian) was identified as the planet Venus in both its morning and evening rôles since the late 4th millennium BCE – see, conveniently, van der Sluijs 2011c: 70; 2011d: 20 notes 58 and 59; James & van der Sluijs 2008: 61 note 9. An Akkadian text (VAT 8577 + 13655 and others) refers to Ištar as *ki-ṣi-ru ša šamê*, which might mean 'meteor of the sky' (*cf.* Oppenheim *et al.* 1971: 441 *s. v.* '**kiṣru**'), but 'knot, lump of the sky' cannot be ruled out. And in Albuquerque (New Mexico) on 23 March 2014, Diné botanist and tradition keeper Arnold Clifford (b. *c*1967), of the Tahchiini clan, was kind enough to tell me an abridged version of the creation myth as he had heard it from his grandmother – presumably Sarah Charley. He mentioned that, according to the Big Star chant, Venus, known as *Sûtso* ('big star'), "was once a comet", with "a tail like hair, which was chopped off": "Venus had horns. ... It was just a celestial body like a new star ... It was a new heavenly body, which created chaos." Within the relative chronology of events, this one occurred when the ancestors were still living in the underworlds (compare 2011b: 99-100; 2011c: 88 note 379, 243), probably between the two floods. However, because of Arnold's keen interest in catastrophist approaches to the world's mythology, more assurance of the authenticity of this tradition would help to rule out the possibility that affinity with the very similar ideas of Velikovsky (1950) coloured the narrative.

[150] van der Sluijs 2011d: 169-170, 217-219 (where confusion with the sun is also noted), 225, 231-232, 248, 303. Compare: '... they honoured and worshipped a certain star (I could not learn which star it was) more than any other creature either celestial or terrestrial, because they held it as certain that their god Quezalcovatl, the highest god ... of those of Chololla, when he died trans-

latter identification, the Spanish-Mexican historian and Franciscan missionary Gerónimo de Mendieta (1525-1604) wrote in 1596 CE:

> And that the soul of the said Quetzalcoatl turned into a star, and that it was that which is sometimes seen to project a ray like a spear from itself: and sometimes such a comet or star has been seen in this land, and after it pestilences have been seen to follow among the Indians, and other calamities; and the fact is that such comets are signs which God placed to denote some remarkable thing or event which he wishes to work or allow in the world.[151]

The contradictory takes on Quetzalcōātl's celestial identity can be reconciled if the original idea was that of a tailed morning star, however that is to be understood astronomically. The relationship of the incident to 'creation' is complicated; although the versions in which Quetzalcōātl's heart turns into Venus were obviously intended to account for the creation of that planet *in illo tempore*, the sources identify the Quetzalcōātl in question as the semihistorical Cē Ācatl Topiltzin (895-947 CE), king of the Toltecs, whose biography is inextricably intertwined with the god's. Apparently, the Aztecs – and probably the Toltecs before them – imagined that this exemplary ruler had lived not long after the creation of the world, having been born only 208 years after the ancestors' emergence from caves at a time of primeval darkness and a mere 92 years after the first appearance of the current, fifth sun.[152]

Meanwhile, the Skidi band of the Pawnee (Nebraska) "sang of the origin of the Morning Star itself that they thought had come from a meteor."[153] That this "meteor" may actually have been a "comet" is perhaps

---

formed into that star', Bartolomé de las Casas (c1484-1566 CE), *Apologética historia sumaria* (*Summary Apologetic History*), 3. 174, ed. de Tudela Bueso 1958: 140 (•); *cf.* Christenson 2003: 218 note 569. 'Quezalcovatl' is an old spelling for 'Quetzalcōātl', 'Chololla' for 'Cholula'. The continuation of the account leaves no doubt that the 'star' was Venus, as the astronomers 'had very certain knowledge of the day when it was to appear in the East and of that when it was to set and disappear in the West' (•).

[151] Gerónimo de Mendieta, *Historia eclesiástica Indiana* (*Indian Ecclesiastical History*; 1596 CE), 2. 5, ed. Icazbalceta 1870: 82 (•).

[152] *Annals of Cuauhtitlan* (*Codex Chimalpopoca* [1610-1628 CE]), 1. 24 - 3. 56, tr. Bierhorst 1992: 24-28, with reconstructed dates in the Christian calendar and a date range of 817-895 CE for the life of Cē Ācatl Topiltzin.

[153] Mark Evarts *alias* Sun Chief (b. c1861), a Skidi, recorded 1928-1936 at Pawnee (Oklahoma), with Henry Chapman *alias* Wolf that Howls (d. c1950) as interpreter, in Weltfish 1965: 113, *cf.* Murie 1981 (1921): 121. It is not clear on which source del Chamberlain (1982: 57, *cf.* 65-66, 245) based the following statement regarding the morning star: "... as he traveled he carried a fireball either in his bundle or in his moccasins. The Morning Star and flint were both associated

more likely, for "the great comet of 1882 was believed ... to be the Morning-Star, who is spoken of as Opriiskisku, the Downy-Feather-Star, who was traveling from the north back to the east in a hurry."[154] And the Jicarilla Apache (New Mexico) knew a long story in which, at one point, Morning Star returns two sky visitors to the earth in the following manner:

> Morning Star journeyed to the west and Morning Glow followed. When Morning Star got directly over the holy place he threw himself down as a meteor. And when Morning Star flew down, the light flashed all over.[155]

More commonly, a possible past or present cometary or meteoric aspect in the perception of the morning or evening star remains implicit in a sudden change in the object's course or even a fall (§359*); suggestive metaphors such as its association with a tail, a string, feathers, hair, smoke or horns; its representation as a fabulous mythical creature such as a giant celestial dragon, snake or bird (compare §§306, 312, 357, 398); or its alleged emission of greater brightness or heat than would be physically possible under the current astronomical circumstances.[156]

To begin with the case of an appendaged crepuscular star, among the Sakha (northeast Siberia) Venus, known as Čolbon, was said to be "the daughter of the Devil and to have had a tail in the early days":

> If it approaches the earth, it means destruction, storm and frost, even in the summer; 'Saint Leontius, however, blessed her and thus her tail disappeared'.[157]

---

with meteorites. ... These beliefs ... indicate a Skidi awareness of the entire range of phenomena associated with meteorite fall, from the brilliant fireball to the fragments striking the ground."

[154] George Amos Dorsey (no date), in del Chamberlain 1982: 60 note 2. The more correct spelling of the indigenous name was u:pirikucu' ('Big Star'), 1982: 48, 54-57, 232. Compare van der Sluijs 2009b: 464-465, 472-473.

[155] Cevero Caramillo (1896-1976), John Chopari, Alasco Tisnado (b. c1863) or Juan Julian, recorded spring 1934 - spring 1935, in Opler 1938: 175.

[156] An example of a horned Venus may be seen in a Samoan myth about "Lady Tapuitea" who "became wild, horns grew out of her head, she ate human flesh" and eventually turned into Venus as evening star, recorded 1840-1880, in Turner 1884: 260, 262; cf. van der Sluijs 2011d: 199. It must be noted, however, that the horns appear here on a human female before she "turned into Venus". Astronomically, 'horns' on Venus might also be an expression of the planet's phases, but no undisputed naked-eye observations of this phenomenon are on record.

[157] recorded 1877 in Namsky District (Sakha Republic), in Seroshevskiy 1896: 668, tr. Mándoki 1968: 489. On the adverse effects of Venus' approach to the earth and two errors in Mándoki's discussion, see §359*.

Various Australian groups presented Venus' possession of a cometoid appurtenance as a parontomyth, that is to say, an ongoing reality. The Yolngu (eastern Arnhem Land) adjudged Barnumbir, which is Venus as a female morning star, to be a tuft of feathers held on a string by one or two women in Purelko – the 'island of the dead' towards the far east – as she emerges from the basket or bag in which she is kept during the day:

> The morning star has a string tied to it because the men on this island made it and it belongs to them. ... Now an old woman owns and controls Barnumbir, the morning star. Her power name was Mar-lum-bu. ... When she sleeps she lies on her baskets where she keeps the morning star and puts her arms around it so that no one can see it. ... It comes from this Island of Perelko. ... she turned it loose, for it was early morning, and it flew away. ...
>
> The old woman held on to the string. Barnumbir sailed away like a kite. She keeps the star going in the direction she wants it. On this island of ghosts there is a tremendously high pandanus tree. Barnumbir flies up there first and rests. ... that old woman holding the rope with one hand and with the other she pulled out the string from her basket. While she did this she cried out her commands to Morning Star. ... She pulled Barnumbir back, pulling as though she had caught a very big shark. She pulled her right into her basket and hid her there again.[158]

The Yolngu at Yirrkala told another visiting anthropologist that Barnumbir is composed of a ceremonial object made from the yam (*mawoka*; *Dioscorea* sp.) and its flower.[159] They continued:

> Two women, *Dunjun-jina* and *Mitjuna*, live at Purelko and keep the morning star, *barnumbir*, in a string bag, guarding it jealously all the day and most of the night, lest it should escape. A little before dawn, *Jaualin-wura*, the head man of Purelko, says to the women: 'It's time that you let the morning star out of that bag so that it can visit the *dua* camps on earth both to wake up the men, women and children and to give them the messages from the dead.' The woman *Mitjuna* objects strongly to this suggestion, because she is afraid that she might lose *barnumbir*, but *Jaualin-wura* overrules her, and releases the morning star, which is already struggling to get out of the bag to perform its allotted tasks.

---

[158] recorded 1926-1929, in Warner 1958: 525-527. In the story, a man named Yaolngura visits the island of the disembodied souls to see the morning star. 'Perelko', like 'Buralku' and 'Bralgu', is a different spelling of 'Purelko'. The pandanus tree corresponds to the botanical genus *Pandanus*.
[159] recorded July-September 1948, in Mountford 1956: 325 note 46.

> At first *barnumbir* rests on the top of a tall pandanus tree from which it can see a long distance. This causes the women to cry out in fear that they might lose the star, and to ask that it be returned to them. To pacify the women *Jaualin-wura* pulls the morning star back again – it is on a string – and puts it in the bag.
>
> But, though the women are pleased, *Jaualin-wura* thinks of the aborigines on earth waiting for their messages. So he opens the bag again and allows *barnumbir* to escape. For a while the morning star dances along the surface of the water, but soon climbs rapidly into the sky. It visits each *dua* place in turn, wakes the aborigines and then gives them messages from their relatives and friends at Purelko. Just as dawn is breaking *Jaualin-wura* takes hold of the string, pulls in the star and, placing it in the carrying-bag, gives it to the women, who guard it until the next morning.[160]

Minor variation is found among the Yolngu at Milingimbi, too:

> Djiraia, the home of the dead and the morning star, is situated on a rocky island somewhere east of the English Company Islands ... Two spirit men, *Jumundik* and *Dalnuranu*, are in charge. ... The morning star, *barnumbir*, is kept in a cave under the care of two women, who sleep all day and most of the night. But just before dawn these women wake up and tell the two men, *Jumundik* and *Dalnuranu*, that it is time they stopped their singing and let the morning star out of the cave to wake up mankind, otherwise they will sleep all day long.
>
> When *barnumbir* is first released it dances up and down on the surface of the sea. It then climbs up a tall pandanus tree, then flies through the air to visit a number of localities where the aborigines live. When the dawn breaks the women take hold of the string attached to *barnumbir*, pull it back and imprison it in the cave until the next morning.[161]

Later still, a Yolngu informant submitted another slightly different account:

> On Buralku, the island of the spirits of the dead, the two spirits, Naikala and Birrowarr, made the rranga of the morning-star. From the

---

[160] recorded as above, in Mountford 1956: 326-327; *cf.* 481 note 9; Bhathal 2009: 18-19; Haynes 1992: 133-134; Worms 1986: 104. The *dua* is one of the Yolngu's moieties.
[161] recorded as above, in Mountford 1956: 328-329. In one bark painting (1956: 316 Plate 101A), Barnumbir is depicted as a "white circle" surmounting a "long rectangle" which represents "the rays of light, called *balai-aba*, which issue from it." The English Company's Islands form the northeasternmost part of Arnhem Land.

skin of the banyan-tree they made the string called rraki, with the white down-feathers of birds twisted in it. ... When the two spirits Naikala and Birrowarr want to speak with spirits in other countries, they throw the pul-pul, the tuft of white feathers, which is the morning-star, into the sky and, when it is daylight, they pull the morning-star, on the end of its string, down again to Buralku, the island of the spirits of the dead.

The morning-star on the end of its string lies coiled up in the dilly-bag of one old-man spirit. This dilly-bag, called Battee, is the mother of the morning-star. It is the womb. The tuft of white feathers, the morning-star, is the child looking out of the dilly-bag. And the string, coiled in the dilly-bag, is the cord by which the child is joined to its mother. ...

The spirit Naikala dances, holding the dilly-bag with the morning-star in it. He looks round and he dances and sees a pandanus-tree. He throws the morning-star out of the dilly-bag and the star climbs up the pandanus and goes into the dark sky. ... The morning-star goes into the sky and then it is daylight. Then Naikala pulls the star down and puts him back in the dilly-bag.[162]

Similarly, the Ringu Ringu, a subdivision of the Pitta Pitta (around Boulia, western Queensland), were found to "call the star Venus *mimungoona* or *big-eye*, and believe that it is a fertile country covered with *bappa*, the name of a sort of grass, the seeds of which the tribes here on earth convert into flour, and is inhabited by Blacks", yet "no water exists in the star, but there are ropes which hang from its surface to the earth, by means of which the dwellers visit our planet from time to time, and assuage their thirst. A big old man of great power is also said to dwell in the star."[163] As a celestial object attached to the underworld or the earth by one or more ropes, the morning star of these Australian traditions parallels the 'tied sun' (§445), while the connecting string or strings serve as an *axis mundi* (compare §86).

As for the motif of a feathered or hairy appearance of the morning or evening star, among the Shuswap (interior of southern British Columbia), a sobriquet for the morning star was "one with hair standing out

---

[162] Manuwa Wongupali (1917-1979), of the Djambarrpuyŋu clan of the Yolŋu, recorded 1954-1956 at Milingimbi, in Robinson 1956: 49-50; *cf.* van der Sluijs 2011d: 245-246. A *rranga* is a sacred ceremonial object, a dilly bag a traditional bag used for the transportation of food. The story continues with the episode in which Barnumbir escapes and the respective colours and trajectories of morning stars are sorted out (§359*).
[163] recorded by Alexander McLean, in McLean 1886: 351.

round his head" (*wō-pk-ā´*).¹⁶⁴ Insofar as the wording suggests that the planet was believed to be still decorated thus, this, too, qualifies as a parontomyth. 'Hairy One' (*Shiʻraj*) seems to have been an Arabic name for the planet Venus, while an Arab counterpart to the legendary queen Semiramis was apparently called 'Hairy One' (*Zebbaj*) as well.¹⁶⁵ And admitting eyelashes as a type of hair, a possible parallel from ancient Egyptian literature centres on the goddess Ḥathor or Saḫmet as the destructive 'eye of Ra'.¹⁶⁶ This episode was firmly embedded in the mythology of creation.

The morning or evening star may also have been conceived of as a comet under the guise of a mythical celestial beast. For example, the god Quetzalcōātl – who was counted among the Tzontemoc or Tzitzimime, a group of stellar deities which once fell from the sky (§359*) – could have owed the meaning of his name, 'feathered serpent', to a very conspicuous tailed comet. Although the extant Spanish texts make it seem as if the historical ruler Cē Ācatl Topiltzin was merely named after this serpentine deity, the myth of his posthumous transformation into a *quetzal* bird could originally have been a variant of a tradition in which the god thus acquired his reptilian form; in myth, avian and ophidian traits are frequently combined or interchangeable. The Sumerian Enḫeduanna (23rd century BCE), high priestess of Ur, invoked the goddess Inanna – who, as seen, was the planet Venus – as a frightening "dragon" (*ušumgal*), tormenting the world with thunderous roars, floods, hurricanes and fires in what appears to have been an ongoing or repeated plight (§306).

As late as the 20th or early 19th century BCE, Sumerians continued to invoke Venus in its evening aspect – as Inanna – in terms that would be wildly exaggerated or inaccurate if applied to the planet's familiar appearance, though without reference to a dragon or terrestrial devastation. In a hymn of that date celebrating the ritual of the goddess' *hieros gámos* ('sacred marriage') with Iddin-Dagān, king of Isin, the planet is praised as a celestial prodigy, visible even at noon and filling the sky with daylight:

> I shall greet the holy torch who fills the heavens, the light, Inana, her who shines like daylight, the great lady of heaven, Inana! I shall greet the Mistress, the most awesome lady among the Anuna gods; the re-

---

[164] recorded 1877 or 1888-1890, in Dawson 1892: 39.
[165] Winckler 1901: 43. Considerable caution is advised, as Winckler's sources could not yet be identified.
[166] van der Sluijs 2011d: 24-25, 183-184, 195, 227-229, 238-239, 248.

spected one who fills heaven and earth with her huge brilliance; the eldest daughter of Suen, Inana! For the young lady I shall sing a song about her grandeur, about her greatness, about her exalted dignity; about her radiantly ascending at evening; about her filling the heaven like a holy torch ...

When at evening, the radiant star, the Venus star, the great light which fills the holy heavens, the lady of the evening, ascends above like a warrior, the people in all the lands lift their gaze to her.

The lady exalted as high as the heaven, her grandeur reaches the borders of heaven.

At night the skilled and beautiful one (?), the joy of An, the ornament of broad heaven, appears like moonlight; in the heat of the noon she appears like sunlight.[167]

Later still, Babylonian scribes twice addressed the goddess Ištar, the Akkadian equivalent of Inanna, as *akukūtu*, a word which has been translated as 'fire', but is really an Akkadian term used for the *aurora borealis*:[168]

... fire that blazes against the enemy ...[169]

Wild cow, which knocks down the parts of the world,
fiery glow, which penetrates into the middle of sky and earth,
high Ištar, who governs the parts of the world ...[170]

---

[167] a *šir-namuršaĝa* to Ninsiana for Iddin-Dagan (Iddin-Dagan A), 4-12, 89-91, 126 = 167 = 225 (*cf.* 110), 112-114, trs. Black *et al.* 1998-2006: 2. 5. 3. 1, translating *izi-ĝar kug an-e si-a-ra* as "the holy torch who fills the heavens", *ud* as "daylight", ^{mul}*dili-bad* as "the Venus star", *an-zag* as "the borders of heaven" and *an-bar$_7$* as "noon". 'Inana' is another spelling of 'Inanna'. Suen is the moon god, An personified the sky.

[168] The Akkadian word *akukūtu* is thought to have meant "flame, blaze" and "red glow in the sky (as a rare meteorological phenomenon)": "Since *akukūtu* denotes an exceptional meteorological phenomenon of bad portent, it probably refers to the aurora borealis." Oppenheim *et al.* 1964: 285 s. v. '**akukūtu**'. Weidner (1912: 5) interpreted the term as 'THE COMMON NAME FOR MORNING AND EVENING TWILIGHT' (•), while Neugebauer & Weidner (1915: 37, 62, *cf.* 55) translated 'shiny red clouds' (•) or 'a heap of clouds irradiated with red (by the morning or evening twilight)' (•), but these opinions are long obsolete. In the annals of king Sargon II (d. 705 BCE) and in 'a hymn' *ḫakukutum* was apparently used in the sense of 'firebrand', Neugebauer & Weidner 1915: 61; Weidner 1912: 6.

[169] "*a-ku-ku-ú-tu$_4$* (var. *a-ku-ku-ti*) *ša ana ajābī napḫat*", K. 26187, obverse, 37, trs. Oppenheim *et al.* 1964: 285 s. v. '**akukūtu**'; *cf.* King 1902: 228-229.

[170] incantation to Ištar and Dumuzi, A (K 2001+, BM 76976, VAT 8261, A 165), 2. 42-44, tr. Hecker 2008: 117 (•). Oppenheim *et al.* (1964: 285 s. v. '**akukūtu**') translated line 43, "*a-ku-ku-tu$_4$ ša qablat*

This suggests that Venus was associated with 'flames' which were similar to the polar aurora.

Exceptional brightness befitting a bolide or comet more than a planet is also ascribed to Venus, along with an erratic course (§359*), in a Chinese astronomical treatise:

> Once, moreover, Venus was visible in full daylight and, while moving across the sky, rivaled the sun in brightness.[171]

false positives

Velikovsky alleged that the Jewish *Talmūd* in "very concrete form" mentions "this luminous tail, which Venus had in earlier centuries" in the following sentence: "Fire is hanging down from the planet Venus."[172] Yet far from being specific about a tail or indeed anything suspended from Venus, the passage in question was concerned with ordinary astrological ideas. On his Procrustean bed, Velikovsky had expediently hacked off the information about the other planets supplied in the same text; the full passage reads:

> Not the constellation of the day but that of the hour is the determining influence.
>
> He who is born under the constellation of the sun will be a distinguished man: he will eat and drink of his own and his secrets will lie uncovered; if a thief, he will have no success.
>
> He who is born under Venus will be wealthy and unchaste [immoral]. What is the reason? Because fire was created therein.
>
> He who is born under Mercury will be of a retentive memory and wise. What is the reason? Because it [Mercury] is the sun's scribe.
>
> He who is born under the Moon will be a man to suffer evil, building and demolishing, demolishing and building, eating and drinking that which is not his and his secrets will remain hidden: if a thief, he will be successful.

šamê u erṣeti ṭerât", as "fiery glow which envelops heaven and earth to the very core ..."; *cf.* the earlier edition and translation in Langdon 1916: 108, 113.
[171] cited in Huáng Cháng, *Sūzhōu Shíkè Tiānwéntú* (*Sūzhōu Astronomical Chart*; 1193 CE), trs. Rufus & Tien 1945: 5.
[172] Velikovsky 1950: 164.

> He who is born under Saturn will be a man whose plans will be frustrated. Others say: All [nefarious] designs against him will be frustrated.
>
> He who is born under Ẓedeḳ [Jupiter] will be a right-doing man [ẓadḳan]. ...
>
> He who is born under Mars will be a shedder of blood.[173]

The words "fire was created therein" (*'ytylyd byh nwr'*) doubtless refer to a basic astrological property.[174] The obvious meaning is simply that Venus is the brightest of all planets.

In August 1618, the Jesuit priest, astronomer and architect Orazio Grassi (1583-1654) was initially sceptical of reports of a comet then seen in the sky for the following reason:

> Suddenly, men had no greater concern than that of observing the sky; if Venus chanced to shine more brightly than usual, it was changed into a comet; if at sunset a cloud did not immediately disappear but formed a cross, it was considered as a monstrous thing. But these were the views of the mass of the people, of less weight than a feather ...
>
> In the month of August, news was brought to us from many parts of Italy that during that period a comet was seen licking the hind feet of the Great Bear. But we, knowing that the ignorant mass of the people had considered Venus as a comet, suspected the same on this occasion and considered that those vigilant watchers had been readily deceived.[175]

Velikovsky construed these words as evidence for a surviving popular memory of Venus as a comet.[176] This is disingenuous, however, because the populace was obviously not sustaining a tradition about Venus as a comet, but mistook it for one where trained astronomers did not see one,

---

[173] Ḥanīnā bar Ḥāmā (d. c250 CE), in *Babylonian Talmūd: Šabbāt*, 24 (156a), ed. Freedman 1972: 156a, tr. 1938: 799. The Aramaic names of the planets used in this passage are respectively Ḥammā for the sun, Kōkab Nōgah for Venus, Kōkāb for Mercury, Ləbānā for the moon, Šabbəta'ī for Saturn, Ṣedeq for Jupiter and Ma'ădīm for Mars.

[174] The editor's note (Freedman 1938: 799 note 7) is of little help: "During the hours ruled over by Mercury."

[175] Grassi 1619: 4-5, trs. Drake & O'Malley 1960: 6-7 (•). For the comet, see Kronk 1999: 334.

[176] Velikovsky 1967: 8, followed by Cochrane 1989: 61. Note Velikovsky's subtle misquoting of "had considered Venus as a comet" into "consider Venus as a comet", as if the error was not committed once by the uneducated, but was a veritable folk belief.

rather in the same way that contemporary reports of 'unidentified flying objects' (UFOs) sometimes turn out to involve nothing more than sightings of Venus by naïve observers.

Greek astronomers associated the planet Venus with a type of comet called 'horseman' (Greek *Hippeús*, Latin *Hippius*): "Of the comets, the 'horseman' is also called the sacred star of Aphrodite. It is the size of the whole full moon, swift in motion, tail flickering and dissipating at the end. It is carried in the same direction as the *kosmos* [east to west] through the 12 signs of the zodiac. When it appears it brings about falls for kings and tyrants, and the changes in those lands from which it sends forth its tail."[177] "... it has been named thus from its speed. It draws oblique and fiery locks and extends a trail of light and, in turn, contracts itself into a small disk with uncustomary quickness and speed, at one time sprinkling around and at another time contracting its so-called trails."[178] However, the link between Venus and 'horseman'-comets was part of a system assigning each of the seven traditional planets to a category of comets.[179] This system was probably devised only during the Hellenistic period, knew several minor variations and was not rooted in folk traditions about the planets. It would be cherry-picking to cite Venus' correlation with 'horseman'-comets as evidence for belief in a cometary phase of Venus while ignoring the other 'planetary' comets.

Chinese literature contains multiple passages in which "Venus generates white comets".[180] A famous ancient historian and scientist put it thus:

> If its color is white with five rays and if it appears ... late it means celestial anomalies and a *Broom-star* [comet] will emanate toward states ...[181]

---

[177] pseudo-Petosiris (late 4th century BCE?), Fr. 10, in Hephaestio of Thebes, *Apotelesmatica* (*Horoscope Casting*; c415 CE), 1. 24. 5, ed. Pingree 1973: 74, trs. Irby-Massie & Keyser 2002: 89-90.
[178] Campester (sometime between 100 BCE and 400 CE), in John of Lydia, *De Ostentis* (*On Celestial Signs*), 4 (Greek 17), ed. Bandy 2013: 76, tr. 91-93 (odd). Compare further John's own discussion, 2 (Greek 15), ed. 2013: 74, tr. 87; and Avienus (305-375 CE), in 'Servius Auctus', *Commentary on Virgil's Aeneid*, 10. 272, ed. Thilo 1884: 421-422.
[179] pseudo-Petosiris, Fr. 10, in Hephaestio of Thebes, *Apotelesmatica*, 1. 24. 5-12, ed. Pingree 1973: 74-76, trs. Irby-Massie & Keyser 2002: 89-90; Avienus, in 'Servius Auctus', *Commentary on Virgil's Aeneid*, 10. 272, ed. Thilo 1884: 421-423; Campester, in John of Lydia, *De Ostentis*, 4-9 (Greek 17-22), ed. Bandy 2013: 76-86 (even), tr. 91-105 (odd); and John's own discussion, 1-2 (Greek 14-15), ed. 2013: 70-74 (even), tr. 85-87 (odd). See further van der Sluijs 2006: 79; van der Sluijs & James 2013: 292.
[180] Schafer 1977: 65, *cf.* 48-49, 64.

Such events were claimed to have occurred, for example, in the summer of 770 CE[182] and on 18 May 905 CE.[183] One chronicle states that once "*T'ai-pai* (= Venus) dispersed and became *T'ien-kou*";[184] the latter term – *Tiān-gǒu* in modern transliteration – literally means 'sky dog' and refers to electrophonic bolides and associated meteorites.[185]

As in the classical world, however, these statements arose within the framework of a wider system – the 'Five Activity doctrine' – in which Mercury, Saturn, Mars and Jupiter also produce comets with characteristic colours.[186] One exposition of this doctrine includes the 'sky dog', which "has a white colour, but a yellow centre like the trace left by fire", among the types of "ominous stars" engendered by Venus.[187] Another, later one incorporates Venus' transformation into a 'sky dog', along with

---

[181] Sīmǎ Qiān, *Shǐjì* (*Scribe's Records*) = *Tàishǐgōng Shū* (*Records of the Grand Historian*; c109-91 BCE), 27 (*Tiānguān Shū* [*Treatise on the Celestial Offices*]): 1327, tr. Pankenier 2013: 485; *cf.* 1333-1334. Schafer (1977: 87) also cited the following passage: "A *Long-Lived* [*Star*] is like a bolt of cloth hanging in the sky. When this star appears, armed combat arises." Sīmǎ Qiān, *Shǐjì*, 27. 1336, tr. Pankenier 2013: 496; also in Lǐ Fǎng (ed.), *Tàipíngyùlǎn* (*Imperial Readings of the Tàipíng Era*; 977-983 CE), 7. 5a. The record does not link this with Venus at all and most likely refers to the *aurora borealis*, *cf.* 2013: 496 note 260. However, it is reminiscent of this one for 25 November 868 CE: "There was a 'star' which came forth like a strip of shimmering satin; it extended across the void, was transformed into clouds, and then disappeared. This was in the 'allotment' of Ch'u, and refers to an appearance of 'prolonger of *keng*', at which armed men will rise up." Ōuyáng Xiū & Sòng Qí (eds.), *Xīn Tángshū*, 32. 10b, tr. Schafer 1977: 87. As Schafer pointed out, the term "prolonger of *keng*" (*chánggēng*) was a name for Venus as evening star, but "The connection with Venus is obscure: it seems possible that the name 'prolonger of *keng*' may, despite our dictionaries, have been applied to more than one kind of fire in the sky." Might it have referred to any object serving as evening star, that is to say, the first object visible in the sky after sunset? Schafer leaned towards an auroral explanation in both cases, but also allowed a cometary or meteoric one; the passage is not included in the archaeoastronomical catalogue of Xu *et al.* 2000. Finally, Schafer (1977: 48-49) also cited an occasion in the late spring of 760 CE, based on Lǐ Bái (701-762 CE), *Ni Ku, Shih Erh Shou*, no. 6, in Liú Xù (ed.), *Jiù Tángshū* (*History of Early Táng*; 945 CE), 3. 6. 23. 2b; however, this poem is not explicit about the connection between Venus and comets at all: "Comets scatter ethereal light. Venus rises in the east." tr. Hinton 1996: 94.

[182] Ōuyáng Xiū & Sòng Qí (eds.), *Xīn Tángshū* (*History of Later Táng*; 1060 CE), 32. 6a, tr. Schafer 1977: 65.

[183] Ōuyáng Xiū & Sòng Qí (eds.), *Xīn Tángshū*, 32. 7b, tr. Schafer 1977: 115.

[184] *Hé Tú* (*Yellow River Chart*), in Xiāo Zǐxiǎn (ed.; 489-537 CE), *Nán Qí Shū* (*Book of Southern Qí*), 13, tr. Keimatsu 1973: 3 #118. Compare this translation: "... the essence of T'ai-Pai [Venus] changed into a meteor of the class T'ien-Kou ['celestial dog']", Rufus & Tien 1945: 5.

[185] This is clear from Sīmǎ Qiān, *Shǐjì*, 27. 1335, tr. Pankenier 2013: 496; Xiāo Zǐxiǎn (ed.), *Nán Qí Shū*, 13, tr. Keimatsu 1973: 2-3 #118; Fáng Xuánlíng (ed.), *Jìnshū* (*History of Jìn*; 648 CE), 12. 2 (*Tiānwénxué* [*Astronomy*; ed. Lǐ Chúnfēng]): 7b, tr. Ho 1966: 138; Toqtogha = Tuōtuō (Mandarin) & Ālǔtú (eds.), *Sòng Shǐ* (*History of Sòng*; 1346 CE), 23, tr. Keimatsu 1975: 32 #330, where earlier sources are cited.

[186] *Hé Tú*, and Jīng Fáng (78-37 BCE), *Fēngjiǎo Shū* (*Book of Wind Angles*), both in Fáng Xuánlíng (ed.), *Jìnshū*, 12. 2. 5a-6b, tr. Ho 1966: 134-135.

[187] Fáng Xuánlíng (ed.), *Jìnshū*, 12. 2. 7b, tr. Ho 1966: 138, citing again the *Hé Tú*.

an enumeration of meteoric or cometary apparitions of Jupiter, Mars, Mercury, Sun and Moon, in a list illustrating how in "very serious cases the planets changed into phantom stars [stars of evil omen]".[188] Again, this seems to have been not ancient folk tradition, but learned interpretation of contemporary observations, tracing back to the 1st century BCE or earlier, but certainly not to prehistory:

> ... comets were temporary emanations of planets, bearing messages decipherable by the wise.[189]

A modern scholar who apparently only saw the application of the theory to Venus tried to make sense of it by suggesting that "comets are usually first noticed as they approach or recede from the sun, the celestial realm of what we now refer to as the inferior planets."[190] Whether that is true or not, the idea is inadequate with respect to the complete Chinese system of 'planetary comets'. A more plausible rationale for the latter, whether or not historically related to the similar Greek system discussed above, may well be perceived in a comment by the mathematician and astronomer Lǐ Chúnfēng (602-670 C.E.):

> Whenever a planet fails to make its appearance at the expected time we generally look (for the 'ominous star' or stellar vapour) produced by the essence of the planet concerned.[191]

In order to prop up his hypothesis of a cometary Venus, Velikovsky pretended that "the peoples of Mexico" passed on "early traditions ..., written down in pre-Columbian days" according to which "Venus smoked".[192] The savant does not appear to have consulted the single primary source he adduced for this claim, misspelling the name of an early editor of it.[193] This is the Aztec *Codex Telleriano-Remensis* annotated by Spanish friars (1553-1563 CE), which contains several illustrations of Venus' 'smoking' as a hemispheric, oval or circular "patch of sky ... with a

---

[188] Huáng Cháng, *Sūzhōu Shíkè Tiānwéntú* (*Sūzhōu Astronomical Chart*; 1193 CE), trs. Rufus & Tien 1945: 5, *cf.* 3-4.
[189] Schafer 1977: 65.
[190] Trenary 1987-1988: 110.
[191] Fáng Xuánlíng (ed.), *Jìnshū*, 12. 2. 6b, tr. Ho 1966: 135.
[192] Velikovsky 1950: 163; *cf.* 1967: 8; Cochrane & Talbott 1987: 22; Cochrane 1989: 61; 1997b: 125; Talbott 1994: 12-14.
[193] Velikovsky (1950: 163 note 1) misspelled Hamy (1899) as "Hammy".

large central star and smoke volutes arising from the form."[194] The accompanying Spanish text records a series of puzzling contemporary observations of Venus:

> Year of two houses [2 House] and 1533 there was an earthquake. And they show smoke coming from the star they called *citlal choloha*, which is the one we call Venus, a star they considered to be very important.
>
> Year of three rabbits [3 Rabbit] and 1534 don Antonio de Mendoza came as viceroy of New Spain. They say that the star was smoking. ...
>
> In this year of four reeds [4 Reed] and 1535 the star was smoking.
>
> This year of six houses [6 House] and 1537 the blacks tried to rebel; in the city of Mexico the instigators were hanged. The star was smoking and there was an earthquake, the worst I have seen, even though I saw many of them in these lands. ...
>
> Year of eight reeds [8 Reed] and 1539 ... The star was smoking.[195]

As these entries preserved historical observations of Venus between 1533 and 1539 CE, they were neither traditional nor pre-Columbian or shared by multiple "peoples", exposing Velikovsky's wording as disingenuous on all counts – what was he smoking?

Despite Velikovsky's smoke screen, it is clear that the Aztec chronicler recorded some type of genuine unusual transient event. Ignoring the stated association with Venus, the German ethnologist Ulrich Köhler (b. 1937) related these reports to sightings of comets,[196] which the Aztecs are known to have called 'smoking stars' (*citlalin popoca*).[197] Taking Venus into account, the American astronomer and anthropologist Anthony Francis Aveni (b. 1938) had earlier suggested:

---

[194] Quiñones Keber 1995: 235, *cf.* 236, 321-323. A similar image is also shown for 1531 CE, fol. 44 recto, 1995: 91, *cf.* 234.

[195] 'hand 5', in *Codex Telleriano-Remensis* (MS. Mexicanus 385, Bibliothèque Nationale, Paris), fols. 44 verso - 45 verso, ed. Quiñones Keber 1995: 92-94, tr. 275-276. For the Spanish text, see de Rosny 1869: 227.

[196] Köhler 1989: 290-291; 2002: 2, followed by Quiñones Keber 1995: 234-236.

[197] *e. g.*, Bernardino de Sahagún, *Historia general de las cosas de Nueva España* (*General History of the Things of New Spain*, 1569 CE; *Codex Florentinus*), 7. 4, trs. Anderson & Dibble 1953: 13; de Molina 1571: 22 verso s. v. 'Citlalimpopoca'; Köhler 1989: 289, 291-292; 2002: 1-2.

> Perhaps a cometary object appeared near the planet.[198]

Could it be that the Aztecs – not unlike the Graeco-Roman and Chinese speculations examined above – viewed comets as emanations from Venus whenever they were first detected in the region around that planet, which – as also noted – is frequently the case?[199] A prominent compiler of historical sightings of comets endorsed this take on Venus' smoking, noting that the comet spotted between June and September 1533 (C/1533 M1) "was less than 8° from Venus on the morning of June 22, and about 12° away on June 27",[200] while the one recorded in January 1538 (C/1538 A1) would, around 16 December 1537, "have risen more than two hours before sunrise for observers in Mexico" and "would have been even brighter in the mornings that followed, although its elongation steadily decreased."[201] Obsessed with Venus as they were, Aztec astronomers could well have scanned the sky diligently enough to discover so many comets in such a short span of time, yet this interpretation does not explain why the *Codex Telleriano-Remensis* clearly distinguishes the Venus events from comets by depicting the latter as snakes and explicitly labelling them 'comet' (Nahuatl *xihuitli*, Spanish *cometa*).[202] Even if the Spanish word *cometa* could at times have meant 'meteor',[203] one would have to assume that the editor of the codex used it exclusively in that sense, while classifying all true comets as instances of Venus smoking. This stretches credulity. Is the cometary angle to this puzzle all smoke and mirrors?

Velikovsky relied on the Prussian naturalist and explorer Friedrich Alexander, baron von Humboldt (1769-1859), for these Aztec data. This gentleman suspected a volcanic trigger and tried to accommodate Venus as follows:

> I am ignorant of the phenomenon, which in the commentary is often designated by these words ... The volcano of Orizava bore the name of

---

[198] Aveni 1980: 27.
[199] Milbrath 1999: 251.
[200] Kronk 1999: 304.
[201] Kronk 1999: 306. Kronk (1999: 305, 307) suggested cometary candidates for the smoking events of 1534 (no official name) and 1539 (C/1539 H1) as well, but did not list any evidence for a comet in 1535.
[202] 'hand 5', in *Codex Telleriano-Remensis*, fols. 39 verso (for 1489 CE) and 44 recto (for 1529 CE), ed. Quiñones Keber 1995: 82, 91, *cf.* 225-226, 233, 274-275, 319, 321. See Izeki (2008) and compare §427 on the very complex semantic range of the word *xihuitl*.
[203] Köhler 1989: 289-290, 292, 294; 2002: 1, 4-5. This interpretation makes a mockery of the clear description of the object of 1489 as 'very big' (*muy grande*), unless a large bolide was intended.

> Citlaltepetl, *mountain of the star*; and we may presume, that the annals of the empire contained the different epochas of the eruptions of this volcano. ... Now, I ask, what optical illusion could give Venus the appearance of a star throwing out smoke? Was it a kind of halo formed around the planet? As the volcano of Orizava is placed to the east of the city of Cholula, and its fiery crater resembles during the night a rising star, the volcano and the morning star may in symbolic language perhaps have been confounded with each other.[204]

An important clue comes from an anonymous informant of the Izalco branch of the Pipil (western El Salvador), who are modern-day relatives of the ancient Aztecs. Commenting on Venus as morning star (*nešta-maláni*) in relation to the fixed stars, this person said:

> But he, when they seize each other and when they hit each other, can catch fire: This morning star once burned. When he had finished burning, the smallpox epidemic began. Only decaying huts remained, all their owners died. I have seen it myself, when this morning star burned, – it was twice twenty and ten and another four years ago.[205]

The anthropologist who recorded these words in 1930, unaware of the parallel with the *Codex Telleriano-Remensis*, resorted to a comet again for an explanation:

> In combat with the fixed stars, Venus can catch fire. With a memory error of two years, the date which the narrator gives could point to the comet 1877 III discovered by Coggia, which came so close to the earth around mid-July that it was visible to the naked eye in the evening sky of Salvador at a stellar magnitude of 1.3 ... Around the same time, Venus was evening star, but the comet stayed far away from it, – the Indian will have subsequently connected this appearance with an old belief which could have rested on more reproachless observations.[206]

The naked-eye appearance of Coggia's comet (C/1874 H1) actually occurred in the summer of 1874, not 1877. And despite its superficial appeal, the explanation is too contrived because Venus and the comet were never seen in proximity to each other, a nebulous memory must be assumed for the date and the native source was concerned with the morn-

---

[204] de Humboldt 1814: 174. The modern name for the "volcano of Orizava" is Pico de Orizaba, the highest mountain in Mexico.
[205] recorded August-October 1930, in Schultze Jena 1935: 100-101 (•), *cf.* 98.
[206] Schultze Jena 1935: 100-101 (•).

ing star, not the evening star – a confusion which is unlikely even taking into account that the Pipil were aware of the astronomical identity of Venus as morning and evening star.[207] Close, but no cigar.

Whatever the explanation, it would seem that Venus' 'smoking' is the same as its 'burning' and that observers in Mesoamerica witnessed such incidents – regarded as portents – throughout the historical period on a biennial to centennial timescale, ruling out any dramatic scenarios such as Velikovsky's Venus comet. Other thought experiments fail to convince as well. The adventurous suggestion of a temporary visibility of Venus' magnetotail[208] cannot be invoked, because it would be against all odds that western astronomers would never have observed such over the past 500 years of diligent observation, while indigenous Mesoamericans did. The conflict of the Pipil morning star with the stars suggests some turbulence, like a meteor shower (compare §§359*), but it is not clear how this could affect the brightness of Venus. And the zodiacal light can appear to encompass Venus, but not emanate from it in any way and occupies a vastly larger segment of the sky. The most promising solution remains an atmospheric optical effect, as suggested by von Humboldt.

Three possibilities arise. First, it is possible that Venus can produce its own *Gegenschein* ('counterglow'), a subtle roughly circular reflection of sunlight off dust particles in the ecliptic plane, closely related to the zodiacal light but with a higher angle of reflection. Second, von Humboldt's "kind of halo formed around the planet" corresponds to the phenomenon known as a planetary aureole or corona, as described in meteorological textbooks:

> At times small, feebly luminous coronae are to be seen even round Venus, Jupiter and the brighter stars.[209]

This is an attractive option, because the annular or oval shape of an aureole could evoke the propensity of smoke to form rings, both with human smokers and some volcanoes. And third, perhaps Venus' 'fuming' referred to scintillations or the so-called red, green or blue flash on the planet, often occurring in heliacal positions due to disturbances in the earth's atmosphere; "... Venus and Mercury, which at times are observed as fairly narrow crescents, do occasionally scintillate quite appreciably,

---

[207] Schultze Jena 1935: 99.
[208] Scott (2006: 137) suggested visibility of Venus' magnetotail as an explanation for aspects of Venus' mythology in general.
[209] Minnaert 1954: 216.

and ... Venus can even show changes of colour when very close to the horizon. When the disturbance in the air is very pronounced and the planets are low in the sky, one will almost invariably notice some changes of intensity."[210] Certainly, ancient Chinese astrologers were familiar with these various optical effects, including aureoles, on Venus and even associated them with battle:

> When [Venus] is small and its rays scintillate, fighting breaks out. ... If [Venus] is rayed, dare to do battle; if it scintillates vigorously, be vigorous; if it is round and quiescent, be quiescent. ... If its rays are red, there will be war; if white, there will be obsequies; if it is dark and round then rayed, [it means] affliction and matters of a Watery kind; if it is green and round with smallish rays, [it means] affliction and matters of a Woody kind; if it is yellow and round and mildly rayed, there are matters of an Earthy kind, and there will be a harvest. ...
>
> When its aspect is larger and encircled with glossy yellow, good things may be accomplished; when it is ringed with bright red, military forces are plentiful, but will not do battle.
>
> The whiteness of *Supreme White* compares with the *Wolf* [*Star*]; when red, it compares with *Heart* ...; when yellow, it compares with the left shoulder of *Triaster*; when it is green, it compares with the right shoulder of *Triaster*; when black, it compares with the big star of *Stride* ... If its color is white with five rays and if it appears early, it means a lunar eclipse, if late it means celestial anomalies and a *Broom-star* [comet] will emanate toward states {below which have lost the Way}.[211]

The depictions of Venus' 'smoking' in the Aztec codex are consistent with the optical-atmospheric approach: an orange aureole surrounds the central 'star' Venus and various other stars or sparks, while the bits of emitted smoke could represent a wispy cloud. Venus' aureole is variously oval and circular, just like the enclosure seen in the pictures. The general Mesoamerican obsession with Venus would guarantee the significance imputed to the innocuous diffractions.

The respective optical effects are strongly modulated by changes in the composition of the atmosphere, including the dispersion of fine vol-

---

[210] Minnaert 1954: 71, *cf.* 63; van der Sluijs & James 2013: 299-303.
[211] Sīmǎ Qiān, *Shǐjì* (*Scribe's Records*) = *Tàishǐgōng Shū* (*Records of the Grand Historian*; c109-91 BCE), 27 (*Tiānguān Shū* [*Treatise on the Celestial Offices*]): 1324-1325, 1327, tr. Pankenier 2013: 483-485. "*Supreme White*" was a title of Venus. *Wolf* is Sirius, *Heart* Antares, the left shoulder of *Triaster* Betelgeuse, the right one Bellatrix and *Stride* Mirach (2013: 484 notes 214 to 218).

canic dust. The events logged in the Aztec chronicle may not be unrelated to the eruption of Cotopaxi (Ecuador) in 1532 and 1534, at a 'cataclysmic' magnitude of 4 on the volcanic explosivity index (VEI).[212] And it is tempting to relate the Pipil account of Venus' incandescence to the great eruption of Krakatoa in 1883; the remarkable sunrises and sunsets seen in the following years could have something to do with the 'battling stars', but a memory slip would again have to be postulated – of at least 7 years.

Be that as it may, a volcanic component is not requisite; Venerean aureoles and scintillations occur regardless. Thus, von Humboldt's hunch of an "optical illusion" deserves resuscitation, but although a direct relation between Pico de Orizaba's eruptions and Venus' flare-ups as perceived by the locals is still possible, it is not needed. Given Venus' significance in Mesoamerican culture, the volcano's designation as *"mountain of the star"* could have been based solely on its nocturnal glow and its orientation towards the east – and hence the morning star – as seen from Cholula, without a connection to Venus' recurrent 'smoking'.

Bringing their designation of comets as 'smoking stars' back into the equation, it would appear that the Aztecs and their descendants used words for 'smoking' and 'burning' in relation to any sort of transient glow in the night sky, including distant lava, cometary tails and planetary haloes. This practice is comparable to the theory of some classical philosophers that comets, aurorae and meteors were 'exhalations' of the earth.[213] Comets or a cometary phase of Venus are almost certainly not indicated by the Aztec chronicle entries and the Pipil account under investigation, which concern far more anodyne events.

The Maya of Yucatán present a puzzle similar to that of the Aztec 'smoking Venus'. A set of poems which could date from any time between the 15th and 18th centuries CE, but may incorporate far older contents, refers to the "smoking star" (*budz ek*) on four occasions:

> I want you to look
> Glorious
> And beautiful,
> So that you appear like the smoking star.[214]

---

[212] anonymous 1968-.
[213] *e. g.*, Aristotle, *Meteorology*, 1. 4 (341b-342a), 1. 7 (344a-b); Manilius, *Astronomy*, 1. 817-926; Proclus, *Commentary on Plato's Timaeus*, 1. 110. 1-23, on 22c3-7.
[214] *Songs of Dzitbalché*, 2, tr. Edmonson 1982: 178.

> To await the appearance
> Of the beautiful smoking star over the forest.[215]
>
> Hence the sun;
> Hence the moon;
> Hence the smoking star …[216]
>
> The beautiful star
> Is flaming
> Over the forest,
> Smoking
> As it sinks,
> And sinks.[217]

The object's 'flaming' and 'smoking' again appear to be closely related functions. As in the *Codex Telleriano-Remensis*, the reference was evidently to a contemporary astronomical phenomenon. Considered on their own, the passages strongly suggest that the 'smoking star' was Venus,[218] widely recognised as the third brightest object in the night sky and regarded as beautiful. However, dictionaries of the Yucatec Maya language define *budz ek* as 'comet'.[219] Thus, the situation is different than in the *Codex Telleriano-Remensis*, which carefully distinguishes Venus' 'smoking' from comets. One specialist argues that the Maya regarded comets as "cigars smoked by Maya gods", while "a discarded cigar could refer to a meteor, more commonly known as a shooting star."[220] The east jamb of the Temple of the Cross at Palenque contains an image of God L, a god of the underworld, smoking a cigar;[221] the god, who "wears the 'quincunx' glyph as his buckle",[222] has been thought to represent Venus, the smok-

---

[215] *Songs of Dzitbalché*, 5, tr. Edmonson 1982: 183.
[216] *Songs of Dzitbalché*, 9, tr. Edmonson 1982: 191.
[217] *Songs of Dzitbalché*, 12, tr. Edmonson 1982: 196-197.
[218] *Cf.* Milbrath 1999: 251.
[219] For Motul: 'hairy comet, like the one which appeared in the year 1577', ed. de Ciudad Real c1577: 58 verso s. v. 'buɔ ek, buɔalek, buɔilek' (•). For Hocabá: Bricker et al. 1998: 37 s. v. 'b'ùuȼ''.
[220] Milbrath 1999: 251, adding that the smoking of cigars by the hero twins in the Quiché *Popol Vuh* (*Book of the People*) was "possibly alluding to a connection with comets." Although the text itself (3, tr. Tedlock 1996: 141) matches these twins, Hunahpu and Xbalanque, to the sun and the moon, compelling arguments suggest that, throughout the narrative, the lads' adventures describe the career of Venus as morning and evening star (1996: 37-38, 43, 225, 240, 256-260, 265-266, 278, 285, 287). The Warao (central Orinoco Delta, Venezuela) associated meteors with cigars smoked by the souls of dark shamans, Wilbert 1973-1974: 93 = 1993: 143; 1993 (1975): 98.
[221] Robertson 1991: Fig. 43, *cf.* 34-35.
[222] Robertson 1991: 35.

ing the passage of Halley's comet in 684 CE[223] – but these are no more than conjectures. If true, the poems cited above may have been composed when a conspicuous comet was in the sky, perhaps as an evening star or concurrently with Venus. Alternatively, the solution may be as suggested for the Aztecs: perhaps Mesoamericans interpreted any transient glows in the night sky – including aureoles and comets – as smoke. In that case, the "smoking star" in the poems could have been Venus undergoing apparent transformations caused by subtle changes in the earth's atmosphere. At any rate, the Yucatec poems do not appear to have anything to do with myths about a distant past.

Finally, Velikovsky buttressed his case for 'comet Venus' by claiming that it is "said in the *Vedas* that the star Venus looks like fire with smoke."[224] The primary source in question, which he plainly did not peruse, is the *Mahābhārata*, which does not belong to the corpus of Vedas. The pertinent passage is a difficult one, which enumerates a large number of omens foreboding the great war on which this epic centres. Among the astronomical omens are the following:

> The white planet has passed beyond the constellation Chítra and dwells there, by which one foresees the destruction of the Kurus in particular. A horrible comet has attacked the constellation Pushya. This great planet will cause terrible misfortune for both armies. Mars moves retrograde in the constellation Magha, and Jupiter in the constellation Shrávana. The Sun's son Saturn has approached the constellation Bhaga and impinges on it. Venus shines, having ascended toward Purva Bhadra and, moving around in the junction, looks toward Úttara Bhadra. The white planet, glowing like a smoky fire, has entered Indra's bright constellation Jyeshtha and remains there. The Polar star is shining intensely and moving to the right. The fierce planet Rahu, positioned between the constellations Chitra and Svati, is eclipsing Róhini as well as the moon and the sun. The red-bodied planet Mars, blazing like fire, has gone retrograde in the Shrávana constellation and now resides in the constellation Brahma·rashi to which it has returned.[225]

---

[223] Milbrath 1999: 251.
[224] Velikovsky 1950: 164, citing Scheftelowitz 1929: 4.
[225] Vyāsa, in *Mahābhārata*, 6 (*Bhīṣma Parva* [*Book of Bhīṣma*]): 1 (*Jambūkhaṇḍa-Nirmāṇa Parva*): 3. 12-18, tr. Cherniak 2008: 24-25. The Sanskrit text does not give a separate name for Saturn, but identifies it only by its title "The Sun's son" (*Sūryaputreṇa*). On this, see van der Sluijs & James 2013: 282 note 18. The respective star groups listed are the lunar mansions (*nakṣatra*) Citrā (Spica), Puṣya (γ, δ and θ Cancri), Maghā (Regulus), Śrāvaṇa (α, β and γ Aquilae), Bhāga which equals Uttara Phālgunī (Denebola), Pūrva Bhādrapadā (α and β Pegasi), Uttara Bhādrapadā (γ

The consensus has been that this list mentions a variety of bodies, including planets, comets and the pole star. If the appearance of the 'white planet' (*śveto grahaḥ*) were of a cometary nature, the text would probably have said so, as a "horrible comet" (*dhūmaketur mahāghoraḥ*) is explicitly mentioned in the same passage. And dramatic though it may be, the planet's "glowing like a smoky fire" (*prajvalitaḥ sadhūma iva pāvakaḥ*) is apparently more akin to Mars' "blazing like fire" (*pāvakaprabhaḥ*) than to a comet's coma or tail.[226] It may be explained in the same way as the Mesoamerican concept of Venus' burning and smoking – planetary scintillations and aureoles. Velikovsky seems to have been oblivious to these fluctuations, even though several ancient societies viewed them with great apprehension.[227]

That said, it is by no means certain that this white planet refers to Venus; the text rather seems to distinguish it from Venus (*Śukraḥ*). Some philologists have emended the name to *śyāma grahaḥ* as "dark planet (to refer to Mercury)",[228] while an earlier translator identified it as Ketu,[229] the descending lunar node in Hindū astrology, which – like the ascending node, Rāhu – was counted among the planets to make nine.[230] A modern scientist has asserted that the two instances of the 'white planet' – along with the "fierce planet", Lohitāṅga ("Mars") and Dhruvaḥ ("Polar star") – in this segment all refer to types of comets, some of which were regarded as the offspring of planets.[231] Hindū astrologers classified *ketu* – a class of transient lights including comets and meteors – according to their perceived kinship with a range of deities, mostly representing natural phenomena such as fire (Agni), wind (Vāyu) and the planets;[232] the system defining most comet types as 'sons of planets' is analogous to the classi-

---

Pegasi and α Andromedae), Jyeṣṭhā (α, σ and τ Scorpionis), Rohiṇī (Aldebaran) and Svāti (Arcturus). On the displacement of the pole star (*Dhruvaḥ*), see §359*. The word "red-bodied" translates *Lohitāṅgo*; the word "Mars" behind it is interspersed by the translator, as is "Rahu".

[226] *Prajvalita* can also be translated as "flaming, blazing, burning, shining" (Monier-Williams 1979: 659 s. v. 'pra-jvalita') instead of "glowing".

[227] Perhaps the Babylonian belief in flare-ups of the planet Mars and a classical theory that the planets Mars, Jupiter and Saturn, especially when in conjunction, can produce comets, lightning or thunderbolts (van der Sluijs 2006: 75-86) were also motivated by observations of such planetary affectations.

[228] Narahari Achar 2003: 20, *cf.* 19.

[229] Roy 1887: 7.

[230] Compare van der Sluijs 2009c: 63.

[231] Narahari Achar 2003: 20.

[232] Varāhamihira (505-587 CE), *Bṛhat-Saṃhitā* (*Great Treatise*), 11. 10-52, tr. Iyer 1987: 65-69. Varāhamihira cited the works of various ancient precursors, including Garga, Parāśara and Asita Devala.

cal, Chinese and possibly even Aztec paradigms of 'planetary comets'. An entry for Venus reads:

> The Comets that appear in the North and North East are 84 in number; they are the sons of Venus; they have large, white and shining discs and when they appear mankind will not be happy.[233]

These 'sons of Venus' were distinct from the *Śveta Ketu* ('white comet')[234] and many others, including the *Dhruva Ketu* ('pole comet'), which "is a comet possessing no fixed course color or shape and appears anywhere in the heavens, in the sky and on Earth (*sic*)".[235] Returning to the vexing passage in the *Mahābhārata*, the authority in question translated the line with which Velikovsky was concerned quite differently, accepting the emendation mentioned above and treating the words for "like a smoky fire" as two additional designations of comets: "*śyamagraha* is luminous and together with *dhūma* and *pāvaka* has crossed over to *jyeṣṭhā*, the bright asterism ruled by Indra".[236] The jury is still out; it hardly inspires confidence that this author failed to recognise "The Sun's son" (*Sūryaputreṇa*) as a common title of Saturn.

451
hot flood

Some traditions portray the waters of the deluge (§§303-305, 308, 310-317, 336, 356, 397) – whether arriving in rain or a tidal wave – as *boiling*.[237] For example, in a flood myth from the Mansi (western Siberia), those who have not built any boats perish 'in the hot water.'[238] A member of the Salinan of San Antonio Mission (central coast of California) told: "Many long years ago before there were any people on the earth the sea suddenly rose, boiling hot and flooded the whole world."[239] And incorpo-

---

[233] Varāhamihira, *Bṛhat-Saṃhitā*, 11. 17, tr. Iyer 1987: 65.
[234] Varāhamihira, *Bṛhat-Saṃhitā*, 11. 37-39, tr. Iyer 1987: 67-68.
[235] Varāhamihira, *Bṛhat-Saṃhitā*, 11. 41, tr. Iyer 1987: 68.
[236] Vyāsa, in *Mahābhārata*, 6. 1. 3. 16, tr. Narahari Achar 2003: 19.
[237] *e. g.*, van der Sluijs 2011d: 15, 22-23 (Jewish), 284 (Zuñi); Anderson 1923: 3-4, 33; Bellamy 1936: 126-128; 1945: 132-133.
[238] recorded 1843-1844 by Antal Reguly (1819-1858; in Russian), in Adam 1874: 12 (•).
[239] Juan Quintana, recorded January 1916 at Jolon (Monterey County, California), translated from Spanish into the Salinan dialect of San Antonio Mission by Maria Jesusa Encinales (c1876 - after 1936), in Mason 1918: 82, *cf.* 81.

rating the theme of a 'strong sun' (§429), the Apurinã (along the Purús River, Amazonas, Brazil) had a kettle on the sun pour down a stream of boiling water, thereby burning the earth and its waters:

> A large kettle with boiling water was formerly located in the sun (*atukatšĭ*). ... The storks' chief, indeed the creator of all birds, was Mayuruberu. This one threw, when the water in the kettle was almost finished, a round stone (*pingitšina*) into it. The kettle fell over, the hot liquid poured towards the earth and burned up everything, the forest and also the water. ... It was dark on Earth, Sun and Moon were hidden. ... The kettle still stands in the sun, but is empty.[240]

The cosmic conflagration (§§302, 304-305, 309-312, 312*, 314-317, 335, 396, 453-454) was often thought to have produced the effect of heating up seas, lakes or rivers to boiling point.[241] In Greek myth, this happened during the Titanomachy, in which the Titans were pitted against the Olympian gods: "All around, the life-giving earth roared as it burned, and all around the great immense forest crackled; the whole earth boiled, and the streams of Ocean and the barren sea."[242] The East Pomo (northern California) held that Marumda, the creator, having wiped out the first race of 'people' by a deluge, some time later cleansed the second race by fire:

> Marumda therefore sent a wild fire over the face of the earth. When the fire came some of the people ran into the water to remain there until the fire was out. But the water commenced to boil, and it killed the people in that way.[243]

In Dakota and Minnesota, the Sioux describe a primeval combat between 'water monsters' (*Unktehi*), who had caused a flood which ended up "killing most of the people", and 'Thunderbirds' (*Wakinyan*), who were on the side of the humans and employed lightning as their principal weapon (§459). The ensuing conflagration caused the waters to evaporate:

---

[240] recorded December 1888 - February 1889, in Ehrenreich 1891: 71-72 (•). See further §§439, 441 for the resulting condition of weak sunlight and §429 for a note concerning the kinship of this myth with flood mythology.
[241] *e. g.*, van der Sluijs 2011d: 5, 7-9.
[242] Hesiod, *Theogony*, 693-696, tr. Most 2006: 58-59. Compare van der Sluijs 2011d: 29.
[243] William Ralganal Benson (1862-1937), an East Pomo storyteller and artist, recorded winter 1924-1925, in Loeb 1926: 493.

> Then all the thunderbirds flew up into the sky. 'When I give the signal', said the Wakinyan Tanka, 'let's use our lightning and thunderbolts together!' So the thunder beings shot off all their bolts at the same instant. The forests were set on fire, and flames consumed everything except the top of the rock on which the humans had taken refuge. The waters boiled and then dried up.[244]

Also on record are traditions in which water brought to a boil by a fire floods the land.[245] Yet other accounts have a deluge putting out a fire,[246] carrying the implication that the water was heated in the process.

The sources frequently employ suggestive wording lacking the specificity required to determine whether a flow of a scalding substance involved water, flames or light alone or intermixed. For example, the Samogitians (northwestern Lithuania) derived the origin of all surface waters from a 'sea of fire' (*Feuermeer*) which gushed out when God forgot to shut the door of heaven, just after the mountains and valleys had formed on Earth and before animals were created:

> Then God became angry and returned to the sky full of wrath. In his anger, he forgot to close the door which led to the sky: then a sea of fire poured down from the sky onto the earth; it collected in the depressions and gradually cooled down. Out of this cooled-off sea of fire developed the waters of the earth, seas, lakes and rivers.[247]

And the 'fire flood' (*Feuerflut*) in a story from the Mansi of the Upper Severnaya Sosva River consists in the overflowing of boiling water from the bath of 'the world-observing man' onto the earth on two occasions, a third one being narrowly prevented.[248]

In other cases, the tradition at hand is concerned with an outburst of fire, but reads like a double of a typical flood myth.[249] The 'fire rain' (*Feuerregen*) in a tradition of the Oraon (northeast India)[250] and the 'fire flood' in other accounts from the Mansi as also the distantly related

---

[244] Tȟáȟča Hušté *alias* John (Fire) Lame Deer (1900/1903-1976), a Miniconjou Lakȟóta medicine man, recorded 1969 in Winner (Rosebud Indian Reservation, South Dakota), in Erdoes & Ortiz 1984: 220-221. For other examples of flood preceding fire, see §305.
[245] *e. g.*, van der Sluijs 2011d: 18 (Nuxalk).
[246] van der Sluijs 2011d: 17-18.
[247] recorded 1878-1882, in Veckenstedt 1883: 215 (•). For 'sky holes' permitting a flow of liquids, compare §292.
[248] recorded 1843-1844 by Reguly (in Russian), in Munkácsi 1908: 261-262 (•).
[249] Compare the structural kinship between deluge myths and the 'ice age' of Zoroastrian tradition (§449).
[250] recorded 1876-1904, in Hahn 1906: 83-84; Grignard 1931: 144-146.

Khanty[251] were apparently expressions of conflagration, even though the Siberian myths mirror familiar flood mythology in several respects – such as prior announcement to a select few and their survival in a vessel – and explicitly mention 'fiery water' (*nājiŋ vit*). Some of the Uralic tales specifically contrast the 'fire flood' with a deluge by water,[252] as also in the myths cited above from the Mansi. And in the "flood of light" which, according to many traditions from the Pacific northwest coast of North America, caused the disappearance of "the first people" (§440), one scholar recognises a conscious parallel to the deluge:

> The breakage of the daylight box at the end of the Theft of Daylight causes the great flood which is so ubiquitous to creation myths worldwide, but in this case the flood is not water but light, drowning the stars ...[253]

452
humans placed above other animals

Belief in *the right to control and exploit other animals* than the human species was rampant especially in patriarchal cultures. A speaker in one of Plato's dialogues casually remarked that "man, being an animal of different and more divine nature than the rest, now tends the lower species of animals."[254] And in Hermetism, the spirit Poimandres reveals that man is endowed with "all authority over the cosmos of mortals and unreasoning animals", for "unlike any other living thing on earth, mankind is twofold – in the body mortal but immortal in the essential man."[255]

Traditional societies less tainted by male arrogance and violence often treated humans as equals of other animals, but exceptions are attested fairly commonly.[256] For example, the Lenape people (originally of the Delaware River region) told the polymath, founding father and former president of the United States of America, Thomas Jefferson (1743-1826), an early proponent of the despicable policy of 'Indian removal',

---

[251] recorded 1888-1889, in Munkácsi 1891: 109-114; 1908: 258-271; *cf.* Herrmann 1893: 336-338.
[252] Gondatti (in Russian), in Munkácsi 1908: 266.
[253] Vogt 1996: 43.
[254] Eleatic Stranger, in Plato, *Politicus* (*Statesman*), 15 (271E), tr. Fowler 1925: 58-59.
[255] *Discourse of Hermes Trismegistus*, 1 (*Poimandres*): 14-15, eds. Nock & Festugière 1945: 11, tr. Copenhaver 1992: 3, translating "of ... unreasoning animals" for *tōn alógōn zōiōn*.
[256] Compare van der Sluijs 2011d: 172 (Sikuani).

that "the bear, deer, elks, buffaloes, and other animals ... had been created for the use of the Indians".[257]

Human supremacy over other animals was often placed in the mouth of a mythical creator or culture hero as a divine sanction, along with instructions for hunting, fishing and other practices (§379). In the Hebrew Bible, the creator, Yahweh, teaches the first pair of humans as follows:

> Be fruitful and multiply; fill the earth and subdue it; have dominion over the fish of the sea, over the birds of the air, and over every living thing that moves on the earth.[258]

> And the fear of you and the dread of you shall be on every beast of the earth, on every bird of the air, on all that move on the earth, and on all the fish of the sea. They are given into your hand. Every moving thing that lives shall be food for you. I have given you all things, even as the green herbs.[259]

Natives in the area around Roebourne (central-western Western Australia), possibly of Jaburrara, Ngarluma or Kariyarra stock, informed that Gnurker, the creator, had instructed the first people to live in a communist way, but be custodians of all other animals:

> They were given control over the fishes of the waters, the birds of the air, all animals, insects, and every living thing – that by a ceremony of will they could cause them to multiply and increase, they and their children for ever; and they were to set apart a hallowed spot called Tarlow for this purpose. Their God gave the men spears, throwing stick, and shields for protection and purposes of hunting; to the women he gave wooden scoops and paper bark from the Cajeput tree for the gathering of seeds and other uses. They were given power even over rain, and provision was made that every food they possessed should be held for the common good.[260]

According to the East Pomo nation (northern California), the creator, Marumda, "told the people how they should kill and eat the animals",

---

[257] a chief of the Lenape, probably Koquethagechton *alias* 'White Eyes' (c1730-1778), in Jefferson 1787: 64-65.
[258] *Genesis*, 1. 28, tr. Farstad 1982: 2.
[259] *Genesis*, 9. 2-3 (*cf.* 1, 7), tr. Farstad 1982: 7.
[260] recorded c1865-c1895, in Withnell 1901: 1-2. 'Cajeput tree' is a name for some species of the tea tree genus, *Melaleuca*, notably *M. cajuputi*, *M. leucadendra*, *M. linariifolia*, *M. viridiflora* and *M. quinquenervia*.

"made the shell fish, and other fishes of all kinds" for the first race of people to eat and, having formed the sun along with the stars, instructed them that "when it shines then you must hunt".[261] And a member of the Salinan of San Antonio Mission (central coast of California) presented a breathtakingly anthropocentric view of the rôle of non-human animals, combined with a perverted interpretation of friendship:

> The Horse begged God for permission to kill men. But God replied, 'No! You are his friend; he must command you always. It is better that you do not kill him. It is his place to command, yours to do your friend's orders. It is not good to do as you ask. Your friend is poor also. Do you not see that it is not painful to be commanded when it is your friend who commands you? Therefore you must carry him to the place where he wishes; you are his foot. So it is not well that you should kill him, for he is your friend. Likewise you are a friend of his. It is well that he should command you and that you should not do him any harm.'
>
> The Ox also begged God for permission to kill people; he wished to gore them so that they would die. But God replied, 'No, you are his food. When they kill you they do not throw you aside. You would not do that; you would only kill them. You have no need to kill them for you could not eat them. You would only kill the poor fellows; you would not do as they, for they kill you merely to eat you.'[262]

Perhaps the inclusion of the horse, which was a recent addition to the North American fauna, indicates that this story was not a tradition of great antiquity.

Some groups went as far as claiming that human dominion was beneficial to other animals. Thus, a Hindū text advised "Be merciful to all creatures, and devoted to their good", "Love all creatures, scorning none" and "subjugating the whole Earth, rejoice thou and let happiness be thine", all in one breath as if oblivious to the contradiction in the claim that forced subordination be merciful or loving.[263]

---

[261] William Ralganal Benson (1862-1937), an East Pomo storyteller and artist, recorded winter 1924-1925, in Loeb 1926: 490-491.
[262] David Mora (c1870 - after 1936), a Salinan of San Antonio Mission, recorded January 1916 at Jolon (Monterey County, California), in Mason 1918: 77.
[263] Mārkaṇḍeya, in *Mahābhārata*, 3 (*Vana Parva* [*Book of the Forest*]): 191, tr. Roy 1884: 581. Dutt (2008: 556) translated "Be king" instead of "Be merciful".

453
a long object, flood and fire

Some traditions suggest a close, even causal relationship between a cosmic disaster, such as flood or fire (§§302-312), and *a long object* – typically a hand-held implement traversing the air or sky. For example, from the East Cree come two myths associating "the burning of the world" with the dispatch of arrows.[264] The archer was conceived of as a "boy" who later changed into a grey jay (*Perisoreus canadensis*) or a blackbird (family *Icteridae*). And the Wurundjeri (Melbourne, Australia) told of a deity's "long staff" – wielded during the primordial time "when it was 'plenty dark'" and people were cold in the winters – which caused the near-extinction of monsters and the temporary availability of fire (compare §449):

> For a long time after the creation, in the winter they were very cold, for they had no fire; their condition as it regarded their food was not better than their dogs, for they were compelled to eat the kangaroo raw; and to add to their misery, the whole land was full of deadly snakes and guanos; but good Karackarock, their truly womanly divinity, did not forget or forsake them.
>
> ... Karackarock, a native divinity of the true feminine sort, a worker, came a long way armed with a long staff – native women carry such – and with this she went over the whole land killing the reptiles; but just before she had killed them all the staff broke, and the kind did not all perish. Misery there was in the breaking of that weapon, but there was also mercy, for Karackarock had so warmed it as well as herself with such a great slaughter, that when the staff snapped there came out of it fire. Fire they now had to warm themselves, and to cook with.[265]

454
a comet, flood and fire

Cosmic misfortunes such as devastating fires and floods are in some traditions directly *blamed on one or more comets, meteors or unusual 'stars'* (compare §312). Thus, a traditional song from the Kimberleys (northwestern

---

[264] Skinner 1911: 95, 107-108.
[265] recorded April 1840 - 1844, in Howitt 1845: 191-192. The deluge occurred at a later time.

Australia) "told about a flood, long before the last, that was brought on by *Kallowa Anggnal Kude*, a star with trails."²⁶⁶ The locals of Ancasmarca (near Cusco, southeastern Peru), either Aymará or Southern Quechua, related the deluge to an unfamiliar grouping of 'stars':

> They say that a month before the Flood arrived, the rams they owned showed great sadness. During the day they did not eat, and at night they were watching the stars to such a degree that the shepherd who took care of them asked them what was happening. To which they [answered by] asking him to look at a group of stars that were assembled [and] there they agreed that the world was to be destroyed by water.²⁶⁷

Unless the reference was to a conjunction of planets, a swarm of comet fragments was perhaps intended. Further, a shaman from an Ojibwe band in Ontario shared the detailed tradition of a 'golden age' (§§407, 407*, 448-449) which was ended when a flyby comet burned the land and thereby exterminated the large animals:

> That star with the long, wide tail is going to destroy the world some day when it comes low again. That's the comet called GE-NON-DAH-WAY-ANUNG (Long Tailed Heavenly Climbing Star). It came down here once, thousands of years ago. Just like a sun. It had radiation and burning heat in its tail. The comet burnt everything to the ground. There wasn't a thing left.
>
> Indian people were here before that happened, living on the earth. But things were wrong; a lot of people had abandoned their spiritual path. The holy spirit warned them a long time before the comet came. Medicine men told everyone to prepare. Things were wrong with nature on the earth. All of these big animals were tearing up the trees, fighting one another. These creatures were even eating one another. They would have destroyed the forests; then nobody would survive. So the holy spirit said, 'Go in there, someplace in the swamp.' The spirit told the good Indians to hide in the muskeg (bog) or crawl into holes in the ground. He was going to send that CHI-ANUNG-NAH-WAY – Long Tailed Star. That's a comet.

---

²⁶⁶ David Bungal Mowaljarlai (1925-1997), a Ngarinyin, recorded before 1993, in Mowaljarlai & Malnic 2001: 194.
²⁶⁷ Cristóbal de Molina, *Relación de las fábulas y ritos de los Incas* (*Account of the Fables and Rites of the Incas*; c1575 CE; MS. Madrid 3169), trs. Bauer *et al.* 2011: 12. The version in the *Huarochirí manuscript* (MS. Madrid 3169, fols. 64 *recto* - 114 *recto*; 1598-1608 CE; 3), trs. Salomon & Urioste 1991: 51-52) omits the celestial portent.

The Indians rolled up in mud to get protection from the heat. That's why they survived. They had educated people (medicine men who fasted), and they knew what to do. The Indians took the air sac (air bladder) from a sturgeon. It's white and long like a tube. They swallowed that tube and breathed through it under the swamp.

Then that CHI-GAH-NUN-NAH-WAY-ANUNG went through here. The comet had a long, wide tail, and it burnt up everything. It flew low so the tail scorched the earth. It was just so hot that everything, even the stones, were cooked. It is said that the comet came down and spread his tail for miles and miles. That's what I was told. OH-ZHOH-WAH. A tail.

It went through here, and it burnt this country down flat. Flat. When the land around Lake Superior was flat, there was nothing here. It burnt right to the ground. Everything burnt. Even, you see, the Indians in those days were hairy. That's where they burnt their hair off. They were like an animal in the start. Then they cross-bred to make a human being. That's the reason why today pure Indians have very little hair on them. They got no hair. And those Indians got baked in the mud. They had brown skin after that. Some of the Indians were destroyed too. Like the bad ones.

That comet made a different world. After that, survival was hard work. The weather was colder than before. But soon after, the holy spirit sent Nanabush along to teach the people how to live. That's the story, but that's just the beginning.

These rocks are all burnt. One time before the fire went through here, the rocks were all solid. There was no broken rock. But the rock was cooked. And it tumbled down out of the mountains. Then the big cracks opened up. And this metal, like gold and copper, it melted. It ran across these cracks, you see. It might run for miles and miles. Maybe you'll find that mineral here. Or maybe you'll go thirty miles to find it. The reason why these lakes are all black is the comet burnt everything. You see, all the minerals run south. Every vein you see is south. The lakes are black. That's where the mineral is. The reason why they are black, whenever it cooled off the mineral, that lake never cleared up. You'll see the rocks in the black river. All black. They're all black from being burnt and from the ashes. There's a big deposit some place here because tons and tons were taken out from the veins of minerals. Not the main lode. They just took what was in the vein. After the comet came, the earth was bare. It was people that fertilized the country with their feet. And I really believe that with all of my heart. Their bare feet helped to spread the ashes and nourish the soil. Old Nanabush came after that fire. The rocks were still soft from the heat, and there are places today where you can see his footprints in the rock.

> What happened with the comet was a long time ago. I'm talking about way beyond two thousand years ago. There is a prophecy that the comet will destroy the earth again. But it's a restoration. The greatest blessing this island (earth) will ever have. People don't listen to their spiritual guidance today. There will be signs in the sun, moon and stars when that comet comes down again.[268]

A revised edition of this report published a few years afterwards adds several nuances.[269] The people "killed some of the animals" before the comet passed through. Seasonality was absent before the coming of the comet (§§407*, 448): "Before the comet came, life on the earth was easy for the Indians. The moon never died [waxed and waned] at that time. There were no cycles of more food and less food. No seasons, until that comet burnt up the country." The words "holy spirit" are clarified with the appended name 'Chimanitou'. The people "were warned a long time before". The women believed that they were "going to get rid of these evil creatures" and indeed "The giant animals were killed off. You can find their bones today in the earth. ... After that comet, new animals were put on the earth. Where they came from, I don't know." (compare §459) The hitherto intimate bond with other animals (compare §34*) was severed in the aftermath of the catastrophe:

> When the people woke up, they were talking. Before that, people were all like beasts. They followed one another like dogs. They mated like animals.

As for geological damage done by the burning, "There were no trees. Just sand and gravel." And Nanabush, a culture hero, "came from the morning star", *Wabanung*, "soon after the comet"; with these words, the narrator was perhaps reflecting an earlier memory that the comet itself had

---

[268] Wabmaymay ('Dawn Pileated Woodpecker'), a storyteller of the Ketegaunseebee (Garden River) band, prior to 1910, to Sah-kah-odjew-wahg-sahor ('Sun Rising over the Mountain') *alias* Fred Pine (b. 1897), of the same band, recorded 1980-1985 at the Garden River reservation (near Sault Ste. Marie, Ontario), in Conway 1985: 99-100. The Ojibwe explicitly identified the fateful comet as Halley's comet (1P/Halley), which changed its course when it burnt the earth, Conway 1985: 102. In rock art images from the region, the editor – perhaps following his informant – recognised a probable depiction of the comet (1985: 102 Figure 4; *cf.* 103 Figure 5) and mythological creatures representing animals which were either destroyed by or survived the comet (1985: 100 Figure 2, 101 Figure 3, *cf.* 102). In an interview he gave on 10 January 1984 (Nickerson *et al.* 1984: 6, 14, 17-19, 21, 24-25), Fred Pine referred to a 'star' falling down to and burning the land, exposing copper, as well as the significance of petroglyphs.

[269] Wabmaymay to Sah-kah-odjew-wahg-sahor, as above, in Conway 1992: 243-245.

served as a morning star (§450).[270] Finally, the explicit comparison of the comet to a sun allows a structural link of the myth with the motifs of a 'strong sun' and a 'descending sun' (§§429, 437).

Meanwhile, a Zulu tradition (§§372*, 436, 449, 457) blames inversion of sky and earth, disturbance of the sun's movement and an onslaught of fire, flood and ice on interference with a giant comet:

> I am told by the great storytellers of our tribes that fresh water is not native to our earth. Once, many thousands of years ago a terrible star, the kind of star with a very long tail, descended very close upon our skies. So close that the earth turned upside down and what had become the sky became down, and what was the heavens became up. The whole world was turned upside down. The sun rose in the south and set in the north. Then came drops of burning black stuff, like molten tar, which burned every living thing on earth that could not escape. After that came a terrible deluge of water accompanied by winds so great that they blew whole mountaintops away. And after that came huge chunks of ice bigger than any mountain and the whole world was covered with ice for many generations. After that the surviving people saw an amazing sight. They saw rivers and streams of water that they could drink, they saw that [sic] some of the fishes that escaped from the sea and were now living in these rivers. That is the great story of our forefathers.[271]

And as the Ojibwe raconteur predicted the return of the comet, so some groups feared fiery or watery devastation of the earth by means of a comet or bolide as a theoretical possibility, perhaps coming to pass in the future at the juncture between epochs. Thus, the Apurinã (along the Purús River, Amazonas, Brazil) associated a meteor with a termination by fire: 'When a meteor appears in the sky, the sorcerer sinks into a narcotic sleep through tobacco snuff and upon awakening explains that he ascended to the sky and extinguished the fire which would otherwise have consumed the whole world.'[272] And in a Hindū text, the god Brahmā announces that, upon the completion of the four Yugas, "Rudder with the ten spirits of dissolution shall roll a comet under the moon, that shall

---

[270] Compare Conway 1985: 101. See the note in §§33*, 38* on the name 'Nanabush'.
[271] Vusamazulu Credo Mutwa (b. 1921), a Zulu shaman of the Msimango tribe, on 2 October 1999, in anonymous 2000: 11. The type of star is called *mu-sho-sho-no-no*, presumably a word for 'comet'. See the notes in §§436, 440 regarding Mutwa's credibility and the garbling of the first sentence about the inversion. Compare the story Mutwa told in Tucker 2003: 68.
[272] recorded December 1888 - February 1889, in Ehrenreich 1891: 69 (•).

involve all things in fire, and reduce the world into ashes. God shall then exist alone, for matter will be totally annihilated."[273]

455
cosmic impact

Some traditions directly describe *the fall of rocks, fireballs, comets or 'stars' such as the morning or evening star from the sky onto the earth*, singly or in larger numbers, landing in water or on the ground, typically with devastating consequences and sometimes in association with the mythology of creation or the termination of a past world.[274] The event is usually set in the past, but occasionally predicted for the future or viewed as merely theoretical. Like suns, moons and countless other natural phenomena, the falling entities are frequently personified. In the case of a familiar celestial body, the impact constitutes a special case of 'erratic motion' (§359*). The crash of a sun or moon (§437), for example as resulting from an attack by shooting (§444), forms a subcategory of impacts of cosmic objects insofar as the object strikes the earth.

A descent of flames is on occasion presented in positive terms as the original gift of fire to humanity (compare §168). The prevailing perception of 'falls', however, is that they were catastrophes, often adversely affecting life on Earth in at least some areas. The Hebrew prophet Isaiah (8th to 7th century BCE) is thought to have alluded to a myth involving the fall of the morning star when he mockingly compared the king of Babylon to Hēlēl ben-Šaḥar ('Hēlēl, son of Dawn'):

> How you are fallen from heaven,
> O Hēlēl, son of Dawn!
> *How* you are cut down to the ground,
> You who weakened the nations!
> For you have said in your heart:
> 'I will ascend into heaven,
> I will exalt my throne above the stars of 'Ēl;

---

[273] 'Vyāsa Muni', 'Vedānta', 1, edited by a 'Sirrider Swāmi', tr. Dow 1768: xlv. This text does not seem to have been identified by modern scholars, but displays Purāṇic features, Herling 2006: 65. As noted (§443), "Rudder" probably represents the god Rudra, the "ten spirits of dissolution" may stand for multiple suns and the "comet" might correspond to the "meteors" or Rāhu mentioned in a similar passage in the *Mahābhārata*.

[274] Iyengar (2004) presented a treasure trove of impact myths drawn from ancient Hindū writings.

> I will also sit on Mount Congregation
> On Ṣāpōn's recesses;
> I will ascend above the heights of the clouds,
> I will be like 'Elyōn.'
> Yet you shall be brought down to Sheol,
> To a pit's recesses.[275]

The Greek poet and scholar Callimachus of Cyrene (c307-240 BCE) recorded the following dedicatory inscription from a lamp in a temple in Canopus (north Egypt):

> To the god of Canopus did Callistion, daughter of Critias, dedicate me – a lamp enriched with twenty nozzles: a vow for her child Apellis. Looking on my light thou wilt say, 'Hesperus, how art thou fallen?'[276]

Although the limited information forbids a firm conclusion, the thematic agreement between the two texts convinces that they were alluding to the same myth. As one scholar observed: "The lamp's use of the Hesperos(-Phaethon) myth is metaphorical. This implies that the myth was well known, since successful metaphors are only composed from readily recognizable material." [277] However, the strong lexical resemblance between the statement on Hesperos, the evening star (*Héspere pōs épeses*), and Isaiah's taunt of the morning star (*pōs exépesen ... ho heōsphóros*) points to a more direct connection between the lamp and

---

[275] *Isaiah*, 14. 12-15, eds. Elliger *et al.* 1997: 696, tr. adapted from Farstad 1982: 609-610, with replacement of "Lucifer, son of the morning" by "Hēlēl, son of Dawn", "God" by "'Ēl", "the farthest sides of the north" by "Ṣāpōn's recesses", "the mount of the congregation" by "Mount Congregation", "the Most High" by "'Elyōn", "the lowest depths of the Pit" by "a pit's recesses". The words "the stars of God" translate *kōkabē-'ēl*, "Mount Congregation" *har-mō'ēd*, "the farthest sides of Ṣāpōn" *yarkatē ṣāpōn*, "Sheol" – which refers to the realm of the dead – *šə'ōl*, and "a pit's recesses" *yarkatē-bōr*. The *Septuagint* (ed. Rahlfs 1950: 585) rendered 'Hēlēl' as *heōsphóros*, the *Vulgate* (4th century CE; ed. Tvveedale 2005: 488) as *Lucifer*, both of which were common designations of the morning star. Mount Ṣāpōn, identified as a 'mount of congregation' by the *parallelismus membrorum*, is widely recognised as a Canaanite expression of an *axis mundi*. For further discussion, see, conveniently, van der Sluijs 2008: 227-228, 233; 2009a; 2011a: 155 note 486; 2011b: 3, 32, 109 note 527, 118-119, 126-127, 215-216; 2011d: 39 note 105, and of the general theme of cosmic rebellion, §§165, 209, 311-312, 329, 358-361.
[276] Callimachus, *Epigram*, 56, tr. Mair 1921: 176-177. The god of Canopus was Sarapis.
[277] Poirier 1999: 384. Poirier (1999: 381) argued that Callimachus' Hesperus and Isaiah's Hēlēl were separate reflexes of the Greek myth of Phaethon, that "independently attest to a stock expression of mock lament, fashioned from a popular myth". The suggestion that "both Isa. 14. 12 and Callimachus' Epigram 56 reflect a common human experience of the fading of the Evening/Morning Star" (Day 2000: 175 note 89) fails to persuade, as Venus' fading does not remotely resemble a fall and descent into hell; compare the insightful comment in Forsyth 1987: 134 note 41.

the *Septuagint* reading: was Callistion familiar with the *Septuagint*, which could then have been produced in Egypt?

The Santal (northeast India) "do not know what a comet is, but it is known that if it falls on the earth it will cause destruction."[278] The Salinan of San Antonio Mission (central coast of California) told with tantalising brevity of a fall of the morning star with lethal consequences: "In the beginning the morning star fell from heaven. When it reached earth then came Prairie-Falcon and found the people dead. Then he revived the people. But it was God who made people."[279] According to the Tuscarora (between North Carolina and New York), the close of the "age of monsters" saw not only the demise of the monsters by means of combat and thunderbolts (§459), but also the calamitous fall of an object from the sky:

> A blazing star fell into their fort, situated on the banks of the St. Lawrence, and destroyed the people. Such a phenomenon caused a great panic and consternation and dread, which they regarded as ominous [*sic*] of their entire destruction.[280]

And the French ethnographer, historian and archaeologist Charles-Étienne Brasseur de Bourbourg (1814-1874), upon introducing to the western world the Aymará or Quechua myth of a peculiar grouping of stars foreboding the flood (§454), drew a parallel between this portent and 'the six *tzontemocque*, or stars which fell from the sky, at the time of the deluge, according to the Mexican traditions.'[281] The tradition in question concerns an annual festival in November dedicated to the fall of a group of deified stars variously called *Tzontemoc* and *Tzitzimime*:

> The feast of the descent of Mictlantecuhtli and of Zontemoc and the others; and thus they depict him with the accoutrements of war because he brought it into the world. ... Properly it should be called the fall of the demons, who they say were stars; and thus there are now stars in the sky that they call (by the) names they had, which are the

---

[278] Mukherji 1935: 111. *Cf.* Hussain 1935: 116 for a parallel from the unrelated Oraon people.

[279] José Cruz, an old man, recorded September 1910 at San Antonio Mission (Monterey County, California), revised late 1910 by Pedro Encinales (c1856-1921), in Mason 1918: 93.

[280] Tawennaki ('Two Things of Equal Value') *alias* Yutana Nire ('Lone Pine Tree') *alias* Elias Johnson (1837-1913), chief of the Tuscarora, in Johnson 1881: 42.

[281] Brasseur de Bourbourg 1864: 40 note 2 (•), *cf.* 48. He (1864: 39-40) unaccountably embellished de Molina's statement with the detail that the congregated stars numbered six and the addition of a solar 'eclipse' of five days, coinciding with the flood. 'Tzontemocque' is an alternative spelling of 'Tzontemoc'.

following: Yacatecuhtli, Tlahuizcalpantecuhtli, Ce Acatl, Achitumetl, Xacopancalqui, Mixcoatl, Tezcatlipoca, Zontemoc like gods. They called them this name before they fell from heaven (and ...), and now they call them Tzitzimime, which means monstrous or frightening thing.[282]

Among these deities are Cē Ācatl Quetzalcōātl, generally associated with the planet Venus (§450), and Tlāhuizcalpantēuctli, whom the same text in another passage equates with Quetzalcōātl as well as Venus both as morning and evening star:

> Tlahuizcalpantecuhtli, or the Venus star
> one reed
> the first light in which Cipactonal was created before the flood
> They say that this light or star was created before the sun.
>
> ... This Tlahuizcalpantecuhtli or Venus star is Quetzalcoatl. ... They say that it is the star that we call the morning star, and thus they show him with one reed [1 Reed], which was his day ... When he went away or disappeared, he took this name. ... This Tlahuizcalpantecuhtli means lord of the morning when day breaks, as well as lord of that light when night is ready to fall. ... Properly speaking, the first light that appeared in the world. ... Properly speaking, it is the light over the houses or surface of the earth.[283]

The description suggests that the astral beings were believed to have landed onto the earth, where they instigated war. Why extant stars should be named after fallen ones is not clear. Regardless, the tradition appears to be akin to the Judaeo-Christian theme of the fall of Hēlēl or Lucifer and his retinue of angels,[284] while Brasseur de Bourbourg compared it to Varro's statement on Venus (§359*).[285] Regrettably, Brasseur

---

[282] Pedro de los Ríos (d. c1563 CE), in *Codex Telleriano-Remensis* (MS. Mexicanus 385, Bibliothèque Nationale, Paris; 1553-1563 CE), fol. 4 *verso*, ed. Quiñones Keber 1995: 12, tr. 255, *cf.* 147. The word "Quetzalcoatl" (*queçalalquatl*) directly after "Ce Acatl" (*çeyacatl*) has here been omitted from Quiñones Keber's translation, as it is clearly crossed out in the original Spanish text (*cf.* de Rosny 1869: 195). The list of names was supplied by one of de los Ríos' collaborators; some of the more modern spellings with length signs are 'Mictlāntēuctli', 'Tzontemoc', 'Yacatēuctli', 'Tlāhuizcalpantēuctli', 'Cē Ācatl', 'Mixcōātl' and 'Tēzcatlepōca'. Compare Pedro de los Ríos and others, *Codex Ríos = Codex Vaticanus A* (MS. Vaticanus 3738; c1566 CE), pl. III and IV, ed. Kingsborough 1831: 164-165, 170.
[283] 'hand 1', 'hand 2' and 'hand 3' (Pedro de los Ríos), in *Codex Telleriano-Remensis*, fol. 14 *verso*, ed. Quiñones Keber 1995: 32, tr. 262, *cf.* 174-175. For the Spanish text, see de Rosny 1869: 205.
[284] Quiñones Keber 1995: 147.
[285] Brasseur de Bourbourg 1864: 48.

de Bourbourg – whose work is generally marred by a strong pseudoscientific inclination – was cutting corners, because he seems to have derived the association with the deluge from the Bacab, a group of beings in Maya mythology which resemble the Tzontemoc in their aspect as personifications of the four *axes mundi* at the cardinal directions (§§231-236), but were not unambiguously identified as 'stars'.[286]

The impactor may splinter into myriad pieces, which may become impactors themselves and in some reports turn into permanently visible aspects of the sky or landscape – a fate shared elsewhere by the 'fragmented sun or moon' (§447). For example, the Samogitians (northwestern Lithuania) thanked the smashing of a star into the earth for the eradication of a powerful neighbouring tribe, which enabled them to annex their land:

> In olden days, fortune favoured the Żamaites so much that everything redounded to their good: soon their number was so great that the land they inhabited became too small for them. So it came about that they strove to enlarge their land. Their neighbours were a bellicose and magically adept people; they worshipped a big star in the sky, this indicated to them everything they had to do; as a result, it happened that the Żamaites always succumbed to them. So they turned to God and complained about the star.
>
> God got angry about the star, he threw it down onto the earth with terrible force, so that it slew the entire magically adept people, which had just gathered for the celebration of Saint John's feast. The star shattered into countless splinters, which flew over the entire earth. Now the Żamaites could appropriate the land of their former enemy unhindered.[287]

The fragments of the star changed into glow worms (*Lampyris noctiluca*), whose annual congregation around the summer solstice was understood to be an attempt to recreate the star.

The falls are repeatedly associated with a crater or a lake, the latter perhaps a filled-in crater. One of several *cruces* in the Biblical passage about Hēlēl is the grammatical definiteness of the word *bōr* ('pit') in the genitive phrase *yarkətē-bōr*. Rendering the *nomen regens*, *yarkətē*, as 're-

---

[286] See, conveniently, van der Sluijs 2011d: 76, where the association of the Tzontemoc with eclipses is also mentioned.
[287] recorded 1878-1882, in Veckenstedt 1883: 223 (•). 'Żamaites' is an alternative spelling for 'Samogitians'.

cesses' in the sense of 'extreme parts',[288] the absence of the definite particle *ha-* before *bōr* means that the phrase as a whole can only be definite if *bōr* is a proper noun: 'the recesses of Pit'. In this case, 'Pit' would have to be an alternative designation of Šə'ōl, the netherworld. The much simpler alternative 'recesses of a pit' has apparently never been considered. It would suggest that Šə'ōl was held to be accessible through any deep cavity, including a freshly dug one – like a tomb.[289] In 1925, a lone traveller near Tilcara (Jujuy, northwest Argentina) heard of "a vast crater, which, according to natives, was bored by a fiery rock from another world".[290]

The notion of oceanic impact is illustrated in a prophecy contained in the syncretistic *Sibylline Oracles* (6th century CE):

> The stars shall all fall down into the sea,
> Many stars one by one, and the bright star
> Men call a comet is a sign of evil,
> Of much war and calamity to come.[291]

In more than one tradition, the destruction accompanying or resulting from impact takes the form of a deluge, a fire, drought, evaporation of the sea, darkness or poisoning of air or water,[292] similar to the motif of a comet or other long object visiting such disasters upon the world (§§453-454). Thus another, damaged passage in the *Sibylline Oracles*: "But when after the fourth year a great star shines, which shall of itself destroy the whole earth ... and from heaven a great star shall fall on the dread ocean and burn up the deep sea, with Babylon itself and the land of

---

[288] Brown *et al.* 1906: 438 s. v. 'יְרֵכָה'.
[289] The *Septuagint* (ed. Rahlfs 1950: 585, trs. Pietersma & Wright 2007: 835) offers *eis ta themélia tēs gēs* ("into the foundations of the earth"), but this is more of an interpretation than a translation. Because Latin lacks articles, the reading of the *Vulgate* (ed. Tvveedale 2005: 489), *in profundum laci*, might equally be taken as "into the depth of the pit" (Kinney 2012: 58-59) and 'into the depth of a pit', while *lacus* could even mean 'lake' instead of 'pit'.
[290] Tschiffely 1929: 142 figure top.
[291] *Sibylline Oracles*, 8. 237-240, ed. Geffcken 1902: 151-152, tr. Terry 1890: 183, translating *ástra* as "the stars", *aktinóenta ... astéra* (accusative) as "the bright star" and *komētēn* (accusative) as "a comet".
[292] The Greek myth of Phaethon burning the world before crashing into the river Eridanus can equally be classified as a fallen 'sun' (§437) and a fallen planet. The Greeks did not directly equate Phaethon with the morning or evening star, either during his mythical life or in his catasterised form, but several lines of evidence – besides his resemblance to the Hebrew 'son of Dawn' – suggest that such an association may once have been a part of the myth. *e. g.*, van der Sluijs 2008: 237-238; 2011d: 215-216, 230; *cf.* 2009a: 275-276. Cochrane (2017) defends the position that Phaethon was a mythical 'morning star', though not Venus but Mars.

Italy, by reason of which many of the Hebrews perished, holy and faithful, and the people of truth."[293] Within the framework of Judaeo-Christian eschatology proper, the future coming of the divine saviour is preceded by a large number of torments, including burning of the world and impact events with toxic effects. One of the latter reads exactly like an oceanic impact:

> Then the third angel sounded: And a great star fell from heaven, burning like a torch, and it fell on a third of the rivers and on the springs of water. The name of the star is Wormwood. A third of the waters became wormwood, and many men died from the water, because it was made bitter.[294]

A subsequent incident matches the image of a crater-forming impact on land:

> Then the fifth angel sounded: And I saw a star fallen from heaven to the earth. To him was given the key to the bottomless pit. And he opened the bottomless pit, and smoke arose out of the pit like the smoke of a great furnace. So the sun and the air were darkened because of the smoke of the pit. Then out of the smoke locusts came upon the earth. And to them was given power, as the scorpions of the earth have power. ... They had tails like scorpions, and there were stings in their tails. Their power *was* to hurt men five months. And they had as king over them the angel of the bottomless pit, whose name in Hebrew *is* Abaddon, but in Greek he has the name Apollyon.[295]

The angels' pouring out of seven vials or bowls (*phiálas*, accusative), each with catastrophic consequences,[296] also suggests precipitation of unusual substances from the sky. It is more than likely that ancient cosmologists saw a relation of some sort between these forecasts and a similar fall of stars linked to the past destruction of the world by water. According to

---

[293] *Sibylline Oracles*, 5. 155-163, ed. Geffcken 1902: 111, tr. Bate 1918: 100, translating *mégas astḗr* and *astḕr mégas* as "a great star". The "fourth year" seems to refer to 74 CE, counting from the fall of Jerusalem during the First Jewish Revolt. In 5. 512-531 (cited in van der Sluijs 2011d: 122), all stars are smitten down upon the ocean, setting the whole earth on fire. *Cf.* 3. 334-336; Bousset 1896: 233.
[294] *Revelation of John* (late 1st century CE), 8. 10-11, eds. Nestle *et al.* 1993: 647-648, tr. Farstad 1982: 1085, translating *astḕr mégas* as "a great star" and *Ápsinthos* as "Wormwood", referring to species of the genus *Artemisia*.
[295] *Revelation of John*, 9. 1-3, 10-11, eds. Nestle *et al.* 1993: 648-649, tr. Farstad 1982: 1085-1086, translating *astéra* (accusative) as "a star" and *phréar tēs abýssou* as "the bottomless pit".
[296] *Revelation of John*, 16. 1-21, eds. Nestle *et al.* 1993: 663-665.

two passages in the *Talmūd*, the flood of Noah ensued when two stars were dislodged:

> For at the time when the Holy One, blessed be He, wanted to bring a flood upon the world, He took two stars from *Kimah* and brought a flood upon the world. And when He wanted to stop it, He took two stars from *'Ayish* and stopped it.[297]

> That day was the seventeenth of Iyar, a day on which the star group *Kimah* sets during the daytime, and the fountains become depleted. But because they altered their practices, the Holy One, blessed be He, altered upon them the works of creation. And he brought the star group *Kimah* up during the daytime. And he took two stars from *Kimah* and brought a flood to the world.[298]

These fragments do not enunciate in what way the two stars brought about the deluge; for example, was the idea that they delivered the water or that their landing in marine water generated a tidal wave?

Further, a traditional Finnish song entitled 'the birth of fire' (*tulen synty*) details the forging of a flame by Ilmarinen and Väinämöinen in one of the very highest heavens in the north, which falls from the sky, causes a massive conflagration on the earth and drops into a lake:

> ... Fire's procreation is from heaven.
> There fire was (softly) rocked,
> Fire's glow lulled to sleep,
> In a box of (yellow) copper,
> In a groundless gold vessel.
> Struck the fire Ilmarinen,
> Fire flashed Wäinämöinen,
> In the nightly dark north,
> With five feathers from the tail,
> With three feathers of an eagle,
> With fire-steeled sword,
> At the end of an iron seat,

---

[297] *Babylonian Talmūd: Bərākōt (Blessings)*, 9 (59a), tr. Simon 1948: 366; *cf. Midraš ha-Gādōl* (*The Great Midraš*; 14th century CE): *Barēšīt: Noaḥ*, ed. Schechter 1902: 156-157; Šəmu'ēl bęn Nissīm Masnūt (12th or 13th century CE), *Ma'yyan Gannīm* (*Fountain of Gardens*), ed. Buber 1889: 125-126; and the sources cited in Ginzberg 1913: 162; 1925: 183 note 40. In the translation of Funk (1913: 214 #736) the positions of Kīmā and 'Ayiš are accidentally reversed, but they are given correctly in the parallel Hebrew text.
[298] Joshua ben Levi (3rd century CE), in *Babylonian Talmūd: Rōš ha-Šānā* (*New Year*), 1 (11b), tr. adapted from Schorr & Malinowitz 1999: 11b. See the note in §359* regarding the translation and meaning of 'Iyyar and Kīmā.

Above nine of the heavens above,
On the cloud, then, of the tenth.
Sparkled up a fire's spark,
Fell down a red clew,
Fell down a blue clew;
Fire's flame sparkled down,
Rolled in its rolling,
Rolled in its journey,
There in Liemo's lake's water,
To the fishless inland lake.
To the bassless inland lake,
In the tips of the seagrass.
...
From that it is known as fire
From that it was found to be fire.
...
Came a youth down from the north,
Tall man from Pimentola ...
Said he upon his arrival,
Arriving at the fire's raging:
...
Ukko you, you golden king,
Bring a cloud from the northwest,
Throw 'nother one over from the west,
Flash the third one from the east,
Throw them arm in arm each other,
Thunder between them all the time!
Rain snow and rain water,
Rain hail, hard like iron,
On the badly burned locations!
Render fire's glow harmless,
render fire impotent!
Make it now as nameless,
Under my eyes' supervision ...
...
Maid Mary, little mother!
...
Throw the water of your lap
On the badly burned locations![299]

---

[299] *Tulen Synty* (*The Birth of Fire*), 3-26, 140-141, 162-163, 167-168, 175-187, 231, 244-245, recorded 1818-1819, tr. (to German) von Schröter 1819: 6-7, 14-21 (•), *cf.* 154-156. The wildfire occurred after a fish had swallowed up the flame, had itself been gobbled up by another fish and so forth, until fishermen had retrieved the flame. Lake Liemo is called Alavo in line 87. Ukko was the thunder god. As discussed (§437), the editor of the *Kalevala* in his reworking of this tale lacked traditional support for presenting the fireball as a substitute for the sun and moon, which had

The Barkindji (western New South Wales) identified a "BIG CIRCLE OF ROCK" on an outcrop in a river 10 km north of the town of Wilcannia as the site where a 'star' fell, causing fires, flooding and countless casualties:

> MALKARRA WOULD DO A LOT OF BAD THINGS ... BUT THEN AGAIN, MALKARRA DID **HELP** THEM IN A LOT OF WAYS. HE COULD DO ALL KINDS OF MIRACLES, HE COULD FEEL AND SEE THINGS IN HIS MIND THAT WAS [sic] GOING TO HAPPEN, ... HE WAS SOMETHING LIKE A ... **DOCTOR**. ... HE TOLD THEM THERE WAS GOING TO BE SOMETHING VERY DANGEROUS HAPPENING, ONE DAY VERY SOON. ... MALKARRA TOLD THEM THEY HAD TO GET READY TO **MOVE**! ...
>
> AND THEY COULD SEE THE SKY WAS **LIT UP** ... AND THERE WASN'T ANY MOON, SO THEY TOOK NOTICE OF THIS, AND THEY GOT **SCARED** ... THEN THEY HEARD THIS RUMBLING NOISE FROM THE SKY, LIKE THUNDER ...
>
> AND AS IT CAME DOWN CLOSE, THERE WAS RED STREAKS, AND A GREAT BIG BALL OF FIRE COMING DOWN ... AND THERE WAS SMOKE ... AND A LOT OF THEM GOT TRAPPED ... THEY JUST **COULDN'T** MOVE BECAUSE IT CAME DOWN TOO QUICK ... AND WHERE IT FELL, SOME OF THEM DIED THERE, AND SOME OF THEM GOT BURNT ... THERE WAS FIRE IN IT. ... THE OTHERS DIED THERE. ... THEY HAD TO **MOVE QUICK** BECAUSE OF THE RAIN THAT WAS COMING BEHIND. ...
>
> THIS BIG CIRCLE OF ROCK IS WHERE THE STAR FELL. YOU CAN ONLY SEE IT WHEN THE RIVER DRIES UP. THE OLD PEOPLE CALLED THIS BEND **'PURLI NGRANGKALITJI'**... THAT'S 'THE FALLEN STAR' IN PARKANTJI LANGUAGE. YEARS AGO, WHEN WE CAME OUT HERE, THERE WAS SOME DIFFERENT COLOURED STONE AS WELL AS WHAT YOU SEE NOW. THERE WAS A LOT OF **BLACK** STONE HERE ... THAT SORT OF DULL BLACK LIKE YOU SEE IN OUR PEOPLE'S OLD FIREPLACES. AND IT HAD **SHINY** BITS LIKE BLACK MARBLE, TOO, AND BITS OF **GREEN**, AND BITS THAT WERE **WHITE-ISH** LIKE THE FAT IN A SHEEP. ...
>
> THEN IT STARTED TO RAIN, LIKE MALKARRA SAID IT WOULD ... AND IT RAINED FOR DAYS ... AND DAYS ... AND DAYS ... AND THEY KEPT MOVING, THIS GROUP OF PEOPLE ... THEY HAD TO GET TO THE

---

been imprisoned. According to the version given earlier by Ganander (1789: 106-107 s. v. 'WEENKUNINGAS', 4 s. v. 'ALAMAN-JÄRWI', 'ALOEN-JÄRWI' = ed. Peterson 1821: 66, 70-71, 78 note 2), the flame resulted from a battle of the two deities with a 'colourful snake' (*kirjawalla kärmehellä*) (•). See §§187-211 for more on layered heavens.

HIGHER GROUND. ... ALL THE SWAMPS WAS [sic] FULL, THERE WAS JUST A SEA OF WATER EVERYWHERE.[300]

The Cherokee of North Carolina submitted an account which is somewhat reminiscent of the Hebrew report about the cause of the flood, especially if the star group Kīmā matches the Pleiades (§359*). According to this, just seven days after "the Seven Stars of the Pleiades" had been placed in the sky, "one fell to earth, leaving a fiery trail":

> All the Indians gathered together to know what this might mean. They found that the star had become a bearded man, who sat down and warned them of the coming of the flood. He remained on earth seven years, and then disappeared, leaving his footprint on a rock. The stars are still called the Seven Stars, although there have since been but six.[301]

In a 'preview' to this information published some years earlier, the messenger is "a star with fiery tail", presumably a comet, which "falls from heaven and becomes a man with long hair, who warns the people of the coming deluge."[302] Within the context of the creation of the world, the setting of the story is the time "before there were any stars in the sky", when "the Great Star" – evidently the morning or evening star – was installed as "the only star in the sky", followed by "the seven stars of the Pleiades", whose purpose was – as the Great Rabbit "told the people" – "to warn them of the approach of the Deluge".[303] And a 16th-century Spanish text reports that the local Maya traced the origin of Lake Yocah Ek' near Chauacá (Chikinchel, northeast Yucatán) to an impact accompanied by rain showers:

> ... it was called Yocajeque [Yocah-Ek'] because of having a great lake with deep water in it, the natives say that a star fell into it with great rains, and thus it can be understood, since they call the morning star Noch Eque [Nohoch Ek']; this one sets to the west, leaving forty

---

[300] Dick Willow to Sarah Cabbage in 1927 and others, recorded before 1989 by Elsie Rose Jones (1917-1996), half Scottish and half Barkindji, ed. Jones 1989: no page numbers given, capitals and boldface in the original. 'Parkantji' is an alternative spelling of 'Barkindji'.
[301] recorded 1898, in Hagar 1906: 359.
[302] Hagar, in Mooney 1900: 445. The variant in Mooney 1900: 258-259 omits the deluge, but adds that a pine tree grew up on the spot where the seventh Pleiad fell.
[303] recorded 1898, in Hagar 1906: 361.

leagues from there to the port of Conil to the east, and that is the final end of the mainland ...³⁰⁴

Just like comets could be represented indirectly through the use of metaphors (§450), so cosmic impacts may be indicated in traditions about the fall of other entities from the sky, like deities not directly described in terms of fire, astral bodies or rocks; their organs, such as eyes; or their belongings, such as chariots and combs. The same types of catastrophes may be stated to accompany these falls. The Quiché Maya (Guatemala) listed "things of wood and stone" as objects which had fallen during the deluge, before the sun had yet risen:

> Again there comes a humiliation, destruction, and demolition. The manikins, woodcarvings were killed when the Heart of Sky devised a flood for them. A great flood was made; it came down on the heads of the manikins, woodcarvings. ... They were not competent, nor did they speak before the builder and sculptor who made them and brought them forth, and so they were killed, done in by a flood:
>
> There came a rain of resin from the sky.
> ...
>
> The earth was blackened because of this; the black rainstorm began, rain all day and rain all night. Into their houses came the animals, small and great. Their faces were crushed by things of wood and stone. ... The people were ground down, overthrown.³⁰⁵

This bombardment with "things of wood and stone" is redolent of the landing of "stones" and "sticks" during the battle between the nine gods of the underworld and the thirteen of the sky (§312*), prior to the deluge, according to a liturgical text from the Maya of Chumayel (Yucatán):

> And then there were finished
> The 13 who are Gods
> By the 9 who are Gods.
> They then brought down fire;

---

³⁰⁴ anonymous, *Relación de la villa de Valladolid* (1579 CE), 8, ed. de la Garza 1983: 33 (•). The location of Conil is hard to determine. Köhler (2002: 5) translated *Yocah Ek'* as 'star has pierced' and suggested that the tradition be "a vague reminiscence of the impact at Chicxulub" – a most curious assertion considering that the latter occurred some 65 million years ago and was unknown to science until the 20th century. The story surely references a much more recent event.
³⁰⁵ *Popol Vuh* (*Book of the People*), 1, tr. Tedlock 1996: 71-73. 'Heart of Sky' (*Uk'ux kaj*) was a designation of the creator, Juraqan, *cf.* van der Sluijs 2011a: 94.

Then they brought down the rope;
Then they brought down stones
And sticks.
Then came beating with sticks
And stones.
And then were finished
The 13 who are Gods.[306]

false positives

A few groups in North Carolina other than the Tuscarora and the Cherokee have been claimed to have preserved memories of an impact event, which caused the formation of new lakes but not a deluge, mass deaths or the end of an era. The Waccamaw (southeastern North Carolina) allegedly explained the origin of one of the Carolina Bays, Lake Waccamaw, in a tradition of an impacting bolide:

> Countless years ago a huge meteor appeared in the sky toward the southwest. It flamed in the atmosphere to a brilliance of many suns as it sped earthward. As suddenly as it appeared, it struck, and buried itself deep in the alluvial mire. The waters of the surrounding swamps and rivers flowed into the crater and cooled it, creating a gem of blue, in a setting of verdent [sic] green.[307]

The legend's authenticity has been cast into doubt and it must be noted that it was recorded after 1933, when the scientific hypothesis that the Carolina Bays were caused by impact was first formulated.[308] Nevertheless, a tradition from the related Catawba nation involving a comet was certainly recorded earlier. According to this, Ugni ('comet') was an evil woman who attempted to follow a mother and her son along a rope to

---

[306] Juan Josef Hoíl, *Book of Chilam Balam of Chumayel* (1782 CE), 29. 3 (42-43; 3040-3050), tr. Edmonson 1986: 154-155; *cf.* van der Sluijs 2011d: 13, 76 note 223. See the earlier note (§312*) on the ritual character of the text and the identity of the thirteen gods and the nine gods. Bolio (1941: 62) translated *tab* as 'ash' instead of "rope" and *che* as 'trees' instead of "sticks" (••); for the latter, Roys (1967: 99-100) gave "trees", Luxton (1995: 76-77, at 17. 6 [1692]) "tree". Bolio (1941: 63) had a subsequent collapse of the sky (compare §§300, 300*, 353, 466): 'the firmament collapsed and the earth sank' (•). Roys (1967: 99) agreed: "Then the sky would fall, it would fall down upon the earth". But none occurs in the more recent translations, which offer: "Who radiated in heaven / And radiated also on the land" (Edmonson 1986: 156, at 29. 7 [43; 3091-3092]) and "In the breadth of the sky / [And] the width of the world" (Luxton 1995: 76-77, at 17. 15 [1725-1726]).

[307] apparently recorded 1949-1950, in Alexander 1950: 30, *cf.* 31. Firestone *et al.* (2006: 196) seem to have relied on this account.

[308] Melton & Schriever 1933.

the sky, but "fell down [through the sky] a tailed star" when the rope broke.[309] The motif of the severed rope to heaven allows a connection between the comet and the disintegration of an *axis mundi* (§§318-340). A very cautious assessment would be that the ancestors of the Waccamaw had passed on some tradition involving a comet, but the notion of the impact or the association with the Carolina Bays was the fruit of exposure to science. Then again, the tradition might just be genuine as given.[310]

A no less challenging case study centres on Lake Mattamuskeet (northeastern North Carolina), another Carolina Bay. Daniel W. Barefoot, a writer of travel guidebooks, retold a legend from the local indigenous people to the effect that the lake came into being following the fall of a star, which ended a drought:

> Long, long ago, the Indians inhabiting the area now covered by the lake were blessed with an abundance of game, fish, fruits, and vegetables until an extreme drought came. Suddenly, the animals died of thirst or ran away in search of water. Streams and creeks where the Indians had once fished dried up. Fields that once yielded maize and other crops in copious quantities were parched.
>
> As the drought lingered for several years, the Indians grew desperate for food, some of their number dying of starvation. As a last resort, the survivors built a great ceremonial bonfire to appease the rain gods. To the dismay of the Indians, the gods were outraged. Fanned by strong winds, the fire spread into the nearby forests. For a year, the conflagration raged.
>
> Once again, the Indians attempted to appease the gods. When they selected their finest young brave to be offered as a human sacrifice, a beautiful Indian maiden interceded on his behalf. Kneeling at a sacrificial altar, she prayed to the Great Spirit to save the brave and her perishing people. After her invocation, a star fell to the earth, and rain soon followed. Days and days of rain quenched the fire. Great holes burned in the earth by the fire were filled, forming a great inland sea.[311]

---

[309] recorded 1913-1934, in Speck 1934: 2-4.
[310] Extant correspondence between Alexander and Speck in October-November 1949, preserved in the collection of Frank G. Speck Papers (Mss. Ms. Coll. 126, box 17) held by the American Philosophical Society in Philadelphia (Pennsylvania), sheds no further light on this matter.
[311] Barefoot 1995: 267-268. Firestone *et al.* (2006: 193-194) followed Barefoot's account uncritically.

Although Barefoot did not identify his source, he assuredly relied on the work of Charles Harry Whedbee (1911-1990), a local judge. However, most other essential details matching, a notable difference is that, in this earlier telling, the relieving rains – much more logically – result from a thunderstorm instead of a stellar impact:

> For more than thirteen moons it burned, destroying large areas of the hunting grounds but always, mercifully, being fanned away from the Indian village by a persistent wind. ... She prayed with all her heart. Great tears rolled down her crimson cheeks, and her voice shook with the urgency of her pleading until, finally, she fell over and lay prostrate upon the sand, exhausted.
>
> At that very instant a great clap of thunder was heard in the smoke-darkened skies. And then another and yet another, as the lightning blazed brilliantly and seemed to light up the whole of creation. This was followed by the most torrential downpour of rain anyone had ever seen, even in the great autumn storms. It rained and it rained. It rained so hard that it was impossible to see more than a few feet in front of your eyes. ... The rain finally stopped, but not before it had completely filled the burnt-out cavities in the earth and there was born a beautiful, sparkling lake in their stead.[312]

Whedbee, too, failed to state the provenance of his story. While his application of the known tribal names 'Pamlico' and 'Coree' and the hydronym 'Wacheeta' to individual characters suggests his own creative input, his mention of "more than thirteen moons" for the duration of the burning demonstrates debt to a written source. This would be the following discussion by Bill Sharpe, which does not include the element of a falling "star" either:

> Lake Mattamuskeet ('Great Dust' in Indian) undoubtedly is of fire origin, since ancient charred tree trunks have been dredged from its shallow bottom. Peaty soil characterizes the territory, and even today, the 'ground' sometimes burns for months after a forest fire.
>
> The Indians told early settlers that long ago there was no lake at all. Then one year there was a great drought, and the woods and swamps were disastrously dry. To propitiate the rain gods, a huge ceremonial fire was built. But the gods looked with disfavor on this worship, and the very ground blazed, the fire spreading wide and deep, burning for thirteen moons. The game fled and the Indians faced starvation, until

---

[312] Whedbee 1978: 119, 121-122.

> one day a simple maid went into the woods and invoked the mercy of the rain gods. Almost instantly, the heavens opened, and rain fell for many days. When the Indians crept to the site again, the fire was extinguished and they found before their eyes a great inland sea, limpid, teeming with fish, and upon whose waters floated succulent birds, and around whose shores were plentiful deer, bear, and other game.[313]

It must be noted that the etymology "bad dust" or "much dust" does not pertain to the name 'Mattamuskeet', but to 'Machapunga', the ethnic name of the people in question.[314] Nevertheless, Sharpe clearly relied on an unknown published source. This may well be another unreferenced tradition cited in 1893 to the effect that "for 13 moons (one year) the fires continued to burn", before they were checked by the rains and Lake Mattamuskeet was formed.[315]

A pair of writers paraphrased Sharpe's version without citing him and added: "Other theories state that the lake has a meteoric origin or that it is a natural depression and was once an arm of the sea."[316] Whereas they clearly intended this as a reference to contemporary scientific thought, Barefoot or another of his sources seems to have understood the "meteoric origin" as a native tradition, thus introducing the star into the story where it may not have existed before. Writing just before Sharpe, the marine biologist Rachel Carson (1907-1964), in fact, included a meteor shower among the tales that were circulating:

> Try to learn the origins of this vast inland lake and at once you stumble upon a collection of local legends in which it is hard to separate fact from fiction. Of all the stories of the genesis of Mattamuskeet, local opinion divides its support between two. According to one story, the Indians long ago set fires in the peat bogs, fires that burned so long and deeply that a huge, saucer-like depression was formed. This caught the rains and the drainage water, creating a lake. The other story has it that a shower of giant meteors once struck the Carolina coastal plain, the impact of the largest ones digging out the beds of Lake Mattamuskeet and the smaller, but otherwise similar, Lakes Alligator, Pungo, and Phelps that lie northwest of Mattamuskeet.[317]

---

[313] Sharpe 1948: 13, repeated *verbatim* in 1958: 900-901, except that the "undoubtedly" is changed into "may be".
[314] Hodge 1907: 781 s. v. '**Machapunga**'.
[315] Jeffers 1893.
[316] Hamnett & Thornton 1953: 40.
[317] Carson 1947: 1-2.

Carson's admission that fact was hard to separate from fiction does not inspire much confidence in the meteoric alternative as authentic folk tradition. As seen, it was in 1933 that scientists had first proposed that the Carolina Bays were formed by impact. It may have been talk of that hypothesis which Carson carelessly classified as a 'legend' – inadvertently generating a new myth. In that case, as so often, a purported myth falls apart when it is attempted to track it down to its earliest written expression. On the other hand, the Tuscarora tradition of a falling "star" was committed to writing a few years before Ignatius Loyola Donnelly (1831-1901) published his celebrated monograph on encounters with comets enshrined in myth[318] and more than a decade before the first hint of a theory of cosmic impact appeared in print.[319] And the clustering of traditions about a fallen star or comet in North Carolina among the Tuscarora, the Cherokee and just possibly also the Waccamaw, the Catawba and the Machapunga counts as a powerful argument in favour of the authenticity, if not also the antiquity, of all of them, as well as the impressive Ojibwe tradition cited elsewhere (§§407*, 448-449, 454). It is not impossible that future recovery of additional evidence will help to settle the matter.

456
rock art produced by mythical beings

People living in the vicinity of sites with prehistoric rock art often *attributed the art* not to ordinary people such as their own human ancestors, but *to a temporally distant race of supernatural beings*, typically associated with the time of 'creation'. For example, an old Tibetan 'told that, in the mountains, there were rupestral figures, *rimudong*, works of divinity, which sometimes disappeared and only showed themselves still to a few privileged ones ...'[320] The Nanai (Middle Amur basin, northeast Asia) traced the carving of local petroglyphs – which include 'face masks', 'separatrices' and a 'thunder dragon'[321] – to the time when the primordial three suns were shot (§§443-444), just after the earth had been formed by 'earth diving':

---

[318] Donnelly 1883.
[319] Gilbert 1896.
[320] Chen 1988: 43 (•).
[321] Laufer 1899: 746-749.

> Ka´do went to where the Sun rises. He dug a pit, in which he hid; and when the first Sun rose, he shot him. He missed the second Sun; but when the third Sun rose, he killed him also. Then he returned. Now it was no longer too hot. Ma´milji drew pictures on stones. Julchu´ said, 'The people have seen that my husband has killed two Suns.' After the Suns had been killed the stones began to harden.[322]

With respect to "a large block of sandstone lying at .wòtàem·i-", the indigenous people of the Andaman Islands (Bay of Bengal) believed that "the deep incisions visible on its surface are hieroglyphics inscribed by .tô·mo-, the first man, giving a history of the Creation, which event ... is believed ... to have occurred at this very spot .wòtàem·i-. The art of deciphering the supposed record has, it is said, been lost for many ages, and no attempt is made to assign a specific meaning to any of the marks which form the mythical inscription. Many of the legends regarding their ancestors picture the scene of their exploits at .wòtàem·i- ..."[323]

The divine authorship of works of parietal art was an especially widespread belief in Australia. Here, "the Aborigines ... in some cases ... were not apparently aware of engravings pointed out to them by whites in their own territory and they usually say that the work was done by spiritual ancestors in the Dreamtime when the land was inhabited by spirits."[324] "Aboriginals today do not carve on stone and say the carvings which surround them are the work of Dreaming Ancestors, or people who lived long, long ago."[325] The Ngadjuri people (South Australia) contended that several carvings in their land, including one of a "magic stick" (*yarida*) at Panaramittee North that scholars had interpreted as a crocodile head, were "made in the Ancestral Times (*Widmakara*), and are associated with two spirit beings":[326]

> ... the country around Yunta, Panaramittee, Manna Hill, as far as Bimbowrie (Bombowie), was rocky and contains many rock engravings. Among these lived two spirits named Budla-bila. They could be seen

---

[322] probably recorded 1898-1899, in Laufer 1899: 749-750. Ma´milji, for whom 'Julchu´' seems to have been another name, was Ka´do's wife.

[323] recorded 1869-1880 by Edward Horace Man (1846-1929), in Man 1883: 171.

[324] McCarthy 1958: 24-25, *cf.* 37 for stencils and 65 for other paintings. "They will admit to painting some figures, and to re-touching sacred pictures at appropriate times of the year ..." 1958: 65.

[325] Isaacs 1980: 250, *cf.* 251; Layton 2001: 316. See Hernández 1961-1962: 116 for an example from one of the Drysdale River nations, probably the Miwa or the Gamberre (Kimberleys).

[326] Gudjari (d. c1900), a Ngadjuri man, to his grandson Barney Gunaia Ngadjibuna Waria (1873-1948), partly of Ngadjuri descent, recorded 1932 - April 1944, in Elkin 1949: 150 note 52.

on sunny mornings, and were responsible for causing mirages (*marragabi*, fresh water, because they looked like that). These rock engravings were said to have been made in the creative era of the Dreaming, and traditionally there were songs associated with many of the figures depicted. The famous Panaramittee stone, identified by Mountford as a crocodile head, was said to be really a *yarida* that had been engraved by the Budla-bila. To accomplish that task they used quartz chisels from stone obtained from Waruni hill ...[327]

Visiting the Ngadjuri's northern neighbours, the Adnyamathanha (Flinders Ranges, South Australia), the Australian anthropologist Charles Pearcy Mountford (1890-1976) learned that some mythical being must have produced the petroglyphs in the Red Gorge – but this seemed to be little more than a secondary, considered opinion:

> When C. P. M. visited the Gorge in 1937 he intentionally did not tell his aboriginal companions the object of the visit. As the party walked along the floor of the Gorge the aborigines passed group after group of clearly defined engravings without apparently having seen them. Even when their attention was drawn to some engravings and they were asked, 'What are these things?' the old men, after a casual examination said, 'Oh, they're just marks in the rocks' and walked away.
>
> Later when the resemblance between some of the engravings and the tracks of kangaroos, emus, lizards and so on, was pointed out, the natives were most surprised and searched enthusiastically for additional examples. But even though they agreed that the marks were not the result of natural agencies they were definite that no aboriginal had made them. Nevertheless they were just as ready as some of the white men to give meanings to the engravings. ...
>
> The following morning two of the old men came to my camp to tell me that, after discussing the engravings among themselves on the previous evening, they had agreed that the examples we had seen in the Red Gorge had been engraved by *Iti*, a mythical lizard-man of creation times, who also made the piles of small stones on the saddles of some of the low ranges.[328]

---

[327] Gudjari to Waria, recorded 1942 - April 1944 at Murray Bridge and Adelaide, in Berndt 1987: 20, *cf.* 15, 21-22, 26-27. The chisels were made of the white quartz (*yudla-gadna*) believed to be the metamorphosed pus (*gaba*) from a wound in the leg of Eaglehawk, 1987: 25.
[328] recorded 1937 by Mountford, in Mountford & Edwards 1964: 849-850; compare 1962: 98; Mountford 1960: 145. "C. P. M." refers to Mountford.

At various locations in Warlpiri, Luritja and Arrernte lands (central Australia), Mountford received similar indigenous information with more confidence: "... I found rock engravings at the Korporilya and Iromba waterholes in central Australia ... On that occasion, my aboriginal companions knew of the existence of the markings, but were definite that they had not been cut in the rock by human hands, but by some mythical hero during the creation period. Similarly, in more recent years, the aborigines at Kamalba, Watelbring and Ngama ... attributed a mythical origin to the rock markings at these places."[329] Later again, Mountford had reason to be sceptical about local claims concerning the origins of the rock art at Gallery Hill in Nyamal territory (Pilbara region, Western Australia):

> When I asked the local aborigines about the origin of the rock pictures at Gallery Hill, I was told that they had been made by the *Minjiburu*, a group of mythical women whom the aborigines believe had created most of the topographical features in the surrounding country.[330]

He went on:

> Later, one of the old men, in conversation, said to me:
>
> 'Them fellows say *Minjiburu* women made those marks but they're only guessing. We blackfellows don't know who made them; we only think it was the *Minjiburu*.' ...
>
> There is a tendency on the part of some investigators to accept the statements of aborigines as absolute fact, whereas they may have no specific knowledge, but merely be expressing an opinion. This has happened to me both at Gallery Hill and, many years earlier, at Red Gorge in South Australia ...[331]

The petroglyphs at Nappa Merrie (southwest Queensland), which include one "somewhat like a small anchor", "a ring", "certainly one crescent-shaped figure" and "concentric arcs and upright lines", were said by a native – probably of the Yandruwandha tribe – "to have been made by

---

[329] recorded 1942 by Mountford, in Mountford 1960: 145; cf. Mountford & Edwards 1964: 850; 1962: 99.
[330] probably recorded 1945-1955, in Mountford 1965: 102.
[331] recorded as above, in Mountford 1965: 102, 100.

two 'dog women', Witdjini and Kilki *mura* (heroines) who camped at the spot and used to sit under two big ti-trees near by":

> A third slab was similarly and distinctly marked. ... it represented *poa*, a grass seed. The concentric arcs represented the falling of the grass seed on a heap under the grinding stones. Witdjini and Kilki rested, ate grass seed and grew strong at this camp. They had 'come out', that is had first arisen, from a cave near the top of another rocky point about two hundred yards up the stream. ... After their 'birth', the two women travelled underground (as through a tunnel) for a short distance and came out of the ground at the camp already mentioned. They remained there until they had become strong enough to travel above ground, after which they went round the rocky corner, and up the stream to Malgara, where they can be seen as white stone.[332]

The anthropologist who recorded this tradition commented: "The interesting point ... is that the petroglyphs of arcs and straight lines had *mura mura* or 'dream-time' mythological and heroic reference, and were therefore sacred."[333]

As for the Americas,[334] the Nlaka'pamux (British Columbia) "claim that some of the rock paintings to be found in their country, especially those on the rocks which overlook water, are the work of the spirits of those places. One of these was on a rock facing the pool between the little and big waterfalls of Waterfall Creek, near Spences Bridge. The pictures were made in red paint, and represented the sun, the stars, the coyote, wolf, grisly bear, etc. They were at one time very plain, but within the last few years have become obliterated. The Indians say that this is a sign that the 'spirit' has left the place. Another painting of this description was above NEqa'umîn Waterfall, near Thompson Siding. Still another was on a cliff overhanging Nicola Lake, not far from Kwîlca'na. This painting is said to be still visible. ... Another painting is on a rock overlooking Kamloops Lake, not far from Savona. This picture is also ascribed by most Indians to a supernatural agency, while some claim that it was painted by the Shuswap ..."[335] The British anthropologist Robert Layton (b. 1944) observed that the rock art of the Columbia Plateau (Washington, Oregon and Idaho) is located in a landscape with a strong mythological resonance:

---

[332] Elkin 1949: 140-141. The *tī* tree, also known as the cabbage tree, is *Cordyline australis*.
[333] Elkin 1949: 141.
[334] Other examples are in Layton 2001: 315, 321; Lewis-Williams & Dowson 1988: 205, 238.
[335] Teit 1900: 339.

> The location of engravings or paintings in the cultural landscape may be critical to their meaning. The rock art of the Columbia Plateau appears to be preferentially located at two types of sites: places considered gateways to the spirit world and, probably, graves. Many features of the landscape bearing rock art are the transformed remains of the bodies and artifacts of heroic beings.[336]

According to some legends in the region, "these picture rocks fell from the sky just as they are, while others say that some mythical person made them."[337] The Sioux articulated that the petroglyphs at Pipestone National Monument (southwestern Minnesota) had been carved by a curious 'thunder being':

> The Pipe Stone Quarry is a place of great importance to the Sioux. From it they obtain the red stone clay – Catlinite – of which their pipes and images are formed; and a peculiar sacredness is, in their minds, attached to the place. Numerous high bluffs and cliffs surround it; and the alluvial flat below these, in which the quarry is situated, contains a huge boulder that rests upon a flat rock of glistening, smooth appearance, the level of which is but a few inches above the surface of the ground.
>
> Upon the portions of this rock not covered by the boulder above and upon the boulder itself are carved sundry wonderful figures – lizards [sic], snakes, otters, Indian gods, rabbits with cloven feet, muskrats with human feet, and other strange and incomprehensible things – all cut into the solid granite, and not without a great deal of time and labor expended in the performance. The commoner Indians, even to this day, are accustomed to look upon these with feelings of mysterious awe, as they call to mind the legend connected therewith.
>
> A large party of Ehanktonwanna and Teetonwan Dakotas, says the legend, had gathered together at the quarry to dig the stone. Upon a sultry evening, just before sunset, the heavens suddenly became overclouded, accompanied by heavy rumbling thunder, and every sign of an approaching storm, such as frequently arises on the prairie without much warning. Each one hurried to his lodge expecting a storm, when a vivid flash of lightning, followed immediately by a crashing peal of thunder, broke over them, and, looking towards the huge boulder beyond their camp, they saw a pillar or column of smoke standing upon it, which moved to and fro, and gradually settled down into the outline of a huge giant, seated upon the boulder,

---

[336] Layton 2001: 316.
[337] Erwin 1930: 43.

> with one long arm extended to heaven and the other pointing down to his feet. Peal after peal of thunder, and flashes of lightning in quick succession followed, and this figure then suddenly disappeared.
>
> The next morning the Sioux went to this boulder, and found these figures and images upon it, where before there had been nothing; and ever since that the place has been regarded as *wakan* or *sacred*.[338]

And regarding the local rock art, which includes an abundance of abstract forms, the natives of Guyana – probably Macushi, in this case – "scout the idea of their having been made by the hand of man, and ascribe them to the handiwork of the Makunaima, their great spirit."[339]

By leaving physical marks as they went, mythical beings are at times stated to have produced rock art inadvertently instead of deliberately. Among the original residents of the northern Flinders Ranges (South Australia), by whom the Adnyamathanha are most likely meant, "the impression was generally that the curious forms on the weather-beaten faces of the rocks represented the fossil-imprints of strange, prehistoric monsters"; they "know nothing about the carved productions of art here discussed" and "barely recognise in them the handicraft of a people who, in all probability, were their direct ancestors."[340] Some groups acknowledged a combination of intentional art and unpurposed imprints of body parts. Thus, the Wiljali (northwestern New South Wales) reported of the "many markings in a rocky place along the creek near Euriowie" (some 80 km north of Broken Hill), which "represented tracks of men, babies, and animals and also outlines of animals", that "the 'Seven Sisters' had made the petroglyphs with chisels before going up to the sky to live."[341] And the Barkindji (western New South Wales) connected the features seen on the rock overhangs at Mount Grenfell, east of Wilcannia, with the disastrous time when an impacting bolide and a massive flood of rain wiped out many people (§455):

> AND THEY KEPT MOVING, THIS GROUP OF PEOPLE ... THEY HAD TO GET TO THE HIGHER GROUND. ... ALL THE SWAMPS WAS [*sic*] FULL,

---

[338] recorded 1853-1862 by James William Lynd (1830-1862), ed. Riggs 1865: 59-60. The modern spellings of the names 'Ehanktonwanna' and 'Teetonwan' are respectively 'Iháŋkthuŋwaŋna' and 'Thítȟuŋwaŋ'.
[339] Brown 1873: 255.
[340] recorded 1906-1914, in Basedow 1914: 195-196, 198.
[341] a mixed-blood Wiljali man (b. c1875), recorded 1930 at Nappa Merrie, in Elkin 1949: 139, who observed: "The significance of this statement is that the petroglyphs were given a mythological origin by the old men of fifty years ago ..." *Cf.* 1949: 149.

> THERE WAS JUST A SEA OF WATER EVERYWHERE. ... THERE'S A PAINTING IN ONE OF THE CAVES OF PEOPLE STANDING ON EACH OTHER'S SHOULDERS. THAT MIGHT BE THESE PEOPLE I'M TALKING ABOUT, CLIMBING UP THE ROCKS. THERE'S A PAINTING IN ONE OF THE CAVES HERE OF A VERY UGLY FACE. IT COULD BE MALKARRA.[342]

> THAT'S WHY YOU'LL SEE FINGERPRINTS AND FOOTPRINTS IN THE ROCKS THERE TODAY ... BECAUSE THEY WERE THE PEOPLE GOING UP AND COMING DOWN THESE HILLS; AND THE ROCKS USED TO BE SOFT.[343]

Apparently, the Barkindji believed that depressions in the rock were accidentally created by the people as they were trying to escape, while the paintings depicting the scene were created afterwards.

From the opinion that rock art was the result of mythical beings leaving accidental impressions of their own bodies, it is only a small step to the conviction that some images were self-portraits or even physical transformations of mythical beings. "... in certain regions in the North and Northwest, where the nicely executed, mythological totemic beings of anthropomorphic form are portrayed, the natives are adamant in their insistance [sic] that neither they nor their forebears are responsible for them, but that the totemic beings themselves are the ones who painted their own likenesses upon the cave walls. The natives do admit that each year they touch up these sacred paintings as a part of the ritual in certain ceremonies, if not for other reasons."[344] The indigenous population of Gunbalanya (west Arnhem Land, Northern Territory), probably of Gunwinggu stock, supposed a group of "spirit people" known as *Mimi* "to have been responsible for the single-line rock paintings in the caves of the Arnhem Land plateau, adjacent to Oenpelli, particularly those of human beings."[345] They also recounted that, during "the time of creation", "many of the stars came down from the sky, transformed themselves into cycad-nut men, called *Mundiga*, and wandered round the rugged plateau adjacent to Nimbawah, near Oenpelli. After a while the

---

[342] Dick Willow to Sarah Cabbage in 1927 and others, recorded before 1989 by Elsie Rose Jones (1917-1996), half Scottish and half Barkindji, ed. Jones 1989: no page numbers given, capitals in the original.
[343] Polly Brown, recorded as above, ed. Jones 1989: no page numbers given, capitals in the original. At Mount Mara, too, the same ancestors reputedly left knee marks (*thinki yapa*), elbow marks (*kupu yapa*) and foot and hand prints (*thina yapa* and *mara yapa*).
[344] Davidson 1936: 18-19.
[345] recorded September-November 1948 or 1949 at Oenpelli, in Mountford 1956: 181, *cf.* 182-183; McCarthy 1958: 51.

Mundiga, deciding to stay at a place called Gunulkjau, transformed themselves into paintings of cycad nuts."[346] Nor are these images the only ones so held to have been produced:

> There are many records at Oenpelli of ancestral beings transforming themselves into paintings ...[347]

The Wardaman (southwest of Katherine, Northern Territory) "divide rock art into two categories: *buwarraja* or Dreaming pictures, which were *not* made by people but by creator beings in the Dreamtime, and *bulawula*, pictures made by people. ... both types exist as both paintings and petroglyphs."[348] Of special interest within the former category is the case of the Lightning Brothers, depicted at Yiwarlarlay (Delamere Station):

> The story concerns moral injustice demonstrated by a fight between two unequally-matched tribal brothers, the older, less well-endowed *Jabirringgi*, and *Yagjabula* who is young, handsome, with more sex appeal and twice as tall. *Jabirringgi* is married to *Garnayanda*, but one day he discovers, when he returns from hunting, *Yagjabula* seducing his wife. A violent fight follows, creating lightning in the sky, which strikes the sandstone outcrop and splits the rock in two. ... At the same time the Rainbow Serpent, *Gorrondolmi*, flashes his forked tongue at the rain to warn him not to go on to *Yingalarri* ... Eventually *Yagjabula* won the fight by knocking *Jabirringgi*'s head-dress off with his boomerang, and 'they painted themselves onto the wall' ...[349]

> In respect to the human-like figures the natives were very emphatic in denying that they, or any other human beings, had been responsible for their portrayal. Indeed, they maintained with dogmatic assurance that these pictures were the work of the personages portrayed. In other words, the Lightning Brothers, themselves, were responsible for their own depiction.[350]

In the Kimberleys (northwestern Australia), the Wandjinas are believed to have been "creator heroes who made the landscape and its fauna and

---

[346] recorded as above, in Mountford 1956: 238.
[347] Mountford 1956: 238 note 32. Compare Berndt & Berndt 1989: 57-59 for Gunwinggu examples.
[348] Flood & David 1994: 9, *cf.* 21; Chippindale 2004: 39.
[349] Nonomarran *alias* Elsie Raymond (c1930-1997) and Tarpot Ngamunugarri, recorded 1989 at Yiwarlarlay, in Flood & David 1994: 10; compare the versions in Barrett 1946: 63 and the discussion in McCarthy 1958: 57-58. The archaeological evidence suggests that the painting is less than a century old, Flood & David 1994: 12.
[350] Davidson 1936: 111-112. The Lightning Brothers' names are here spelled 'Yagtchadbulla' and 'Tcabuinji'. *Cf.* 110, 113-120.

flora, its rivers and caves", as well as "the first men whose journeys are marked by sacred landmarks such as pools, rocks, and bottle trees."[351] Such a clan ancestor eventually "painted his or her image upon the wall of a rockshelter within the territory, sometimes in quasi-human form, sometimes in an animal transformation."[352] For example, the Woljamidi, a subgroup of the Ngarinyin, considered the Wandjina paintings to be "the work of Wolaro:, who put them there as a memorial to keep the natives mindful of himself and his work. For strangely enough, Wolaro: is thought of not as a great spirit, but as a man who died like other men."[353] Another Ngarinyin group linked 'Ngurulin painting' in Wodongari country to Waránа, the eaglehawk (*Aquila audax*):

> They say that the eaglehawk, Waránа, laid two eggs in his nest on the top of a tree. While he was out kangaroo hunting, a small bird called *wodoi*, apparently a species of rock pigeon, and very, very important in mythology, took them down to the ground and sat on them to hide them. Warana came back and missed them. Looking about he saw *wodoi* and guessed he was the culprit. So he gave chase, up and down, up and down, yet failing to catch *wodoi*. *Wodoi*'s mate, *djuŋgun*, a species of owl, got a boomerang and throwing stick and waited for Warana. When Warana got tired, Djunggun was able to kill him. Warana then turned into a painting, and the eggs into two stones which are seen just outside the cave.[354]

The curious conversion of Wandjinas into paintings was inseparably related to funerary ritual:

> There is always the story explaining how this Wandjina came to be a painting … The phrase 'turned into a painting' is peculiar. … Sometimes the Wandjina in the story says *ganda ɲio:de*, 'here I shall become a painting.' With this idea of a person turning into a painting is coupled always the phrase *wed' auwani*, 'he lay down' (Ungarinyin). First he lies down, and another Wandjina paints an outline around him; then he goes down into sacred *Uŋgud* water, and the details that could not be painted while he lay against the rock are added. These paintings are not done nowadays, they belong to the *lalai* times. They are simply touched up periodically with fresh paint … The essential fea-

---

[351] McCarthy 1958: 56.
[352] Layton 2001: 313. Bryant (2008: 263-266 = 2014: 187-190) judged that, of the rock paintings of Wandjinas, "None is older than four centuries", although "Their origin may be much older and traceable to the flood myths in the Dreamtime".
[353] Capell 1939: 388.
[354] Capell 1939: 389-390.

ture of the Wandjina story, then, is the lying down, descent into sacred water, and turning into a painting. ... These things all suggest that the real explanation of the 'lying down' mentioned is dying ..."[355]

The term *lalai* refers to "the old time when the creatures were at once man and bird or man and beast",[356] the 'age of myth', in other words (§34). A contemporary Ngarinyin distinguished between two stages of rock art. The *Birrimitji* or "Before Ice Age mob" – which included the "Lightning Spirits" and had witnessed the presence of the sun, the moon and some stars on Earth (§430) – "turned into rocks", *i. e.* into rock art, on occasion of an event variously called the "Flood" and the "Ice Age", while the subsequent race of Wandjinas was responsible for the younger rock art of that description (§456):

> Those earlier people who lived before the Flood, they got destroyed. The second mob, they were the Wandjina men that manifested, painted themselves, at Wanalirri ... When the Wandjina walked back to their homes, they waded knee-deep through the roots in floodwater. They put the pattern down again after the wipe-out, they started Life all over again. What they manifested then is what we are looking at today. ... That's why we call ourselves Wandjina people. Everything started all over again after the Ice Age. It was Creation again! What happened after the Ice Age is this mob now – Wandjina again. ...

> Those animals and people who turned into rocks, they were the Before Ice Age mob, the *Birrimitji*. They painted the Ngolngol Rain Spirit, the Hopping Djua and the Lightning Spirits. We don't know about these, they were here before the Ice Age. ... Every Aborigine knows that after the Ice Age everything started all over again. As a whole, I have come to understand this myself only not so long ago. The people that painted the Ngolngol, the Lightning Spirits and the Djua, they are the oldest kind, before the Flood, people called *Munggugnangga*, from Ancient Time, when this land was all one big continent: *Bandaiyan*. ... The Ice Age left the old rock art. After that, Wandjina started to put his print again on his chosen caves.[357]

---

[355] Capell 1939: 390-391. 'Ungarinyin' is a different spelling for 'Ngarinyin'. Capell proceeded to give a Euhemerist explanation for the Wandjinas.
[356] Capell 1939: 390.
[357] David Bungal Mowaljarlai (1925-1997), recorded before 1993, in Mowaljarlai & Malnic 2001: 181, 187. See the note in §430 on the confusion introduced by Mowaljarlai's editor and Mowaljarlai's use of the term 'ice age'.

457
inversion of sky and earth

Several cultures related that *the sky and the earth or the worlds above and below once changed places*. For an inversion of the actual physical realms this implies that a 'collapse of the sky', as known from many other traditions (§§300, 300*, 353, 466), formed a part of the process; the sky was widely perceived as a solid expanse (§§276-281). However, partly due to the lexical confusion resulting from the inversion, it is not always straightforward to determine whether it was sky and earth themselves, their respective denizens or all of the above which were believed to have swapped positions. For example, the Efé tribe of the Mbuti (northern Ituri Forest, northeastern Congo) shared the following tale:

> Long ago, at the beginning, the earth was up there where heaven is now, and heaven was down here. The Efé were hungry, and therefore they appealed about their plight to Tore, whereupon the earth with all its food supplies fell down below, to the position it is now, and heaven then went up in its place.[358]

The logic seems to be that the ancestors were already living in the lower realm and were not transported upwards together with what is now the sky. By contrast, the people apparently come down in a fuller version of the tradition, recorded later by another anthropologist, in which lightning plays a key part:

> In the beginning, earth was above and heaven was below. Earth was crowded with people. Their camps covered the land. When the great famines came, God said to the lightning, 'Leap out of the earth!' The lightning split the earth with a deafening boom and sprang up to the sky. God followed, then the moon. That is how the world turned upside down. ... 'Heaven and earth changed places' or 'the world turned upside down', according to many Efé elders.[359]

Told in this form, the story only makes sense if the lightning jumped from the original sky down below to the original earth up above – that is to say, with the introduction of the lightning the narrator switches to

---

[358] Tebi, chief of the Andeporu clan of the Efé, recorded 1929-1930, in Schebesta 1932: 217-218, tr. 1933: 236 (•). The words for "about their plight", "to the position it is now" and "in its place" are not in the German original. 'Tore' is a name for the supreme deity.
[359] recorded 1957-1958 at Ebuya (southeast Ituri Forest) by Jean-Pierre Hallet, in Hallet & Pelle 1973: 309-310.

the terminology appropriate for the current condition. The upshot is that the abodes of sky and earth were not themselves interchanged, but only their inhabitants. This leaves unclear how the famine was resolved; perhaps the lightning killed off many eaters. In other versions of the myth 'which is told in the whole Efe territory from Beni to the Nepoko', the trigger to change is not famine, but contamination of food:

> In the beginning, the earth was above, but the sky, *i. e.* the seat of the deity, below. Together with God was [sic] the moon and the lightning ... Dust and dirt constantly floated down from above and contaminated God's food, until he got fed up with it and looked for another place of residence. He ordered the lightning to locate a place above the earth. With a big crash, the lightning split the earth and moved up. After the sky had been prepared, God and the moon followed. The moon dwelled above, the lightning below God ...[360]

This account corroborates the impression that the sky and earth were primarily defined by their residents, but the dust fluttering down was effectively a descent of parts of the physical earth as well. A variant transmitted in French confirms that 'earth' fell down and sheds additional light on the conundrum by revealing that 'people' were present on both sides:

> Formerly, it was thus: the sky was below and the earth above. Every day as the men went out to collect food, earth fell on them. So one day Alu says:
>
> We need to change that. The earth will be down and the sky up.
>
> So the men planted food which matures very well. ... But before everything changed, there were men above and men below. And the men who were above descended and those who were below went up. But these last ones became bad. Nobody has seen these men, but it is known that they are bad. The moon and the stars are equally inhabited by many men.[361]

---

[360] recorded 1934-1935, in Schebesta 1936: 123 (••). According to Hallet & Pelle (1973: 310), Paul Schebesta (1887-1967) heard this myth from Evadu, an elder of the Efé of the Oruendu region, but Schebesta's text does not bear this out. The indigenous name of 'God' is Arebati in this case. Schebesta (1936: 124) interpreted the moon as the first human being and Arumei, the chamaeleon.

[361] Mbene, of the Andibepe clan, recorded 1932-1948, in Joset 1948: 142 (•).

Foul rain also provides the impetus to an inversion in a story from the Bira (southern Ituri forest), another tribe of Mbuti, comprising the Kango and Sua. In this, "the water" is substituted for the 'sky' and trades places with the earth, making no mention of people:

> Many, many moons ago the water was down below, and the earth was way up in the sky. When it rained it rained dirt, and the dirt ruined all the water vegetables and spoiled all the water food, so that it had to be thrown away. The Water said to the Earth: 'You are spoiling my water gardens by raining dirt. You come down here and I'll go up there.'
>
> The Earth agreed, and so the Water moved up and the Earth came down. When they had changed places, the Water said: 'Now I'm going to rain on *you*, but *I'm* going to rain water.' And the Water rained on the Earth. The earth vegetables flourished and the earth gardens grew. The Water said, 'See, when I rain I don't spoil your food like you spoiled mine. It is good like this.' And from then onwards the Water stayed up in the sky and the Earth stayed down below.[362]

The water's ascent is comparable to the lightning's in the Efé versions and no contradiction exists if a thunderstorm is the underlying image. Thus, the common denominator in all these variants is apparently that the earth went through a stage of dusty air, drought and evaporation of surface waters before lightning ushered in the present habitable condition of an open sky replete with moist air.

Some tied the inversion of sky and earth to the earth's overturning (§372, §372*), presumably on the logic that the earth did not roll over in relation to the sky above it, but together with the sky – as if sky and earth formed a single unit within a larger whole. As noted (§372*), this appears to be what a shaman of the Zulu (southern Africa) envisioned in the following report:

> ... the earth turned upside down and what had become the sky became down, and what was the heavens became up. The whole world was turned upside down. The sun rose in the south and set in the north. Then came drops of burning black stuff, like molten tar, which burned every living thing on earth that could not escape. After that came a terrible deluge of water accompanied by winds so great that they blew whole mountaintops away. And after that came huge

---

[362] recorded 1953-1954 by Anne Eisner Putnam (1911-1967), in Turnbull 1959: 47.

chunks of ice bigger than any mountain and the whole world was covered with ice for many generations.[363]

In the mythology of the Nivaclé (Paraguay and northwest Argentina), the inversion of sky and earth involves the sky's collapse and a decimation of human life:

> Once the earth, which used to be the sky, turned upside down. Our earth used to be the sky, and the sky was the earth. They turned upside down one day. Nearly everyone died when the sky fell. Nine people were saved. When they saw that the sky was going to fall, they fled to the forest. All the rest ran to the forest too, but could not find a safe place. Those nine people, though, took refuge under a very hard tree. They were under the tree which was very strong; the sky could not break it.
>
> ... this earth that was the sky before was very low, very close to the other earth, the one that is the sky now.[364]

It is noteworthy that the storyteller draws attention to the proximity between this former sky and earth, confirming that the inverting sky was also the low sky (§3), at least in this instance. The translation used here suggests that the inversion also involved the sky and the earth each turning upside down (§§372, 372*), but it will be necessary to consult the original Spanish or Nivaclé text to ensure that this is not simply a clumsy rendition of the earth and sky changing places. If sky and earth were treated as two parallel surfaces in a fixed system which was overturned as a whole, it would be seen that each would have its top and bottom reversed, so that the wording quoted above would be accurate. But this is clearly not the intended meaning, as the story goes on to tell how the survivors on the surface of the original earth cut through the collapsed sky (§466) and began to inhabit its surface as a new earth; the old earth crushed beneath the old sky presumably rose up to become the new sky.[365] In a variant, the inversion is – as in Mbuti lore – motivated by deposition of filth and the old earth's ascent is explicitly stated:

---

[363] Vusamazulu Credo Mutwa (b. 1921), a Zulu shaman of the Msimango tribe, on 2 October 1999, in anonymous 2000: 11. See §436 on the disturbance in the sun's course, §458 on the molten tar and §449 on the ice. See also the notes of caution regarding Mutwa's credibility in §§436, 440.
[364] Leguán (b. c1916), a shaman, recorded 1986, translated by Pascual Benítez (b. early 1960s), of Laguna Escalante, in Wilbert & Simoneau 1987: 105.
[365] In the immediate aftermath of the cataclysm, the direction of the sun's appearance had to be rediscovered by the first "father" (§§436, 466).

> In the very beginning, in that remote period of time when the ancient Nivaklé were first put on Kotsxáat, the earth, Earth was touchy. She did not like for those men to urinate and defecate on her, and since she wanted nothing to do with such filth she decided to go up into the sky. Then the sky, Vá·as, who did not mind having any kind of dirty thing being piled on him, came down to the earth. Sky was not as sensitive as Earth. That is why he remained down here and she went up above. What we walk on up to this day (the earth) is what in that time was the sky, while what used to be the earth is what we now see up above and what we call the sky.[366]

A third narration likewise cites pollution from above as the reason for the old earth's displacement, but complicates the matter by its report on the whereabouts of the people throughout the event:

> After the collapse of the sky, the earth came into being immediately below it. Fitsakajich told people that the two levels were going to be reversed: 'I will take what is below up into the sky, and the sky will be placed below. Don't move from where you are while this reversal is taking place.' When the earth on which the Nivaklé were living had begun to tilt, Fitsakajich told the people: 'This tilting is a sign that the sky and the earth will be reversed.'
>
> The earth had begun to rotate before and was just about to take her place above the sky, but she was not yet quite there because she was waiting for Fitsakajich to take her there. When the sky changed its position, the Nivaklé remained stuck to it because Fitsakajich was still with them; otherwise they would have fallen off. Earth was very delicate. She did not want to have all kinds of filth deposited on her. That is why there was a reversal in the position of Earth and Sky, because Earth did not like having urine and excrement thrown on her.[367]

Though the ancestors are stated to have "remained stuck to" the sky, the only consistent interpretation of this cryptic account is that they stayed put in the lower region, while the sky and earth changed places. The old earth's tilting refers to a peculiar type of earthquake. This explanation requires that the dirt spoiling it came from the people directly on its surface, not – as was the case among the Mbuti – from the old sky above it. Perhaps consultation of the original Spanish or even Nivaclé text can

---

[366] Nuxaché *alias* Alejandro Fleitas (b. c1905), recorded 1980, in Wilbert & Simoneau 1987: 103. The word Vá·as used here for the old sky recurs in a variant (§300*) as vôôs, the fallen sky.
[367] As·etí *alias* Comisario (b. c1912), of the Jotoy Ihavós ('grassland people'; around the Santa Teresita mission, near Mariscal Estigarribia), recorded 1980, in Wilbert & Simoneau 1987: 103-104.

clarify whether "remained stuck to" should not be read as something like 'clung to', 'grasped' or 'held on to'. In this case, the event commences with a sort of tectonic unrest and ends with the survivors' attachment to their new territory. According to the remainder of the story, the sky only received its two supports – in the form of trees planted at the ends of a "Rainbow" (§343*) – following the above events.[368]

The Huni Kuin (Acre, northwestern Brazil, and adjacent area in Peru), too, equated a fall of the sky with its changing places with the earth, in a story which again highlights mass deaths and the rôle of lightning and rain:

> The Caxinauás are living, made houses, live in very beautiful villages, lots of vegetables abound.
> The Caxinauás do not think about anything (they fear nothing), they are very happy, they live, far from the mighty river on the border they live.
> All Caxinauás are living.
> It rains a long time, it rains, it rains under the high sun, in the dark it rains, it is raining much for a long time.
> A Caxinauá cannot go far from another, all are lying in their houses.
> The lightning is breaking, (it thunders), they are frightened, all are lying down.
> The sky broke, came, came down, killed all those, killed also the game, killed also the fish, killed all those, it terminated them, not leaving any beings, killed those, terminated them.
> It killed, it terminated, the earth changed sides, high up being sky, the sky turned into earth.
> The earth was being sky, on top of the Caxinauás whom the sky killed. The sky changed sides, those souls took it away, they dwelled inside the sky.
> They live in the sky, healthy and happy they now live in the sky.
> In the sky is a large pond, in the sky flow many rivers.
> On the earth not many things were left (nothing remained alive) ...
>
> The sky broke, came, killed those, terminated them.
> The sky broke, came, killed all those, terminated them, the sky changed sides, it took them away.
> But the Caxinauás were generated again.[369]

---

[368] As·etí, as above, in Wilbert & Simoneau 1987: 104, *cf.* 40-41, 97-98.
[369] Bô-rô *alias* Vicente Penna Sombra, a Huni Kuin, recorded c1908, in Capistrano de Abreu 1914: 481-483 (•), with addition of capital letters.

This tale does not presuppose a migration of living people, but only of their souls, while a new race is subsequently created on Earth, as the story goes on to relate. The intended meaning is assuredly that the fall of water and possibly other materials from above to below amounted to 'the sky becoming earth', while the migration of the living beings from the world below to the world above, as souls, effected 'the earth becoming sky'. As a physical rollover of the sky or the earth – by which top and bottom are reversed – is thus not indicated, it seemed preferable to translate the Portuguese verb in question *revirou-se* (Huni Kuin *karabökökī*) as 'changed sides' or perhaps 'swapped' rather than 'turned over' or 'turned round'.[370] If, then, the souls of the victims rose from the ground into the sky, do the words 'The sky changed sides' refer to the new sky, formed from the old earth, or do they concern a second interchange, by which the effect of the first one was undone? A German translator opted for the latter:

> The earth changed places with the sky. The sky fell on the Kashinaua and killed them. The sky turned itself over again and the souls which lived in the sky took it with them.[371]

Simpler is to assume that the narrator was in this sentence referring to the new sky: 'The (new) sky changed sides, those souls took it away ...' Whereas *levaram* ('took') in 'those souls took it away' appears to describe the souls' ascent, *levou* ('took') in the later phrase 'it took them away' would seem to describe the people's death, without reference to their souls. Perhaps someone capable of reading the Huni Kuin language can settle this matter definitively. Regardless, all this was stated to have transpired when it was always daytime, before darkness and the night had made their appearance (§§435, 440); the mention of 'the dark' in the passage quoted above is probably a minor narrative inconsistency.

Finally, it is instructive to compare these myths to the account given by the Barasana (concentrated in southeastern Colombia) of the sky falling down and becoming either the earth or the underworld (§300*). Because the earth or underworld does not convert into the sky but a new sky is forged, the Barasana tale contains only an approximation of the

---

[370] Aillaud (1813: s. v. 'Revirar-se') defined the Portuguese verb as "to turn, or to change sides again". The Huni Kuin word is presumably related to *bö-kö-i-ba*, 'on the other side, frontier', Capistrano de Abreu 1914: 557 s. v. 'bö-kö-i-ba' (•), cf. 579 s. v. 'ka-ra-bö-kö'.
[371] Koch-Grünberg 1927: 229 (•). Though much more legible, Koch-Grünberg's rendition is closer to a paraphrase than a translation. 'Caxinauá' or 'Kashinaua' is an exonym for the Huni Kuin.

complete inversion of sky and earth. A deeper relationship between the respective stories is nevertheless likely on the ground of other parallels: the implication of ashes precipitating from the griddle which was the old sky compares to the deposition of filth in the myths related above; and the cosmic conflagration which led to the collapse of the old sky may be akin to the lightning in the Huni Kuin and Efé traditions.

458
rain of flammable materials

Some traditions involve a *rain of flammable materials*, typically with catastrophic consequences.[372] Unless the combustibles are of volcanic origin, the incident qualifies as a subtype of cosmic impacts (§455) and possibly a collapse of the sky itself (§§300, 300*, 353, 466), in shattered form. It is closely related to a 'rain' of fire (§451), a conflagration and even a deluge (§§302-305, 308-313, 335-336, 356, 396-397), whether or not visited upon the earth by a comet or other long object (§§453-454) and ending one of the former ages recognised in myth (§§407-413). For example, according to a shaman of the Zulu (southern Africa) the fall of "drops of burning black stuff, like molten tar, which burned every living thing on earth that could not escape" followed a diversion of the sun and an inversion of sky and earth, while preceding a "terrible deluge of water", hurricanes and an ice age (§§372*, 436, 449, 454, 457).[373] The Quiché Maya (Guatemala) described an incendiary component of the flood which, along with a bombardment of objects (§455), wiped out an earlier race of people before the sun had yet risen:

> Again there comes a humiliation, destruction, and demolition. The manikins, woodcarvings were killed when the Heart of Sky devised a flood for them. A great flood was made; it came down on the heads of the manikins, woodcarvings. ... They were not competent, nor did they speak before the builder and sculptor who made them and brought them forth, and so they were killed, done in by a flood:
>
> There came a rain of resin from the sky.
> ...

---

[372] Compare the examples in Allan & Delair 1995: 162-164 Table 3B.
[373] Vusamazulu Credo Mutwa (b. 1921), a Zulu shaman of the Msimango tribe, on 2 October 1999, in anonymous 2000: 11. See the earlier notes of caution (§§436, 440) regarding Mutwa's credibility.

> The earth was blackened because of this; the black rainstorm began, rain all day and rain all night. Into their houses came the animals, small and great. Their faces were crushed by things of wood and stone. ... The people were ground down, overthrown.[374]

Regarding the "rain of resin", a contemporary Quiché authority remarked: "This was turpentine that fell, and it was burning as it fell."[375] Meanwhile, the Barasana (concentrated in southeastern Colombia) remembered the precipitation of a "resin-like substance" causing dermatological problems from a box opened in a primordial time when it was ever daytime (§§435, 440):

> The *Ayawa* ... decided to ask Night Father for night. They said to him, 'Mother's son, give us night.' He gave them a box telling them not to open it without first carrying out the appropriate blowing. They went home and after blowing spells on the box, they opened it. A resin-like substance fell out and covered their bodies with sores. They were angry with Night Father saying that they had asked for night (*nyami*) not sores (*kami*).[376]

When the protagonists obtained a second receptacle and released the true night from it prematurely, catastrophe ensued:

> They went back to Night House and asked once again for night. Night Father gave them a pot ... He also warned them not to open the pot until they got back to their house. They were very suspicious of the pot, thinking that it too would contain sores. When they reached the edge of their manioc garden they decided to open the pot and see what was inside. As they opened it, the lid flew off and covered the eyes of the sun. Everything became pitch black with heavy rain falling and wind whistling through the trees. The rivers rose and flooded the land and the *Ayawa* were very frightened. The night was very long.[377]

---

[374] *Popol Vuh* (*Book of the People*), 1, tr. Tedlock 1996: 71-73.
[375] Andrés Xiloj Peruch (d. before 2005), a 'daykeeper' from Momostenango (Guatemala), recorded 1968-1996, in Tedlock 1996: 235. The Aztecs preserved an equivalent tradition of a 'rain of fire and gravel' concluding the era of the 'third sun', *Annals of Cuauhtitlan* (*Codex Chimalpopoca* [1610-1628 CE]), 2. 34-38, tr. Bierhorst 1992: 26; *Leyenda de los soles* (*Legend of the Suns*; 1558 CE; *Codex Chimalpopoca*), 75. 25-33, tr. 1992: 143; *cf.* van der Sluijs 2011d: 3, 266-267.
[376] Bosco, the brothers Pau and Pasico, and Maximilliano, recorded September 1968 - December 1970 at Caño Colorado (Pirá-paraná region), in Hugh-Jones 1979: 267-268.
[377] Bosco, Pau, Pasico and Maximilliano, as above, in Hugh-Jones 1979: 268. It is not clear whether this flooding was conceived of as a global deluge.

The "pitch black" and "very long" night of "heavy rain" following the earlier dispersion of the "resin-like substance" sounds almost identical to the "black rainstorm" which the Quiché Maya thought succeeded the "rain of resin". The two traditions are probably related.

At least one account incorporates a recognisable reference to an *axis mundi*. The Klamath (southwestern Oregon) told that the creator, K'múkamtch, resorted to several strategies to exterminate his son, Aíshish. An episode involving a fast-rising pine tree, identifiable as an *axis mundi* (§§54-56, 58-60, 63-64, 66, 171, 212, 240, 267, 294, 403), was followed by a "general conflagration by which the earth and its inhabitants were consumed through a rain of burning pitch". In a word-for-word translation:

> Long after again K'múkamtch became alive; he then proceeded against his son. There (he) all over pitch daubed on the sky; then he set on fire the sky so after doing. ... The pitch turned into a lake all over the world, Aíshish's home only remained dry.[378]

Finally, the inflammable matter may take its origin from the sun or a previous sun (§428). For example, in Hindū myth Manu is able to survive by being warned beforehand that the sun is to spew forth burning charcoal (*prataptāṅgāra*), consuming the world together with flames seemingly appearing from below the earth's surface, and the deluge is to follow (compare §429):

> From this day forward a drought shall visit the earth for a hundred years and more, with a tormenting famine. Then the seven harsh rays of the sun, bringing destruction to weaklings, shall be raining burning charcoal. At the close of the yuga the submarine fire shall burst forth, while the poisonous flame issuing from the mouth of Sankarshaṇa (shall blaze) from Pātāla, and the fire from Mahādeva's third eye shall issue from his forehead. Thus kindled the world shall become confounded. When, consumed in this manner, the earth shall become like ashes, the æther too shall be scorched with heat. Then the world, together with the gods and planets, shall be destroyed.[379]

---

[378] Minnie Froben (b. c1860), daughter of a pure-blood Klamath woman and a French settler Froben or Frobine, recorded October 1877 in the Klamath Lake dialect, in Gatschet 1890: lxxxi-lxxxii, 96; *cf.* 1879: 161.

[379] *Matsya Purāṇa* (250-500 CE), 2. 3-8, tr. Muir 1868: 206-207, except the sentence beginning with "Then the seven harsh rays", where the translation by Peter Bisschop (personal communication, 28 April 2015) is followed instead of Muir's "Then the seven direful rays of the son [sic], of little power, destructive, shall rain burning charcoal." *Cf.* Hohenberger 1930: 11: 'Then the seven

Reports of the shooting (§444), downfall (§437) and fragmentation (§447) of one or more suns or moons frequently draw attention to such liquid substances as 'tears' and 'blood' pouring from the wounded object onto the earth. The solar origin of these fluids presupposes an igneous nature. According to the Abkhaz (southwestern Caucasus), Amra "hit the centre of the sun" with an arrow in order to obtain fire (§444), but received more than he bargained for:

> The sun began trembling with the pain, dropping a little tear. Very soon the little tear reached the ground, and a thousand-year-old forest burst into hot flame.[380]

The Blang of Sipsongpanna Dǎi Autonomous Prefecture (southern Yúnnán, China) described what happened when Gumiya, the creator, disposed of eight suns and nine moons (§444):

> One after another, suns and moons were shot dead. A rain of blood poured from the sky, and made the earth much cooler.[381]

The Yuchi (northeastern Oklahoma) provide another example (§444):

> Then the Shawnee shot at the sun, and the earth was covered all over with black blood ...[382]

Such traditions of 'bleeding suns' may also bear a relationship of some sort to the myth bequeathed by the Aztecs in which the sun – and in some versions also the moon – would only move after much bloodshed on Earth (§444).

---

merciless rays of the sun, which cause ruin to the little creatures, will let it rain burning coals.' (•) Other translators omit the reference to charcoal. Thus anonymous 1916: 6: "After that, all the inferior beings of the universe would be scorched to death by the seven ordinary rays of the sun which shall become seven times more powerful." And Joshi 2007: 4: "Thereafter at the time of the delusion [sic] at the end of the yuga, the seven scorching rays of the sun shall start destruction of the petty creatures." These translations are not reliable (Peter Bisschop, personal communication, 28 April 2015). A *yuga* is a cosmic period. 'Saṅkarṣaṇa', here spelled 'Sankarshaṇa', is an epithet of Śeṣa, the world-supporting serpent, *cf.* van der Sluijs 2011a: 160 note 506; 2011b: 74-75; 2011c: 239; 2011d: 286. 'Pātāla' refers to the seven underworlds or only the lowest of these, *cf.* 2011c: 61, 87; 2011d: 286. 'Mahādeva' is a title of Śiva.

[380] recorded before 1986 in Pachulia (in Russian), tr. Hunt 2012: 338.
[381] recorded before 1979 by Zhu Jialu, tr. Miller 1994: 90.
[382] Maxey Simms (b. c1876) of Sapulpa (Oklahoma), Andy Johnson of Sapulpa, or George, Sally or Ida Clinton of Bristow (Oklahoma), recorded summer 1928 or winter 1929, in Wagner 1931: 166.

459
fossils as mythical beings

Around the world, indigenous cultures tended to view *local fossils - often in deposits which can be identified today - as the remains of mythical beings*. Frequently, these 'ancestors' were conceived of as giant humans, other animals or a curious mixture of these, with evil inclinations (§§33-35, 33*, 38, 38*), wiped out by natural disasters such as floods and fires or in mighty combat (§§302-305, 308-313, 335-336, 356, 396-397) and in many cases 'converted to rocks' – a possible reference to fossilisation (§§362-363). Fossils of smaller species, such as belemnites and echinoderms, are more commonly mythologised as 'thunderstones',[383] although examples of their traditional interpretation as the remains of small and perhaps innocuous species do occur.[384]

Europe

Pleistocene species, extinct during the Holocene, were common in the Mediterranean Basin, along with much older creatures.[385] In some places, the bones are embedded in lignite soil, which is highly combustible. Classical writers identified various rich fossiliferous locales as the stage for the Gigantomachy, the epic clash between Giants and Olympian gods following Kronos' 'golden age' and the Titanomachy, in which Herakles played no minor part and Zeus wielded his thunderbolts to great advantage, ushering in the present era under his dominion. The main contenders were Pallene *alias* Phlegra or Phlegrae (Chalcidice, northeast Greece),[386] Trapezus (Peloponnesus, Greece)[387] and the Phlegrean Fields around Mount Vesuvius (southern Italy).[388] Woolly rhinoceroses and

---

[383] On thunderstones, see van der Sluijs 2011b: 193-194, 233 note 1089.
[384] Perhaps the petrified 'frogs' in a Tsimshian myth (§440) belong in this category.
[385] Mayor 2000: 64, 70-71, 99; 2007: 245.
[386] pseudo-Apollodorus, *Bibliotheca* (*Library*), 1. 6. 1; Diodorus of Sicily, *Bibliotheca Historica* (*Historical Library*), 5. 71. 4; Pausanias, *Graecae Descriptio* (*Description of Greece*), 1. 25. 2; 8. 29. 1; Strabo, *Geography*, 7. 25, 27; Solinus (3rd century CE), *Collectanea Rerum Memorabilium* (*Collection of Curiosities*) = *De Mirabilibus Mundi* (*On the Wonders of the World*), 9. 6-7, tr. Brodersen 2014: 108-111; an unidentified writer and Theagenes, *Macedonica*, both in Stephen of Byzantium, *Ethnica*, s. v. 'Pallḗnē', trs. Billerbeck & Neumann-Hartmann 2016: 10-11 s. v. 'Παλλήνη'; Philostratus, *Heroicus* (*On Heroes*; 213-214 CE), 8. 16.
[387] Pausanias, *Graecae Descriptio*, 8. 29. 1.
[388] Philostratus, *Heroicus*, 8. 15; Strabo, *Geography*, 5. 4. 4. Diodorus of Sicily, *Bibliotheca Historica*, 4. 15. 1; 4. 21. 5-7; 5. 71. 4, apparently relying on Timaeus of Tauromenium (*c*345-*c*250 BCE).

mastodons were found at Pallene.[389] Remains of "ancestral mammoths and other Ice Age mammals" at Phanagoria (near Sennoi on the Taman Peninsula, Black Sea coast) may have been the subject of a legend that Aphrodite and Herakles slaughtered giants there in a cave, presumably as a part of the Gigantomachy:[390] "... the peninsula's high cliffs and sand-clay pits bear incredibly rich Neogene remains continually exposed by the sea."[391]

Similarly, it is possible that the legends of the strongman clearing Crete and Libya of wild animals, including reptilians,[392] drew on discoveries of fossils in these regions, which were identified as the remains of the victims; the same might apply to the various other monsters he disposed of, such as the Nemean Lion, the Lernean Hydra and the Erymanthian Boar. In these cases, however, the fossil deposits remain yet to be identified.

Adapting the mindset of fossils as legendary giants to a Christian outlook, the African theologian Augustine of Hippo (354-430 CE) cited a giant tooth he had seen in Utica (Tunisia) as evidence of the antediluvian giants known from Hebrew tradition:

> ... some people refuse to believe that men's bodies were of much larger size then than they are now. ... in those days the earth used to produce larger bodies. How much more so then was that true before that celebrated and far-famed flood when the world was younger! As far as the size of bodies is concerned, however, sceptics are generally persuaded by the evidence in tombs uncovered through the ravages of time, the violence of streams or various other occurrences. For incredibly large bones of the dead have been found in them or dislodged from them.
>
> On the shore of Utica I myself, not alone but with several others, saw a human molar so enormous that, if it were divided up into pieces to the dimensions of our teeth, it would, so it seemed to us, have made a hundred of them. But that molar, I should suppose, belonged to some giant.

Claudian (*Gigantomachy*, 4, tr. Platnauer 1922: 280-281), Ovid (*Metamorphoses*, 10. 150-151) and Statius (*Thebaid*, 6. 358) offered no further clues as to which Phlegra they meant.

[389] Sources are given in Mayor 2000: 317 note 10.

[390] "... the Giants attacked the goddess there; but she called upon Heracles for help and hid him in a cave, and then, admitting the Giants one by one, gave them over to Heracles to be murdered through 'treachery'." Strabo, *Geography*, 11. 2. 10, tr. Jones 1928: 200-201.

[391] Mayor 2000: 196, citing palaeontologist Alexey Tesakov.

[392] Diodorus of Sicily, *Bibliotheca Historica*, 4. 17. 3-5.

> For not only were bodies in general much larger then than our own, but the giants towered far above the rest, even as in subsequent times, including our own, there have almost always been bodies which, though few in number, far surpassed the size of the others. ... the size of ancient bodies is disclosed even to much later ages by the frequent discovery of bones, for bones are long-lasting.[393]

Pre-Christian Latvians had the concept of 'giant's bones' (*milsenu kauli*).[394] Presumably, these were fossils of large prehistoric animals.

Asia

The Śiwalīk Hills (northern India) are awash with fossils. Although fossil remains of much older life forms, such as dinosaurs, are common in other parts of India, those in the Śiwalīk Hills represent much more recent groups, including many species of mammal and other vertebrate animals, from the middle of the Miocene to the end of the Pleistocene epoch:

> ... in Upper Siwaliks, wet condition might have returned, in which more modern proboscideans, artiodactyls, carnivores and others thrived. Towards the end, climate went cold ultimately coinciding with cooling effects of late Pleistocene glaciation.[395] [*sic* throughout]

Locals interpreted some of the bones in the Śiwalīk Hills as the remains of *Rákṣasa*'s,[396] primordial monstrous giants, many of whom were slain by mythical heroes as told in the epics *Mahābhārata* (4th century BCE to 4th century CE) and *Rāmāyaṇa* (5th or 4th century BCE).[397, 398]

---

[393] Augustine, *De Civitate Dei* (*On the City of God*), 15. 9, tr. Levine 1966: 456-459.
[394] Stender 1783: 266 s. v. 'Milsenu kauli'; 1789: 482 s. v. 'Riese' (•).
[395] Ray 2008: 316, *cf.* 314; Gupta 2011: 256.
[396] Falconer & Cautley 1846: 2; *cf.* van der Geer *et al.* 2008: 83; Mayor 2000: 133, 135.
[397] *e. g.*, *Mahābhārata*, 1 (*Ādi Parva* [*Book of the Beginning*]): 9 (*Hidimva-Vadha Parva*): 154-156; 3 (*Vana Parva* [*Book of the Forest*]): 11, 157, 285, 288; 7 (*Droṇa Parva* [*Book of Droṇa*]): 109, 180, 183.
[398] Mayor (2000: 133) conflated these fossils with the "lightning bones" (*Bijli ca har*) which natives of the Kumaon region (Uttarakhand, northern India) obtained from further north, according to Herbert 1831: 269. A reviewer of the latter study (anonymous 1832: 148) spelled "*bijlì ka har*". Falconer, in a lecture delivered to the Royal Asiatic Society of Great Britain on 1 or 8 June 1844 (ed. Murchison 1868: 4), offered the false spelling "Bijli ki har", which was adopted in van der Geer *et al.* 2008: 83, but further corrupted to "*Bijli ki bar*" by Mayor. These bones hailed from north of Mount Kailāśa and were said by the 'Tatars of Daba' (western Tibet), presumably Tibetans, "to have fallen from the clouds, and to be the bones of genii." (Buckland 1823: 223) Examples collected by Captain William Spencer Webb (1784-1865) prior to March 1819 (*cf.* Colebrooke

Both Pliocene and Pleistocene fossils from China – especially from the red Lower Pliocene clay of Bǎodéxiàn (northwest Shānxī) and often retrieved from limestone caves – used to be sold as dragon bones (*lóng gǔ*) and dragon teeth (*lóng chǐ*).[399]

Australia

The Arabana, Dieri and Dhirari nations (west and east of Lake Eyre, northern South Australia) shared a legend concerning the Kadimarkara, Kadimakara or Woma, "creatures which in the Mura-mura times descended from the sky-country to the earth, by means of great trees which grew on the eastern shores of Lake Eyre, and supported the sky."[400] On one hand, the myth is a transparent variation on the global theme of giant primordial beings travelling between the sky and the earth along sky-supporting *axes mundi*, until sudden disruption of the columns forces them to remain either on the earth or in the sky.[401] On the other, it appears to commemorate biological species that used to roam the region long ago and left fossil traces:

> This legend professes to account for the origin of the fossilised marsupials and other creatures which are found in several places in the Lake Eyre district ...[402]

And:

> At times when the country is wasted by prolonged drought, or the floods from the Queensland hills lie too long upon the hunting-grounds, the aborigines make pilgrimage to the bones of the Kadimakara. There corroborees are held, at which blood sacrifices are offered and dances performed to appease the spirits of the dead Kadi-

---

1820: 68) proved to be remains of horse, deer and bear species. The notion of their fall from the sky is akin to that of 'thunderstones'.

[399] "The workmen in the mine know well enough the real nature of the skulls. They recognize that *Hipparion* skulls, for instance, are those of a kind of horse." Oakley 1965: 123. *Cf.* van der Geer *et al.* 2008: 71-72; Prothero & Schoch 2002: 108, 241, 247, 253, 271; Kahlke 1961: 104-105; Owen 1870: 433 note *, 434.

[400] recorded 1894-1902 by Otto Siebert (1871-1957), in Howitt 1904: 800-801. In 1904: 433, Howitt locates the trees "on the western side of Lake Eyre", but the reading "eastern" appears in the text of which this was a paraphrase. The term 'Mura-mura' connotes a legendary race that preceded the current one.

[401] Compare van der Sluijs 2011a: 142; 2011c: 147-148; 2011d: 78, 144-145.

[402] recorded 1894-1902 by Siebert, in Howitt 1904: 800. See also the comment in McCarthy 1958: 29.

makara, and persuade them to intercede with those who still dwell in the sky, and control the clouds and rain.[403]

According to the myth cited elsewhere concerning the Nullarbor Plain (§407*), a catastrophic rising of the ocean obliterated the strange animals associated with the original luxuriant phase: "The only evidence we have of their existence is found in bones or casts or impressions on stone."[404]

In the region of Gowrie (west of Brisbane, Queensland), an indigenous man told naturalist and physician George Bennett (1804-1893) that the fossil *Diprotodon* specimens they had collected were "those of an animal long since extinct, known to the natives by the name of 'Gyedarra'":

> Tradition among them has handed down the appearance and habits of this animal for generations ... he spoke most positively, and asserted that the bones we have been finding are those of the animal of which he was speaking, and that at one time the bones were very numerous about the Gowrie water-holes, where his forefathers had seen the animals themselves sporting about.[405]

'Gyedarra' may have been a local designation for the beast known in other parts of eastern Australia as the Bunyip. Though the latter is often thought to still exist, natives would identify it with fossils, too: "Big fossil bones that were found, the blacks declared, were those of the Bunyip, and many settlers accepted them as proof of its existence: they were fossil remains of Diprotodon, and of giant kangaroos which became extinct thousands of years before the coming of the white man to Australia."[406] One colonist observed in 1845:

---

[403] Gregory 1906: 4.
[404] Smith 1930: 181. In this account, a "Reptile Age" followed by a "Bird Age" precedes the present era. As noted, influence from the evolutionary theories developed in the European culture of colonists seems likely.
[405] Charlie Pierce, possibly a Barunggam, cited in a letter of unknown authorship to George Bennett (1 December 1871), in Bennett 1872: 315. *Cf.* 321: "The 'old bones' ... they never imagined could be so treated by palæontologists, who they were not aware possessed the power, until they saw these works, of depicting the ancient race of Australian animals, re-forming them into living structures, imparting to these long extinct animals the motion of animated life ..."
[406] Barrett 1946: 9, *cf.* 31; Dugan 1980: 266; Vickers-Rich & Archbold 1991: 2. Barrett allowed that the Bunyip, if extant, "might be a 'living fossil' – a survivor from the Age of giant reptiles, or at least, the era of Diprotodon, that huge wombat-like marsupial whose fossil remains have been found in abundance nearly all over our island-continent."

> It may not be amiss to state that all the Natives throughout these Northern Districts have a tradition relative to a very large animal having at one time existed in the large Creeks & Rivers & by many it is said that such animals now exist & several of the Fossil bones which I have at various times shown to them they have ascribed to them.[407]

In January 1846, an Athol(l) T. Fletcher found a skull of recent date on the banks of the Lower Murrumbidgee River, near the junction with the Lachlan River (New South Wales). While "Every black to whom the skull was afterwards shown agreed that it belonged to the dreaded monster of the lakes", known by various names including 'Bunyip' among the Gunditjmara people,[408] naturalists variously judged it to be that of a juvenile "large herbivorous animal",[409] "a mishapen [sic] foal or foetus of a mare" incompatible with the Bunyip identification,[410] "a calf"[411] and – a surprisingly attractive candidate – a stray specimen of the Malay tapir (*Tapirus indicus*).[412]

Another example of fossil lore concerns the study of the Adnyamathanha culture (Flinders Ranges, South Australia) conducted by the Australian linguist Dorothy Tunbridge:

> During her work on the language she collected about a dozen language terms for mammal species which were no longer in existence.[413]

When palaeontologists unearthed bones of *Diprotodon* in the area, "the Adnyamathanha 'recognized' these bones as those of the *yamuti*. ... stories of the giant *yamuti* were the subject of Adnyamathanha myth, and associated sites were within 160 km of the bone sites."[414]

Even if entities such as the Bunyip and the Yamuti were not explicitly incorporated by the land's first nations in the framework of creation mythology, their general association with the 'dream time' does suggest this relationship.

---

[407] Frederick Neville Isaac (1845), in Dugan 1980: 266.
[408] Hovell 1847.
[409] James Grant (19 February 1846), in Gunn 1847: 148.
[410] Macleay 1847.
[411] Richard Owen (1804-1892) and William John Broderip (1789-1859), in Buckland 1867: 304-305.
[412] Tompson 1847.
[413] Sharpe & Tunbridge 1997: 351-356.
[414] Sharpe & Tunbridge 1997: 357.

America

The American continent has yielded a plethora of traditions concerning the – often collective and violent – demise and fossil preservation of past giants or monsters. People in the Willamette Valley (western Oregon), probably of Kalapuya descent, linked local fossils with a dragon which Coyote had once slain: "Not far from Bethel, Polk county, a large number of fossil remains were found some years ago, which the Indians stated were the bones of a monster dragon inhabiting the Willamette valley in the ages past."[415] Because the feat involved a chain of arrows (§§192-193) and 'sun shooting' (§444), it likely belongs to the cycle of creation myths.

The deluge is sometimes fingered as the cause of the disappearance of these beings. For example, the Pawnee recognised a former race of giant humans, destroyed by flood, in the fossils deposited at Swimming Mound (Kansas):

> ... many years ago, before we lived upon this earth, Tirawa placed wonderful human beings upon the earth. We knew of them as the wonderful beings or the large people. These people lived where the Swimming Mound is in Kansas. The bones of these large people were found upon the sides of the hill of the Swimming Mound. The old people told us that at this place the rain poured down from the heavens, and the water came from the northwest upon the earth so that it became deep and killed these wonderful beings.[416]

Lightning, too, is frequently cited as the primary instrument of the animals' destruction.[417] As recorded by former American president Thomas Jefferson, the Lenape (originally of the Delaware River region; §452) related that the giant animals "whose bones were found at the Saltlicks, on the Ohio", including allegedly carnivorous mammoths, were wiped out with lightning by the supreme deity when they incited his anger:

---

[415] Saylor 1900: 317. See the note in §444 on the myth's provenance.
[416] a woman to her grandson Ari-Wa-Kis *alias* Young Bull *alias* Captain Jim (c1835-1916), shaman of the Pitahawirata band of the Pawnee (Nebraska), recorded 1896-1906, in Dorsey 1906: 134, *cf.* 490; van der Sluijs 2011d: 134. The location of Swimming Mound is no longer known, but might have been in Hitchcock County (Nebraska), Mayor 2005: 177-180.
[417] Compare van der Sluijs 2011d: 143 (Zuñi) and the Diné account in §§33*, 38*, in which a belief that the slain "enemies", including "great giants", left fossil remains is not stated, but probably existed. In the Tsimshian story of "the Frogs" turning into "stone" as "the daylight" is released from a box (§440), one wonders if the "rock" was fossiliferous.

> That in antient times a herd of these tremendous animals came to the Big-bone licks, and began an universal destruction of the bear, deer, elks, buffaloes, and other animals, which had been created for the use of the Indians: that the Great Man above, looking down and seeing this, was so enraged that he seized his lightning, descended on the earth, seated himself on a neighbouring mountain, on a rock, of which his seat and the print of his feet are still to be seen, and hurled his bolts among them till the whole were slaughtered, except the big bull …[418]

Among the Sioux, it was held that the 'water monsters' (*Unktehi*) caused a flood "killing most of the people" and were subsequently defeated in combat by the 'Thunderbirds' (*Wakinyan*), friends of men, whose lightning engulfed the earth in flames which reduced them to bones (compare §451):

> Then began the great battle between the thunderbirds and the evil water monsters. It lasted many years, during which the earth trembled and the waters burst forth in mighty torrents, while the night was like day because of the flashes of lightning. … The Wakinyan used their claws, their teeth, their lightning to fight the water monsters. …
>
> Then all the thunderbirds flew up into the sky. 'When I give the signal', said the Wakinyan Tanka, 'let's use our lightning and thunderbolts together!' So the thunder beings shot off all their bolts at the same instant. The forests were set on fire, and flames consumed everything except the top of the rock on which the humans had taken refuge. The waters boiled and then dried up. The earth glowed red-hot, and the Unktehi, big and small, burned up and died, leaving only their dried bones in the Mako Sicha, the Badlands, where their bones turned to rock.[419]

The natives confidently identified remains of mammoths or mastodons as the "bones of the Onkteri", holding them in high esteem at least in

---

[418] a chief of the Lenape, probably Koquethagechton *alias* 'White Eyes' (c1730-1778), in Jefferson 1787: 64-65. The 'fable' given by David Thompson (written c1840, ed. Tyrrell 1916: 191) and apparently attributed to the Osage appears to be a paraphrase of this passage. The site is now Big Bone Lick State Park in northern Kentucky. It would be interesting to establish whether the imprints on the rock are petroglyphs (§456).

[419] Tȟáȟča Hušté *alias* John (Fire) Lame Deer (1900/1903-1976), a Miniconjou Lakȟóta medicine man, recorded 1969 in Winner (Rosebud Indian Reservation, South Dakota), in Erdoes & Ortiz 1984: 220-221. Badlands National Park is in southwestern South Dakota. For the Wakinyan, compare Pond 1867: 228-229; Lynd 1865: 66, 79; Pond 1908: 403. See also van der Sluijs 2011d: 34, 142-143.

Minnesota.⁴²⁰ The Lakȟóta supposed that these Proboscideans were "still in existence, and, as they were not seen on land and their bones were found in low and wet places, they concluded that their dwelling was in the water."⁴²¹ Ossified corpses of the thunderbirds were also recognised in fossils:

> Dreamers have told us of these great birds in the sky, enwrapped in the clouds. If the bear and other vicious beasts are regarded as dangerous, how much more should we fear the thunderbirds that cause destruction on the face of the earth. It is said that the thunderbirds once came to the earth in the form of giants. These giants did wonderful things, such as digging the ditches where the rivers run. At last they died of old age, and their spirits went again to the clouds and resumed their form as thunderbirds. ... The bodies of these giants became stone, and parts of them are found in many places, indeed the whole body of more than one of these giants has been found in the land of the Dakotas.⁴²²

Again, at least one group pinpointed close contact with a comet as the reason why the former giants whose bones we see have vanished. A shaman from an Ojibwe band in Ontario taught that the conflagration

---

⁴²⁰ recorded 1834-1860, in Pond 1860: 643, 645; cf. 1867: 230; Riggs 1852: 205 s. v. 'Uŋ-kte'-ȟi'. 'Onkteri' – like 'Onktehi' – is an alternative spelling used for 'Unktehi'.

⁴²¹ recorded as above, in Pond 1908: 403, cf. 414; Riggs 1852: 205 s. v. 'Uŋ-kte'-ȟi'; Pond 1860: 643; 1867: 219; Lynd 1865: 68. According to Pond (1867: 230), the conflict between the two parties is ongoing, in which case one is entitled to speak of a 'parontomyth', but the connection with fossil bones is less obvious. The belief that mammoths are subterranean creatures was also sustained by the Central Alaskan Yup'ik at the lower Yukon River (recorded 1877-1881, in Nelson 1899: 443) and by the Sakha, Tungus and Ket or Khanty (Siberia); for the latter groups, this was documented in October 1692 by the Danish traveller and diplomat Eberhard Isbrand Ides (1657-1708; 1704: 31), as he travelled on the Ket River near Makovskoye (Krasnoyarsk Krai): 'Not far from here in the mountains to the northeast one finds the mammoth's teeth and bones; they are also found particularly at the rivers Jenize, Trugan, Mongamsea, on the river Lena, and at Yakutskoi, as far as the Ice sea; ...The pagans, like the Yakuti, Tungusi and Ostiakky, say that these animals continuously dwell and move about in the earth, no matter how hard it freezes because of the severe winter; also relate that they often witnessed that, when such an animal had moved, the earth welled up above it and then collapsed again and made a deep hole. They further suppose that when this animal comes high enough to smell or see the air, it dies at once and that consequently many were found dead at the high banks of the river, where they inadvertently emerge.' (•) Doubtless, the depressions here blamed on mammoths are methane bubbles, vents or blow-holes. The 'Jenize' is the Yenisei; the 'Trugan' the Turukhan; 'Mongamsea' is bound to refer to Mangazeya on the Taz River; and 'Yakutskoi' must be Yakutsk, on the Lena.

⁴²² Oku'te alias Shooter, a Lakȟóta of the Húŋkpapȟa band, recorded 1911-1914 at Standing Rock Reservation (North and South Dakota), in Densmore 1918: 157-158. The excavation of riverbeds is elsewhere ascribed to dragons or serpents (§317).

brought on by a low-flying comet spelled the end of the hegemony of large animals and, paradoxically, a golden age (§§407*, 448-449, 454):

> Things were wrong with nature on the earth. All of these big animals were tearing up the trees, fighting one another. These creatures were even eating one another. They would have destroyed the forests; then nobody would survive. ... What happened with the comet was a long time ago. I'm talking about way beyond two thousand years ago.[423]

> The giant animals were killed off. You can find their bones today in the earth. ... After that comet, new animals were put on the earth. Where they came from, I don't know.[424]

In Mesoamerica, the Aztecs similarly considered that, during the second one of four past epochs (compare §§410-413), which was called *nahin ocelutl*, 'there were the giants, and that theirs are the big bones which I said are now found in the mines and elsewhere below the ground: those who are now asked tell us according to what their ancestral fathers and grandfathers told them. These bones are of some very big and very tall men who supposedly came from elsewhere, where before them there were people in this second era.'[425] It was with respect to 'the innumerable fossil deposits of elephants which have been discovered in different directions, and which correspond to such a remote epoch', that 'the Spanish chroniclers held those fossils for giants' bones.'[426] And the notion of the Quiché Maya (Guatemala) that mythical beings and fearful animals alike were petrified on the occasion of the sun's first rising (§429) may reflect a belief that fossils represented creatures exterminated towards the end of the 'age of myth' in a flash of light.

---

[423] Wabmaymay ('Dawn Pileated Woodpecker'), a storyteller of the Ketegaunseebee (Garden River) band, prior to 1910, to Sah-kah-odjew-wahg-sahor ('Sun Rising over the Mountain') *alias* Fred Pine (b. 1897), of the same band, recorded 1980-1985 at the Garden River reservation (near Sault Ste. Marie, Ontario), in Conway 1985: 99-100.
[424] Wabmaymay to Sah-kah-odjew-wahg-sahor, as above, in Conway 1992: 243-244.
[425] Toribio de Benavente *alias* Motolinía, *Memoriales* (*Memorials*; 1536-1541 CE), 2. 28, ed. Pimentel 1903: 346-347 (•). This passage was paraphrased and expanded by de Gomara (1553: fol. 118 verso): 'There were giants then, and it was their bones which our Spaniards have found while digging mines, and graves. From the measure and proportion of which it appears that they were men twenty spans high. The stature is very great, but very certain.' (•).
[426] Chavero 1880: 29-30 (••).

460
volcanic eruption

Some societies recalled a natural disaster identifiable as a *volcanic eruption*, occasionally in association with an 'age of myth' or its termination. Accounts devoid of mythical acts or actors read more like sober eye-witness reports than myths. For example, an indigenous group in western Victoria (Australia), quite likely the Djabwurung, reminisced on a time "long ago, when the volcanic hills were in a state of eruption" and "some very large birds, which were incapable of flight, and resembled emus", still roamed the land.[427] And the Spokane (northeastern Washington State) remembered the disappearance of a former lake accompanied by volcanism and earthquakes:

> Centuries ago, long before the paleface was known on this continent, where Spokane is now situated and for many days' travel east of it, was an immense and beautiful lake, with many islands resting on its surface. The country swarmed with game and the lake abounded with fish – veritably a hunter's paradise. Many well-populated villages lay along the shores of the lake.
>
> One summer morning the entire population were startled by the rumbling and shaking of the earth. The waters of the lake began raising [sic], and pitching, and tossed into mountainous waves, which threatened to engulf the entire country. To add to the horrors of the situation, the sun became obscured by an eclipse, and darkness added its horrors to the scene. The terror-stricken inhabitants fled to the hills for safety. The shaking of the earth continued for two days, when a rain of ashes began to fall, and so heavy was the fall of them that there was little difference between day and night. The fall of ashes continued for several weeks.
>
> The game abandoned the country, the waters of the lake receded and dry land filled its place, and desolation spread over the entire country. The Indians died by thousands from starvation. The remnant who escaped starvation followed the course of the receding waters until they arrived at the Falls (now Spokane). Their first village was located in the neighborhood of where the Galland-Burke brewery now stands.[428]

---

[427] recorded 1840-1900, in Dawson 1881: 92. On the birds, see §§33*, 38*.

[428] Whis-tel-po-sum *alias* Lot (c1842-1902), chief of the Lower Spokane, recorded 1886-1893 by Rickard Daniel Gwydir (1844-1925), in Gwydir 1907. See the comments in §439.

The volcanoes may be named and even geographically identified. According to the Quiché Maya (Guatemala), the monster Zipacna raised a number of volcanic mountains in the wake of the deluge and before the sun had risen for the first time:

> And this is Zipacna, this is the one to build up the great mountains: Fireplace, Hunahpu, Cave by the Water, Xcanul, Macamob, Huliznab, as the names of the mountains that were there at the dawn are spoken. They were brought forth by Zipacna in a single night. ... 'Here am I: I am the maker of the earth', said Zipacna.[429]

The mountains listed in this passage correspond to known volcanoes.[430] A native Australian nation in the Blue Mountains (New South Wales), presumably the Dharug, reported a combined earthquake and volcanic eruption occurring in the remote past:

> There was a camp one time on a volcanic field (presumably that of which Mount Wilson is the highest point) that was a scene of a weird and awesome happening. ... Then the world shook. The rumbling of an earthquake sped upon them and rolled beneath them and the hillside tumbled. The country rolled first one way and then another. The trees leaned with the rolling and righted when the earth righted.
>
> ... between them and the top of the hill an opening came and tongues of flame shot out. A few hot stones rolled down into the clearing, though no one was hurt. Then smoke arose and fire flared and the camp was seen to be ablaze. Cries and lamentations filled the air. ... the rocking of the earth had ceased, but the fire burned on and the tongues of flame still leapt along the whole length of the great crack that came in the mountain-side.
>
> ... both Camoola and Wombat-skin dropped down into the cave. ... They came to a bend, and rounding this they came in sight of the fire. It seemed to be coming up from a depth below, and it swept along the crack that passed here through the cave. ... Camoola was left in the cave, and many years afterwards – many centuries – his bones were found by the botanist Cayley. Cayley penetrated the Blue Mountains to a spot where a great rock wall prevented his further exploration.

---

[429] *Popol Vuh (Book of the People)*, 2, tr. Tedlock 1996: 77. Zipacna met his demise at the hands of the brothers Xbalanque and Hunahpu (2, tr. 1996: 85), who had also eliminated the despotic bird Vuqub-Kaqix (§444); on the theme of twin heroes cleansing the world of monsters, compare §§33*, 38*.
[430] Tedlock 1996: 241 *ad* 77; Christenson 2003: 96 notes 171-176.

> Here he erected a cairn of stones, and the place is called now Cayley's Repulse.[431]

The Gungganyji (Cape Grafton, northern Queensland) related that what appears to be a volcanic eruption halted a flood: "The waters rose rapidly as the fugitives climbed to the heights of the Murray Prior Range. This range is called by the aborigines 'Wambilari' … They succeeded in reaching the top of the highest peak in the range, and there they made a fire, and heating large stones rolled them down the mountain side, and succeeded in checking the flood. The sea, however, never returned to its original limits."[432] A member of the Yidindji (south and east of Cairns) told a variant of the same event in which the water does recede somewhat:

> Soon they bombarded the [rising sea] water [with hot stones], bombarded [it] all the time. The water moved away; [it] was bombarded with hot [stones]. Kapamari stones were heated up. [They they [sic]] hit the ground, and cut it. The water started to subside, and now lay [there] peacefully.[433]

In two other tales of what seems to be the same flood, the same narrator presents volcanic activity as a precursor of the flood rather than a way to check it and traces the origin of Lake Eacham, a crater lake on the Atherton Tableland (northern Queensland), to the incident:

> [And I saw] a cloud high up [in the sky] getting yellower. (This indicated that there was trouble brewing.) … I went and saw the wind blowing strongly (like a whirlwind). A cold wind was rising up. … By-and-by I saw the water (rushing up and engulfing everything). The cassowary came running. The grey wallaby came running. The scrub-turkey, the pademelon, the dilly-bag and all the animals came running. The short-nose bandicoot and the black-nose wallaby came running. (All were running to escape the rushing waters; they were in fact partly blown by the wind.) …
>
> Lots of people were drowned in the water; we were covered by the water. Our people had done wrong. Then [a body] of water stood

---

[431] Peck 1933: 170-176. Despite the difference in spelling, the botanist was indubitably the English George Caley (1770-1829). Were the bones fossils (§459)?
[432] recorded 1892-1909 at Yarrabah by Ernest Richard Bulmer Gribble (1869-1957), in Gribble 1932: 56-57.
[433] Jarriyi *alias* Dick Moses (b. c1898), a Yidindji, recorded 22 August 1973 at Yarrabah, in Dixon 1991: 94. A *kapamari* is an earth oven.

> [there] up [in the tableland] – Lake Eacham. The people had drowned there. [It came about] from the initiated men not having paid attention, none of them listened [to the old men, who told them, as initiands not to touch certain sacred things]. ... The newly initiated men were all covered by water; [they] sank down (and were drowned).[434]

And:

> [He] saw the ground burning a yellow colour (that is, it was a yellow colour, as if something were burning). ... [He looked up and saw] yellow clouds lying [in the sky], red and yellow [clouds] lying [there]. 'Hey! the sky at this place is a burning yellow colour.' ... [So, the old man] beat the ground with bushes, because of the yellow colour burning all around now, the sky burning up now. ...
>
> He came and saw water [there]. 'Hey! this camp has water. What have those people [newly-initiated men] been doing? ...' [The old man] cut the ground, cut the ground, kept on cutting to stop [the flood]. [He] called out [to the rainbow-serpent] in the camp, for the water to recede. A big flood went pouring [into the camp], and the dilly-bag came running away. The grey wallaby, and the cassowary, and the pademelon, and a half-sewn dilly-bag, together with the people, all ran away, frightened of the water. [All these animals, and the dilly-bag] came and disappeared [swallowed up by the water] there [just in front of] all the initiated men. Where did [the water] stop? [All the animals] came and disappeared [in the water] there. ... There were too many people of another sort, and they were now floating in the water, drowned – drowned in the water. ... Then water burst out, against the people. They were all drowned, at [that] place, in [that] water. (And the water formed Lake Eacham.)[435]

A related story from the Ngadyan, a subgroup of the Dyirbal (northeast Queensland), also suggests seismic activity: at a time when "the country round the lakes was 'not jungle – just open scrub'", "two newly initiated men broke a taboo and so angered the rainbow serpent, major spirit of the area ... As a result 'the camping-place began to change, the earth under the camp roaring like thunder. The wind started to blow down, as if a cyclone were coming. The camping-place began to twist and crack. While this was happening there was in the sky a red cloud, of a hue never

---

[434] Jarriyi, recorded 17 December 1971 at Yarrabah, in Dixon 1991: 42-44. The 'I' is the narrator, who "has here taken over the identity of the old man" figuring in the story, 1991: 42. The pademelon is a small marsupial of the genus *Thylogale*.
[435] Jarriyi, recorded late May 1974 at Yarrabah by Carolyn Strachan and Alessandro Cavadini, in Dixon 1991: 106-108.

seen before. The people tried to run from side to side but were swallowed by a crack which opened in the ground ...'"[436] The eruption resulted in the formation of Lake Eacham (Yidyam) and the neighbouring lakes Barrine (Barany) and Euramoo (Ngimun) *alias* The Crater.

false positives

Velikovsky stated that, according to the "Midrashic sources", "during the Deluge, all volcanoes erupted", but referred only to the *Sēpər ha-Yašar* (mid-16th century CE), not even identifying a specific passage or edition.[437] Presumably, he was referring to the following passage:

> And on that day, the Lord caused the whole earth to shake, and the sun darkened, and the foundations of the world raged, and the whole earth was moved violently, and the lightning flashed, and the thunder roared, and all the fountains in the earth were broken up, such as was not known to the inhabitants *before* ...[438]

These words are highly suggestive, yet it would be premature to interpret the raging of the *mūsdē tēbēl*, here translated as "foundations of the world", as a proven reference to volcanism – though this meaning is not impossible. Did the Hebrew notion of these 'foundations'[439] come with a belief that they protuberate above the surface as volcanoes? As no erupting fire or boulders are mentioned, it is more prudent to limit the meaning of the phrase to an earthquake. And for the words rendered above as "all the fountains in the earth were broken up", the Hebrew actually reads 'the voice of the mighty prevailed over the whole earth' (*yigbor qōl 'āṣūm bəkol hā'āręṣ*); the use of the same verb *gābar* ('to prevail') in the flood narrative of *Genesis*[440] suggests that this referred to the outpouring of water.

A paraphrase of a creation myth from Jeju Island (to the south of the Korean peninsula) makes it seem as if volcanic outbursts accompanied the separation of sky and earth (§§39, 46-47, 56-57, 77-80, 212, 240, 267, 294, 339, 339*, 350, 374, 404, 408):

---

[436] Nyiyija *alias* George Watson (c1899-1991), of the Dulgubarra Mamu subgroup of the Dyirbal, recorded 1964 by Robert Malcolm Ward Dixon (1939-), in Dixon 1972: 29; *cf.* 1991: 41.
[437] Velikovsky 1979: 9.
[438] *Sēpər ha-Yašar* (*The Book of Jasher*), 6. 11, ed. Dan 1986: 58, tr. Samuel 1887: 12.
[439] Compare van der Sluijs 2011b: 23, 68-69, 177 note 832; 2011c: 133, 193-194, 199-201.
[440] *Genesis*, 7. 18, 24, eds. Elliger *et al.* 1997: 11.

> ... in the beginning there was no distinction between sky and earth, and all was chaos. Then the sky and earth were separated, and under the arching sky, mountains erupted and water appeared.[441]

However, upon inspection of the original bilingual Korean and Japanese text the words "mountains erupted" are exposed as an unfortunate 'Konglish' translation; the intended meaning is that mountains rose up from the earth – that is to say, were created.[442]

Finally, the Hopi (northeastern Arizona) allegedly listed the following as the dire consequences of Sótuknang's discovery of corruption among the first race of people:

> He rained fire upon it. He opened up the volcanoes. Fire came from above and below and all around until the earth, the waters, the air, all was one element, fire, and there was nothing left except the people safe inside the womb of the earth. This was the end of Tokpela, the First World.[443]

Yet as discussed (§§34*, 449), Frank Waters' book is an unreliable source.

461
abstract concepts acquired in containers

A motif perhaps never heretofore recognised is that some mythical heroes are stated to have *retrieved from heaven concepts which modern people would consider to be abstract – such as wisdom, blessings or evil – held in one or more containers*, such as bags or boxes. The theme is similar to the acquisition of the sun, light, heat, darkness or other meteorological phenomena from enclosures in remote places (§440) and the temporary sojourn on Earth of a mythical hero or ancestor imparting essential, sacred knowledge to the people (§§166, 379).

In a few cases, the receptacles are reached by means of a form of *axis mundi*, such as a tree or stairway (compare §§157-163, 166-168). For example, the Māori (New Zealand) claimed that their forebears acquired

---

[441] Kim 1998: 101.
[442] shaman Bak Bongchun, *Chogamje* (*Song of First Invitation*), recorded October 1931 by Akamatsu Chijō or Akiba Takashi, eds. Akamatsu & Akiba 1937: 371. See the note in §443 on the relationship of this song to the *Cheonjiwang Bonpuri*.
[443] purportedly Oswald 'White Bear' Fredericks (1906-1996), to Waters before 1963, in Waters 1978: 14; compare van der Sluijs 2011d: 263.

the sacred knowledge (*wānanga*), not long after the separation of sky and earth, in the form of three baskets (*kete*). The god Tāne collected these upon invitation from the supreme god Io in "the uppermost heaven" (*Tikitiki-o-rangi*) or "the overhanging (overcast) summit of Heaven" (*Te Toi-o-nga-rangi-taupuru*). On his way, he availed himself of a staircase called Ara-tiatia ("the way of steps") and the help of deities personifying various types of whirlwinds:

> Tāne replied to this, 'I can do it! ... I will ascend by the Ara-tiatia, the Toi-hua-rewa of the family of my elder brother, Tawhiri-matea [god of winds], who dwells above in Tihi-o-manono.' ... Tāne now reached Te Pu-motomoto of Tawhiri-rangi [the guardhouse of the uppermost heaven], and there entered the house ... After the above occurrence, Tāne was conducted into Matangi-reia [the house of Io – Sun's path in the Heavens] where Io was awaiting him. ... Io added, 'What is thy reason for ascending here?' 'The sacred contents of the 'baskets' pertaining to the Sky-father and Earth-mother to obtain; hence have I ascended up to thee, O Io, ē ī!' ... they entered the temple Rangiatea [treasure house ...]. It was here that the Whatu-kuras gave into Tāne's charge, the three 'baskets' and the two sacred stones. ... These are the names of the three 'baskets' and two stones: –
>
> 1. The *kete-uruuru-matua*, of peace, of all goodness, of love.
> 2. The *kete-uruuru-rangi* (or *tipua*), of all prayers, incantations, ritual, used by mankind.
> 3. The *kete-uruuru-tau* (or *tawhito*), of the wars of mankind, agriculture, tree or wood-work, stone-work, earth-work – of all things that tend to well-being, life, of whatsoever kind. ...
>
> 1. Te Whatu-kura, Huka-a-tai (the translation is, Foam-of-Ocean).
> 2. Te Whatu-kura, Rehu-tai (the translation is, White-sea-mist).
>
> Those stones are both white in colour, like sea-foam, that is, they were white according to description handed down; they are stones that may indicate either good or evil according to man's desire. They are sacred stones ... The *kete*, or 'baskets' are the three great divisions of knowledge taught in the Maori College; we may call each *kete* a syllabus ... The two *whatu*, or stones, are said by the Scribe to be not ordinary stones of this earth, but were brought from Heaven. ...
>
> Now, after the three 'baskets' of the *wānanga* [knowledge] and the two stones had been acquired, the Whatu-kuras [gods] escorted Tāne-te-wānanga and his properties to the next lower Heaven. ... And now the face of Rangi-nui [the sky above, lowest Heaven] flashed forth in brilliant red. Hence did Tupai, Uepoto, Tamakaka, Uru-roa, Tama-te-

kapua, Tu-mata-uenga, Tangaroa, and Tawhiri-matua, know that the *wānanga* had been acquired by Tāne-matua.[444]

In a Samoan myth, the "Child of the Sun", taking advice from his mother Mangamangai, mounts a tree and obtains a gift in the form of "blessings done up in a basket" from his father, whom he had to snare to this end (§445):

> Following her directions, he went one morning with a long vine from the bush, which is the convenient substitute for a rope, climbed a tree, threw his rope with a noose at the end of it, and caught the sun. He made known his message, and (Pandora like) got a present for his bride. The sun first asked him what was his choice – blessings or calamities. He chose, of course, the former, and came down with his store of blessings done up in a basket.[445]

Many a story revolves around the negative consequences of the – perhaps proscribed – opening of a container or the explosive scattering of its contents.[446] In the famous Greek tale of Pandora's 'box', Prometheus steals fire (*pyr*) from Zeus "in a hollow fennel-stalk" (*en koílōi nárthēki*) for the benefit of humans and Zeus exacts revenge by sending Pandora and her "storage jar" (*píthou*, genitive) to mankind:

> For previously the tribes of men used to live upon the earth entirely apart from evils, and without grievous toil and distressful diseases, which give death to men. ... But the woman removed the great lid from the storage jar with her hands and scattered all its contents abroad – she wrought baneful evils for human beings. Only Anticipation remained there in its unbreakable home under the mount of the storage jar, and did not fly out; for before that could happen she closed the lid of the storage jar ... But countless other miseries roam among mankind; for the earth is full of evils, and the sea is full; and

---

[444] Nepia Te Ika Pohuhu (c1802-1882), priest of the Ngāti Hinepare subtribe of the Ngāti Kahungunu tribe (around Napier, North Island), recorded spring 1863 by Hoani Te Whatahoro Jury (1841-1923), tr. Smith 1913: 125-126, 129-132, 135, omitting the bracketed numbers following proper nouns; *cf.* 131 note 38; Moihi Te Matorohanga (c1804-1884) of Wai-rarapa, shaman and historian of the Ngāti Kahungunu tribe, recorded February 1865, in 1913: 94. Tāne's full name on this occasion, apart from Tāne-te-wānanga ('Tāne the Knowledge'), was Tāne-nui-a-rangi ('Great Tāne of the Heavens') and Io's was Io-taketake ('Io, Origin of All Things'). Tawhai (1988: 861 = 2002: 247) added: "Tane-nui-a-rangi has the three baskets with him at the moment in his fourth heaven." On layered heavens, see §§187-211.
[445] recorded 1840-1859, in Turner 1861: 248; *cf.* 1884: 200.
[446] For an example from the Ashanti (Ghana), see van der Sluijs 2011d: 110-111. See §§440, 458 for the Barasana story of a box disclosing a resin-like substance which caused sores.

some sicknesses come upon men by day, and others by night, of their own accord, bearing evils to mortals in silence ...[447]

Hesiod presented this myth as a separate story from that of the 'ages of men', but in both accounts the paradisiacal age ends with or during the reign of Zeus.

462
drowned land

Many traditions claim that coastlines have changed significantly and *areas now under water were once dry land*. In the case of former land bridges, the drowned land used to enable pedestrian traffic between two or more landmasses now separated by water, be they continents or islands. The inundation itself may be portrayed as a gradual or a rapid and catastrophic process, set at an unspecified time in the past – in some cases identifiable as a mythical age of heroes or creation.

Europe

In antiquity, the natives of Iberia seem to have believed that a legendary strongman – whom the Greeks naturally recognised as Herakles – divorced the continents of Europe and Africa by opening the Strait of Gibraltar:

> At the narrowest part of the Straits stand mountains on either side, enclosing the channel, Ximiera in Africa and Gibraltar in Europe; these were the limits of the labours of Hercules, and consequently the inhabitants call them the Pillars of that deity, and believe that he cut the channel through them and thereby let in the sea which had hitherto been shut out, so altering the face of nature.[448]

> Some authorities ... say ... that the two continents were originally joined and that he cut a passage between them, and that by opening

---

[447] Hesiod, *Opera et Dies* (*Works and Days*), 50-52, 90-103, tr. Most 2006: 90-91, 94-95. For the theft of fire, compare §§167-168.
[448] Pliny the Elder, *Natural History*, 3. 1 (4), tr. Rackham 1942: 4-5, translating *Abyla* and *Calpe* by their more modern equivalents "Ximiera" and "Gibraltar". The former is currently known as Monte Hacho, in Spanish Africa. On the pillars, see the comment in §§444.

the passage he brought it about that the ocean was mingled with our sea.[449]

Another tradition had it that Europe and Africa were once joined at Sicily and what must have been Tunis. Thus, Valerius Flaccus (d. *c*90 CE) wrote of the separation of "the shores of Sicily and Libya, when Janus and Atlas, lord of the sunset mountains, were struck aghast at the crash."[450] In a catalogue of similar events, Pliny the Elder (23-79 CE) did not mention Sicily's severance from Libya, but rather from the Italian mainland – by the formation of the Strait of Messina: "For another way also in which nature has made islands is when she tore Sicily away from Italy, Cyprus from Syria, Euboea from Boeotia, Atalantes and Macrias from Euboea, Besbicus from Bithynia, Leucosia from the Sirens' Cape."[451] Diodorus of Sicily (1st century BCE), himself born on the island, elaborated on Sicily's separation from Italy at Rhegium, which is today's Reggio di Calabria:

> The ancient mythographers, that is, say that Sicily was originally a peninsula, and that afterward it became an island, the cause being somewhat as follows. The isthmus at its narrowest point was subjected to the dash of the waves of the sea on its two sides and so a gap (*rhegma*) was made (*anarrhegnusthai*), and for this reason the spot was named *Rhegion*, and the city which was founded many years later received the same appellation as the place. Some men say, however, that mighty earthquakes took place and the neck of what was the mainland was broken through, and in this way the Strait was formed, since the sea now separated the mainland from the island.[452]

---

[449] Diodorus of Sicily, *Bibliotheca Historica* (*Historical Library*), 4. 18. 5, tr. Oldfather 1935: 402-403. However, much to his credit Diodorus (4. 18. 4-5, tr. 1935: 402-403) also included a variant reporting "just the opposite": "When Heracles arrived at the farthest points of the continents of Libya and Europe which lie upon the ocean, he decided to set up these pillars to commemorate his campaign. And since he wished to leave upon the ocean a monument which would be had in everlasting remembrance, he built out both the promontories, they say, to a great distance; consequently, whereas before that time a great space had stood between them, he now narrowed the passage, in order that by making it shallow and narrow he might prevent the great sea-monsters from passing out of the ocean into the inner sea ..."
[450] Valerius Flaccus, *Argonautica*, 2. 619-620, tr. Mozley 1936: 120-121. Barich (2009: 82) renders *Libycum* as "Africa" and swaps its position with "Sicily".
[451] Pliny the Elder, *Natural History*, 2. 90 (204), tr. Rackham 1949: 334-335.
[452] Diodorus of Sicily, *Bibliotheca Historica*, 4. 85. 3-4, tr. Oldfather 1939: 86-87. 'Rhegium' is Latin for Greek 'Rhégion'. Again, Diodorus (4. 85. 5) tagged on a contrary opinion which he attributed to Hesiod: "But the poet Hesiod states the very opposite, namely, that when the sea extended itself in between, Orion built out the headland which lies at Peloris and also erected there the sanctuary of Poseidon which is held in special honour by the natives ..." Peloris, on Sicily's northeastern promontory, is now known as Capo Peloro or Punta del Faro. Strabo (*Geography*, 1.

Asia

Several classical authors referred to the severance of a former land bridge between Europe and Asia in the Turkish Straits. Comparing this event with the Sicilian one, Flaccus poetically identified the agents as "Neptune's trident" (*Neptunia ... cuspis*), probably connoting earthquake activity, and a slow process like erosion or flooding:

> Then onward he steered the ship, and flew on between cities on either hand, where the race boils with its narrow waters, and Europe, grimmer with its cliffs, breaks away from pursuing Asia. These lands, too, these fields with their once linked peoples lashed by the ocean, Neptune's trident, I think, and the slow workings of time the enemy sundered of yore, even as they did the shores of Sicily and Libya, when Janus and Atlas, lord of the sunset mountains, were struck aghast at the crash.[453]

And Pliny the Elder wrote:

> Cases of land entirely stolen away by the sea are, first of all (if we accept Plato's story), the vast area covered by the Atlantic, and next, in the inland seas also, the areas that we see submerged at the present day, Acarnania covered by the Ambracian Gulf, Achaea by the Gulf of Corinth, Europe and Asia by the Sea of Marmora and the Black Sea.

---

3. 10, tr. Jones 1917: 198-199) aired a third opinion: "And in a similar way settlings in the bed of the sea, both great ones and small, may also occur, if it be true, as people say, that yawning abysses and engulfments of districts and villages have been caused by earthquakes – as happened in the case of Bura and Bizone and several other places; and as for Sicily, one might conjecture that it is not so much a piece broken away from Italy as that it was cast up from the deeps by the fire of Aetna and remained there; and the same is true both of the Lipari Islands and the Pithecussae." Bura lay in Achaea (Greece), Bizone *alias* Byzone was a Greek colony at modern-day Kavarna (Bulgaria).

[453] Valerius Flaccus, *Argonautica*, 2. 613-620, tr. Mozley 1936: 118-121. The words "time the enemy" (*adversi ... aevi*) belong together. Slavitt (1999: 43) omits the trident from his translation, applies the words "in ancient times" (*quondam*) – here rendered as "of yore" – to the Sicilian incident and distinguishes the latter from an allusion to the flooding at Gibraltar: "The ship sailed on through the Dardanelles, with Europe's cliffs / on the one side and, on the other, Asia's gentler slopes. / These lands were connected once and their peoples lived together, / but over the eons the force of the thrashing ocean tore them / apart, as in ancient times they sundered Sicily's coast / and cut it off from the mainland, or Atlas and Janus struggled / to tear with a mighty roar Gibraltar from Africa's coast." This translation has to be rejected as far too fanciful. Barich (2009: 82) translates much more literally.

> Also the sea has made the channels of Leucas, Antirrhium, the Dardanelles and the two Bospori.[454]

Pliny thus seems to have thought that the Black Sea expanded into the region corresponding to the Turkish Straits. The Greek philosopher Strato of Lampsacus (c335-c269 BCE) likewise contended that "the Euxine Sea formerly did not have its outlet at Byzantium, but the rivers which empty into the Euxine forced and opened a passage, and then the water was discharged into the Propontis and the Hellespont."[455] The ancient inhabitants of Samothrace (northern Aegean Sea) remembered a deluge, otherwise known as Dardanus' flood, in which water burst out from the then lacustrine Black Sea into the Mediterranean Sea:

> And the Samothracians have a story that, before the floods which befell other peoples, a great one took place among them, in the course of which the outlet at the Cyanean Rocks was first rent asunder and then the Hellespont. For the Pontus, which had at the time the form of a lake, was so swollen by the rivers which flow into it, that, because of the great flood which had poured into it, its waters burst forth violently into the Hellespont and flooded a large part of the coast of Asia and made no small amount of the level part of the land of Samothrace into a sea; and this is the reason, we are told, why in later times fishermen have now and then brought up in their nets the stone capitals of columns, since even cities were covered by the inundation.[456]

Australia

According to the Bunurong – a branch of the Kulin – on the Mornington Peninsula (south of Melbourne), it was formerly possible to traverse Port Phillip Bay by foot:

> 'Plenty long ago ... along Corio, men could cross, dry-foot, from our side of the bay to Geelong.' They described a hurricane – trees bend-

---

[454] Pliny, *Natural History*, 2. 92 (205), tr. Rackham 1949: 334-337. The words "the Atlantic" translate *Atlanticum mare*, "the Sea of Marmora" *Propontide* (ablative), "the Black Sea" *Ponto* (ablative), "the Dardanelles" *Hellespontum* (accusative) and "the two Bospori" *Bosporos duos* (accusative). Acarnania, Leucas and Antirrhium are in west-central Greece. Note also that Pliny here locates Atlantis in the Atlantic Ocean; as Latin lacks articles, *immenso spatio* is better translated as 'a vast area' than "the vast area".
[455] Strato of Lampsacus, in Strabo, *Geography*, 1. 3. 4, tr. Jones 1960: 182-183. Byzantium is today's Istanbul.
[456] Diodorus of Sicily, *Bibliotheca Historica*, 5. 47. 3-4, tr. Oldfather 1939: 228-229. 'Cyanean Rocks' (*Kyanéas* [accusative]) was another designation for the Symplegades, situated at the Bosphorus. Diodorus (5. 48) went on to discuss the life of Dardanus.

ing to and fro – then the earth sank, and the sea rushed in through the Heads, till the void places became broad and deep, as they are today.[457]

One is told:

> Port Phillip was once dry land and the Kulin were in the habit of hunting kangaroos and emus there. One day the men were away hunting and the women had gone off collecting roots and yams, while some little boys, who had been left behind, were playing in the camp. They were hurling little toy spears at each other, just like their fathers did. In the camp there were some wooden troughs full of water, and one of the spears upset one of these. However, this was no ordinary bucket, but a magic one, and it held a tremendous amount of water, which came rolling down engulfing all the land, and threatening to drown all the people. Bunjil felt sorry for them, and placed a rock where Mornington now is, and told the water not to go any further. Then with two other rocks he made the heads, and told the water to run out between them and meet the ocean. This is how Port Phillip was made.[458]

As for Hobson's Bay, which is part of Greater Melbourne, the Bunurong "recollected when Hobson's Bay was a kangaroo ground; they say, 'Plenty catch kangaroo, and plenty catch opossum there'", adding "that the passage up the bay, through which the ships came, is the River Yarra, and that the river once went out at the heads, but that the sea broke in, and that Hobson's Bay, which was once hunting ground, became what it is."[459] "… *Hobson's Bay* and the Valley, north of the Yarra River, were once united, and that what is now an inland sea of some 100 miles in circumference, was a splendid country abounding in Kangaroo, Emu, &c."[460]

From the Gungganyji (Cape Grafton, northern Queensland) comes the information that "the Barrier Reef was the original coastline of the country", but the coastline moved to its current position further west in a memorable flood:

---

[457] recorded 30 October 1850 at Arthur's Seat by a Mr. Cobb, to Robert Russell, to Georgiana McCrae (1804-1890), in McCrae 1934: 176.
[458] Massola 1968: 47-48. Massola's source has not yet been identified. Bunjil was the creator and supreme deity in the belief system of this cultural group.
[459] Yankee Yankee *alias* Robert Cunningham (c1823-1846), Murray and Old Bembo, all Bunurong, recorded 9 November 1858 by William Henry Hull (1795-1874), in anonymous 1858-1859: 12.
[460] Hull 1846: 4.

> The waters rose rapidly as the fugitives climbed to the heights of the Murray Prior Range. This range is called by the aborigines 'Wambilari' … They succeeded in reaching the top of the highest peak in the range, and there they made a fire, and heating large stones rolled them down the mountain side, and succeeded in checking the flood. The sea, however, never returned to its original limits.[461]

Perhaps this flood, apparently concomitant with a volcanic outburst, was the same one that, in two other myths (§460), formed Lake Eacham (Atherton Tableland). A storyteller from the Dyirbal (northeast Queensland) also "remarked that in Giɾugar's day it was possible to WALK across to the islands (Palm Island, Hinchinbrook Island, and so on)", Giɾugar being a mythical character.[462]

Africa

On the Arabian peninsula and in the Horn of Africa, the idea circulated that the Red Sea originally was not a sea:

> The Arabs tell us that the Red Sea is simply water that did not dry up after Noah's deluge; the Somalis say that when their ancestors crossed from Arabia to Africa there was a land connection across the straits of Babel-Mandeb.[463]

South America

A flood myth of the Mapuche of Chiloé Island (central-western Chile) centres on two antagonistic snakes – Kaikai Vilu ('water snake') and Tenten Vilu or Trentren Vilu ('land snake'), the former of which floods the land, while the latter raises the mountains in order to help living beings survive. Although most versions, including the earliest one on record,[464] refrain from commenting on any lasting changes in the local geography produced by the interactions, there appears to have been a belief – of which the authenticity cannot yet be verified – that the Chiloé archipel-

---

[461] recorded 1892-1909 at Yarrabah by Ernest Richard Bulmer Gribble (1869-1957), in Gribble 1932: 56-57. A version of this tradition was also told by Jarriyi *alias* Dick Moses (b. c1898), a Yidindji (south and east of Cairns), on 22 August 1973 at Yarrabah, in Dixon 1991: 91-94.
[462] Dixon 1972: 29.
[463] Gregory 1894: 290 = 1896: 5. It is not clear whether Gregory based this information on textual or oral testimony.
[464] e. g., the version recorded 1629-1674, in Diego de Rosales, *Historia general del reino de Chile; Flandes Indiano (General History of the Kingdom of Chile, Indian Flanders*; 1674 CE), 1. 1, ed. MacKenna 1877: 4-6; Cárdenas Tabies 1978: 17-18; Grenier 1984: 140; Bengoa 2000: 16.

ago was formed on the occasion, with some areas remaining permanently inundated. In the words of one account:

> As to the waters introduced into the valleys by Caicaivilu, they gave rise to the formation of the gulfs, channels and fjords. For its part, the prominences raised by Tentenvilu originated that seedbed of islands of all forms and sizes which make up the southern archipelagoes, beyond parallel 41°.[465]

According to the Selk'nam (northeastern Tierra del Fuego), their ancestor Kwányip used to enter Tierra del Fuego from the mainland of South America by foot, as is no longer possible today:

> *Kwányip* came from the north by foot to our country. He drove his guanacos in front of him, his dogs helped him with that. At that time [= upon his first arrival] he moved until Cabo San Pablo. Here one still sees in the stones the footprints of his first herd of tame guanacos, which he had brought with him. ... When all his guanacos had been consumed, he moved back to the north. There he fetched another herd of tame guanacos. These he drove in front of him. With that he returned to our country.[466]

Other reports clarify that the flooding occurred in unison with an earthquake:

> At that time there were still narrow crossings. On these anyone could get from one shore to the other by foot. ... Thus, on those crossings one could reach the mainland in the north from our island.
>
> When, one day, very many people had gathered here on the big island again, in order to hunt guanacos, there was unexpectedly a tremendous commotion in nature and a strong quaking of the earth, high waves rolled over and penetrated deep into the land. Only then did people recover from their great anxiety again, when calmness had set in. As soon as possible they wanted to rush back to their homeland. But the usual crossings were now covered by water. Thus the people saw themselves shut off from their homeland and deprived of any return. As getting away was no longer possible, the people scattered across the island in all directions.[467]

---

[465] Barría 1997: 63 (•). 'Caicaivilu' is a Spanish spelling of 'Kaikai Vilu'.
[466] Tenenésk *alias* Ventura (c1859 - mid-1925), in April 1923, in Gusinde 1931: 585 (•). Cabo San Pablo is close to the southern border of the Selk'nam territory.
[467] Gusinde 1931: 134-135 (•).

463
anthropomorphic creator or culture hero

A *mythical being with human appearance, typically male, manifests in the sky or on the 'waters of chaos'* (§§5, 7). He may represent the creative deity, the earliest teacher of cultural institutions or a combination of these and is often celebrated as the 'first' or paradigmatic human being. Examples from Pentecost Island (Vanuatu, Melanesia) and South Africa[468] can be supplemented with a Tahitian memory of the age before 'creation', when 'an expanse of water ... covered the abyss, and the god Tino taata floated on the surface', for the god's name was stated to mean 'human body'.[469] The Ukomno'm (Round Valley, Mendocino County, California) told a similar myth about the first appearance of their creator and civiliser:

> There was only water, and over it a fog. On the water was foam. The foam moved round and round continually, and from it came a voice. After a time there issued from the foam a person in human form. He had wing-feathers of the eagle on his head. This was Taikó-mol ['solitude walker']. ... He stood on the foam, which still revolved. There was no light.[470]

The 'sky man' or 'water man' overlaps with the *axis mundi* in its animate or personified aspect, often doubling as a cosmic mountain, pillar or tree (§146).[471] Many traditions, though certainly not all, present him or the *axis mundi* as luminous (§§153, 431).

464
edible sky

According to a common belief which could be documented *ad nauseam*, the *sky* was *formerly edible*.[472] This curious trait is intimately associated

---

[468] van der Sluijs 2011b: 224-225; 2011d: 174-175.
[469] recorded 1843-1854, in de Bovis 1855: 516 (••). The translation "to the surface" (1976: 41) is misleading; *cf.* Fornander 1878: 64; Emory 1939: 24. The translation of *Tino taata* as 'human body' is refined as 'the type or source god of the human race', de Bovis 1855: 517 (•).
[470] recorded 1915, 1916, 1922 or 1924 from an Ukomno'm, in Curtis 1924: 169; *cf.* Kroeber 1907: 184. On the primeval darkness, see §§6-7.
[471] Compare van der Sluijs 2011a: 188-191; 2011b: 60-61; 2011c: 92-94.
[472] Berezkin (no date) cites instances from western New Guinea, northeast India, the Chuvash, the Serbians and a large number of African groups. The K'ahsho Got'ine, a group of the Sahtú (around Fort Good Hope and Colville Lake, Northwest Territories, Canada), shared a tradition of

with the 'low sky' (§3).⁴⁷³ A 19th-century 'modern' Greek myth concerning the separation of sky and earth (§§39, 46-47, 56-57, 77-80, 212, 240, 267, 294, 339, 339*, 350, 374, 404, 408) opens with the words: 'In ancient times the sky was so close to the earth that the cows were able to lick it.'⁴⁷⁴ And to "account for the separation of Divinity from men below", the Cic Dinka (near Bor, South Sudan) told "how there was once a wall in the sky, which held a man in until he ate part of the wall, and was therefore pushed below by Divinity."⁴⁷⁵

Some myths introduce a form of *axis mundi*, such as a rope or ladder, into the narrative. Thus, the inhabitants of Nias (off the west coast of Sumatra) 'assume that the sky was formerly near the earth; the priests arrived in the sky along a ladder. The fat then used to be scraped off the sky with alang-alang leaves. One time a man ordered his wife again to fetch fat; in her distress she took an axe and hacked into the sky; this was then lifted up and the woman was taken with it.'⁴⁷⁶ And the Ngaju Dayak (eastern Kalimantan) related:

> The sky was … in the beginning close above the earth; it consists of an edible, oily substance and served the people for food. But the Anak Mahatara, the son of Mahatara, the highest god, taught the people to plant rice, etc., which outraged Mahatara and he moved the sky further away from the earth.⁴⁷⁷

A Dutch anthropologist was informed that it was coconut flesh that the sky used to be made of and that the name of the 'son of Mahatara' was Manjamei. As icing on the cake, he learned that the latter figure subsequently retreated into the sky along a rope⁴⁷⁸ – a familiar expression of an *axis mundi* (§§160-174).

---

pieces of meat falling from the sky (Petitot 1887: 232-233, paraphrased in 1886: 231-232 and loosely translated in 1976: 58), but this looks suspiciously like a direct borrowing of the Hebrew legend of manna (*mān*; *Exodus*, 16; *Numbers*, 11. 4-9).

⁴⁷³ *e. g.*, van der Sluijs 2011a: 153 (Kassena).

⁴⁷⁴ Georgios Kremos (1839-1926), recorded in Aráchoba (Boeotia), in Schmidt 1877: 133 (•). A more elaborate version from Cyprus adds the detail that, at that time, 'God could be seen and touched', Louka 1874: 1 (•), *cf.* Schmidt 1877: 243.

⁴⁷⁵ recorded 1947-1950, in Lienhardt 1961: 35. The formation of a sky hole (§293) is implied.

⁴⁷⁶ Kruijt 1906: 494 (•), not citing his source. *Alang alang* is *Imperata cylindrica* or 'cogongrass', a species of grass.

⁴⁷⁷ recorded 1839-1845 or 1849-1858 by August Hardeland (1814-1891), in Hardeland 1859: 295 s. v. 'LANGIT' (•); *cf.* van der Sluijs 2011a: 153.

⁴⁷⁸ Kruijt 1906: 493-494.

465
ugly male

A universal theme in myth is *a male character - generally in the rôle of a hero - cursed with physical deformities,* such as facial or corporeal scars or ulcers, progeria, a hunched back and other repulsive dermatological or anatomical features.[479] Typically, the affliction is lifted permanently or temporarily in the course of the story (compare §393).[480] Some other person – often a divine parent or a partner of the opposite sex – is usually involved in the removal of the repugnant condition.[481]

In many versions, the entity is or becomes a celestial body.[482] Where the latter is identified, the 'morning star' is sometimes named as the bearer of the hideous physical traits.[483] Alternatively, the protagonist is the sun or moon. For example, the Aztecs equated the current sun with the diseased god Nānāhuatl *alias* Nānāhuatzin (compare §§435, 391*, 444), on the understanding that the god's fiery transformation had taken care of his ailments.[484] Another case is a myth from the Emberá (eastern Panama and northwestern Colombia) in which a character identified in one version as the moon dons a shirt which causes him to be covered in sores; he removes it and is thereby transformed into an attractive man at a party, enabling him to make love with his wife, who is unaware of the metamorphosis and believes she is cheating – he scratches her and so

---

[479] *e. g.,* van der Sluijs 2011b: 133-134 (Kiribati); Ouwehand 1964: 83 (Japan). The theme seems to have been first recognised by Cochrane (*e. g.,* 1988: 27; 1991a: 68, 70-71; 1991b: 64-66, 69-70; 1993: 63, 66-68, 72; 1994a: 90; 1994b: 79; 1996: 55; 1997a: 50, 126, 129, 131, 149-150, 154, 163, 168-170, 177-179; 1997c: 82; 1997d: 72; 2002: 91-95; 2006: 56-62, 64-65, 67-69, 82-84, 103, 111-113; 2015: 31-33; 2017: 12-14, 20-23, 58-61, 107, 111; personal communication, 3 January 2017); compare Talbott 1989: 42 #109. A related motif may be the facial contortions seen in many iconographic representations, 'ancestral' tattoo patterns and shamanic expressions.

[480] *e. g.,* van der Sluijs 2011c: 240; Boas 1917: 43 (both Nlaka′pamux).

[481] *e. g.,* van Hasselt 1876: 176-178 (Numfor); Wissler & Duvall 1908: 61-65 (Piegan); McCleary 1997: 45 (Crow); Boas 1900: 69 (Nuxalk); Wilbert & Simoneau 1987: 51 (Nivaclé); 1992: 10, 105-111 (Sikuani).

[482] *e. g.,* van der Sluijs 2011c: 240; von Weiher 1971: 52, 80, 84-85 (Babylonia); Wissler & Duvall 1908: 61-65 (Piegan); Boas 1917: 43 (Nlaka′pamux); Frazer 1921: 390-391 (Nuxalk); Wilbert & Simoneau 1992: 10, 105-111 (Sikuani).

[483] *e. g.,* van der Sluijs 2011d: 167, 217-218, 294 (all Aztec), 203 (Sikuani); *Annals of Cuauhtitlan* (*Codex Chimalpopoca*), 5. 45-46, tr. Bierhorst 1992: 32 (Aztec); Seler 1923: 142-143 (Aztec); Brundage 1982: 224-226 (Aztec); Lehmann 1928: 772, 781 (Mixe). Other stories feature the morning star, but distinguish it from the ugly hero – *e. g.,* van Hasselt 1876: 176-178 (Numfor); Wissler & Duvall 1908: 61-65 (Piegan).

[484] van der Sluijs 2011d: 218 (Aztec).

exposes her later.[485] In variants from the Catío Emberá[486] and the Baudó Emberá,[487] the person is called respectively 'Caragabí' and 'Carabí' and is not explicitly identified with the moon, although in the latter version the unfaithful wife is changed into a "moon bird".[488] Based on parallels such as that documented among the Selk'nam (§391*), the comparativist suspects that, in the common progenitor of these variants, the husband was the sun, who branded his wife, the moon, with its familiar spots.

466
appearance of the sun, light or heat at elevation or dissipation of low or collapsed sky

Some traditions attest to *a correlation between light levels, density of the sky and height of the sky*, such that a dense and low sky – whether fallen (§§300, 353) or primordial (§3) – corresponds to darkness and the present, 'high' one to daylight.[489] The Vili people (Loango, western Congo) illustrate the theme:

> Fog or dark cloud cover or the sky which lay dark over the earth, it pressed until someone or something lifted it and pushed it ever higher, so that it became bright.[490]

Another striking example is the richly documented myth from the Nivaclé (Paraguay and northwest Argentina) concerning the collapse of the thick, heavy sky (§300*):

> In the meantime, it had dawned. One of the men remembered the teeth of *Majôctsi*, the tucu-tucu. He had kept them for many years in a rolled-up string. This saved them. He cut the sky with the *Mâjoctsi* teeth. He cut fast. Suddenly the sky opened above this man. He went running to the others and distributed among them the *Majôctsi* teeth

---

[485] a woman from the area of Río Tarasito to her grandson Selimo Huacoríso, an Emberá shaman originally from the Río Docamparó (Colombia; c. 5° N), recorded 1927 on the shore of the Río Sambú (eastern Panama) by Erland Nordenskiöld (1877-1932), in Wassén 1933: 110-111, tr. Isacsson 1993: 296-297; *cf.* Nordenskiöld, in Wassén 1933: 131 note 1.
[486] Severino de Santa Teresa, in Rivet 1929: 82; Wassén 1933: 131.
[487] Pardo 1984: 29-33, tr. Isacsson 1993: 297-298.
[488] Pardo 1984: 33, tr. Isacsson 1993: 298 (•).
[489] Compare also the Sumerian and Nuxalk examples in §49, which are there blended in with cases of enclosed light or heat (§440).
[490] recorded 1874-1876, in Pechuël-Loesche 1907: 137 (•).

which he had. All worked to cut the sky above them. Very soon it opened, making it possible to see, once again, the day. They were very happy. ... The man who was the owner of the *Majôctsi* teeth was the one who saved those of his clan. ... Each time when he caught a *Mâjoctsi*, he kept them, because he used to listen to the old men who said:

– Keep the teeth of the *Majôctsi* well. Have them ready for when *vôôs* falls.

When cutting the sky, it suddenly became smoke and it went up. Because, it is said, it was quite thick when it fell. ... Only those who stayed near the man who had the *Majôctsi* teeth were saved. All those years he guarded them. Those were the only ones who were saved.[491]

A rival version (§300*) concurs that the light was restored by cutting through the sky, but does not mention the dissipation into smoke:

They could not see anything because there was total darkness. They were covered by the sky, and it was completely dark there underneath the tree. ... Then Fitsakajich told the young man to try to cut into the sky that was covering them. It was hard as a rock. ... The young man tried again, and he cut through the sky with his knife as if it were an animal hide. He said to Fitsakajich: 'It's no longer hard.' 'Well, if that is so, then we are saved.' However, the sky was hard as a rock and only Fitsakajich's mediation made it soft. If he had not been there, the people would not have been able to get out from beneath the sky. Fitsakajich told him: 'Now cut vigorously. Dig in your knife and bring it down hard.'

The young man cut into the sky on top and then he brought the knife down. He brought it back up again, then cut down, until he had cut a square. Then a piece of the sky fell down, but they still could not see anything and it was still dark. Fitsakajich told him to keep cutting, so the young man did and cut out another square piece of the sky, which fell down. He continued to cut and then a bit of light flickered through. Fitsakajich told him not to get discouraged but to go on cutting into the sky.

The next time they could see a small hole and realized that he was about to cut through the sky, which had a very thick layer. Fitsakajich

---

[491] Chajanaj, of the Tovok Ihavós of the Pilcomayo, recorded mid-1971 - mid-1972, in Chase-Sardi 1981: 94-95 (•). The circumflex accent is variously placed on the first and second syllable of '*Majoctsi*'. Wilbert & Simoneau (1987: 101-102) translated this word as "tuco-tuco", a rodent of the genus *Ctenomys*.

continued to encourage the young man, asking him to keep cutting into the sky and soon they saw light coming through the hole. Now the men and women and young people who were totally disoriented under that tree were able to see and recognize one another.[492]

Another variation (§457) contains the same element of experiencing the sunlight after cutting through a collapsed sky, but blends it with the motif of an inversion of sky and earth in such a way that the protagonists continue their existence on top of the old sky instead of beneath it. In this story, the sky is positioned low above the earth (§3) before it falls and effectively becomes a new earth as the survivors, owing their salvation to a tree, dug through it and begin to live on its surface:

The oldest person in the group had tools, different things, and they tried them out. Then they looked for tuco-tuco teeth and dug with them, because this earth that was the sky before was very low, very close to the other earth, the one that is the sky now. They dug to be able to go through to the other side. They dug and they dug, and the earth was still soft, like wax, sticky. Then all of a sudden the old man had to climb up to the other side so he could get the others out, too. They climbed up to what is now our earth. When they got there, the earth was still soft; the water had just dried up, and the sun still had not come out. The whole family got out; there were nine people.[493]

Although the text seems to imply that the old earth turned into the current sky, it does not explicitly state as much. The impenetrable darkness is not mentioned, but the light of the sun and moon is restored soon after the people's emergence from the hole:

After two days the sun came out. ... A little later wild plants came up too ... Many things appeared, one by one. ... The earth was getting harder and harder, because the sun had come out. The first day the sun came out it began to dry out little by little, but as the sun shone more and more, the earth got a bit harder every day. ... They had been a long time without eating, because of the falling of the sky, which is now the earth. ... When the first day was over, that man went to inspect the new earth, which had been the sky. ... Many years went by, without trees, wild plants, grass; they did not exist then. ...

---

[492] As·etí *alias* Comisario (b. c1912), of the Jotoy Ihavós ('grassland people'; around the Santa Teresita mission, near Mariscal Estigarribia), recorded 1980, in Wilbert & Simoneau 1987: 98-100. Compare §§276-282, 293 for the creation of a hole in a solid sky.

[493] Leguán (b. c1916), a shaman, recorded 1986, translated by Pascual Benítez (b. early 1960s), of Laguna Escalante, in Wilbert & Simoneau 1987: 105. On the initial softness of the earth, compare §31.

Then that man began to think of which direction the sun had come from, where north was, and south, and west. He studied the names (he had not forgotten the other world which had disappeared). There was still no wind, either from the south or from the north. So then the man began to study which direction the sun rose from, which had to be east. Then he said to his sons: 'This is the east; afterward the sun will go in that direction, and that is the west. North then must be there, and the south over there.' They were getting better acquainted with the new world they were living in.

Where they were then there was no wind, only rain. It rained every day, it never stopped raining. The years went by. One day all of a sudden there was a wind, a north wind. ... At that time there was still no grass, or trees. They planted corn seeds ... When the earth was changed, the sun came out after two days and began to dry the earth. On the third day the moon appeared.[494]

༄༅

---

[494] Leguán, as above, in Wilbert & Simoneau 1987: 105-107.

quotations in other languages

footnote:

8   "tous les animaux qui, alors, demeuraient et conversaient avec l'homme"
22 "... se cayó el cielo, vôôs, en aquellos tiempos. Comenzó lloviendo largamente, hasta que, empezó a bajar. Los hombres tenían mucho miedo. Les pedían a los chamanes para que ordenen parar la lluvia. Pero ni siquiera aquellos que cantaban a la lluvia sabían hacer nada. Al día siguiente vieron como se caían las nubes. – Ya llegó el momento terrible. – dicen que decían los hombres. Vôôs aplastaba las chozas matando a todos los que se refugiaban dentro. Era muy pesado."
23 "Entre los hombres había uno que advirtió a los demás para que busquen un árbol de molle, ôtjayuc, para refugiarse. Porque a todos los demás árboles el cielo los tumbaba. Solamente ôtjayuc, lo resitió. No lo pudo aplastar ni voltear. Reventaron todos los hombres que se colocaron bajo otros árboles. Unicamente, otjayuc pudo aguantar el peso de vôôs. Los hombres salieron corriendo hacia la selva y encontraron algunos árboles de otjayuc para guardarse de vôôs que se caía; llevando a sus mujeres, sus hijos y unas cuantas ovejas que se dejaron arrear rápido. Los cubrió una obscuridad muy intensa. No podían verse más unos a otros. Estaban desorientados. No sabían que hacer. ... No sabían qué hacer porque tenían mucho miedo. No era como de día. Ni podían verse, pues estaba más oscuro que durante la noche. / – ¿Estás vivo todavía? – preguntaban unos. / – Sí, estoy vivo. – contestaban los otros. ... / Muchos años escuchamos que los antiguos decían que iba a caer el cielo y así ocurrió. Murieron todos los que se refugiaron bajo el quebracho blanco, el quebracho colorado y los demás árboles. Todos fueron tumbados por el cielo. Solamente los árboles ôtjayuc han resistido, salvándose los que se protegieron bajo ellos. ... La gente de todas las aldeas murieron."
24 "Sólo se salvaron aquellos que estaban cerca del hombre que tenía los dientes del Majôctsi. Todos los años los venía guardando. Aquellos fueron los únicos que se salvaron. ... Pero desde entonces no se ha caído más el cielo."
27 "Era el momento en que acababa de despertar la tierra"
27 "la nivelación"
29 "Y fué robada su Serpiente de Vida"
29 "fué robada la Gran Serpiente"
34 "Der Anfang ist, daß Jeli gefällt wurde. Von der einen Seite hackte ein Hûl-Baumkänguruh und von der anderen Seite ein Hîsalî-Baumkänguruh. Die Splitter warfen sie hinter sich, so daß sie in alle Richtungen flogen. Das sind die sakralen Steine. Der Baum stand in Konowî, am Sarukfluß. Als er gefällt war, richtete er sich weit im Osten in der Richtung von Koropun am Ort Masamlu wieder auf. Aber Hûl und Hîsalî folgten ihm und fällten ihn aufs neue. Dann richtete er sich auf dem Pasinpaß auf und überschritt den Berg. Wieder folgten sie ihm und fällten ihn, und als er niederstürzte, zersplitterte der eine Ast völlig. Die Splitter flogen überall umher. Der andere Ast machte sich selbständig

und ging in Richtung der Dörfer Npsan, Serekasi und Mîmbanam den nördlichen Weg. ... Von dort ging Jeli nach Tanggusene (bei Sanggalpunu) und stürzte dort nieder (sahûng-tîbag). Dabei gab es ein so gewaltiges Erdbeben, daß die Limlim-Leute alle umkamen. Von dort aus ging er nach Luruk und stürzte nieder (sahûng-tîbag). Alle Flüsse führten sein Blut mit. Von dort ging er über Wanijok und Pilijam über den Îlît-Berg nach Sîjelma, an den Feraweberg. Von dem Berg sagt man, daß er ein Splitter von Jeli sei. Die Leute ... trugen die Splitter von Jeli bei sich und steckten sie in die Erde, um die Erde zu beruhigen und zu festigen, denn die Erde war zu Schlamm geworden, Jeli hatte sie zu Schlamm gemacht. Auch auf die Berge legten sie die Splitter von Jeli, und so bekamen die Berge Namen."

35 "Es war ein Baum, der in Koropun stand. Die Spitze war mit dem Himmel verwachsen. Die Leute aus Koropun und aus Turam versuchten ihn zu fällen, aber es gelang ihnen nicht. Da holten sie den Sama-Mann Kuwilahun. Der brachte die Zähne vom Hûl- und vom Hîsalî-Baumkänguruh. Als er an den Baum kam, begann er zu hacken. Den ersten Splitter, der sich löste, legte er für sich weg und sagte: 'Damit werde ich mein sakrales Männerhaus bauen'. Dann hackten sie weiter, das Hûl an der Hinterseite, das Hîsalî an der Vorderseite. Der Baum fiel um. Als sie auch die Spitze abhackten, die mit dem Himmel verwachsen war, hob sich das Himmelsgewölbe. Als der Baum umfiel, wurde er zum Schwein. Er wurde Jeli, das Jeli-Schwein. Das Schwein kam hierher und machte dabei Geräusche wie ein Flugzeug."

63 "le soleil et la terre"

63 "les cinq planètes"

65 "goberno"

78 "... ehe die große Fluth das Land überschwemmte; aber da die Erde sich umwälzte, kam das unten, was vorher oben war."

79 "... le ciel va tomber, la terre tourne!"

82 "... daß der Himmel vor diesem auf den Gipfeln der Berge ruhte, aber nach der großen Fluth, die die ganze Erde überschwemte, wurde er zu der Höhe hinauf gehoben, welche er jetzt hat."

84 "Anfangs erscheinen zwei Sonnen am Himmel, dann vier, dann sechzehn, und durch die Hitze wird Alles verbrennen. Diese Folgen werden sich selbst dem Altan melekei (dem goldenen Frosche) bemerkbar machen, der das Bild des Uran Mandsu-schirin vorstellt, als unter dem Berge Sumber befindlich, die ganze Erde umhüllend. Indem dieses Thier bemerkt, dass die sein Leben bedingende Feuchtigkeit sich vermindert, muss es seine Lage verändern und kopfüber schlagen, und mit dieser Umdrehung wird auch die ganze Welt überschlagen."

85 "La terre se retourne sur elle-même"

85 "D'abord le soleil se lève vers (à l'est) les Courtisanes ... demeuraient. Les Kolloches donc des chiens étaient, puis hommes ils sont devenus. Alors les Dènè (hommes) l'ouest vers demeuraient, nous or des hommes nous sommes. ... Alors tout à coup la terre ainsi fit: d'un côté à l'autre elle s'est retournée ça a fait, elle a pirouetté c'est comme si [sic]; et puis lors depuis au même instant les Kolloches l'ouest à, les bighorns-montagnes sur l'autre versant demeurent, et nous là de ce côté-ci nous sommes venus. Tout d'abord donc la grande mer au

bord de nous demeurions, et cette terre sur elle sur il n'y avait personne. ... Avant cela l'ouest à on demeurait. Cela il y a longtemps très ne pas."

85 "Au commencement, les Fantômes demeuraient au Levant. Ces Fantômes furent d'abord des chiens qui se métamorphosèrent en hommes. Alors nous, les Hommes (*Dènè*), nous demeurions à l'Occident (*Tahan*) ... Alors tout à coup la terre fit ainsi: elle tourna sur elle-même en intervertissant les points cardinaux. Ce fut comme si elle avait pirouetté sur le talon. Depuis lors, les Fantômes demeurent à l'Ouest des Montagnes Rocheuses; tandis que nous sommes venues à l'Est de ces mêmes montagnes. Donc, tout au commencement, au bord de la grande mer occidentale nous habitions, alors qu'à l'Est du Mackenzie, il n'y avait encore aucun habitant; car nous sommes des habitants des plateaux des hautes montagnes. Nous ne connaissions pas encore le *Nakotsia-kotchô* (le Mackenzie) et nous demeurions au milieu des Montagnes Rocheuses."

85 "étoile flamboyante"

85 "Souvenir récent d'une éruption volcanique à l'occident"

94 "os caxinauás moram, casas fizeram, muito aldeias bonitas com moram, muito legumes abundam. / os caxinauás em coisa alguma pensam não (nada receiam), muito felizes são, moram, longe-não de rio caudaloso á beira moram."

94 "legumes havia não"

102 "Anticamente però non era così, ma tutti gli alberi avevano sempre le foglie verdi. Or avvenne che un giovane di nome Camschoat andò verso il nord lontano, lontano, dove fa più caldo e ritornò dicendo che in quei paesi molti grandi alberi avevano foglie verdi d'estate e rosse d'autunno. Gli Onas non vollero prestargli fede per cui quel giovane sdegnato partì di nuovo per il nord e poi ritornò sotto forma di *cotorra* (un piccolo papagallo della Terra del Fuoco, tutto verde eccetto il petto che è rosso) carico di foglie rosse per mostrarle agli increduli. Arrivato si posò sugli alberi, le cui foglie alla sua vicinanza diventarono rosse. ... Cotorra è nome spagnuolo mentre l'indigeno Ona è *Kerrkperrk*."

114 "Anfangs hatten die Pygmäen kein Feuer, darum mußten sie alles roh essen; sie saßen vor ihren Hütten mit ausgestreckten Beinen und froren."

117 "Anfangs bewohnte Gott den Himmel allein, dann schuf er Engel, welche ihm im Himmel dienen und Menschen, welche auf der Erde, die früher unbewohnt war, ihn verehren sollten. Aber es war überall Finsterniß und Kälte und die Engel und Menschen klagten Gott, daß sie die große Kälte und die dichte Finsterniß nicht ertragen könnten."

125 "allgemeine Dunkelheit mit viel Schnee und Eis"

126 "Es war in alter Zeit. Wieder einmal nahte der Frühling. ... Die *Léxuwa* ist aber sehr zartfühlend und empfindlich, sie will besonders vornehm behandelt werden. Als nun jene Männer, Weiber und Kinder so laut und lange schrien, hörte sie diesen Lärm und erregte sich darüber sehr. Tief beleidigt, ließ sie in ihrem Zorn plötzlich einen dichten Schneesturm kommen, begleitet von starkem Frost und viel Eis. Seitdem fiel Schnee und immer wieder Schnee durch ganze Monate. Andauernd fiel Schnee und die ganze Erde bedeckte sich mit Eis; denn es herrschte auch eine sehr empfindliche Kälte. In allen Wasserstraßen gefror das Wasser. Da starben viele, viele Menschen; denn sie konnten ihre Kanus nicht besteigen und hinausfahren, um Nahrung zu suchen. Nicht einmal die

Wohnhütten konnten sie verlassen, um Brennholz zu sammeln; denn überall lag sehr viel Schnee. Immer mehr Menschen starben. Endlich nach langer, langer Zeit hörte der Schneefall auf. ... die ganze Erde war bis hoch über die Bergspitzen damit bedeckt. ... so dick war die Eisdecke, die damals auf der ganzen Erde lagerte. Damals herrschte ein außerordentlich starker Frost und eine erschreckliche Schneemasse war gefallen. Das alles hatte die Léxuwakīpa veranlaßt, sie ist eine sehr feinfühlige, empfindsame Frau. Seit jener Zeit behandeln die Yamana jede Bandurria mit höchster Ehrfurcht."

127 "Die sehr empfindliche Léxuwakīpa fühlte sich durch die Menschen beleidigt. Aus Rache ließ sie sehr viel Schnee fallen. Eine ungeheure Eismasse überdeckte schließlich die ganze Erde. ... Jenes Weib trug sich mit der Absicht, die ganze Welt und alle Menschen zugrunde zu richten."

128 "Die Vereisung vollzog sich gerade zur Zeit der allgemeinen Umwälzung in Yáiaašága, als die Männer ihren Kampf gegen die Weiber führten und sich des kína bemächtigten."

129 "Nu kwam de ijsbergenvloot der witte winterreuzen uit het Noorden aangedreven ... Veel droeve tijden verliepen, waarin de ontzaglijke winterreus opperheerschappij voerde."

131 "... og Vandet strømmede til overalt. Da Jorden blev til paany, var den fuldstændig dækket med Isbræ. Denne gik efterhaanden bort, og der faldt to Mennesker ned fra Himlen, fra hvilke Jorden blev befolket. Man kan hvert Aar se, at Isbræen er i Aftagende."

132 "Au commencement on habitait sur cette terre tout comme aujourd'hui; car ce qui est a toujours été, ce qui se fait s'est toujours fait. L'homme a toujours été pèlerin sur la terre, il a toujours chassé et pêché pour gagner sa subsistance, il a toujours bu, mangé et dormi, il a toujours dormi avec sa femme et procréé des enfants. Or, durant un hiver, il arriva une chose qui n'avait pas toujours été: il tomba tant et tant de neige que la terre en était comme ensevelie, et que le faîte des plus hauts sapins seul paraissait. Ce n'était pas tenable. Aussi tous les animaux qui, alors, demeuraient et conversaient avec l'homme, partirent pour le ciel, en quête de chaleur; car sur cette terre, convertie en glacier, on se mourait de froid et de besoin. ... il faisait sombre et froid sur la terre."

132 "Au commencement des temps ... eut lieu au mois de septembre un déluge de neige. ... la neige qui la couvrait jusqu'au sommet des plus hauts sapins ..."

137 "... cuando llegó la época y sopló el viento Sur, trajo el humo de la helada de Jive'cla y al siguiente día estaba a esta altura (muestra con la mano) una gran helada. Venía de Jive'cla."

144 "... el Ehecatonatiuh en que acabó por nieves y huracanes ... En el Ehecatonatiuh, cuatro cabezas de Ehécatl, el dios de los vientos, soplan huracanes en todas direcciones, y Quetzalcoatl deja caer de los cielos lluvia de nieve que concluye con la humanidad, salvándose tan sólo otro par en una gruta."

145 "... la seconda Età, quale dicono durò anni 4010, dappoi delli quali dicono che ebbe fine il mondo per impeto dei venti fortissimi"

150 "... honraban y adoraban cierta estrella (no pude saber qué estrella era) más que a otra criatura ninguna celestial, ni terrena, porque tuvieron por cierto que su dios Quezalcovatl, dios principalísimo ... de los de Chololla, cuando murió se había convertido en aquella estrella"

150 "tenían sciencia certísima del día que había de aparecer en Oriente y del que se había de poner y desaparecer en Occidente"

151 "Y que el alma del dicho Quetzalcoatl se volvió en estrella, y que era aquella que algunas veces se ve echar de sí un rayo como lanza: y algunas veces se ha visto en esta tierra la tal cometa ó estrella, y tras ella se han visto seguir pestilencias en los indios, y otras calamidades; y es que las tales cometas son señales que Dios puso para denotar alguna cosa ó acaecimiento notable que quiere obrar ó permitir en el mundo."

168 "DER GEMEINSAME NAME FÜR MORGEN- UND ABENDRÖTE"

168 "rotglänzendes Gewölk"

168 "einen (von der Morgen- oder Abendröte) rötlich durchstrahlten Wolkenhaufen"

170 "Wildkuh, die die Weltteile niederstößt, / Feuerschein, der in die Mitte von Himmel und Erde eindringt, / hohe Ištar, die die Weltteile beherrscht ..."

175 "factumq; est aliquando, vt nulla iam sollicitudo maior hominum sit, quam Cæli suspiciendi, ac si forte Venus solito splendidius scintillarit, in Cometam abierit: Si nubes ad Solis occasum non se subitò abdiderit, crucemq; formauerit, monstri id loco habeatur. Sed hæc sibi habeat vulgus pluma leuius ... Augusto mense ex pluribus Italiæ partibus perlatum ad nos fuit, visum per eos dies Cometam Vrsæ maioris postremos pedes lambentem. At nos, qui Venerem subinde ignaræ plebi Cometæ loco fuisse audieramus, simile quid etiam eo tempore suspicati, vigiles illos excubitores facilè hallucinatos existimauimus ..."

205 "Der nun, wenn sie einander packen, und wenn sie einander schlagen, kann Feuer fangen: Es brannte einst dieser Morgenstern. Als er dann ausgebrannt hatte, da fing die Pockenseuche an. Es blieben nur verfallene Hütten übrig, alle ihre Herren starben. Ich selbst hab's gesehen, als dieser Morgenstern brannte, – es sind zweimal zwanzig und zehn und dazu vier Jahre her."

206 "Im Kampf mit den Fixsternen kann die Venus Feuer fangen. Die Datierung, die der Erzähler gibt, könnte mit einem Erinnerungsfehler von zwei Jahren auf den von Coggia entdeckten Kometen 1877 III weisen, der um Mitte Juli der Erde so nahe kam, daß er bei 1,3 Sterngröße mit bloßem Auge am Abendhimmel Salvadors sichtbar war ... Um dieselbe Zeit war die Venus Abendstern, aber der Komet hielt sich fern von ihm, – der Indianer hat diese Erscheinung wohl nachträglich mit einem alten Glauben verbunden, der sich auf einwandfreiere Beobachtungen stützen mag."

219 "cometa crinita, como lo q̂ aparecio el año de 1577"

238 "dans l'eau chaude."

240 "In der Sonne (*atukatši*) befand sich ehemals ein grosser Kessel mit kochendem Wasser. ... Der Häuptling der Störche, überhaupt der Schöpfer aller Vögel, war Mayuruberu. Dieser warf, als das Wasser im Kessel zu Ende ging, einen runden Stein (*pingitšina*) hinein. Der Kessel fiel um, die heisse Flüssigkeit strömte zur Erde und verbrannte Alles, den Wald und auch das Wasser. ... Auf Erden war es finster, Sonne und Mond waren versteckt. ... Der Kessel steht noch in der Sonne, ist aber leer."

247 "Da ward Gott zornig und kehrte voll Grimm in den Himmel zurück. In seinem Zorn vergaß er die Thür, welche zum Himmel führte, zu schließen: da ergoß sich ein Feuermeer vom Himmel auf die Erde nieder; in den Niederungen

	sammelte es sich und kühlte allmählich ab. Aus diesem abgekühlten Feuermeer entstand das Gewässer der Erde, Meere, Seen und Flüsse."
248	"der Weltbeobachtende Mann"
272	"Erscheint am Himmel ein Meteor, so versenkt sich der Zauberer durch Tabakschnupfen in narkotischen Schlaf und erklärt nach dem Erwachen, er sei zum Himmel aufgestiegen und habe das Feuer gelöscht, das sonst die ganze Welt verzehrt hätte."
281	"les six *tzontemocque*, ou étoiles qui tombèrent du ciel, au temps du déluge, d'après les traditions mexicaines."
287	"In alten Zeiten war den Żamaiten das Glück so hold, daß ihnen alles zum Guten gereichte: bald war ihre Zahl so groß, daß ihnen das Land, welches sie bewohnten, zu klein wurde. So kam es, daß sie darnach strebten, ihr Land zu vergrößern. Ihre Nachbarn waren ein streitbares und zauberkundiges Volk; sie verehrten einen großen Stern am Himmel, dieser gab ihnen alles an, was sie zu thun hatten; in Folge dessen geschah es, daß die Żamaiten ihnen stets unterlagen. Da wandten sich diese an Gott und beklagten sich über den Stern. Gott wurde über den Stern böse, er warf denselben mit furchtbarer Kraft hinab auf die Erde, so daß er das ganze zauberkundige Volk, welches gerade zur Feier des Johannisfestes versammelt war, erschlug. Der Stern zersprang in unzählige Splitter, welche über die ganze Erde hinstoben. Nun konnten die Żamaiten sich ungehindert des Landes ihres früheren Feindes bemächtigen."
299	"… Feuers Zeugung ist vom Himmel. / Dort ward Feuer (sanft) gewieget, / Feuers Gluten eingelullet, / In 'nem Korbe (gelben) Kupfers, / In grundlosem Goldgefäße. / Schlug das Feuer Ilmarinen, / Feuer blitzte Wäinämöinen, / In dem nächtig dunklen Norden, / Mit fünf Federn aus dem Schwanze, / Mit drei Federn eines Adlers, / Mit feuergestähltem Schwerte, / Auf 'nes Eisensitzes Ende, / Ueber neun der Himmel oben, / Auf der Wolke dann des zehnten. / Sprühte auf ein Feuers Funken, / Fiel herab ein rothes Knäuel, / Fiel herab ein blaues Knäuel; / Feuers Flamme sprühte nieder, / Rollte unter ihrem Rollen, / Rollte unter ihrer Reise, / Dort in Liemo's Sees Wasser, / Zu fischlosem Binnensee. / Zu barschlosem Binnensee, / In die Spitzen des Seegrases. / … / Daraus kannt' man es als Feuer / Daraus fand man es sei Feuer. / … / Kam ein Jüngling her aus Norden, / Langer Mann aus Pimentola … / Sagte er bei seiner Ankunft, / Ankommend bei Feuers Wüthen: / … / Ukko du, du goldner König, / Bring aus Nordwest eine Wolke, / Wirf 'ne andre her aus Westen, / Blitz' von Osten her die dritte, / Wirf sie Arm in Arm einander, / Donnre sie stets an einander! / Regne Schnee, und regne Wasser, / Regne Hagel, hart wie Eisen, / Auf die argverbrannten Stellen! / Mache Feuers Glut unschädlich, / Mache Feuer unvermögend! / Mache es nun namenlos gleich, / Unter meiner Augen Draufsehn … / … / Maid Maria, kleine Mutter! / … / Wirf das Wasser deiner Schöße / Auf die arg verbrannten Stellen!"
299	"bunten Schlange"
304	"… llamóse Yocajeque [Yocah-Ek'] porque habiendo en él un gran lago de agua muy hondable, dicen los naturales que cayó en él una estrella con grandes pluvias, y así se deja entender, pues a la estrella del alba llaman Noch Eque [Nohoch Ek']; ésta cae al oeste, dejando cuarenta leguas de allí al puerto de Conil al este, y éste es el último término de la tierra firme …"
306	"ceniza"

306	"árboles"
306	"se desplomó el firmamento y hundió la tierra"
320	"racontait que, dans les montagnes, il y avait des figures rupestres, des *rimudong*, œuvres de la divinité, qui disparaissaient parfois et ne se montraient plus qu'à quelques privilégiés ..."
358	"Früher, im Anfange, war die Erde oben, dort wo jetzt der Himmel ist; der Himmel war aber unten. Die Efé hatten Hunger und riefen darum zu Tore, woraufhin die Erde mitsamt allen Nahrungsmitteln nach unten fiel. Der Himmel jedoch verzog nach oben."
360	"die im ganzen Efegebiet von Beni bis zum Nepoko erzählt wird"
360	"Am Anfang war die Erde oben, der Himmel aber, d. h. der Sitz der Gottheit, unten. Zusammen mit Gott war [sic] der Mond und der Blitz ... Von oben herab rieselte ständig Staub und Schmutz und verunreinigte die Speisen Gottes, bis er es überdrüssig wurde und sich nach einem anderen Aufenthaltsort umsah. Er befahl dem Blitz, über der Erde einen Platz ausfindig zu machen. Mit großem Krachen zerteilte der Blitz die Erde und fuhr hinauf. Nachdem der Himmel vorbereitet war, zogen Gott und der Mond nach. Der Mond wohnte oberhalb, der Blitz unterhalb Gottes ..."
361	"Jadis, il en était ainsi: le ciel était en bas et la terre, en haut. Or, comme tous les jours, les hommes sortaient pour prendre de la nourriture, la terre tombait sur eux. Alors, un jour Alu dit: / Il faut que nous changions cela. La terre sera en bas et le ciel en haut. / Alors les hommes plantèrent de la nourriture qui mûrit très bien. ... Or, avant que tout changea, il y avait des hommes en haut et des hommes en bas. Et les hommes qui étaient en haut descendirent et ceux qui étaient en dessous montèrent. Mais ces derniers devinrent mauvais. Personne n'a vu ces hommes, mais on sait qu'ils sont mauvais. La lune et les étoiles sont habitées par beaucoup d'hommes également."
369	"os caxinauás moram, casas fizeram, muito aldeias bonitas com moram, muito legumes abundam [sic]. / os caxinauás em coisa alguma pensam não (nada receiam), muito felizes são, moram, longe-não de rio caudaloso á beira moram. / caxinauás todos moram. / chove compridamente, chove, ao sol alto chove, escuro dentro chove, muito chuvendo compridamente está. / caxinauá outro algum longe ia não, todos casa em deitados estão. / o relampago quebrando-se está, (trovejou), amedrontaram-se, todos deitaram-se. / o ceu quebrou-se, veio, para baixo veio, todos aquelles matou, as caças tambem aquellas matou, os peixes tambem matou, todos aquelles matou, acabou, outro ser algum deixou não, aquelles matou, acabou. / matou, acabou, a terra revirou-se, em cima ceu ser foi, o ceu terra virou. / a terra ceu foi ser, em cima aos caxinauás o ceu áquelles matou. / o ceu revirou-se, áquelles as almas levaram, ceu dentro moraram. / ceu dentro moram, ceu dentro agora são felizes, moram. / ceu dentro a lagoa grande é, ceu dentro muito o rio encheram-se. / terra em muito cousa alguma não muitissimo ha (nada restava com vida) ... o ceu quebrou-se, veio, aquelles matou, acabou. / o ceu quebrou-se, veio, todos aquelles matou, acabou-os, o ceu revirou-se, aquelles levou. / porem os caxinauás outra vez geraram-se."
370	"do outro lado, fronteiro"

371	"Die Erde wechselte mit dem Himmel den Platz. Der Himmel fiel auf die Kaschinaua und tötete sie. Der Himmel wendete sich wieder um, und die Seelen, die im Himmel wohnten, nahmen sie mit sich."
379	"Dann werden die sieben unbarmherzigen Strahlen der Sonne, die den kleinen Wesen Verderben bereiten, durchglühte Kohlen regnen lassen."
394	"Riesenknochen"
421	"Niet verre van hier in het gebergte ten Noord-oosten vind men de Mammuts tanden en beenen … De Heidenen, als de Jakuti, Tungusi en Ostiakky, zeggen, dat deze dieren zich in de aarde, of 't schoon, wegens den harden winter, noch zoo sterk vriest, zich geduriq ophouden, en heen en weêr gaan; verhaalen ook dikwils gezien te hebben, dat, wanneer zoo een dier gegaan had, de aarde boven het zelve zich opwelde, en dan wederom inviel, en eenen diepen kuil maakte. Zy meenen ook verder, dat by aldien dit dier zoo hoog komt, dat het de lucht ruikt of ziet, het zelve aanstonds sterft, en dat 'er daarom, aan de hooge oeveren van den vloed, alwaar zy onvoorziens uitkomen, veele dood gevonden worden."
425	"fueron los gigantes, y que de aquellos son los grandes huesos que dije que agora se hallan en las minas y en otras partes debajo de la tierra: los que agora son preguntados no dicen que segund sus antepasados padres y abuelos, les han dicho. Aquestos huesos son de unos hombres muy grandes y muy altos que de otras partes dizque vinieron, que onde antes de ellos habia gentes en aquesta segunda edad."
425	"hauía entonces gigantes, y que son dellos los huesos que nuestros Españoles han hallado cauando minas, y sepulturas. De cuya medida, y proporciõ, paresce como eran aq̃llos hõbres de veynte palmos en alto. Estature es grãdissima, pero certissima."
426	"los innumerables depósitos fósiles de elefantes que se han descubierto en diferentes direcciones, y que corresponden á época tan remota"
426	"los cronistas españoles tuvieron esos fósiles por huesos de gigantes."
465	"En cuanto a las aguas introducidas en los valles por Caicaivilu, dieron lugar a la formación de los golfos, canales y fiordos. Por su parte, las prominencias elevadas por Tentenvilu originaron ese semillero de islas de todas formas y tamaños que configuran los archipiélagos sureños, más allá del paralelo 41°."
466	"*Kwányip* kam aus dem Norden zu Fuß in unser Land. Seine Guanacos trieb er vor sich her, dabei halfen ihm seine Hunde. Damals [= bei seiner ersten Ankunft] zog er bis zum Cabo San Pablo. Hier sieht man in den Steinen noch die Fußabdrücke der ersten Herde zahmer Guanacos, die er mitgebracht hatte. … Wenn alle seine Guanacos verzehrt worden waren, zog er nach dem Norden zurück. Dort holte er sich eine andere Herde von zahmen Guanacos. Diese trieb er vor sich her. Damit kam er wieder in unser Land."
467	"Damals gab es noch schmale Übergänge. Auf diesen konnte jedermann zu Fuß von einem Ufer zum andern gelangen. … So konnte man auf jenem Übergange von unserer Insel aus das Festland im Norden erreichen. Als eines Tages sehr viele Leute wieder hier auf der Großen Insel zusammengekommen waren, um Guanacos zu jagen, gab es unerwartet eine gewaltige Aufregung in der Natur und eine starke Erschütterung der Erde, hohe Wellen wälzten sich heran und drangen tief ins Land vor. Erst dann erholten sich die Leute wieder von ihrer großen Angst, als Ruhe eingetreten war. Baldigst wollten sie in ihre Heimat

	zurückeilen. Aber die gewohnten Übergänge waren jetzt vom Wasser verdeckt. So sahen sich die Leute von ihrer Heimat abgesperrt und jeder Rückkehr beraubt. Da ein Fortkommen nicht mehr möglich war, verstreuten sie sich auf der Insel nach allen Richtungen hin."
469	"une étendue d'eau … recouvrait les abîmes, et le dieu Tino taata flottait à la surface"
469	"corps humain"
469	"le dieu type ou source de la race humaine"
474	"In alten Zeiten war der Himmel so nahe der Erde, dass die Rinder an ihm lecken konnten."
474	"man Gott habe sehen und berühren können"
476	"… nemen aan, dat vroeger de hemel dicht bij de aarde was; de priesters kwamen in den hemel langs eene ladder. Men schrapte het vet toen van den hemel met alang-alangbladeren. Eens gelastte een man zijne vrouw weer vet te gaan halen; in hare verstoordheid nam zij een bijl en hakte in den hemel; deze werd nu naar boven getrokken en de vrouw werd medegenomen."
477	"Der Himmel war … Anfangs dicht über der Erde; er besteht aus einer essbaren, öhligen Substanz, und diente den Menschen zur Nahrung. Aber der Anak Mahatara, Mahataras, des höchsten Gottes, Sohn, lehrte die Menschen Reiss [sic] pflanzen, etc., worüber Mahatara sich erzürnte, und er rückte den Himmel weiter von der Erde fort."
488	"pájaro luna"
490	"Nebel oder dunkles Gewölk oder der Himmel, der finster auf der Erde lag, sie drückte, bis jemand oder etwas ihn lüpfte und immer höher schob, wodurch es hell wurde."
491	"Mientras tanto había amanecido. Uno de los hombres se acordó de los dientes de *Majôctsi*, el tucutucu. Los había guardado durante muchos años metidos entre una piola arrollada. Esto los salvó. Cortó el cielo con los dientes de *Mâjoctsi*. Cortaba rápido. De repente se abrió el cielo sobre este hombre. Corriendo fue hasta los demás y les repartió los dientes de *Majôctsi* que tenía. Todos trabajaron para cortar el cielo sobre ellos. Muy pronto se abrió pudiendo ver, otra vez, el día. Quedaron muy contentos. … El hombre que era dueño de los dientes de *Majôctsi*, fue el que salvó a los de su clan. … Cada vez que cazaba un *Mâjoctsi*, los guardaba, porque solía escuchar a los antiguos hombres que decían: / – Guarden bien los dientes del *Majôctsi*. Ténganlos preparados para cuando se caiga *vôôs*. / Al cortar el cielo, de súbito se convirtió en humo y se fue para arriba. Porque, se dice, era bastante grueso cuando cayó. … Sólo se salvaron aquellos que estaban cerca del hombre que tenía los dientes del *Majôctsi*. Todos los años los venía guardando. Aquellos fueron los únicos que se salvaron."

bibliography

Adam, L., 'Une Génèse Vogoule', *Revue de philologie et d'ethnographie*, 1 (1874), 9-14
Aillaud, J. P. (ed.), *Dictionary of the Portuguese and English Languages, in Two Parts; Portuguese and English, and English and Portuguese: Wherein I. The WORDS Are Explained in their Different Meanings, by Examples from the Best Portuguese and English Writers. II. The ETYMOLOGY of the Portuguese Generally Indicated from the Latin, Arabic, and Other Languages. Throughout the Whole Are Interpreted a Great Number of Phrases and Proverbs. By Anthony Vieyra, Transtagano. A New Edition, Carefully Corrected, Greatly Enlarged, and very Considerably Improved*, vol. 1: *Portuguese and English* (London: F. Wingrave; J. Walker; Scatcherd and Letterman; Wilkie and Robinson; J. Cuthell; Longman, Hurst, Rees, Orme and Brown; Cadell and Davies; C. Law; Lackington, Allen and Co.; Crosby and Co.; T. Boosey; Black, Parry, and Co; J. Mawman; J. Booker; Dulau and Co; J. Richardson J. M. Richardson; J. Asperne; and J. Faulder, 1813)
Akamatsu Chijō & Akiba Takashi, 朝鮮巫俗の研究 (*Chōsen Fuzoku-no Kenkyū*; 1; Seoul: Ōsakayagō Shoten, 1937)
Alexander, J. E., 'Waccamaw – The Fallen Star', *The American Indian*, 5. 3 (1950), 30-39
Allan, D. S. & J. B. Delair, *When the Earth Nearly Died; Compelling Evidence of a World Cataclysm 11,500 Years Ago* (Bath: Gateway Books, 1995)
Anderson, A. J. O. & Ch. E. Dibble (trs.), *Florentine Codex; General History of the Things of New Spain; Fray Bernardino de Sahagún*, vol. 8: *Book 7 – The Sun, Moon, and Stars, and the Binding of the Years; Translated from the Aztec into English, with Notes and Illustrations* ('Monographs of the School of American Research', 14. 8; Santa Fe, New Mexico: The School of American Research, 1953)
Anderson, W., *Nordasiatische Flutsagen* ('Acta et Commentationes Universitatis Dorpatensis', series B, 4. 3; Tartu: C. Mattiesen, 1923)
anonymous, 'Miscellanies, Original and Select', *The Asiatic Journal and Monthly Register for British and Foreign India, China, and Australasia*, 7 (1832), 145-159
anonymous (ed.), *Report of the Select Committee of the Legislative Council on the Aborigines; Together with the Proceedings of Committee, Minutes of Evidence, and Appendices* (Melbourne: John Perres, 1858-1859)
anonymous ['a taluqdar of Oudh'] (tr.), *The Matsya Puranam* (1; 'The Sacred Books of the Hindus Translated by Various Sanskrit Scholars', 17. 1; Allahabad: Apurva Krishna Bose, 1916)
anonymous, 'Last of the Paka-Jakes', *Time; The Weekly Newsmagazine*, 41. 14 (5 April 1943), 28
anonymous, *Global Volcanism Program* (Washington, District of Columbia: Smithsonian Institution National Museum of Natural History, 1968-)
anonymous, 'International Living Lakes Conference; Credo Mutwa: Keynote Address', *Mono Lake Newsletter*, 22. 3 (Winter 2000), 10-11
Aston, W. G. (tr.), *Nihongi, Chronicles of Japan from the Earliest Times to A. D. 697. Translated from the Original Chinese and Japanese* (1; 'Transactions and Proceedings of the Japan Society, London', 1; London: Kegan Paul, Trench, Trübner & Co., 1896)

Aveni, A. F., *Skywatchers of Ancient Mexico* ('The Texas Pan American Series'; Austin, Texas: University of Texas Press, 1980)

Bandy, A. C. (tr.), *On Celestial Signs (De Ostentis); Ioannes Lydus; Translated and Edited* (Lewiston, New York: The Edwin Mellen Press, 2013)

Barefoot, D. W., *Touring the Backroads of North Carolina's Upper Coast* (Winston-Salem, North Carolina: John F. Blair, 1995)

Barich, M. (tr.), *Valerius Flaccus,* Argonautica (Gambier, Ohio: Xoxox Press, 2009)

Barrett, Ch., *The Bunyip and Other Mythical Monsters and Legends* (Melbourne: Reed & Harris, 1946)

Barría, N. G., *Tesoro mitológico del Archipiélago de Chiloé; Bosquejo interpretativo* (Santiago, Chile: Editorial Andres Bello, 1997)

Basedow, H., 'Aboriginal Rock Carvings of Great Antiquity in South Australia', *The Journal of the Royal Anthropological Institute of Great Britain and Ireland*, 44 (1914), 195-211

Bastian, A., *Reisen in China von Peking zur mongolischen Grenze und Rueckkehr nach Europa* ('Die Voelker des oestlichen Asien. Studien und Reisen', 6; Jena: Hermann Costenoble, 1871)

Basu, M. N., 'The Bunas of Bengal', *Journal of the Department of Letters*, 32 (1939), 1-120

Bate, H. N. (tr.), *The Sibylline Oracles; Books III-V* ('Translations of Early Documents', 2; 'Hellenistic-Jewish Texts'; London: The MacMillan Company, 1918)

Bauer, B. S., V. Smith-Oka & G. E. Cantarutti (trs.), *Account of the Fables and Rites of the Incas; Cristóbal de Molina* ('The William & Bettye Nowlin Series in Art, History, and Culture of the Western Hemisphere'; Austin, Texas: University of Texas Press, 2011)

Beals, C., *Stories Told by the Aztecs before the Spaniards Came* (London: Abelard-Schuman, 1970)

Bellamy, H. S., *Moons, Myths and Man; A Reinterpretation* (London: Faber and Faber, 1936)

Bellamy, H. S., *In the Beginning God; A New Scientific Vindication of the Cosmogonic Myths in the Book of Genesis* (London: Faber & Faber, 1945)

Beltran, P., *Arte de el idioma Maya reducido a succintas reglas, y semilexicon Yucateco* (Mexico City: Viuda de D. Joseph Bernardo de Hogal, 1746)

Bengoa, J., *Historia del pueblo Mapuche (Siglo XIX y XX)* ('Biblioteca del Bicentenario', 7; Santiago, Chile: LOM Ediciones, 2000^6)

Bennett, G., 'A Trip to Queensland in Search of Fossils', *The Annals and Magazine of Natural History, Including Zoology, Botany, and Geology*, series 4, 9 (April 1872), 314-321

Berezkin, Y., 'Tale Type and Motif Indices', at http://starling.rinet.ru/kozmin/tales/index.php?index=berezkin (no date; last accessed 6 May 2017)

Berndt, R. M., 'Panaramittee Magic', *Records of the South Australian Museum*, 20 (1987), 15-28

Berndt, R. M. & C. H. Berndt, *The Speaking Land; Myth and Story in Aboriginal Australia* ('Penguin Books'; Ringwood, Victoria: Penguin Books, 1989)

Bhathal, R., 'Pre-Contact Astronomy', *Journal and Proceedings of the Royal Society of New South Wales*, 142. 3-4 (2009), 15-23

Bierhorst, J. (tr.), *History and Mythology of the Aztecs; The Codex Chimalpopoca* (Tucson, Arizona: The University of Arizona Press, 1992)

Billerbeck, M. & A. Neumann-Hartmann (tr.), *Stephani Byzantii Ethnica Recensuerunt Germanice Verterunt Adnotationibus Indicibusque Instruxerunt*, vol. 4: Π-Y ('Corpus Fontium Historiae Byzantinae; Consilio Societatis Internationalis Studiis Byzantinis Provehendis Destinatae Editum', 43. 4; 'Series Berolinensis'; Berlin: De Gruyter, 2016)

Black, J. A., G. Cunningham, J. Ebeling, E. Flückiger-Hawker, E. Robson, J. Taylor & G. Zólyomi (trs.), *The Electronic Text Corpus of Sumerian Literature* (Oxford, 1998-2006), at http://etcsl.orinst.ox.ac.uk/ (last accessed 6 May 2017)

Boas, F., 'The Central Eskimo', *Annual Report of the Bureau of Ethnology to the Secretary of the Smithsonian Institution*, 6 for 1884-1885 (1888), 409-669

Boas, F., 'The Mythology of the Bella Coola Indians', *Memoirs of the American Museum of Natural History*, 2 (Anthropology, 1; *Publications of the Jesup North Pacific Expedition*, 1. 2 for 1898-1900) (1900), 25-128

Boas, F. (ed.), *Folk-Tales of Salishan and Sahaptin Tribes* ('Memoirs of the American Folk-Lore Society', 11; Lancaster, Pennsylvania: The American Folk-Lore Society, 1917)

Bolio, A. M. (tr.), *Libro de Chilam Balam de Chumayel* ('Biblioteca del estudiante universitario', 21; Mexico City: Ediciones de la Universidad Nacional Autonoma, 1941)

Bousset, W., *The Antichrist Legend; A Chapter in Christian and Jewish Folklore* (tr. A. H. Keane; London: Hutchinson and Co., 1896)

Brasseur de Bourbourg, *S'il Existe des sources de l'histoire primitive du Mexique dans les monuments Égyptiens et de l'histoire primitive de l'ancien monde dans les monuments Américains?* (Paris: Maisonneuve et Cie, 1864)

Bricker, V. R., E. Po'ot Yah & O. Dzul de Po'ot (eds.), *A Dictionary of the Maya Language: As Spoken in Hocabá, Yucatán* (Salt Lake City, Utah: University of Utah Press, 1998)

Bridges, E. L., *Uttermost Part of the Earth* (New York: E. P. Dutton & Co., 1948)

Brodersen, K. (tr.), *Gaius Iulius Solinus; Wunder der Welt; Lateinisch und deutsch; Eingeleitet, übersetzt und kommentiert* ('Edition Antike'; Darmstadt: Wissenschaftliche Buchgesellschaft, 2014)

Brown, Ch. B., 'Indian Picture Writing in British Guiana', *The Journal of the Anthropological Institute of Great Britain and Ireland*, 2 (1873), 254-257

Brown, F., S. R. Driver & Ch. A. Briggs (eds.), *A Hebrew and English Lexicon of the Old Testament with an Appendix Containing the Biblical Aramaic Based on the Lexicon of William Gesenius as Translated by Edward Robinson Late Professor in the Union Theological Seminary, New York* (Oxford: Clarendon Press, 1906)

Brundage, B. C., *The Phoenix of the Western World: Quetzalcoatl and the Sky Religion* ('The Civilization of the American Indian Series'; Norman, Oklahoma: University of Oklahoma Press, 1982)

Bryant, E., *Tsunami; The Underrated Hazard* (New York: Springer, 2008[2], 2014[3])

Buber, S. (ed.), *Majan Gannim; Commentar zu Job von Rabbi Samuel ben Nissim Masnuth (Lebte in Aleppo im XII. Jahrhundert.); Zum ersten Male nach einer Oxforder Handschrift herausgegeben, mit Bemerkungen und einer Einleitung versehen* (Berlin: H. Itzkowski, 1889)

Buckland, F. T., *Curiosities of Natural History* (London: Richard Bentley, 1867[6])

Buckland, W., *Reliquiæ Diluvianæ; Or, Observations on the Organic Remains Contained in Caves, Fissures, and Diluvial Gravel, and on Other Geological Phenomena, Attesting the Action of an Universal Deluge* (London: John Murray, 1823)

Cagni, L. (ed.), *L'Epopea di Erra* ('Studi Semitici', 34; Rome: Istituto di Studi del Vicino Oriente, 1969)

Cai, M. (tr.), 'Li Chaowei 李朝威, 'The Tale of the Supernatural Marriage at Dongting', 洞庭靈姻傳', in W. H. Nienhauser junior (ed.), *Tang Dynasty Tales: A Guided Reader* (2; Singapore: World Scientific, 2016), 1-70

Campbell, A. H., 'Aboriginal Traditions and the Prehistory of Australia', *Mankind; The Australian Journal of Anthropology*, 6. 10 (December 1967), 476-481

Capell, A., 'Mythology in Northern Kimberley, North-West Australia', *Oceania; A Journal Devoted to the Study of the Native Peoples of Australia, New Guinea and the Islands of the Pacific Ocean*, 9. 4 (1939), 382-404

Capistrano de Abreu, J., *Rã-txa hu-ni-ku-ĩ; A lingua dos Caxinauás do Rio Ibuaçu; Affluente do Muru (Prefeitura de Tarauacá)* (Rio de Janeiro: Leuzinger, 1914)

Cárdenas Tabies, A., *Usos y costumbres de Chiloé* (Santiago, Chile: Editorial Nascimento, 1978)

Carson, R., *Mattamuskeet: A National Wildlife Refuge* ('US Fish & Wildlife Publications', 4; Washington, District of Columbia: United States Government Printing Office, 1947)

Cawthorne, A. N., *The Legend of Kuperree; Or, the Red Kangaroo. An Aboriginal Tradition of the Port Lincoln Tribe. A Metrical Version* (Adelaide: Alfred N. Cawthorne, 1880s[2])

Chase-Sardi, M. (ed.), *Pequeño Decameron Nivacle; Literatura oral de una etnia del Chaco Paraguayo* ('Ediciones NAPA', 1. 11; Asunción: Ediciones NAPA, 1981)

Chavero, A., 'Explicacion del códice geroglífico de Mr. Aubin', in D. Duran, *Historia de las Indias de Nueva España y Islas de Tierra Firme* (2; Mexico City: Ignacio Escalante, 1880), 1-172

Chen Zhao-Fu, *Découverte de l'art préhistorique en Chine* (tr. A. Didier; Paris: Albin Michel, 1988)

Cherniak, A. (tr.), *Mahābhārata; Book Six; Bhīṣma*, vol. 1: *Including the 'Bhagavad Gītā' in Context* ('The Clay Sanskrit Library'; New York: New York University Press, 2008)

Chippindale, Ch., 'Hunter-Gatherer Imagery in Aboriginal Australia: Interpreting Rock Art by Informed and Formal Methods', in G. Berghaus (ed.), *New Perspectives on Prehistoric Art* (Westport, Connecticut: Praeger, 2004), 31-49

Christenson, A. J. (tr.), *Popol Vuh; The Sacred Book of the Maya; The Great Classic of Central American Spirituality, Translated from the Original Maya Text* (New York: O Books, 2003)

Cochrane, E., 'Velikovsky and Oedipus', *Aeon; A Symposium on Myth and Science*, 1. 6 (1988), 14-38

Cochrane, E., 'On Comets and Kings', *Aeon; A Symposium on Myth and Science*, 2. 1 (1989), 53-75

Cochrane, E., 'Indra: A Case Study in Comparative Mythology', *Aeon; A Symposium on Myth and Science*, 2. 4 (1991a), 49-76

Cochrane, E., 'The Death of Heracles', *Aeon; A Symposium on Myth and Science*, 2. 5 (1991b), 55-72

Cochrane, E., 'On Mars and Pestilence', *Aeon; A Journal on Myth and Science*, 3. 4 (1993), 59-79

Cochrane, E., 'Sothis and the Morning Star in the Pyramid Texts', *Aeon; A Journal on Myth and Science*, 3. 5 (1994a), 77-94

Cochrane, E., 'On Dragons and Red Dwarves', *Aeon; A Journal on Myth and Science*, 3. 6 (1994b), 70-83

Cochrane, E., 'The Milky Way', *Aeon; A Journal on Myth and Science*, 4. 4 (1996), 39-65

Cochrane, E., *Martian Metamorphoses; The Planet Mars in Ancient Myth and Religion* (Ames, Iowa: Aeon Press, 1997a)
Cochrane, E., *The Many Faces of Venus; The Planet Venus in Ancient Myth and Religion* (Ames, Iowa: Aeon Press, 1997b)
Cochrane, E., 'Samson Revealed', *Aeon; A Journal of Myth and Science*, 4. 6 (1997c), 67-84
Cochrane, E., 'Stairway to Heaven', *Aeon; A Journal of Myth, Science and Ancient History*, 5. 1 (1997d), 69-77
Cochrane, E., 'Sky Woman', *Aeon; A Journal of Myth, Science, and Ancient History*, 6. 3 (2002), 80-106
Cochrane, E., *Starf*cker: The Catastrophic Conjunction of Venus and Mars* (Ames, Iowa: Aeon Press, 2006)
Cochrane, E., 'The Light-Bringer', *Chronology & Catastrophism Review* (2015: 2), 29-38
Cochrane, E., *Phaethon; The Star that Fell from Heaven* (Ames, Iowa: Kronos Press, 2017)
Cochrane, E. & D. Talbott, 'When Venus Was a Comet', *Kronos; A Journal of Interdisciplinary Synthesis*, 12. 1 (1987), 2-24
Cojazzi = Coiazzi, A. [anonymous], "Folk-lore" fueghino', *Bollettino Salesiano; Periodico della Pia Unione dei Cooperatori Salesiani di D. Bosco*, 35. 5 (1911), 140-145
Colebrooke, H. T., 'Extract of a Letter from Captain William Spencer Webb, 29th March, 1819, Containing an Account of his Journey in Thibet, and Pilgrimage to the Temple of Kédár Nát'h', *The Quarterly Journal of Science, Literature, and the Arts*, 9. 17 (1820), 61-69
Conway, Th., 'Halley's Comet Legends among the Great Lakes Ojibwa Indians', *Archaeoastronomy*, 8. 1 (1985), 98-105
Conway, Th., 'The Conjurer's Lodge: Celestial Narratives from Algonkian Shamans', in R. A. Williamson & C. R. Farrer (eds.), *Earth and Sky; Visions of the Cosmos in Native American Folklore* (Albuquerque, New Mexico: University of New Mexico Press, 1992), 236-259
Copenhaver (tr.), B. P., *Hermetica; The Greek Corpus Hermeticum and the Latin Asclepius in a New English Translation, with Notes and Introduction* (Cambridge: Cambridge University Press, 1992)
Cranz, D., *Historie von Grönland enthaltend die Beschreibung des Landes und der Einwohner u. insbesondere die Geschichte der dortigen Mission der evangelischen Brüder zu Neu-Herrnhut und Lichtenfels* (Barby, Saxony-Anhalt: Heinrich Detlef Ebers, 1765)
Curtis, E. S., *The North American Indian; Being a Series of Volumes Picturing and Describing the Indians of the United States[, the Dominion of Canada,] and Alaska* (14; Norwood, Massachusetts: Plimpton Press, 1924)
Dalley, S. (tr.), *Myths from Mesopotamia; Creation, the Flood, Gilgamesh, and Others* ('Oxford World's Classics'; Oxford: Oxford University Press, 2000²)
Dan, J. (ed.), ספר הישר (Jerusalem: Mosad Bialiq, 1986)
Darmesteter, J. (tr.), *The Zend-Avesta*, vol. 1: *The Vendîdâd* ('The Sacred Books of the East', 4; Oxford: Clarendon Press, 1880)
Davidson, D. S., *Aboriginal Australian and Tasmanian Rock Carvings and Paintings* ('Memoirs of the American Philosophical Society Held at Philadelphia for Promoting Useful Knowledge', 5; Philadelphia, Pennsylvania: The American Philosophical Society, 1936)
Davidson, M. O., 'No. 23', *Report of the Commissioner of Indian Affairs* (1865), 131-136
Davies, P. V. (tr.), *Macrobius: The Saturnalia* ('Records of Civilization; Sources and Studies', 79; New York: Columbia University Press, 1969)

Dawson, G. M., 'Notes on the Shuswap People of British Columbia', *Proceedings and Transactions of the Royal Society of Canada*, 9. 2 for 1891 (1892), 3-44

Dawson, J., *Australian Aborigines; The Languages and Customs of Several Tribes of Aborigines in the Western District of Victoria, Australia* (Melbourne: George Robertson, 1881)

Day, J., *Yahweh and the Gods and Goddesses of Canaan* ('Journal for the Study of the Old Testament', supplement 265; Sheffield: Sheffield Academic Press, 2000)

de Bovis, E., 'De la Société Tahitienne à l'arrivée des Européens', *Revue Coloniale*, series 2, 14 (1855), 368-408, 510-539 = *Tahitian Society before the Arrival of the Europeans* (tr. R. D. Craig; Laie, Hawai'i: Brigham Young University Press, 1976)

de Ciudad Real, A. (ed.), *Diccionario de Motul Maya* (1; Motul, c1577)

de Gomara, F. L. [anonymous], *Hispania Victrix; Primera y segvnda parte de la historia general de las Indias cõ todo el descubrimiento, y cosas notables que han acaescido dende que se ganaron hasta el año de 1551, Con la conquista de Mexico, y de la nueua España* (Medina del Campo, Spain: Guillermo de Millis, 1553)

de Harlez, C. (tr.), *Textes Tâoïstes traduits des originaux Chinois* ('Annales du Musée Guimet', 20; Paris: Ernest Leroux, 1891)

de Humboldt, A., *Researches, Concerning the Institutions & Monuments of the Ancient Inhabitants of America, with Descriptions & Views of Some of the Most Striking Scenes in the Cordilleras!* (2; tr. H. M. Williams; London: Longman, Hurst, Rees, Orme & Brown, J. Murray & H. Colburn, 1814)

de la Garza, M. (ed.), *Relaciones histórico-geográficas de la Gobernación de Yucatán*, vol. 2: *Mérida, Valladolid y Tabasco* (Mexico City: Universidad Nacional Autónoma, 1983)

de Molina, Alonso, *Vocabvlario en lengva mexicana y castellana* (Mexico City: Casa de Antonio de Spinosa, 1571)

de Rosny, L. (ed.), *Archives paléographiques de l'Orient et de l'Amérique publiées avec des notices historiques et philologiques* (1. 1; Paris: Maisonneuve et Cie, 1869)

de Sahagun, B., *Historia general de las cosas de Nueva España* (2; Mexico City: Pedro Robredo, 1938)

de Smet, P. J., *Oregon Missions and Travels over the Rocky Mountains, in 1845-46* (New York: Edward Dunigan, 1847)

de Tudela Bueso, J. P. (ed.), *Obras escogidas de Fray Bartolome de las Casas*, vol. 4: *Apologetica historia; estudio critico preliminar y edicion* ('Biblioteca de autores españoles desde la formacion del lenguaje hasta nuestros dias (continuación)', 106; Madrid: J. Sánchez de Ocaña y Cía, 1958)

del Chamberlain, V., *When Stars Came Down to Earth; Cosmology of the Skidi Pawnee Indians of North America* ('Ballena Press Anthropological Papers', 26; Los Altos, California: Ballena Press, 1982)

Deloria, V., *Red Earth; White Lies; Native Americans and the Myth of Scientific Fact* (New York: Scribner, 1995)

Densmore, F., *Teton Sioux Music* ('Smithsonian Institution Bureau of American Ethnology Bulletin', 61; Washington, District of Columbia: Government Printing Office, 1918)

Dixon, R. M. W., *The Dyirbal Language of North Queensland* ('Cambridge Studies in Linguistics', 9; Cambridge: Cambridge University Press, 1972)

Dixon, R. M. W., *Words of our Country; Stories, Place Names and Vocabulary in Yidiny, the Aboriginal Language of the Cairns-Yarrabah Region* (St. Lucia: University of Queensland Press, 1991)

Donnelly, I., *Ragnarok: The Age of Fire and Gravel* (New York: D. Appleton and Company, 1883)

Dorsey, G. A., *The Pawnee; Mythology (Part I); Collected under the Auspices of the Carnegie Institute of Washington* ('Carnegie Institution of Washington Publication', 59; Washington, District of Columbia: The Carnegie Institution of Washington, 1906)

Dow, A. (tr.), *The History of Hindostan; From the Earliest Account of Time, to the Death of Akbar; Translated from the Persian of Mahummud Casim Ferishta of Delhi: Together with a Dissertation Concerning the RELIGION and PHILOSOPHY of the BRAHMINS; With an Appendix, Concerning the History of the MOGUL EMPIRE, from its Decline in the Reign of MAHUMMUD SHAW, to the Present Times* (1; London: T. Becket & P. A. de Hondt, 1768)

Drake, S. & C. D. O'Malley (trs.), *The Controversy on the Comets of 1618; Galileo Galilei; Horatio Grassi; Mario Guiducci; Johann Kepler* (Philadelphia, Pennsylvania: University of Pennsylvania Press, 1960)

Dugan, K. G., 'Darwin and *Diprotodon*: The Wellington Caves Fossils and the Law of Succession', *Proceedings of the Linnean Society of New South Wales*, 104. 4 (460) (1980), 265-272

Dutt, M. N. (tr.), *Mahābhārata; Sanskrit Text and English Translation*, vol. 2: Vana Parva ('Parimal Sanskrit Series', 60; Delhi: Parimal Publications, 2008)

Edmonson, M. S., 'The Songs of Dzitbalche: A Literary Commentary', *Tlalocan*, 9 (1982), 173-208

Edmonson, M. S. (tr.), *Heaven Born Merida and its Destiny; The Book of Chilam Balam of Chumayel* ('The Texas Pan American Series'; Austin, Texas: University of Texas Press, 1986)

Egede, P., *Continuation af Relationerne betreffende den Grønlandske Missions Tilstand og Beskaffenhed, forfattet i form af en Journal fra anno 1734 til 1740. Af Colonien Christians-Haab udi Disco-Bugt* (Copenhagen: Johann Christoph. Groth, 1740)

Egede, P., *Nachrichten von Grönland. Aus einem Tagebuche, geführt von 1721 bis 1788* (tr.; Copenhagen: Christian Gottlob Prost, 1790)

Ehrenreich, P., *Beiträge zur Völkerkunde Brasiliens* ('Veröffentlichungen aus dem königlichen Museum für Völkerkunde', 2. 1-2; Berlin: W. Spemann, 1891)

Elkin, A. P., 'The Origin and Interpretation of Petroglyphs in South-East Australia', *Oceania; A Journal Devoted to the Study of the Native Peoples of Australia, New Guinea and the Islands of the Pacific Ocean*, 20. 2 (1949), 119-157

Elliger, K., W. Rudolph & A. Schenker (eds.), תורה נביאים וכתובים *Biblia Hebraica Stuttgartensia* (Stuttgart: Deutsche Bibelgesellschaft, 1997[5])

Emory, K. P., 'The Tuamotuan Creation Charts by Paiore', *Journal of the Polynesian Society*, 48/189 (1939), 1-29

Erdoes, R. & A. Ortiz, *American Indian Myths and Legends* ('Pantheon Fairy Tale & Folklore Library Press'; New York: Pantheon Books, 1984)

Erwin, R. P., 'Indian Rock Writing in Idaho', *Biennial Report of the Board of Trustees of the State Historical Society of Idaho*, 12 (1930), 35-111

Evans, I. H. N., 'Folk Stories of the Tempassuk and Tuaran Districts, British North Borneo', *The Journal of the Royal Anthropological Institute of Great Britain and Ireland*, 43 (1913), 422-479

Falconer, H. & P. T. Cautley, *Fauna Antiqua Sivalensis, Being the Fossil Zoology of the Sewalik Hills, in the North of India*, vol. 1: Proboscidea (London: Smith, Elder and Co., 1846)

Farstad, A. L. (ed.), *The Holy Bible Containing the Old and New Testaments; NKJV; New King James Version; Reference Edition* (Nashville, Tennessee: Thomas Nelson, 1982)

Firestone, R., A. West & S. Warwick-Smith, *The Cycle of Cosmic Catastrophes: Flood, Fire and Famine in the History of Civilization* (Rochester, Vermont: Bear and Company, 2006)

Flood, J. & B. David, 'Traditional Systems of Encoding Meaning in Wardaman Rock Art, Northern Territory, Australia', *Artefact; Pacific Rim Archaeology; The Journal of the Archaeological and Anthropological Society of Victoria*, 17 (1994), 6-22

Fornander, A., *An Account of the Polynesian Race; Its Origin and Migrations and the Ancient History of the Hawaiian People to the Times of Kamehameha I* (1; 'The English and Foreign Philosophical Library', 'Extra Series', 3; London: Trübner & Co., 1878)

Forsyth, N., *The Old Enemy; Satan and the Combat Myth* (Princeton, New Jersey: Princeton University Press, 1987)

Fowler, H. N. (tr.), *Plato in Twelve Volumes*, vol. 8: *The Statesman; Philebus* ('Loeb Classical Library', 164; London: William Heinemann, 1925)

Frachtenberg, L. J., *Lower Umpqua Texts and Notes on the Kusan Dialects* ('Columbia University Contributions to Anthropology', 4; New York: Columbia University Press, 1914)

Frachtenberg, L. J., 'Siuslawan (Lower Umpqua)', in F. Boas (ed.), *Handbook of American Indian Languages* (2; 'Smithsonian Institution Bureau of American Ethnology Bulletin', 40; Washington, District of Columbia: Government Printing Office, 1922), 431-629

Frazer, J. G. (tr.), *Apollodorus; The Library*, vol. 2 ('Loeb Classical Library', 122; London: William Heinemann, 1921)

Freedman, H. (tr.), *Shabbath; Translated into English with Notes, Glossary and Indices* (2; 'The Babylonian Talmud'; '*Seder Mo'ed*', 1; London: The Soncino Press, 1938) = *Shabbath; Translated into English with Notes and Glossary* ('Hebrew-English Edition of the Babylonian Talmud'; '*Seder Mo'ed*'; London: The Soncino Press, 1972)

Funk, S. (ed.), *Bibel und Babel* ('Monumenta Hebraica'; 'Monumenta Talmudica', 1; Vienna: Orion-Verlag, 1913)

Ganander, Ch., *Mythologia Fennica, eller förklaring öfver de Nomina Propria de Astrorum, Idolorum, Locorum, Virorum, &c. eller afgudar och afgudinnor, forntidens märkelige personer, offer och offer-ställen, gamla sedvänjor, jättar, troll, skogs-sjö och bergs-rån m. m. som förekomma i de äldre Finska troll-runor, synnyt, sanat, sadut, arwotuxet &c. samt än brukas och nämnas i dagligt tal; til deras tjenst, som vela i grund förstå det Finska språket, och hafva smak för Finska historien och poësin, af gamla runor samlad och uttydd* (Turku: Frenckellska Boktryckeriet, 1789)

Gatschet, A. S., 'Mythologic Text in the Klamath Language of Southern Oregon', *The American Antiquarian. A Quarterly Journal Devoted to Early American History, Ethnology and Archæology*, 1. 3 (1879), 161-166

Gatschet, A. S., *The Klamath Indians of Southwestern Oregon* (1; 'Contributions to North American Ethnology', 2. 1; Washington, District of Columbia: Government Printing Office, 1890)

Geertz, A. W., 'Book of the Hopi: The Hopi's Book?', *Anthropos; International Review of Ethnology and Linguistics*, 78. 3-4 (1983), 547-556

Geffcken, J. (ed.), *Die Oracula Sibyllina bearbeitet im Auftrage der Kirchenväter-Commission der Königl. Preussischen Akademie der Wissenschaften* ('Die griechischen christlichen Schriftsteller der ersten drei Jahrhunderte herausgegeben von der Kirchenvatercommission der Königl. Preussischen Akademie der Wissenschaften'; Leipzig: J. C. Hinrich'sche Buchhandlung, 1902)

Gilbert, G. K., 'The Origin of Hypotheses, Illustrated by the Discussion of a Topographic Problem', *Science*, 3. 53 (3 January 1896), 1-13

Ginzberg, L. (ed.), *The Legends of the Jews*, vol. 1: *Bible Times and Characters from the Creation to Jacob* (tr. H. Szold; Philadelphia, Pennsylvania: The Jewish Publication Society of America, 1913); vol. 5: *Notes to Volumes I and II; From the Creation to the Exodus* (tr. H. Szold (?); *idem*, 1925)

Grassi [anonymous], *De Tribvs Cometis Anni M. DC. XVIII. Dispvtatio Astronomica Pvblica Habita in Collegio Romano Societatis Iesv* (Rome: Iacobus Mascardi, 1619)

Green, W. M. (tr.), *Saint Augustine; The City of God against the Pagans* (7; 'Loeb Classical Library', 417; Cambridge, Massachusetts: Harvard University Press, 1972)

Gregory, J. W., 'Contributions to the Physical Geography of British East Africa', *The Geographical Journal*, 4. 4 (October 1894), 289-315

Gregory, J. W., *The Great Rift Valley; Being the Narrative of a Journey to Mount Kenya and Lake Baringo with Some Account of the Geology, Natural History, Anthropology, and Future Prospects of British East Africa* (London: John Murray, 1896)

Gregory, J. W., *The Dead Heart of Australia; A Journey around Lake Eyre in the Summer of 1901-1902, with Some Account of the Lake Eyre Basin and the Flowing Wells of Central Australia* (London: John Murray, 1906)

Grenier, Ph., *Chiloé et les Chilotes; Marginalité et dépendance en Patagonie chilienne; Étude de géographie humaine* (Aix-en-Provence: Édisud, 1984)

Griaule, M. & G. Dieterlen, 'The Dogon', in D. Forde (ed.), *African Worlds; Studies in the Cosmological Ideas and Social Values of African Peoples* (London: Oxford University Press, 1954), 83-110

Gribble, E. R. B., *The Problem of the Australian Aboriginal* (Sydney: Angus & Robertson Ltd., 1932)

Grignard, A. (tr.), *Hahn's Oraon Folk-Lore in the Original; A Critical Text with Translations and Notes* (Patna, India: Government Printing, 1931)

Gunn, R. C., 'On the 'Bunyip' of Australia Felix', *The Tasmanian Journal of Natural Science, Agriculture, Statistics, &c.*, 3 (January 1847), 147-149

Gupta, V. J., 'Late Cenozoic Glacial Sediments of the Himalaya', in M. J. Hambrey & W. B. Harland (eds.), *Earth's Pre-Pleistocene Glacial Record* (Cambridge: Cambridge University Press, 2011), 256-257

Gusinde, M., *Die Feuerland-Indianer; Ergebnisse meiner vier Forschungsreisen in den Jahren 1918 bis 1924, unternommen im Auftrage des Ministerio de Instruccion Publica de Chile*, vol. 1: *Die Selk'nam; Vom Leben und Denken eines Jägervolkes auf der grossen Feuerlandinsel* ('Anthropos-Bibliothek; Expeditions-Serie', 1; Mödling bei Wien: Verlag der Internationalen Zeitschrift 'Anthropos', 1931); vol. 2: *Die Yamana; Vom Leben und Denken der Wassernomaden am Kap Hoorn* (*idem*, 2; *idem*, 1937); partial translation of vol. 2: *The Yamana; The Life and Thought of the Water Nomads of Cape Horn* (4; tr. F. Schütze; New Haven, Connecticut: Human Relations Area Files, 1961)

Gusinde, M., *Hombres primitivos en la Tierra del Fuego (de Investigador a compañero de tribu)* (tr. D. B. Camacho; 'Publicaciones de la Escuela Hispano-Americanos de Sevilla', series 3. 5, 63; Sevilla: G. E. H.-A., 1951)

Gwydir, R. D., 'Prehistoric Spokane – An Indian Legend', *The Washington Historical Quarterly*, 1. 3 (April 1907), 136-137

Hagar, S., 'Cherokee Star-Lore', in B. Laufer (ed.), *Boas Anniversary Volume; Anthropological Papers Written in Honor of Franz Boas; Professor of Anthropology in Columbia University; Presented to Him on the Twenty-Fifth Anniversary of his Doctorate; Ninth of August Nineteen Hundred and Six* (New York: G. E. Stechert & Co., 1906), 354-366

Hahn, F., *Blicke in die Geisteswelt der heidnischen Kols; Sammlung von Sagen, Märchen und Liedern der Oraon in Chota Nagpur* (Gütersloh: C. Bertelsmann, 1906)

Hallet, J.-P. & A. Pelle, *Pygmy Kitabu* (New York: Random House, 1973)

Hamnett, W. L. & D. C. Thornton, *Tar Heel Wildlife* (Raleigh, North Carolina: North Carolina Wildlife Resources Commission, 1953)

Hamy, E.-T. (ed.), *Manuscrit Mexicain du cabinet de Ch.-M. Le Tellier, Archevèque de Reims à la Bibliothèque Nationale* (Ms. Mexicain N° 385) *reproduit en photochromographie aux frais du Duc de Loubat et précédé d'une introduction contenant la transcription complète des anciens commentaires Hispano-Mexicains* (Paris: publisher not stated, 1899)

Hardeland, Au. (ed.), *Dajacksch-Deutsches Wörterbuch* (Amsterdam: Frederik Muller, 1859)

Harou, A., 'Les Météores', *Revue des traditions populaires; Recueil mensuel de mythologie, littérature orale, ethnographie traditionelle et art populaire*, 17. 11 (November 1902), 566-573

Haynes, R. D., 'Aboriginal Astronomy', *Australian Journal of Astronomy*, 4. 3 (1992), 127-140

Hecker, K. (tr.), 'Rituale und Beschwörungen', in B. Janowski & G. Wilhelm (eds.), *Omina, Orakel, Rituale und Beschwörungen* ('Texte aus der Umwelt des Alten Testaments', 'Neue Folge', 4; Gütersloh: Gütersloher Verlagshaus, 2008), 61-127

Herbert, J. D., 'On the Organic Remains Found in the Himmalaya [sic]', *Gleanings in Science*, 3. 33 (September 1831), 265-272

Herling, B. L., *The German Gītā; Hermeneutics and Discipline in the German Reception of Indian Thought, 1778-1831* (New York: Routledge, 2006)

Hernández, T., 'Myths and Symbols of the Drysdale River Aborigines', *Oceania; A Journal Devoted to the Study of the Native Peoples of Australia, New Guinea and the Islands of the Pacific Ocean*, 32. 2 (1961-1962), 113-127

Herrmann, A., 'Die Flutsagen der finnisch-ugrischen Völker', *Globus; Illustrierte Zeitschrift für Länder- und Völkerkunde*, 63. 21 (1893), 333-338

Hinton, D. (tr.), *The Selected Poems of Li Po* (New York: New Directions, 1996)

Ho Peng Yoke (tr.), *The Astronomical Chapters of the Chin Shu with Amendments Full Translation and Annotations* ('Le Monde d'Outre-mer passé et présent', 2: 'Documents', 9; Paris: Mouton & Co., 1966)

Hodge, F. W. (ed.), *Handbook of American Indians North of Mexico* (1; 'Smithsonian Institution Bureau of American Ethnology Bulletin', 30; Washington, District of Columbia: Government Printing Office, 1907)

Hohenberger, A., *Die Indische Flutsage und das Matsyapurāṇa* (Leipzig: Otto Harrassowitz, 1930)

Holm, G., 'Ethnologisk Skizze af Angmagsalikerne', *Meddelelser om Grønland*, 10 (1888), 45-182

Horne, G. & G. Aiston, *Savage Life in Central Australia* (London: MacMillan and Co., 1924)

Hovell, W. H., 'The Apocryphal Animal of the Interior of New South Wales', *The Sydney Morning Herald*, 22. 3035 (9 February 1847), 3

Howitt, A. W., *The Native Tribes of South-East Australia* (London: MacMillan and Co., 1904)

Howitt, R., *Impressions of Australia Felix, during Four Years' Residence in that Colony; Notes of a Voyage round the World; Australian Poems, &c.* (London: Longman, Brown, Green, and Longmans, 1845)

Hugh-Jones, S., *The Palm and the Pleiades; Initiation and Cosmology in Northwest Amazonia* ('Cambridge Studies in Social Anthropology', 24; Cambridge: Cambridge University Press, 1979)

Hull, W. ['a colonial magistrate'], *Remarks on the Probable Origin and Antiquity of the Aboriginal Natives of New South Wales. Deduced from Certain of their Customs, Superstitions, and Existing Caves and Drawings, in Connexion with those of the Nations in Antiquity* (Melbourne: J. Pullar & Co., 1846)

Hunt, D., *Legends of the Caucasus* (London: Saqi, 2012)

Hussain, Q. N., 'Further Notes on the Tribes of Palamau', in J. H. Hutton (ed.), *Census of India, 1931*, vol. 1: *India*, part 3: *Ethnographical* (Simla: Government of India Press, 1935), 114-117

Icazbalceta, J. G. (ed.), *Historia eclesiástica Indiana; Obra escrita á fines del siglo XVI por Fray Gerónimo de Mendieta de la Orden de San Francisco* (Mexico City: Antigua Libreria, 1870)

Ides, E. Ysbrants, *Driejaarige Reize naar China, te Lande Gedaan door den Moskovischen Afgezant, E. Ysbrants Ides, van Moskou af, Over Groot Ustiga, Siriania, Permia, Sibirien, Daour, Groot Tartaryen tot in China. Waar in, behalven de Gemelde Landstreeken, de Zeden dier Woeste Volken, ten Aanzien van hunnen Godsdienst, Regeeringen, Huwelyken, Dagelykschen Handel, Kleedinge, Woningen, Onderhoud, Dood en Begraafnissen Naaukeuriglyk Beschreven Worden. Met eene Landkaart, door den Gezant op zyne Reize, naar de Waare Gelegenheit der Plaatzen Getekent, en met Veele Schoone Printverbeeldingen Versiert. Hier is Bygevoegt, eene Beknopte Beschryvinge van China, door eenen Chineeschen Schryver t' Zamengestelt, nu Eerst in 't Neêrduitsch Vertaalt, en met Verscheide Aantekeningen Verrykt* (Amsterdam: François Halma, 1704)

Irby-Massie, G. L. & P. T. Keyser (eds.), *Greek Science of the Hellenistic Era; A Sourcebook* (London: Routledge, 2002)

Isaacs, J. (ed.), *Australian Dreaming; 40,000 Years of Aboriginal History* (Sydney: Lansdowne Press, 1980)

Isacsson, S.-E., *Transformations of Eternity; On Man and Cosmos in Emberá Thought* (PhD dissertation; Göteborg, Sweden: University of Göteborg, 1993)

Iyengar, R. N., 'Profile of a Natural Disaster in Ancient Sanskrit Literature', *Indian Journal of History of Science*, 39. 1 (2004), 11-49

Iyer, N. C. (tr.), *The Bṛhat Saṁhitā of Varāha Mihira; Translated into English with Notes* ('Sri Garib Dass Oriental Series', 43; Delhi: Sri Satguru Publications, 1987^2)

Izeki Matsumoto, *Conceptualization of 'Xihuitl': History, Environment and Cultural Dynamics in Postclassic Mexica Cognition* ('BAR International Series', 1863; Oxford: Archaeopress, 2008)

James, P. & M. A. van der Sluijs, 'Ziggurats, Colors, and Planets: Rawlinson Revisited', *Journal of Cuneiform Studies*, 60 (2008), 57-79

Jeffers, A., 'The Oldest Lumber Company in the United States', *The Wood Worker; A Monthly Journal, Devoted to the Interests of Wood-Working Industries*, 11. 12 (February 1893), 27

Jefferson, Th., *Notes on the State of Virginia* (London: John Stockdale, 1787)

Johnson, E., *Legends, Traditions and Laws, of the Iroquois or Six Nations, and History of the Tuscarora Indians* (Lockport, New York: Union Printing and Publishing, 1881)

Johnston, B. H., 'Sky Tales from the Anishinaubaeg', in V. del Chamberlain, J. B. Carlson & M. J. Young (eds.), *Songs from the Sky; Indigenous Astronomical and Cosmological Traditions of the World; Selected Proceedings of the 'First International Conference on Ethnoastronomy: Indigenous Astronomical and Cosmological Traditions of the World' Held at the Smithsonian Institution, Washington, D. C., 5-9 September 1983* (Bognor Regis: Ocarina Books, 2005) = *Archaeoastronomy: The Journal of the Center for Archaeoastronomy*, 12-13 (1996), 147-150

Jones, E., *The Story of the Falling Star* (Canberra: Aboriginal Studies Press, 1989)

Jones, H. L. *The Geography of Strabo*, vol. 1 ('Loeb Classical Library', 49; London: William Heinemann, 1917); vol. 5 (*idem*, 211; *idem*, 1928)

Joset, P.-E., 'Buda Efeba (Contes et légendes Pygmées); Troisieme partie', *Zaïre; Revue Congolaise*, 2. 2 (February 1948), 137-157

Joshi, K. L. (tr.), *Matsya Mahāpurāṇa (An Exhaustive Introduction, Sanskrit Text, English Translation, Scholarly Notes and Index of Verses)*, vol. 1: *Chapters: 1-150* ('Parimal Sanskrit Series', 93; Delhi: Parimal Publications, 2007)

Kahlke, H. D., 'On the Complex of the *Stegodon-Ailuropoda*-Fauna of Southern China and the Chronological Position of *Gigantopithecus Blacki* v. Koenigswald', *Vertebrata Palasiatica*, 5. 2 (1961), 104-108

Kaster, R. A. (tr.), *Macrobius; Saturnalia; Books 1-2* ('Loeb Classical Library', 510; Cambridge, Massachusetts: Harvard University Press, 2011)

Keimatsu, M., 'A Chronology of Aurorae and Sunspots Observed in China, Korea and Japan; Part IV 6~8 Century', *The Annals of Science; Kanazawa University*, 10 (1973), 1-32

Keimatsu, M., 'A Chronology of Aurorae and Sunspots Observed in China, Korea and Japan; Part VI A. D. 1001-1130', *The Annals of Science; Kanazawa University*, 12 (1975), 1-40

Kim Tae-Kon, *Korean Shamanism - Muism* (tr. Chang Soo-Kyong; 'Korean Studies Series', 9; Seoul: Jimoondang Publishing, 1998)

King, L. W. (tr.), *The Seven Tablets of Creation, or the Babylonian and Assyrian Legends Concerning the Creation of the World and of Mankind*, vol. 1: *English Translations, etc.* ('Luzac's Semitic Text and Translation Series', 12; London: Luzac and Co., 1902)

Kingsborough (ed.), *Antiquities of Mexico: Comprising Fac-Similes of Ancient Mexican Paintings and Hieroglyphics, Preserved in the Royal Libraries of Paris, Berlin, and Dresden; in the Imperial Library of Vienna; in the Vatican Library; in the Borgian Museum at Rome; in the Library of the Institute at Bologna; and in the Bodleian Library at Oxford. Together with The Monuments of New Spain, by M. Dupaix: With their Respective Scales of Measurement and Accompanying Descriptions. The Whole Illustrated by Many Valuable Inedited Manuscripts* (5; London: Rovert Havell, 1831)

Kinney, A. M. (ed.), *The Vulgate Bible*, vol. 4: *The Major Prophetical Books; Douay-Rheims Translation* ('Dumbarton Oaks Medieval Library', 13; Cambridge, Massachusetts: Harvard University Press, 2012)

Knibb, M. A. (tr.), '1 Enoch', in H. F. D. Sparks (ed.), *The Apocryphal Old Testament* (Oxford: Clarendon Press, 1984), 169-319

Koch-Grünberg, Th., *Indianermärchen aus Südamerika* ('Die Märchen der Weltliteratur'; Jena: Eugen Diederichs, 1927)

Köhler, U., 'Comets and Falling Stars in the Perception of Mesoamerican Indians', in A. F. Aveni (ed.), *World Archaeoastronomy; Selected Papers from the 2nd Oxford Inter-*

national Conference on Archaeoastronomy Held at Merida, Yucatan, Mexico 13-17 January 1986 (Cambridge: Cambridge University Press, 1989), 289-299

Köhler, U., 'Meteors and Comets in Ancient Mexico', in Ch. Koeberl & K. G. MacLeod (eds.), *Catastrophic Events and Mass Extinctions: Impacts and Beyond* ('Geological Society of America Special Papers', 356; Boulder, Colorado: The Geological Society of America, 2002), 1-6

Kroeber, A. L., 'Indian Myths of South Central California', *University of California Publications American Archaeology and Ethnology*, 4. 4 (1907), 169-250

Kronk, G. W., *Cometography; A Catalog of Comets*, vol. 1: *Ancient-1799* (Cambridge: Cambridge University Press, 1999)

Krüger, T., *Discovering the Ice Ages; International Reception and Consequences for a Historical Understanding of Climate* (tr. A. M. Hentschel; Leiden: Brill, 2013)

Kruijt, A. C., *Het Animisme in den Indischen Archipel* (The Hague: Martinus Nijhoff, 1906)

Langdon, S., 'A Ritual of Atonement Addressed to Tammuz and Ishtar', *Revue d'Assyriologie et d'archéologie orientale*, 13. 3 (1916), 105-117

Laufer, B., 'Petroglyphs on the Amoor', *American Anthropologist*, new series, 1 (1899), 746-750

LaViolette, P. A., *Earth under Fire; Humanity's Survival of the Apocalypse* (Schenectady, New York: Starlane Publications, 1997)

Layton, R., 'Ethnographic Study and Symbolic Analysis', in D. S. Whitley (ed.), *Handbook of Rock Art Research* (Walnut Creek, California: Altamira Press, 2001), 311-331

Legge, J. (tr.), *The Chinese Classics: With a Translation, Critical and Exegetical Notes, Prolegomena, and Copious Indexes*, vol. 3. 1: *The First Parts of the Shoo-King. Or the Books of T'ang; The Books of Yu; The Books of Hea; The Books of Shang; and the Prolegomena* (London: Trübner & Co., 1865)

Lehmann, W., 'Ergebnisse einer mit Unterstützung der Notgemeinschaft der Deutschen Wissenschaft in den Jahren 1925/1926 ausgeführten Forschungsreise nach Mexiko und Guatemala', *Anthropos; International Review of Ethnology and Linguistics*, 23. 3-4 (1928), 749-791

Levine, Ph. (tr.), *Augustine: The City of God against the Pagans*, vol. 4: *Books XII-XV* ('Loeb Classical Library', 414; Cambridge, Massachusetts: Harvard University Press, 1966)

Lewis-Williams, J. D. & T. A. Dowson, 'The Signs of All Times; Entoptic Phenomena in Upper Palaeolithic Art', *Current Anthropology*, 29. 2 (1988), 201-245

Lienhardt, G., *Divinity and Experience; The Religion of the Dinka* (Oxford: Clarendon Press, 1961)

Loeb, E. M., 'The Creator Concept among the Indians of North Central California', *American Anthropologist*, 28. 3 (1926), 467-493

Louka, G. [Γ. Λουκα], Φιλολογικαι επισκεπεις των εν τω βιω των νεωτερων Κυπριων μνημειων των αρχαιων (1; Athens: Nikolaos Rousopoulou, 1874)

Luxton, R. N. (tr.), *The Book of Chumayel; The Counsel Book of the Yucatec Maya 1539-1638; Translated and Annotated* ('Mayan Studies', 7; Laguna Hills, California: Aegean Park Press, 1995)

Lynd, J. W., 'The Religion of the Dakotas. Chapter Six of Mr. Lynd's Manuscript', *Collections of the Historical Society of Minnesota*, 2. 2 for 1864 (1865), 63-84

MacKenna, B. V. (ed.), *Historia general de el Reyno de Chile; Flandes Indiano por el R. P. Diego de Rosales, de la Compañia de Jesus: Dos veces v. provincial de la v. provincia de Chile, calificador del Santo Officio de la Inquisicion y natural de Madrid dedicada al Rey* de España D. Carlos II N. S. publicada, anotada i precedida de la vida del autor i de una estensa noticia de sus obras (1; Valparaíso: Imprenta del Mercurio, 1877)

Macleay, W. S., 'On the Skull now Exhibited at the Colonial Museum of Sydney, as that of 'The Bunyip'', *The Sydney Morning Herald*, 22. 3162 (7 July 1847), 3

Mair, A. W. (tr.), *Callimachus and Lycophron* ('Loeb Classical Library', 129; London: William Heinemann, 1921)

Major, J. S., S. A. Queen, A. S. Meyer & H. D. Roth (trs.), *The Huainanzi; A Guide to the Theory and Practice of Government in Early Han China; Liu An, King of Huainan* ('Translations from the Asian Classics'; New York: Columbia University Press, 2010)

Man, E. H., 'On the Aboriginal Inhabitants of the Andaman Islands (Part II)', *The Journal of the Anthropological Institute of Great Britain and Ireland*, 12 (1883), 117-175

Mándoki, L., 'Two Asiatic Sidereal Names', in V. Diószegi (ed.), *Popular Beliefs and Folklore Tradition in Siberia* (The Hague: Mouton and Company, 1968), 485-496

Mason, J. A., 'The Language of the Salinan Indians', *University of California Publications in American Archaeology and Ethnology*, 14. 1 (1918), 1-154

Massola, A., *Bunjil's Cave; Myths, Legends and Superstitions of the Aborigines of South-East Australia* (Melbourne: Lansdowne Press, 1968)

Mayor, A., *The First Fossil Hunters: Paleontology in Greek and Roman Times* (Princeton, New Jersey: Princeton University Press, 2000)

Mayor, A., *Fossil Legends of the First Americans* (Princeton, New Jersey: Princeton University Press, 2005)

Mayor, A., 'Place Names Describing Fossils in Oral Traditions', in L. Piccardi & W. B. Masse (eds.), *Myth and Geology* ('Geological Society Special Publication', 273; London: The Geological Society, 2007), 245-261

McBeth, K. C., *The Nez Perces since Lewis and Clark* (New York: Fleming H. Revell Company, 1908)

McCarthy, F. D., *Australian Aboriginal Rock Art* (Sydney: Australian Museum, 1958)

McCleary, T. P., *The Stars we Know: Crow Indian Astronomy and Lifeways* (Prospect Heights, Illinois: Waveland Press, 1997)

McCrae, H. (ed.), *Georgiana's Journal; Melbourne a Hundred Years Ago* (Sydney: Angus & Robertson, 1934)

McLean, A., 'Between the Georgina and Burke Rivers', in E. M. Curr (ed.), *The Australian Race: Its Origin, Languages, Customs, Place of Landing in Australia, and the Routes by which it Spread itself over that Continent* (2; London: Trübner & Co., 1886)

Melton, F. A. & W. Schriever, 'The Carolina 'Bays' – Are they Meteorite Scars?', *The Journal of Geology*, 41. 1 (1933), 52-66

Meyer, E., 'Die Stele des Ḥoremḥeb', *Zeitschrift für Ägyptische Sprache und Alterthumskunde*, 15. 4 (1877), 148-157

Milbrath, S., *Star Gods of the Maya; Astronomy in Art, Folklore, and Calendars* ('The Linda Schele Series in Maya and Pre-Columbian Studies'; Austin, Texas: University of Texas Press, 1999)

Miller, F. J. (tr.), *Ovid*, vol. 3: *Metamorphoses*, vol. 1: *Books I-VIII* ('Loeb Classical Library', 42; Cambridge, Massachusetts: Harvard University Press, 1977³)

Miller, L. (ed.), *South of the Clouds; Tales from Yunnan* (Seattle, Washington: University of Washington Press, 1994)

Minnaert, M., *The Nature of Light & Colour in the Open Air* (tr. H. M. Kremer-Priest; New York: Dover Publications, 1954)

Monier-Williams, M. (ed.), *A Sanskrit-English Dictionary Etymologically and Philologically Arranged with Special Reference to Cognate Indo-European Languages* (Oxford: Clarendon Press, 1979)

Mooney, J., 'The Sacred Formulas of the Cherokees', *Annual Report of the Bureau of Ethnology to the Secretary of the Smithsonian Institution*, 7 for 1885-1886 (1891), 301-397

Mooney, J., 'Myths of the Cherokee', *Annual Report of the Bureau of American Ethnology to the Secretary of the Smithsonian Institution*, 19. 1 for 1897-1898 (1900), 3-548

Most, G. W. (tr.), *Hesiod: Theogony; Works and Days; Testimonia* ('Loeb Classical Library', 57; Cambridge, Massachusetts: Harvard University Press, 2006)

Mountford, Ch. P., *Records of the American-Australian Scientific Expedition to Arnhem Land*, vol. 1: *Art, Myth and Symbolism* (Melbourne: Melbourne University Press, 1956)

Mountford, Ch. P., 'Simple Rock Engravings in Central Australia', *Man; A Monthly Record of Anthropological Science*, 60 (1960), 145-147

Mountford, Ch. P., 'Aboriginal Rock Poundings on Gallery Hill, Northwestern Australia', *Records of the South Australian Museum*, 15. 1 (1965), 89-107

Mountford, Ch. P. & R. Edwards, 'Aboriginal Rock Engravings of Extinct Creatures in South Australia', *Man; A Monthly Record of Anthropological Science*, 62 (1962), 97-99

Mountford, Ch. P. & R. Edwards, 'Rock Engravings in the Red Gorge, Deception Creek, Northern South Australia', *Anthropos; International Review of Ethnology and Linguistics*, 59. 5-6 (1964), 849-859

Mowaljarlai[, D. B.] & J. Malnic, *Yorro Yorro; Everything Standing up Alive* (Broome, Western Australia: Magabala Books, 2001 [1993])

Mozley, J. H. (tr.), *Valerius Flaccus: Argonautica* ('Loeb Classical Library', 286; Cambridge, Massachusetts: Harvard University Press, 1936)

Muck, O., *The Secret of Atlantis* (tr. F. Bradley; New York: Times Books, 1978)

Muir, J. (tr.), *Original Sanskrit Texts on the Origin and History of the People of India; Their Religion and Institutions; Collected, Translated, and Illustrated*, vol. 1: *Mythical and Legendary Accounts of the Origin of Caste, with an Enquiry into its Existence in the Vedic Age* (London: Trübner & Co., 1868²)

Mukherji, C. C., 'Notes on the Santals and Kherias of Manbhum District', in J. H. Hutton (ed.), *Census of India, 1931*, vol. 1: *India*, part 3: *Ethnographical* (Simla: Government of India Press, 1935), 110-112

Munkácsi, B., 'Kosmogonische Sagen der Wogulen', *Ethnologische Mitteilungen aus Ungarn*, 2. 6-8 (1891), 105-133

Munkácsi, B., 'Die Weltgottheiten der wogulischen Mythologie (III)', *Keleti Szemle; Revue orientale pour les études ouralo-altaïques. Subventionnée par l'Académie Hongroise des Sciences. Journal du Comité Hongrois de l'Association internationale pour l'exploration de l'Asie Centrale et de l'Extrême-Orient*, 9 (1908), 206-277

Murchison, Ch. (ed.), *Palæontological Memoirs and Notes of the Late Hugh Falconer ... with a Biographical Sketch of the Author*, vol. 1: *Fauna Antiqua Sivalensis* (London: Robert Hardwicke, 1868)

Murie, J. R., *Ceremonies of the Pawnee*, vol. 1: *The Skiri* ('Smithsonian Contributions to Anthropology', 27; Washington, District of Columbia: Smithsonian Institution Press, 1981)

Mutwa, V. C., *Zulu Shaman; Dreams, Prophecies, and Mysteries* (Rochester, Vermont: Destiny Books, 1996)

Nansen, F., *Eskimo Life* (tr. W. Archer; London: Longmans, Green, and Co., 1893)

Narahari Achar, B. N., 'On Astronomical References in Vyāsa-Dhṛtarāṣṭra-Saṁvāda in the Bhīṣmaparvan of Mahābhārata', *Annals of the Bhandarkar Oriental Research Institute*, 84 (2003), 13-22

Nelson, E. W., 'The Eskimo about Bering Strait', *Annual Report of the Bureau of American Ethnology to the Secretary of the Smithsonian Institution*, 18. 1 for 1896-1897 (1899), 3-518

Nestle, E., E. Nestle, B. Aland, K. Aland, J. Karavidopoulos, C. M. Martini & B. M. Metzger (eds.), *Novum Testamentum Graece* (Stuttgart: Biblia-Druck, 1993[27])

Neugebauer, P. V. & E. F. Weidner, 'Ein astronomischer Beobachtungstext aus dem 37. Jahre Nebukadnezars II. (-567.66)', *Berichte über die Verhandlungen der Königlich Sächsischen Gesellschaft der Wissenschaften zu Leipzig; philologisch-historische Klasse*, 67 (1915), 29-89

Nickelsburg, G. W. E. & J. C. VanderKam (trs.), *1 Enoch; The Hermeneia Translation* (Minneapolis, Minnesota: Fortress Press, 2012)

Nickerson, R., J. McLeod & H. Yaworski, interview with Fred Pine (Archives of Ontario, #IH-OA.030, #130; 10 January 1984), at http://ourspace.uregina.ca/bitstream/handle/10294/1016/IH-OA.030.pdf?sequence=1 (last accessed 6 May 2017)

Nock, A. D. & A.-J. Festugière (trs.), *Corpvs Hermeticvm*, vol. 1: *Traités I-XII* (Paris: Société d'Édition «Les Belles Lettres», 1945)

Oakley, K., 'Folklore of Fossils; Part II', *Antiquity*, 39. 154 (1965), 117-125

Oldfather, C. H. (tr.), *Diodorus of Sicily*, vol. 2: *Books II (Continued) 35 – IV, 58* ('Loeb Classical Library', 303; Cambridge, Massachusetts: Harvard University Press, 1935); vol. 3: *Books IV. 59 – VIII* (idem, 340; idem, 1939)

Opler, M. E., *Myths and Tales of the Jicarilla Apache Indians* ('Memoirs of the American Folklore Society', 31; New York: The American Folk-Lore Society, 1938)

Oppenheim, A. L. & E. Reiner (eds.), *The Assyrian Dictionary of the Oriental Institute of the University of Chicago*, vol. 10. 1: *M* (Chicago: The Oriental Institute, 1977)

Oppenheim, A. L., E. Reiner, R. D. Biggs, J. M. Renger, R. F. G. Sweet, D. B. Weisberg & M. Elswick (eds.), *The Assyrian Dictionary of the Oriental Institute of the University of Chicago*, vol. 8: *K* (Chicago: The Oriental Institute, 1971)

Oppenheim, A. L., E. Reiner, A. K. Grayson, H. E. Hirsch, E. V. Leichty & J. M. Rosenthal (eds.), *The Assyrian Dictionary of the Oriental Institute of the University of Chicago*, vol. 1. 1: *A* (Chicago: The Oriental Institute, 1964)

Ouwehand, C., *Namazu-e and their Themes; An Interpretative Approach to Some Aspects of Japanese Folk Religion* (Leiden: E. J. Brill, 1964)

Owen, R., 'On Fossil Remains of Mammals Found in China', *The Quarterly Journal of the Geological Society of London*, 26. 1 (1870), 417-434

Pankenier, D. W., *Astrology and Cosmology in Early China; Conforming Earth to Heaven* (Cambridge: Cambridge University Press, 2013)

Pardo, M. (ed.), *Zroará Nēburá; Historia de los antiguos; Literatura oral Emberá; segun: Floresmiro Dogiramá* (Bogotá: Centro Jorge Eliécer Gaitán, 1984)

Pechuël-Loesche, E., *Volkskunde von Loango* ('Die Loango Expedition ausgesandt von der Deutschen Gesellschaft zur Erforschung Aequatorial-Africas 1873-1876. Ein Reisewerk in drei Abtheilungen', 3. 2; Stuttgart: Strecker & Schröder, 1907)

Peck, *Australian Legends; Tales Handed Down from the Remotest Times by the Autocthonous [sic] Inhabitants of our Land* (Melbourne: The Lothian Publishing Co., 1933)

Peterson, Ch. J. (ed.), *Christfrid Ganander Thomasson's Finnische Mythologie. Aus dem Schwedischen übersetzt, völlig umgearbeitet und mit Anmerkungen versehen* (Tallinn: Carl Dullo, 1821)

Petitot, E., *Monographie des Dènè-Dindjié* (Paris: Ernest Leroux, 1876)

Petitot, É., *Traditions Indiennes du Canada nord-ouest* ('Les Littératures populaires de toutes les nations; Traditions, légendes contes, chansons, proverbes, devinettes superstitions', 23; Paris: Maisonneuve Frères et Ch. Leclerc, 1886)

Petitot, E., *Traditions Indiennes du Canada nord-ouest; textes originaux & traduction littérale* (Alençon: E. Renaut-de Broise, 1887) = *The Book of Dene; Containing the Traditions and Beliefs of Chipewyan, Dogrib, Slavey, and Loucheux Peoples* (tr.; Yellowknife, Canada: Programme Development Division, 1976) (this translation is only partial)

Pietersma, A. & B. G. Wright (trs.), *A New English Translation of the Septuagint and the Other Greek Translations Traditionally Included under that Title* (New York: Oxford University Press, 2007)

Pimentel, L. G. (ed.), *Memoriales de Fray Toribio de Motolinia; Manuscrito de la coleccion de Señor Don Joaquin García Icazbalceta* (Paris: A. Donnamette, 1903)

Pingree, D. (ed.), *Hephaestionis Thebani Apotelesmaticorum Libri Tres* (1; 'Bibliotheca Scriptorum Graecorum et Romanorum Teubneriana'; Leipzig: B. G. Teubner Verlagsgesellschaft, 1973)

Platnauer, M. (tr.), *Claudian* (2; 'The Loeb Classical Library', 136; Cambridge, Massachusetts: Harvard University Press, 1922)

Poirier, J. C., 'An Illuminating Parallel to Isaiah XIV 12', *Vetus Testamentum*, 49. 3 (1999), 371-389

Pond, G. H., 'Power and Influence of Dacota Medicine-Men', in H. R. Schoolcraft (ed.), *Archives of Aboriginal Knowledge. Containing All the Original Papers Laid before Congress Respecting the History, Antiquities, Language, Ethnology, Pictography, Rites, Superstitions, and Mythology, of the Indian Tribes of the United States* (4; 'Information Respecting the History Condition and Prospects of the Indian Tribes of the United States: Collected and Prepared under the Bureau of Indian Affairs'; Philadelphia, Pennsylvania: J. B. Lippincott & Co., 1860), 641-651

Pond, G. H., 'Dakota Superstitions. Dakota Gods', *Collections of the Minnesota Historical Society*, 2. 3 (1867), 215-255

Pond, S. W., 'The Dakotas or Sioux in Minnesota as they Were in 1834', *Collections of the Minnesota Historical Society*, 12 (1908), 319-501

Powell, J. W., 'Mythologic Philosophy', *The Popular Science Monthly*, 15 (October 1879), 795-808

Powell, J. W., 'Sketch of the Mythology of the North American Indians', *Annual Report of the Bureau of Ethnology to the Secretary of the Smithsonian Institution*, 1 for 1879-1880 (1881), 19-56

Prothero, D. R. & R. M. Schoch, *Horns, Tusks, and Flippers; The Evolution of Hoofed Mammals* (Baltimore, Maryland: The Johns Hopkins University Press, 2002)

Quiñones Keber, E. (tr.), *Codex Telleriano-Remensis; Ritual, Divination, and History in a Pictorial Aztec Manuscript* (Austin, Texas: University of Texas Press, 1995)

Rackham, H. (tr.), *Pliny: Natural History*, vol. 1: *Praefatio, Libri I, II* ('Loeb Classical Library', 330; London: William Heinemann, 1949); vol. 2: *Libri III-VII* (*idem*, 352; *idem*, 1942)

Rahlfs, A. (ed.), *Septuaginta id est Vetus Testamentum Graece iuxta LXX Interpretes*, vol. 2: *Libri Poetici et Prophetici* (Stuttgart: Privilegierte Württembergische Bibelanstalt, 1950⁴)

Ray, A. K., *Fossils in Earth Sciences* (New Delhi: Prentice Hall, 2008)

Reiner, E., R. D. Biggs & M. T. Roth (eds.), *The Assyrian Dictionary of the Oriental Institute of the University of Chicago*, vol. 17. 3: Š (Chicago: The Oriental Institute, 1992)

Reiner, E. & M. T. Roth (eds.), *The Assyrian Dictionary of the Oriental Institute of the University of Chicago*, vol. 14: R (Chicago: The Oriental Institute, 1999)

Riggs, S. R. (ed.), *Grammar and Dictionary of the Dakota Language. Collected by the Members of the Dakota Mission* ('Smithsonian Contributions to Knowledge', 4; Washington, District of Columbia: Smithsonian Institution, 1852)

Riggs, S. R., 'History of the Dakotas. James W. Lynd's Manuscripts', *Collections of the Historical Society of Minnesota*, 2. 2 for 1864 (1865), 57-62

Riordan, J. (tr.), *The Sun Maiden and the Crescent Moon; Siberian Folk Tales* (Edinburgh: Canongate, 1989)

Rivet, P. (ed.), 'Nociones sobre creencias, usos y costumbres de los Catíos del Occidente de Antioquia', *Journal de la Société des Americanistes*, 21. 1 (1929), 71-105

Robertson, M. G., *The Sculpture of Palenque*, vol. 4: *The Cross Group, the North Group, the Olvidado, and Other Pieces* (Princeton, New Jersey: Princeton University Press, 1991)

Robinson, R., *The Feathered Serpent; The Mythological Genesis and Recreative Ritual of the Aboriginal Tribes of the Northern Territory of Australia; the Kuppapoingo, Jumbapoingo, Birrikilli, Miarr-Miarr and Leagulawulmirree Tribes at Milingimbi; the Murinbata and Djamunjun Tribes of Port Keats; the Djauan and Ngalarkan Tribes at the Roper River; and the Arranda, Luritja and Pitjantjara Tribes of the Centre* (Sydney: Edwards & Shaw, 1956)

Roy, P. Ch. (tr.), *The Mahabharata of Krishna-Dwaipayana Vyasa Translated into English Prose (from the Original Sanskrit Text)*, vol. 2: *Vana Parva* (Kolkata: Bharata Press, 1884); vol. 4: *Bhishma Parva* (*idem*, 1887)

Roys, R. L. (tr.), *The Book of Chilam Balam of Chumayel* ('The Civilization of the American Indian Series', 87; Norman, Oklahoma: University of Oklahoma Press, 1967)

Rufus, W. C. & Tien Hsing-Chih (trs.), *The Soochow Astronomical Chart* (Ann Arbor, Michigan: University of Michigan Press, 1945)

Salomon, F. & G. L. Urioste (trs.), *The Huarochirí Manuscript; A Testament of Ancient and Colonial Andean Religion* (Austin, Texas: University of Texas Press, 1991)

Samuel, M. (tr.), ספר הישר *or the Book of Jasher, Referred to in Joshua and Second Samuel. Faithfully Translated from the Original Hebrew into English* (Salt Lake City, Utah: J. H. Parry and Company, 1887)

Saylor, F. H., 'Legendary Lore of the Indians', *Oregon Native Son and Historical Magazine Devoted to the History, Industries and Development of the Original Oregon Comprising the States of Oregon, Washington, Idaho and Part of Montana*, 2. 6 (November 1900), 315-317

Schafer, E. H., *Pacing the Void; T'ang Approaches to the Stars* (Berkeley, California: University of California Press, 1977)

Schebesta, P., *Bambuti; die Zwerge vom Kongo* (Leipzig: F. U. Brockhaus, 1932) = *Among Congo Pigmies* (tr. G. Griffin; London: Hutchinson & Co., 1933)

Schebesta, P., *Der Urwald ruft wieder; Meine zweite Forschungsreise zu den Ituri-Zwergen* (Salzburg-Leipzig: Anton Pustet, 1936)

Schechter, S. (ed.), *Midrash Hag-Gadol; Forming a Collection of Ancient Rabbinic Homilies to the Pentateuch; Edited for the First Time from Various Yemen Manuscripts and Provided with Notes and Preface*, vol.: *Genesis* (Cambridge: Cambridge University Press, 1902)

Scheftelowitz, J., *Die Zeit als Schicksalsgottheit in der indischen und iranischen Religion (Kāla und Zruvan)* ('Beiträge zur indischen Sprachwissenschaft und Religionsgeschichte', 4; Stuttgart: W. Kohlhammer, 1929)

Schmidt, B., *Griechische Märchen, Sagen und Volkslieder gesammelt, übersetzt und erläutert* (Leipzig: B. G. Teubner, 1877)

Schoolcraft, H. R., *Algic Researches, Comprising Inquiries Respecting the Mental Characteristics of the North American Indians*, series 1: *Indian Tales and Legends, Mythologic and Allegoric. Rendered from the Oral Traditions of the North American Indians by Competent Interpreters, and Written out from the Original Notes* (1; New York: Harper & Brothers, 1839)

Schorr, Y. S. & Ch. Malinowitz (trs.), *Tractate Rosh Hashanah* ('Talmud Bavli; The Schottenstein Edition; The ArtScroll Series'; '**The Gemara:** The Classic Vilna Edition, with an Annotated, Interpretive Elucidation, as an Aid to Talmud Study'; 'The Horn Edition of Seder Moed'; New York: Mesorah Publications, 1999)

Schultze Jena, L., *Indiana*, vol. 2: *Mythen in der Muttersprache der Pipil von Izalco in El Salvador* (Jena: Gustav Fischer, 1935)

Scott, D. E., *The Electric Sky; A Challenge to the Myths of Modern Astronomy* (Portland, Oregon: Mikamar Publishing, 2006)

Seler, E., *Gesammelte Abhandlungen zur amerikanischen Sprach- und Alterthumskunde*, vol. 4: *Mythus und Religion der alten Mexikaner. – Die buntbemalten Gefäße von Nasca im südlichen Perú und die Hauptelemente ihrer Verzierung. – Kleinere Aufsätze und Vorträge. – Bruchstücke einer allgemeinverständlichen Darstellung des Landes Mexiko, seiner Bevölkerung und seiner Entdeckungsgeschichte. – Die Tierbilder der mexikanischen und der Maya-Handschriften* (Berlin: Behrend & Co., 1923)

Seroshevskiy, V. L. [В. Л. Сѣрошевскій], *Якуты. опытъ этнографическаго изслѣдованія* (1; Saint Petersburg: Tipografija Glavn. Upravlenija Udelov, 1896)

Sharpe, B., '$17,000,000 Home of Canada Geese', *Wildlife in North Carolina*, 12. 1 (January 1948), 12-13

Sharpe, B., *A New Geography of North Carolina*, vol. 2: *25 Counties* (Raleigh, North Carolina: Sharpe Publishing Company, 1958)

Sharpe, M. & D. Tunbridge, 'Traditions of Extinct Animals, Changing Sea-Levels and Volcanoes among Australian Aboriginals: Evidence from Linguistic and Ethnographic Research', in R. Blench & M. Spriggs (eds.), *Archaeology and Language*, vol. 1: *Theoretical and Methodological Orientations* ('One World Archaeology'; London: Routledge, 1997), 345-361

Shastri, J. L. (tr.), *Brahma Purāṇa* (1; 'Ancient Indian Tradition & Mythology', 33; Delhi: Motilal Banarsidass, 1985)

Simon, M. (tr.), *Rosh Hashanah; Translated into English with Notes, Glossary and Indices* ('The Babylonian Talmud'; '*Seder Moʻed*', 4; London: The Soncino Press, 1938)

Simon, M. (tr.), *Berakoth; Translated into English with Notes, Glossary and Indices* ('The Babylonian Talmud'; '*Seder Zeraʻim*'; London: The Soncino Press, 1948)

Skeat, W. W. & Ch. O. Blagden, *Pagan Races of the Malay Peninsula* (2; London: MacMillan and Co., 1906)

Skinner, A., *Notes on the Eastern Cree and Northern Saulteaux* ('Anthropological Papers of the American Museum of Natural History', 9. 1; New York: American Museum of Natural History, 1911)

Slavitt, D. R. (tr.), *The Voyage of the* Argo; *The* Argonautica *of Gaius Valerius Flaccus* (Baltimore, Maryland: The Johns Hopkins University Press, 1999)

Smith, S. P. (tr.), *The Lore of the Whare-Wānanga; or Teachings of the Maori College on Religion, Cosmogony, and History. Written down by H. T. Whatahoro from the Teachings of Te Matorohanga and Nepia Pohuhu, Priests of the Whare-Wānanga of the East Coast, New Zealand*, vol. 1: *Te Kauwae-runga, or 'Things Celestial'* ('Memoirs of the Polynesian Society', 3; New Plymouth, New Zealand: Thomas Avery, 1913)

Smith, W. R., *Myths & Legends of the Australian Aboriginals* (New York: Farrar & Rinehart, 1930)

Speck, F. G., *Catawba Texts* (New York: Columbia University Press, 1934)

Steiger, B., *Worlds before our own* (New York: Berkley Publishing Corporation, 1978)

Stender, G. F., *Lettische Grammatik* (Jelgava, Latvia: Johann Fried. Steffenhagen, 1783²)

Stender, G. F. (ed.), *Lettisches Lexikon; In zween Theilen abgefasset, und den Liebhabern der lettischen Litteratur gewidmet* (Jelgava, Latvia: J. F. Steffenhagen, 1789)

Stevenson, J., 'Ceremonial of Hasjelti Dailjis and Mythical Sand Painting of the Navajo Indians', *Annual Report of the Bureau of Ethnology to the Secretary of the Smithsonian Institution*, 8 for 1886-1887 (1891), 235-285

Stieglitz, R. R., 'The Hebrew Names of the Seven Planets', *Journal of Near Eastern Studies*, 40. 2 (1981), 135-137

Strehlow, T. G. H., *Aranda Traditions* (Melbourne: Melbourne University Press, 1947)

Talbott, D., 'Servant of the Sun God', *Aeon; A Symposium on Myth and Science*, 2. 1 (1989), 37-52

Talbott, D., 'The Great Comet Venus', *Aeon; A Journal of Myth and Science*, 3. 5 (1994), 5-51

Tawhai, T. P., 'Maori Religion', in S. Sutherland, L. Houlden, P. Clarke & F. Hardy (eds.), *The World's Religions* (Boston, Massachusetts: G. K. Hall & Co., 1988), 854-863 = in G. Harvey (ed.), *Readings in Indigenous Religions* (London: Continuum, 2002), 237-249

Tedlock, D. (tr.), *Popol Vuh; The Definitive Edition of the Mayan Book of the Dawn of Life and the Glories of Gods and Kings* ('Touchstone'; New York: Simon & Schuster, 1996)

Teit, J., 'The Thompson Indians of British Columbia', *Memoirs of the American Museum of Natural History*, 2 (*Anthropology*, 1; *The Jesup North Pacific Expedition*, 1. 4) (1900), 163-390

Teit, J. A., 'The Shuswap', *Memoirs of the American Museum of Natural History*, 2. 7 (*Publications of the Jesup North Pacific Expedition*) (1909), 443-813

Terry, M. S. (tr.), *The Sibylline Oracles Translated from the Greek into English Blank Verse* (New York: Hunt & Eaton, 1890)

Thilo, G., (ed.), *Aeneidos Librorvm VI-XII Commentarii* ('Servii Grammatici qvi Fervntvr In Vergilii Carmina Commentarii', 2: Leipzig: B. G. Tevbnerus, 1884)

Tompson, F. A., letter, *The Sydney Morning Herald*, 22. 3167 (13 July 1847), 2

Trenary, C., 'Universal Meteor Metaphors and their Occurrence in Mesoamerican Astronomy', *Archaeoastronomy; The Bulletin of the Center for Archaeoastronomy*, 10 (1987-1988), 99-116

Tschiffely, A. F., 'Buenos Aires to Washington by Horse: A Solitary Journey of Two and a Half Years, through Eleven American Republics, Covers 9,600 Miles of Mountain and Plain, Desert and Jungle', *The National Geographic Magazine*, 55. 2 (February 1929), 135-196

Tucci, G., *The Religions of Tibet* (tr. G. Samuel; Bombay: Allied Publishers, 1980)

Tucker, L., *Mystery of the White Lions; Children of the Sun God* (Mapumulanga, South Africa: Npenvu Press, 2003)

Turnbull, C. M., 'Legends of the BaMbuti', *The Journal of the Royal Anthropological Institute of Great Britain and Ireland*, 89. 1 (1959), 45-60

Turner, G., *Nineteen Years in Polynesia: Missionary Life, Travels, and Researches in the Islands of the Pacific* (London: John Snow, 1861)

Turner, G., *Samoa; A Hundred Years Ago and Long Before together with Notes on the Cults and Customs of Twenty-Three Other Islands in the Pacific* (London: MacMillan and Co., 1884)

Tvveedale, M. (ed.), *Biblia Sacra juxta Vulgatam Clementinam; Editio Electronica* (London: Council of Bishop's Conference of England and Wales, 2005)

Tyrrell, J. B. (ed.), *David Thompson's Narrative of his Explorations in Western America; 1784-1812* ('The Publications of the Champlain Society', 12; Toronto: The Champlain Society, 1916)

Unaipon, D., *Legendary Tales of the Australian Aborigines* (1-2; typescript, 1924-1925)

van Beek, W. E. A., 'Dogon Restudied; A Field Evaluation of the Work of Marcel Griaule', *Current Anthropology*, 32. 2 (1991), 139-167

van de Wall Perné, G., *Veluwsche Sagen* (Amsterdam: Scheltens & Giltay, 1911²)

van der Geer, A., M. Dermitzakis & J. de Vos, 'Fossil Folklore from India: The Siwalik Hills and the *Mahâbhârata*', *Folklore*, 119. 1 (2008), 71-92

van der Sluijs, M. A., 'Phaethon and the Great Year', *Apeiron; A Journal for Ancient Philosophy and Science*, 39. 1 (2006), 57-90

van der Sluijs, M. A., 'On the Wings of Love', *Journal of Ancient Near Eastern Religions*, 8. 2 (2008), 219-251

van der Sluijs, M. A., 'Hll: Lord of the Sickle', *Journal of Near Eastern Studies*, 68. 4 (2009a), 269-281

van der Sluijs, M. A., 'Multiple Morning Stars in Oral Cosmological Traditions', *Numen; International Review for the History of Religions*, 56 (2009b), 459-476

van der Sluijs, M. A., review of L. Piccardi & W. B. Masse (eds.), *Myth and Geology* ('Geological Society Special Publication', 273; London: Geological Society, 2007), *Myth & Symbol*, 5. 2 (2009c), 58-74

van der Sluijs, M. A., *Traditional Cosmology; The Global Mythology of Cosmic Creation and Destruction*, vol. 1: *Preliminaries; Formation* (London: All-Round Publications, 2011a); vol. 2: *Functions* (idem, 2011b); vol. 3: *Differentiation* (idem, 2011c); vol. 4: *Disintegration* (idem, 2011d); vol. 5: *Solar and Lunar Anomalies* (Vancouver, Canada: All-Round Publications, 2018)

van der Sluijs, M. A. & P. James, 'Saturn as the 'Sun of Night' in Ancient Near Eastern Tradition', *Aula Orientalis*, 31. 2 (2013), 279-321

van Hasselt, J. B., 'Die Noeforezen', *Zeitschrift für Ethnologie. Organ der Berliner Gesellschaft für Anthropologie, Ethnologie und Urgeschichte*, 8 (1876), 134-139, 169-202

Veckenstedt, E., *Die Mythen, Sagen und Legenden der Žamaiten (Litauer). Gesammelt und herausgegeben* (1; Heidelberg: Carl Winter's Universitätsbuchhandlung, 1883)

Velikovsky, I., *Worlds in Collision* (New York: The MacMillan Company, 1950)

Velikovsky, I., 'Venus – A Youthful Planet', *Yale Scientific Magazine*, 41. 7 (April 1967), 8-11, 32

Velikovsky, I., 'On Saturn and the Flood', *Kronos; A Journal of Interdisciplinary Synthesis*, 5. 1 (1979), 3-11

Vickers-Rich, P. & N. W. Archbold, 'Squatters, Priests and Professors: A Brief History of Vertebrate Palaeontology in *Terra Australis*', in P. Vickers-Rich, J. M. Monaghan, R. F. Baird & T. H. Rich (eds.), *Vertebrate Palaeontology of Australasia* (Melbourne: Pioneer Design Studio, 1991), 1-43

Vidale, M., 'Protohistory of the Vara. Exploring the Proto-Indo-Iranian Background of an Early Mytheme of the Iranian Plateau', *The Journal of Indo-European Studies*, 45. 1-2 (2017), 27-57

Vogt, D., 'Raven's Universe', in V. del Chamberlain, J. B. Carlson & M. J. Young (eds.), *Songs from the Sky; Indigenous Astronomical and Cosmological Traditions of the World; Selected Proceedings of the 'First International Conference on Ethnoastronomy: Indigenous Astronomical and Cosmological Traditions of the World' Held at the Smithsonian Institution, Washington, D. C., 5-9 September 1983* (Bognor Regis: Ocarin Books) = *Archaeoastronomy: The Journal of the Center for Archaeoastronomy*, 12-13 (1996), 38-48

von Schröter, H. R., *Finnische Runen; Finnisch und Deutsch* (Uppsala: Palmstad & Co., 1819)

von Weiher, E., *Der babylonische Gott Nergal* ('Alter Orient und Altes Testament; Veröffentlichungen zur Kultur und Geschichte des Alten Orients und des Alten Testaments', 11; Neukirchen-Vluyn: Neukirchener Verlag, 1971)

Wagner, G., *Yuchi Tales* ('Publications of the American Ethnological Society', 13; New York: G. E. Stechert and Company, 1931)

Warner, W. Ll., *A Black Civilization; A Social Study of an Australian Tribe* (New York: Harper & Brothers Publishers, 1958[2])

Wassén, H., 'Cuentos de los Indios Chocós; Recogidos por Erland Nordenskiöld durante su expedición al istmo de Panamá en 1927 y publicados con notas y observaciones comparativas', *Journal de la Société des Américanistes*, 25. 1 (1933), 103-137

Waters, F., *Book of the Hopi* ('Penguin Books'; Harmondsworth: Penguin, 1978)

Watson, B. (tr.), *Records of the Grand Historian of China Translated from the Shih Chi of Ssuma Ch'ien*, vol. 1: *Early Years of the Han Dynasty 209 to 141 B. C.* ('Records of Civilization: Sources and Studies', 65; New York: Columbia University Press, 1971)

Weidner, E., 'Zur babylonischen Astronomie: II. ha-ha-ha-tum', *Babyloniaca; Études de philologie Assyro-Babylonienne*, 6 (1912), 1-7

Weltfish, G., *The Lost Universe; With a Closing Chapter on 'The Universe Regained'* (New York: Basic Books, 1965)

Whedbee, Ch. H., *Outer Banks Mysteries & Seaside Stories* (Charlotte, North Carolina: Heritage Printers, 1978)

Wilbert, J., 'Tobacco and Shamanistic Ecstasy among the Warao Indians of Venezuela', in P. T. Furst (ed.), *Flesh of the Gods; The Ritual Use of Hallucinogens* (Long Grove, Illinois: Waveland Press, 1972), 55-83, reprinted as 'Tobacco and Shamanistic Ecstasy' in J. Wilbert (ed.), *Mystic Endowment; Religious Ethnography of the Warao Indians* ('Religions of the World'; Cambridge, Massachusetts: Harvard University Press, 1993), 113-132

Wilbert, J., 'The Calabash of the Ruffled Feathers', *Artscanada*, 30. 4. 184-187 (1973-1974), 90-93, reprinted as 'The Calabash of Ruffled Feathers', in J. Wilbert (ed.), *Mystic Endowment; Religious Ethnography of the Warao Indians* ('Religions of the World'; Cambridge, Massachusetts: Harvard University Press, 1993), 133-143

Wilbert, J., 'Navigators of the Winter Sun', in E. P. Benson (ed.), *The Sea in the Pre-Columbian World; A Conference at Dumbarton Oaks October 26th and 27th, 1974* (Washington, District of Columbia: Dumbarton Oaks Research Library and Collections, 1977), 16-46

Wilbert, J., 'Geography and Telluric Lore of the Orinoco Delta', *Journal of Latin American Lore*, 5. 1 (1979), 129-150, reprinted in J. Wilbert (ed.), *Mystic Endowment; Religious Ethnography of the Warao Indians* ('Religions of the World'; Cambridge, Massachusetts: Harvard University Press, 1993), 3-24

Wilbert, J., 'Warao Cosmology and Yekuana Roundhouse Symbolism', *Journal of Latin American Lore*, 7. 1 (1981), 37-72, reprinted in J. Wilbert (ed.), *Mystic Endowment; Religious Ethnography of the Warao Indians* ('Religions of the World'; Cambridge, Massachusetts: Harvard University Press, 1993), 183-218

Wilbert, J., 'The House of the Swallow-Tailed Kite: Warao Myth and the Art of Thinking in Images', in G. Urton (ed.), *Animal Myths and Metaphors in South America* (Salt Lake City, Utah: University of Utah Press, 1985), 145-182, reprinted as 'The House of the Swallow-Tailed Kite' in J. Wilbert (ed.), *Mystic Endowment; Religious Ethnography of the Warao Indians* ('Religions of the World'; Cambridge, Massachusetts: Harvard University Press, 1993), 145-181

Wilbert, J., 'Eschatology in a Participatory Universe: Destinies of the Soul', in J. Wilbert (ed.), *Mystic Endowment; Religious Ethnography of the Warao Indians* ('Religions of the World'; Cambridge, Massachusetts: Harvard University Press, 1993), 87-111

Wilbert, J. & K. Simoneau (eds.), *Folk Literature of the Nivaklé Indians* ('Folk Literature of South American Indians'; 'UCLA Latin American Studies', 66; Los Angeles: UCLA Latin American Center Publications, 1987)

Wilbert, J. & K. Simoneau (eds.), *Folk Literature of the Sikuani Indians* ('Folk Literature of South American Indians'; 'UCLA Latin American Studies', 79; Los Angeles: UCLA Latin American Center Publications, 1992)

Winckler, H., *Himmels- und Weltenbild der Babylonier als Grundlage der Weltanschauung und Mythologie aller Völker* ('Der Alte Orient. Gemeinverständliche Darstellungen herausgegeben von der Vorderasiatischen Gesellschaft', 3. 2/3; Leipzig: J. C. Hinrichs'sche Buchhandlung, 1901)

Wissler, C. & D. C. Duvall, *Mythology of the Blackfoot Indians* ('Anthropological Papers of the American Museum of Natural History', 2. 1; New York: Order of the Trustees, 1908)

Withnell, J. G., *The Customs and Traditions of the Aboriginal Natives of North Western Australia* (Roebourne: publisher not stated, 1901)

Worms, E. A., *Australian Aboriginal Religions* (trs. M. J. Wilson, D. O'Donovan & M. Charlesworth; 'Nelen Yubu Mythological Series', 3; Kensington, New South Wales: Nelen Yubu Missiological Unit, 1986)

Xu Zhentao, D. W. Pankenier & Jiang Yaotiao (eds.), *East Asian Archaeoastronomy: Historical Records of Astronomical Observations of China, Japan and Korea* ('Earth Space Institute Book Series', 5; Amsterdam: Overseas Publishers Association, Gordon and Breach Science Publishers, 2000)

Zöllner, S., *Lebensbaum und Schweinekult; Die Religion der Jalî im Bergland von Irian-Jaya (West-Neu-Guinea)* (Wuppertal: Theologischer Verlag Rolf Brockhaus, 1977) = *The Religion of the Yali in the Highlands of Irian Jaya* (tr. J. A. Godschalk; Goroka: The Melanesian Institute, 1988)

index

A

Abaddon, 89
'Abbā 'Arīkā, 20
Abkhaz, 120
Abraham, 20
abundance, 30, 32, 96, 105, 125
Abyla, 139
abyss, 17, 146
acacia buds, 32
Acarnania, 141–42
Achaea, 141
Achitumetl, 86
Adam (author), 72
Adelaide, 101
Ādi Parva, 123
Adnyamathanha, 101, 105, 126
Adrastus of Cyzicus, 21
Aegean Sea, northern, 142
Aeneid, 60
aeons. *See* epochs
Aetna, 141
Africa(n), 27, 47, 112, 117, 139–41, 144, 146
age of creation, 33
age of monsters, 2, 85
age of myth, 3, 39, 109, 130–31, 139
ages, paradisiacal, 31, 139
ages of men, 139
Agni, 71
agriculture, 33, 137
Ahakanoko, 17
Ahura Mazdā, 41
Aillaud, 116
air
  dusty, 112
  moist, 112
  parched, 35
air bladder, 80
Aíshish, 119
Akkadian, 50, 57
Akudnirmiut, 43
akukūtu, 57
alang-alang, 147
Alaska, Central, 129
Alavo, 91
Albuquerque, 2, 50
Aldebaran, 71
Alexander (author), 95–96
Alfredo, 42–43
Algonquian, 2
Allan & Delair, 117
Alligator, Lake, 98
alluvial mire, 95
Alps, 38
Alsea, 49
Altan melekei, 29

altar, sacrificial, 96
alternation, regular seasonal, 37
Alu, 111
Ālūtú, 61
Amazonas, 73, 82
Ambracian Gulf, 141
America, Central, 45
American Philosophical Society, 96
Amma, 18
Amra, 120
Amur, Middle, 99
Anacardiaceae, 8
Anak Mahatara, 147
Ancasmarca, 79
anchor, 102
Andaman Islands, 100
Andeporu clan, 110
Anderson, 72
Anderson & Dibble, 63
Andes, 38
Andibepe clan, 111
α Andromedae, 71
Aneki, 35
angels, 40, 86, 89
anger, 42, 74, 127
Angguruk, 13
Ani´-Hyûñ´tĭkwălâ´skĭ, 39
animals, giant, 79, 81, 126–27, 130
Anishinaubaeg, 37
Annals of Cuauhtitlan, 51, 118, 148
annual festival, congregation, 85, 87
Antares, 67
Antirrhium, 142
Ant People, 49
Anuna gods, 56
Apellis, 84
Aphrodite, 60, 122
apocalyptic traditions, 25
Apollodorus, pseudo-, 121
Apollyon, 89
Apologética historia sumaria, 51
Apotelesmatica, 60
Ápsinthos, 89
Apurinã, 73, 82
Aquila audax, 108
α, β and γ Aquilae, 70
Arabana, 124
Aráchoba, 147
Aramaic, 20, 59
Ara-tiatia, 137
arch, 14, 18
archer, 10, 78
archipelagoes, southern, 145
arcs, 14, 103
  concentric, 102–3

Arcturus, 71
Arebati, 111
Argentina, 6, 14, 35, 46, 88, 113, 149
Argonautica, 140–41
Aristotle, 68
Ari-Wa-Kis, 26, 127
Arizona, 3–5, 35–36, 49, 136
arm, 53, 91, 98
  long, 105
Arnhem Land, 20, 53, 106
Arrernte, 32, 102
arrows, 13, 29, 38, 78, 120, 127
art, parietal, 100
Artemisia, 89
Arthur's Seat, 143
artiodactyls, 123
Arumei, 111
ascending, 36, 57, 116, 137
ascent
  old earth's, 113
  water's, 112
Asejetáx, 9
As·etí, 6–7, 14, 114–115, 151
Ashanti, 138
ashes, 80, 83, 95, 117, 119, 131
Asia, 99, 123, 141–42
Asita Devala, 71
Aspidosperma quebrachoblanco, 8
asterisms, 22–23, 72
astḕr mégas, 89
Aston, 15
Atalantes, 140
Atayal, 45
Atherton Tableland, 133, 144
Athol(l), 126
Atlantic, 142
Atlantis, 142
Atlas, 140–41
atmosphere, 66–67, 70, 95
Augustine of Hippo, 21, 122–23
aureoles, 66–67, 70–71
aurora borealis, 57–58, 61
Australia, Central, 31–32, 34, 102
Australian, 132
autumn storms, great, 97
Aveni, Anthony Francis, 63–64
Avesta, 41
Avienus, 60
Ax, John, 4, 39
axe, 6, 147
axis mundi, axes mundi, 6–7, 11, 14–18, 21, 23–24, 32, 39, 47, 49, 55, 84, 87, 96, 119, 146–47
Ayawa, 118

'Ayiš ['Ayish], 90
Aymará, 41–42, 79, 85
A'yûñ'inĭ, 4, 39
Aztecs, 12, 48, 50–51, 62–65, 67–68, 70, 72, 118, 120, 130, 148

B

Babel-Mandeb, 144
Babylon(ian), 23, 57, 71, 83, 88, 148
Babylonian Talmūd, 20, 23, 59, 90
Bacab, 87
Badlands (National Park), 128
bag, 21, 53–55, 136
 dilly, 55
bags, celestial, 44
bahana(rotu), 16, 18
Bak Bongchun, 136
baktun cycles, 11
balai-aba, 54
Baliem Valley, 12
Bamboo Annals, 22
Bandaiyan, 109
bandicoot, short-nose, 133
bandicoots, sharp-nosed, 32
bandurria, 42
Bandy, 60
banks, 31, 85, 126, 129
banyan-tree, 55
Bǎodéxiàn, 124
Barany, 135
Barasana, 5, 116, 118, 138
Barefoot, Daniel W., 96–98
Barich, 140–41
bark, 4, 76
Barkindji, 92–93, 105–6
Barnumbir, 20, 53–55
Barrett, 107, 125
Barría, 145
Barrier Reef, 143
Barrine, lake, 135
Barunggam, 125
Basedow, 105
baskets, 53, 137–38
Bastian, 29
Basu, 36
Bate, 89
Battee, 55
battle, 9, 21, 32, 38, 43, 67, 92, 94, 128
Baudó Emberá, 149
Bauer, 79
Bay of Bengal, 100
Beals, Carleton, 48
Beboon, 37, 41
bees, native, 32
Before Ice Age mob, 109
Bellamy, 72
Bellatrix, 67
Beltran, 11
beṇ Nissīm Masnūt, Šəmu'ēl, 90
Benavente, Toribio de, 130
Bengal, Bay of, 100

Bengal, Central and Eastern, 36
Bengoa, 144
Beni, 111
Benítez, Pascual, 9, 113, 151
Bennett, George, 125
Benson, William Ralganal, 73, 77
Bərākōt, 90
Bərēšīt, 90
Berezkin, 146
Berndt, 101
Berndt & Berndt, 107
Besbicus, 140
Betelgeuse, 67
Bethel, 127
Bhaga, constellation, 70
Bhathal, 54
Bhīṣma Parva, 25, 70
Bibbulmun, 39
Bible, Biblical, 20, 76, 87
Bibliotheca, 121
Bibliotheca Historica, 121–22, 140, 142
Bibliothèque Nationale, Paris, 63, 86
Bierhorst, 51, 118, 148
Big Bar, 38
Big Bone Lick (State Park), 128
Bighorns mountains, 30
Bijli ca har, 123
Billerbeck & Neumann-Hartmann, 121
Bimbowrie, 100
Bira, 112
Bird Age, 125
birds, 4, 24, 32, 38, 45, 50, 52, 55–56, 73, 76, 98, 108–9, 131
 extinct, 1
 forest, 4
 large, 1, 129, 131
bird-spirit, 17
Birrimitji, 109
Birrowarr, 54–55
birth of fire, 90
Bisschop, Peter, 119–20
Bithynia, 140
Bizone, Byzone, 141
Black, Richard, 43
Black Sea, 122, 141–42
black stuff, burning, 28, 82, 112, 117
blacksmiths, 18
Blang, 120
blazes, 30, 57, 70–71, 119
Bleeke Meer, 43
blood, 12, 14, 59, 120
 black, 120
blood sacrifices, 124
blossoms, yellow, 32
blue flash, 66
Blue Mountains, 132
bluffs, high, 104
Boas, 43, 148
body parts, 105
Boeotia, 140, 147
boiling, 72–74

bolide, 58, 64, 82, 95, 105
 electrophonic, 61
Bolio, 11, 95
Bolivia, 41–42
Bolon(tiku), 11
bolts, 9, 61, 74, 128
bombardment, 94, 117
Bombowie, 100
bones, 81, 121, 123–30, 132–33
bonfire, ceremonial, 96
Bön religion, 33
Book of Chilam Balam of Chumayel, 11, 95
Book of Jasher, 135
Book of Southern Qí, 61
boomerang, 107–8
bōr, 87–88
Bor, 147
Bô-rô, 33, 115
Bosco, 5, 118
Bosp(h)orus, 142
boulder, 47, 104–5, 135
 erratic, 38
Boulia, 55
Bousset, 89
bows, 4
box, daylight, 75
boy, 15–16, 78
boys, little, 143
Brahmā, 25, 82
Brahmarashi, constellation, 70
Bralgu, 53
brass, yellow, 35
Brasseur de Bourbourg, Charles-Étienne, 85–87
Brazil, 33, 73, 82, 115
Bṛhat-Saṃhitā, 71–72
Bricker, 69
bridge, 14–17
Bridges, 35
Brisbane, 125
Bristow, 120
British Columbia, 38, 55, 103
Broderip, William John, 126
Brodersen, 121
Broken Hill, 105
Broom-star, 60, 67
brothers, 7, 27, 107
Brown, Polly, 106
Brundage, 148
Bryant, 108
Buber, 90
bucket, 143
Buckland, 123, 126
Buddhism, 29
Budla-bila, 100–101
budz ek, 68–69
buffaloes, 76, 128
Bulgaria, 141
bull, big, 128
Buna, 36
Bunjil, 143
Bunurong, 142–43
Bunyip, 125–26
Bura, 141
Buralku, 53–55

burning, 28–29, 31, 65–66, 68, 71, 73, 78, 80–82, 88–89, 92, 97–98, 112, 117–19, 134
burning pitch, 119
Burt Plain, 32
Bùzhōu, Mount, 23–24
Byzantium, 142
    Stephen of, 121

C

Cabbage, Sarah, 93, 106
Cabo San Pablo, 145
Cagni, 23
Cahuabi, 4, 35
Cai, 10
Caicaivilu. *See* Kaikai Vilu
cairn, 133
Cairns, 144
Cajeput tree, 76
Calderón, Clemente, 9
Caley, George, 133
calf, 126
California, 72–73, 76–77, 85, 146
Callimachus of Cyrene, 84
Callistion, 84–85
Calpe, 139
Camoola, 132
Campbell, 32
Campester, 60
Camschoat, 36
Canaanite, 84
Canada, 3, 29–30, 43–44, 146
γ, δ and θ Cancri, 70
cangel [*canhel*], 11–12
Caño Colorado, 5, 118
canoe-maker, 17
Canopus, 84
Capa, Angel, 9
Cape Grafton, 133, 143
Capell, 108–9
Capistrano de Abreu, 33, 115–16
Capo Peloro, 140
Captain Jim, 26, 127
Cara(ga)bí, 149
Caramillo, Cevero, 52
Cárdenas Tabies, 144
Carolina, 98
Carolina Bays, 95–96, 99
Carson, Rachel, 98–99
carvings, 99–100, 104–5
cashew family, 8
cassowary, 133–34
Castor of Rhodes, 21
catasterised form, 50, 88
Catawba, 95, 99
Categorised Tales, 10
Catío Emberá, 149
Catlinite, 104
Caucasus, southwestern, 120
Cavadini, Alessandro, 134
caves, 32, 47, 51, 54, 103, 106, 108–9, 122, 124, 132
cavity, deep, 88
Cawthorne, 1
Caxinauá, 33, 115–16

Cayley, 132
Cayley's Repulse, 133
Cē Ācatl Quetzalcōātl, 86
Cē Ācatl Topiltzin, 51, 56
ceremonial object, 53, 55
Chajanaj, 8–9, 150
Chakekenapok, 26–27
Chalcidice, 121
Chamba Leko, 45
changers, the four, 10–12
chaos, 50, 136, 146
Chapman, Henry, 51
charcoal, burning, 119–20
chariot, great, 25
Charley, 43
Charley, Sarah, 50
Charlin, 43
Chase-Sardi, 8–9, 46, 150
Chashkilchesh, 35
Chauacá, 93
Chavero, Alfredo, 48, 130
Chayu, 10
Chen, 99
Chén Hàn, 10
Cheonjiwang Bonpuri, 136
Cherniak, 25, 70
Cherokee, 4, 39, 93, 95, 99
Chi-Anung-Nah-Way, 79
Chicxulub, 94
Chi-Gah-Nun-Nah-Way-Anung, 80
Chikinchel, 93
Chilam Balam of Chumayel, Book of, 11, 95
child, 38, 55
child-ancestor, 15
Child of the Sun, 138
children, 3, 8, 26, 38, 42, 53, 76
Chile
    central-western, 144
    southern, 35
Chiloé, 144
Chimanitou, 81
China, Chinese, 9, 20–21, 23–24, 40, 58, 60, 62, 64, 67, 72, 120, 124
Chipewyans, 39
Chippewa, 39
Chippindale, 107
Chisel Tusk, 10
Chogamje, 136
Cholula [Chololla], 50–51, 65, 68
Chopari, John, 52
Christenson, 51, 132
Christian, 122
    calendar, 51
Ch'u, 61
Chumayel, 10, 94
Chumayel, Book of Chilam Balam of, 11, 95
Chuvash, 146
Cic Dinka, 147
cigars, 16, 66, 69
Cipactonal, 86
cities, quadrangular, 32, 41
citlal choloha, 63
citlalin popoca, 63

Citlaltepetl, 65
Citrā, constellation, 70
classical, 34, 61, 68, 71
Claudian, 122
clay, 5
    red Lower Pliocene, 124
    red stone, 104
clew, 91
Clifford, Arnold, 2, 50
cliffs, 104, 122, 141
climate, 33, 38–40, 123
    monsoon, 36
    paradisiacal, 34
Cline Library, 5
Clinton, George, 120
Clinton, Ida, 120
Clinton, Sally, 120
clouds, 8–9, 15, 17, 25, 37, 57, 59, 61, 67, 84, 91, 123, 125, 129, 133–34
    red, 57, 134
    yellow, 134
cloven feet, 104
coastlines, 139, 143
coasts, 14, 30, 47, 142, 147
Cobb, 143
Cochrane, 59, 62, 88, 148
Cochrane & Talbott, 62
coconut flesh, 147
Codex Chimalpopoca, 51, 118, 148
Codex Florentinus, 63
Codex Ríos, 48, 63
Codex Telleriano-Remensis, 63–65, 69, 86
Codex Vaticanus, 48, 86
Coggia's comet, 65
cogongrass, 147
Cojazzi, 36
Čolbon, 21, 52
Cold People, 38
cold period, 34, 38–40, 43–44, 46, 80
Colebrooke, 123
Collectanea Rerum Memorabilium, 121
Colombia, 5, 116, 118, 148–49
colonists, 125
Colorado, 37
column, 12–13, 18, 50, 104, 124, 142
columns, juxtaposed, 14
Colville Lake, 29, 146
comet, Coggia's, 65
comet, Halley's, 70, 81
comet(ary), 25, 27, 32, 34, 43–45, 50–53, 56, 58–65, 67–72, 78–83, 85, 88, 93–96, 99, 129–30
comets
    giant, 52, 82
    hairy, 69
    planetary, 60, 62, 72
    pole, 72
    white, 72
comet's coma, 71
Comisario, 6, 14, 114, 151

conflagration, 6, 73, 75, 90, 96, 117, 119, 129
Congo, 39, 110, 149
Congregation, Mount, 84
Conil, 94
Con Quien, 4, 35
constellations, 22-23, 58
contest, 2, 46
Conway, 33-34, 44, 81-82, 130
cooking, 45, 78
cooling, 45-46, 123
Copenhaver, 75
copper, 80-81, 90
cords, 23, 25, 55
Cordyline australis, 103
Coree, 97
Corinth, Gulf of, 141
Corio, 142
cornel-cherries, 34
coronae, luminous, 66
cosmic egg, 17
Cotopaxi, 68
cotorra, 36
Council Bluffs, 2, 27
counterglow, 66
Courtesans, 29
coyote, 4, 37, 103
Coyote, 127
Cranz, 27
crater, 65, 87-88, 95
Crater, The, 135
crater lake, 133
Creator-Bird of the Dawn, 15-16
Cree, East, 78
creeks, 32, 96, 105
crescents, narrow, 66
Crete, 122
Criollo, 9
Critias, 84
crocodile head, 100-101
Cronus. See Kronos
crow, 45
Crow (nation), 148
Cruz, José, 85
crystal, solid, 31, 39
Ctenomys, 9, 150
Cuauhtitlan, Annals of, 51, 118, 148
culture hero, 2, 76, 81, 146
Cumberland Sound, 43
Cunningham, Robert, 143
Curtis, 146
Cusco, 79
Cyanean Rocks, 142
cycad nuts, 107
cyclones, 48
Cyprus, 140, 147
Cyzicus, Adrastus of, 21

D

Daevas, 41
Daka, 46
Dakota, North and South, 73-74, 128-29
Dalles, 38
Dalley, 23

Dalnuranu, 54
dancing, 54-55, 124
Danish, 129
Dardanelles, 141-42
Dardanus, 142
dark cloud, 149
dark land, 35
darkness, 1, 3, 5-8, 18, 22, 36, 40, 42, 44, 46-47, 88, 90, 115-16, 146, 149-51
dark planet, 71
Darmesteter, 41
daughter, 38, 52, 57, 84, 119
Davidson, 4, 35, 106-7
Davies, 35
Davis Strait, 43
dawn(ing), 6, 10-11, 23, 53-54, 132
Dawn, Creator-Bird of the, 15-16
Dawn Pileated Woodpecker, 33, 44, 81, 130
Dawn, son of, 83-84, 88
Dawson, 1, 56, 131
Dayak, Ngaju, 147
daykeeper, 118
de Benavente, Toribio, 130
de Bovis, 146
de Ciudad Real, 69
De Civitate Dei, 21, 123
De Gente Populi Romani, 21
de Gomara, 130
de Harlez, 22
de la Garza, 94
de las Casas, Bartolomé, 51
de los Ríos, Pedro, 48, 86
de Mendieta, Gerónimo, 51
de Mendoza, don Antonio, 63
De Mirabilibus Mundi, 121
de Molina, Cristóbal, 63, 79, 85
De Ostentis, 60
de Rosales, Diego, 144
de Rosny, 63, 86
de Sahagún, Bernardino, 63
de Santa Teresa, Severino, 149
de Smet, Pierre-Jean, 2, 27
de Tudela Bueso, 51
death, 26-27, 31, 35, 39, 116, 120, 138
deer, 96, 98, 124, 128
deformities, physical, 148
deities
 otiose, 33
 supreme, 110, 127, 143
del Chamberlain, 51-52
Delamere Station, 107
Delaware River, 75, 127
Deloria, Vine, 39
deluge. See flood
Dendrolagus, 13
Denebola, 70
Déné, 29-30
Denésoliné, 39
Densmore, 129
depressions, 74, 98, 106, 129
dermatological problems, 118

descending lunar node, 71
descent, 18, 83-85, 109, 111
desert, central, 30
deus otiosus, 33
Devas, 25
Devil, 52
devils, 42
dew
 deep, 40
 plain of, 40
Dharug, 132
Dhirari, 124
Dhruva(ḥ), 25, 71
Dhruva Ketu, 25, 72
dhūmaketur mahāghoraḥ, 71
Diamantina, 30-31
Dieri, 31, 124
diffractions, 67
dilly-bag, 21, 55, 133-34
Diné, 1-2, 50, 127
Dinka, Cic, 147
Dio of Naples, 21
Diodorus of Sicily, 121-22, 140, 142
Dioscorea, 53
Diprotodon, 125-26
dirt, 111-14, 117
disappearance, 23, 75, 127, 131
disc, 24, 27
diseases, 138
dismembered body parts, 26
diucon, fire-eyed, 42
Dixon, Robert Malcolm Ward, 133-35, 144
Djabwurung, 1, 131
Djambarrpuyŋu clan, 21, 55
Djiraia, 54
Djua, 109
Djunggun, 108
Dogon, 18-19
dog women, 103
dogs, 29-30, 78, 81, 145
Domu Hokonamana Ariawara, 15
Dòngtíng (Lake), 9-10
Dòngtíng Líng Yǐn Zhuàn, 10
Donnelly, Ignatius Loyola, 99
Dorsey, George Amos, 26, 52, 127
Dow, 83
Downy-Feather-Star, 52
dragon, 9-11, 52, 56, 127, 129
 black, 24
 crimson, 9
dragon bones, 124
Dragon Lord, 9
Drake & O'Malley, 59
dreaming, 100-101, 107, 129
Dreamtime, 100, 103, 107-8, 126
Droṇa Parva, 123
drought, 88, 96-97, 112, 119, 124
Drysdale River, 100
dua, 54
Dugan, 125-26
Dulgubarra Mamu, 135

Dumuzi, 57
Dunjun-jina, 53
Durikiyoo, 21
dust, 66, 98, 111
   volcanic, 68
Dusun, Low-Country, 14
Dutch, 147
Dutt, 77
Dyirbal, 134-35, 144
Dzitbalché, Songs of, 68-69

E

Eacham, Lake, 133-35, 144
eagle, 90, 146
Eagle Men, 42
eaglehawk, 108
Eaglehawk, 101
earth diving, 99
Earth-mother, 28, 137
earth oven, 133
earth sinking, 43, 95, 143
earthquakes, 1, 12, 24, 47, 49, 63, 114, 131-32, 135, 140-41, 145
earth's sphericity, 49
Ebuya, 110
echinoderms, 121
eclipses, 21, 67, 85, 87, 131
   partial, 22
ecliptic band, 14, 19
ecliptic plane, 33, 66
ecstatic trance, 16
Ecuador, 68
Edmonson, 11-12, 68-69, 95
Éfé, 39, 110-12, 117
Egede, Poul Hansen, 27-28
eggs, 16-18, 108
Egypt, 56, 84-85
Ehanktonwanna, 104-5
Ehécatl, 48
Ehecatonatiuh, 48
Ehrenreich, 73, 82
elbow marks, 106
Elcho Island, 21
Eleatic Stranger, 3, 75
electrophonic bolides, 61
'Ēl, 83-84
Elkin, 100, 103, 105
elks, 76, 128
Elliger, 84, 135
El Salvador, western, 65
'Elyōn, 84
emanations, 62, 64
Emberá, 148-49
   Baudó, 149
   Catío, 149
emergence, people's, 51, 151
Emory, 146
emus, 1, 101, 131, 143
Encinales, Maria Jesusa, 72
Encinales, Pedro, 85
English Company Islands, 54
engravings, 100-101, 104
Enḫeduanna, 50, 56, 149
Enicognathus ferrugineus, 36
Enoch, 25
entrails, 27

epochs, 3, 20, 35-36, 39, 49, 82, 95, 101, 118, 121, 125, 130
equator, 33
equatorial latitude, 39
eras. *See* epochs
Erdoes & Ortiz, 74, 128
Eridanus, river, 88
Erra and Išum, 23
eruption, volcanic, 1, 30, 65, 68, 131-33, 135
Erwin, 104
Erymanthian Boar, 122
escape, 28, 53-54, 82, 106, 112, 117, 133
Ethiopic Enoch, 25
Ethnica, 121
Euboea, 140
Euhemerist, 109
Euramoo, 135
Euriowie, 105
Euxine (Sea), 142
Evadu, 111
Evans, 14
evaporation, 88, 112
Evarts, Mark, 51
evening, 15, 57, 101, 104
evening star, 20, 50, 52, 55-56, 61, 65-66, 69-70, 83-84, 86, 88, 93
evergreens, 35
exhalations, 68
Exodus, 147
extinction, 1-2, 46, 48, 121, 125
eyelashes, 47, 56
eye of Ra, 56
Eyre, Lake, 30-31, 124

F

face masks, 99
facial contortions, 148
Falconer, 123
Falconer & Cautley, 123
famine, 110-11, 119
Fáng Xuánlíng, 61-62
Faro, Punta del, 140
Farstad, 76, 84, 89
feathered serpent, 56
feathers, 21, 52-53, 55, 59, 90
felling, 12-13
Fēngjiāo Shū, 61
fennel-stalk, hollow, 138
Ferawe mountain, 13
Feuerflut, 74
Feuermeer, 74
Feuerregen, 74
fiery mane, 9
filth. *See* dirt
fingerprints, 106
Finnish, 90
fireballs, 52, 83, 91
fire flood, 74-75
fire rain, 74
fireless condition, 45
Fireplace, 132

fires, 24, 31, 45, 56, 59, 78, 92, 98, 121
Firestone, 95-96
firs, highest, 44
First Jewish Revolt, 89
First World, 136
Fisher, 37-38
fishermen, 142
fishes, 4, 32, 76-77, 82, 91, 96, 98, 115, 131
Fitsakajich, 6-7, 114, 150
Five Activity doctrine, 61
Flaccus, Valerius, 140-41
Flagstaff, 5
flames, 26, 57-58, 69, 71, 74, 83, 90-92, 119-20, 128, 132
flammable materials, 117
Flandes Indiano, 144
flash, blue or green, 66
flattening of the lands, 11
Fleitas, Alejandro, 114
flesh, human, 52
Fletcher, Athol(l) T., 126
flight, 1, 15, 131
   ecstatic, 15
Flinders Ranges, 101, 105, 126
flint(stone), 27, 51
flint, the man of, 26
floating, 43, 134
flood, 9-12, 21-23, 27-29, 33, 41, 43-44, 72-75, 78-79, 82, 85-88, 90, 92-95, 108-9, 117-19, 121-22, 132-35, 141-45
Flood & David, 107
flowers, 15-18, 31-32, 34, 53
foam, 146
Foam-of-Ocean, 137
fog, 146, 149
food, 15, 30, 32-34, 42, 55, 76-78, 81, 96, 110-12, 147
   planted, 111
foot, 77, 106, 142, 145
footprints, 80, 93, 106, 145
forests, 8, 24, 27, 35, 39, 47, 69, 73-74, 77, 79, 96-97, 110, 112-113, 120, 123, 128, 130
Fornander, 146
Forsyth, 84
Fort Good Hope, 29, 146
fossil deposits, 121-22, 127, 130
fossil-imprints, 105
fossil, living, 125
fossils, 1, 121-27, 129-30
foul rain, 112
foundations, 88, 135
fountains, 22, 90, 135
Four Corners Region, 1
Fourth World, 46
Fowler, 3, 75
Frachtenberg, 49
fragmentation, 26, 120
fragments, 12, 27, 52, 87, 90
Franciscan, 51
Frazer, 148
Fredericks, Oswald 'White Bear', 4-5, 49, 136

Freedman, 20, 59
freezing, 47, 129
French, 18–19, 85, 119
fresh water, 48, 82, 101
Froben [Frobine], 119
Froben, Minnie, 119
frog, golden, 29
frogs, 4, 121, 127
frost, 21, 41–42, 46–47, 52
fruits, 34, 96
fugitives, 133, 144
Funk, 90
furnace, great, 89

G

Galland-Burke brewery, 131
Gallery Hill, 102
Gălûṅ'lătĭ, 39
Gamberre, 100
game, 96–98, 115, 131
Ganander, 92
Garden River band, 33, 44, 81, 130
gardens, earth, 112
Garga, 71
Garnayanda, 107
Gatschet, 119
Geelong, 142
Geertz, 5
Geffcken, 88–89
Gegenschein, 66
Ge-Non-Dahway-Anung, 79
Geography (Strabo), 121–22, 140, 142
German, 63–64, 94, 116
Ghana, 138
giant, eastern, 40
giant birds, 1
giant humans, 121, 127
giant kangaroos, 1, 125
giant reptiles, 125
giant tooth, 122
giants, 1–3, 35, 104, 122–24, 126–27, 129–30
Giants (Greek), 121
giants, winter, 43
Gibraltar(, Strait of), 139, 141
Gigantomachy, 121–22
Gilbert, 99
Ginzberg, 90
Giṛugar, 144
glacial condition, 31, 39
glaciation, 42–43, 46
glaciers, 38, 43–44
glow(ing), 70–71, 90–91
 fiery, 57–58
 nocturnal, 68
 red, 57
glow worms, 87
Gnurker, 76
God, 40, 74, 147
gold, 35, 80
golden age, 3, 30, 33–34, 36, 41, 79, 121, 130
golden frog, 29
Gondatti, 75
Gònggōng [Gong Gong], 23–24

Gorge, 101
Gorrondolmi, 107
Gowrie, 125
Graecae Descriptio (Pausanias), 121
Graeco-Roman, 64
grain, 10, 34
granite, solid, 104
Grant, James, 126
grass, 32, 41, 55, 103, 147, 151–52
Grassi, Orazio, 59
grassland people, 6, 14, 114, 151
graves, 104, 130
Great Bear, 59
Great Dust, 97
Great Midraš, 90
Great Rabbit, 93
Great Serpent, 11
Great Slave Lake, 3, 44
great star, 88–89
Great Star, 93
Greece, 121, 141–42
Greenland, 27, 43
Gregory, 31, 125, 144
Grenfell, Mount, 105
Grenier, 144
grey jay, 78
Griaule, Marcel & Dieterlen, 18–19, 85, 119
Gribble, Ernest Richard Bulmer, 133, 144
griddle, 5, 117
Grignard, 74
guanos, 45, 78
guardians, 21, 50
guarding, 3, 8, 35, 40, 53–54
Guatemala, 1, 44, 94, 117–18, 130, 132
Gudjari, 100–101
Gumiya, 120
gum-trees, 31–32
Gunbalanya, 106
Gunditjmara, 126
Gungganyji, 133, 143
Gunn, 126
Gunulkjau, 107
Gunwinggu, 106–7
Gupta, 123
Gusinde, 42–43, 145
Guyana, 105
Gwydir, Rickard Daniel, 131
Gyedarra, 125

H

Hacho, Monte, 139
Hades, 28
Hagar (author), 93
Hahn, 74
Haida, 30
hail, 10, 39, 45, 91
hair, 47, 50, 52, 56, 80, 93
hair standing, 55
Hairy One, 56
Hallet, Jean-Pierre & Pelle, 110–11

Halley's comet, 70, 81
halo, 65–66
haloes, planetary, 68
Hálupens, 42
Hamilton, 1
Ḥammā, 59
Hamnett & Thornton, 98
Hamy, 62
hand, 46, 53, 63–64, 74, 76, 86, 99, 105–6, 124, 141
Ḥanīnā bar Ḥāmā, 59
happiness, 32, 77
Hardeland, August, 147
Harlots, 30
har-mō'ēd, 84
harmony, 3, 32
Harou, 27
Hathor, 56
Haudenosaunee (Confederacy), 2, 46
Haynes, 54
heart, 11, 50, 67, 80, 83, 94, 97, 117
Heart (star), 67
Heart of Sky, 94, 117
heat, 5, 15, 29, 37–38, 44–45, 52, 57, 80, 119, 136, 149
Heavenly Court, constellation, 22
heavens, layered, 92, 138
Hebrew, 41, 76, 83, 88, 90, 93, 122, 135, 147
Hecker, 57
Hēlēl ben-Šaḥar, 83–84, 86–87
heliacal position, 66
Hellenistic period, 60
Hellespont, 142
heōsphóros, 84
Hephaestio of Thebes, 60
Heracles [Herakles, Hercules], 121–22, 139–40
Herbert, 123
herbivorous animal, large, 126
herbs, 10, 32, 76
herd, 8, 128, 145
Herling, 83
Hermes Trismegistus, 75
Hermetism, 75
Hernández, 100
hero, 102, 107, 123, 136
 culture, 2, 76, 81, 146
heroes, age of, 121
heroes, twin, 1, 69, 132
Heroicus, 121
Herrmann, 75
Hesiod, 73, 139–40
Hesperos [Hesperus], 84
Héšpul, 42
Hé Tú, 61
Hidimva-Vadha Parva, 123
hieros gámos, 56
hills, 1, 31–32, 106, 127, 131–32
Hinchinbrook Island, 144
hind feet, 59
Hindū astrology, 71
Hinepare, Ngāti, 28, 138

Hinton, 61
Hipparion, 124
Hîsalî, 12–13
Historia eclesiástica Indiana, 51
Historia general de las cosas de Nueva España, 63
Historia general del reino de Chile, 144
History of Jìn, 61
History of Sòng, 61
Hitchcock County, 127
Ho, 61–62
Hoani Te Whatahoro Jury, 28, 138
Hobson's Bay, 143
Hocabá, 69
Hodge, 98
Hohenberger, 119
Hoíl, Juan Josef, 11, 95
hole, 39, 74, 79, 96, 129, 147, 150–51
Holm, 44
Holocene, 121
honey, 32, 35
Hopi, 4–5, 36, 40, 49, 136
Hopping Djua, 109
horizon, 36, 67
Horn of Africa, 144
Horne & Aiston, 31
horns, 17–18, 50, 52
horse, 77, 124
horseman, 60
House of Smoke, 15–16
houses, 13, 15–17, 33, 48, 63, 86, 94, 115, 118, 137
Hovell, 126
Howitt, 40, 45, 78, 124
Huacoríso, Selimo, 149
Huánánzǐ, 10, 22, 24
Huáng Cháng, 20, 58, 62
Huarochirí manuscript, 79
Hugh-Jones, 5, 118
Huka-a-tai, 137
Hûl, 12–13
Huliznab, 132
Hull, William Henry, 143
Húnán, northeast, 9
Huni Kuin, 33, 115–17
Húŋkpapha band, 129
hunting, 38, 76, 107, 143
hurricanes, 1, 24, 48, 56, 117, 142
Hussain, 85
huts, 8, 39, 42, 47, 65
Hyperboreans, 41

I

Iberia, 139
ibis, black-faced, 42
Icazbalceta, 51
ice, 28, 38–39, 42–44, 47–49, 82, 113
ice age, 47–48, 74, 117
Ice Age, 41, 109, 122
ice sea, 129
iceberg fleet, 43

Icelandic, 19, 43
icicles, 35
Icteridae, 78
Idaho, 103
Iddin-Dagān, 56–57
Ides, Eberhard Isbrand, 129
Ifugao, 30
Iháŋkthuŋwaŋna, 105
Îlît mountain, 12
illness, 47
Ilmarinen, 90
impact, 83, 87–89, 93–99
Imperata cylindrica, 147
imprints, 105, 128
imprisonment, temporary, 47
Ina(n)na, 50, 56–57
incantations, 57, 137
India, 74, 85, 123, 146
Indonesia, 12
Indra, 70, 72
inflammable matter, 119
initiation, 17
inland lake, 91, 98
inland seas, 96, 98, 141, 143
insects, 4, 32, 76
insignia, 12
Inuit, 43
inundation. *See* flood
inversion of sky and earth, 28, 48, 82, 110, 112–13, 117, 151
invisible guide, 15–16
Io-taketake, 138
Iowa, 2, 27
Iran, 41
Irby-Massie & Keyser, 60
Iromba, 102
Isaac, Frederick Neville, 126
Isaacs, 100
Isacsson, 149
Isaiah, 83–84
Isaiah, 20, 84
Isin, 56
island, 39, 53–55, 81, 131, 139–40, 144–45
island-continent, 125
island of the dead, 53
Istanbul, 142
Ištar, 50, 57
Ităgû´năhǐ, 4, 39
Italy, 59, 89, 121, 140–41
Iti, 101
Ituri Forest, 39, 110, 112
Iyengar, 83
Iyer, 71–72
'Iyyar [Iyar], 22–23, 90
Izalco, 65
Izanagi no Mikoto, 15
Izanami no Mikoto, 15
Izeki, 64

J

Jabirringgi, 107
Jaburrara, 76
Jakun, 40
Jambūkhaṇḍa-Nirmāṇa Parva, 25, 70
James & van der Sluijs, 50

Janus, 140–41
jar, storage, 138
Jarriyi, 133–34, 144
Jaualin-wura, 53–54
Jeffers, 98
Jefferson, Thomas, 75–76, 127–28
Jeju Island, 135
Jerusalem, 89
Jesuit priest, 59
jewel-spear, 15
Ji Province, 24
Jicarilla Apache, 52
Jìn, History of, 61
Jīng Fáng, 61
Jìnshū, 61–62
Jiù Tángshū, 61
Jive'cla, 46
John, Saint, 87
John, Revelation of, 89
John of Lydia, 60
Johnson, Andy, 120
Johnson, Elias, 2–3, 85
Johnston, 37, 41
Jolon, 72, 77
Jones, 122, 141–42
Jones, Elsie Rose, 93, 106
Joorningor, 21
Joset, 111
Joshi, 120
Joshua ben Levi, 23, 90
Jotoy Ihavós, 6, 14, 114, 151
Jove. *See* Jupiter
Judaeo-Christian, 86, 89
Judah bar Ezekiel, 20
Judaism, 25
Jujuy, 88
Julchu´, 100
Julian, Juan, 52
Jumundik, 54
Jupiter, 20–21, 34–35, 59, 61–62, 66, 70–71
Juraqan, 94
Jyeṣṭhā, constellation, 70–72

K

Kabî-ngil-ngilibungî, 13
Kabti-ilāni-Marduk, 23
Kadimarkara [Kadimakara], 124
Ka´do, 100
Kahlke, 124
K'ahsho Got'ine, 29, 146
Kahungunu, Ngāti, 28, 138
Kaikai Vilu [Caicaivilu], 144–45
Kailāśā, Mount, 123
Kalaallit, 27–28
Kalapuya, 127
Kalevala, 91
Kalimantan, eastern, 147
Kallowa Anggnal Kude, 79
Kamalba, 102
Kamloops, 38, 103
Kampong Piasau, 14
kangaroo hunting, 108, 143
kangaroos, 78, 101, 143

giant, 1, 125
Kango, 112
Kanobo Mawari, 16
Kansas, 127
Karackarock, 45, 78
Kariyarra, 76
Kashinaua. *See* Caxinauá
Kasin, 14
Kasin-pit-piribungî, 14
Kassena, 147
Kaster, 35
Katherine (town), 107
Kavarna, 141
Keimatsu, 61
Kentucky, northern, 128
Kerrhprrh [Kerrk-perrk], 35–36
Ket (River), 129
kete, 137
Ketegaunseebee, 33, 44, 81, 130
kettle, 73
ketu, 71
Khanty, 75, 129
Kilki (mura), 103
Kim, 136
Kīmā [Kimah], 22–23, 90, 93
Kimberleys, 78, 100, 107
king, 37, 41, 50-51, 56–57, 60, 77, 83, 89, 91
King, 57
Kingsborough, 48, 86
Kinney, 88
Kintu, 47
Kiribati, 27, 148
kiṣru, 50
Klamath (Lake), 45, 119
K'múkamtch, 119
knee marks, 106
Knibb, 25
knife, 2, 150
Koch-Grünberg, 33, 116
Kogi, 45
Köhler, Ulrich, 63–64, 94, 116
Kōkāb, 59
Kōkab Nōgah, 59
Kollouches, 29–30
Konglish, 136
Konowî, 12
Koquethagechton, 76, 128
Korea, 45, 135
Kornelis, 14
Koropun, 12–13
Korporilya, 102
Korupun, 13
Kotsxáat, 114
Krakatoa, 68
Krasnoyarsk Krai, 129
Kreeh, 35
Kremos, Georgios, 147
Kroeber, 146
Kronk, 59, 64
Kronos, 3, 35, 121
Krren, 35
Krüger, 38
Kruijt, 147
Kulin, 142–43
Kumaon, 123

Kun, 42
Kurus, 70
Kuwilahun, 13
Kwányip [Kwonyipe], 35, 145
Kwîlca'na, 103
Kwonyipe. *See* Kwányip

L

Lachlan River, 126
ladder, 147
Laguna Escalante, 9, 113, 151
lake, inland, 91, 98
lakes, 2, 31, 43, 49, 73–74, 80, 87–88, 90, 93, 95–98, 119, 126, 131, 134, 142
Lakȟóta, 129
  Miniconjou, 74, 128
lalai times, 108–9
Lame Deer, John (Fire), 74, 128
lamp, 84
Lampsacus, Strato of, 142
Lampyris noctiluca, 87
land, drowned, 139
land bridges, 139, 141, 144
Land of Perfect Bliss, 32
land snake, 144
Langdon, 58
language, common, 3–4, 44
languages, 4, 126
Lángxīng [Lang-Hsing], 20
lathe, 24
Latin, 60, 88, 140, 142
latitudes, 39–40, 44
Latvians, 123
Laufer, 99–100
lava, distant, 68
LaViolette, 11, 48
layers, 5, 19, 28, 150
Layton, Robert, 100, 103–4, 108
Labānā, 59
Legge, 22
legs, 24, 39, 101
Leguán, 9, 113, 151–52
Lehmann, 148
Lèishuō, 10
Lena, river, 129
Lenape, 75–76, 127–28
Leontius, Saint, 21, 52
Lernean Hydra, 122
Leucas, 142
Leucosia, 140
Levine, 123
Lewis-Williams & Dowson, 103
Lę́x̣uwakīpa, 42–43
Leyenda de los soles, 118
Lǐ Bái, 61
Lǐ Cháowēi, 10
Lǐ Chúnfēng, 61–62
Lǐ Fǎng, 10, 61
Líbahon, 13
Library (pseudo-Apollodorus), 121
Libya, 122, 140–41
lid, 118, 138

Liemo, Lake, 91
Lienhardt, 147
lifting, 12, 28
light levels, 149
lightning, 1–2, 39, 71, 73–74, 97, 104–5, 107, 110–12, 115, 117, 127–28, 135
lightning arrows, 2
lightning bones, 123
Lightning Brothers, 107
Lightning Spirits, 109
light shaman, 16
Limlim people, 12
Lipari Islands, 141
Lisu, 45
Lithraea molleoides, 8
Lithuania, 40, 74, 87
Líu Ān, 10, 22, 24
Liú Xù, 61
lizard-man, 101
lizards, 101
  monitor, 45
Loango, 149
lock, 9
Loeb, 73, 77
Lohitāṅga, 71
Lo-ki-ye-wah, 37–38
Lone Pine Tree, 2, 85
lóng chǐ, 124
lóng gǔ, 124
Long Snake, 10
Louka, 147
Lucifer, 84, 86
lunar mansions, 70
lunar phases, 34
Luritja, 102
Luruk, 12
Luxton, 11–12, 95
Lydia, John of, 60
Lynd, James William, 105, 128–29

M

Ma'ădīm, 59
Macamob, 132
Mac-Donnell ridges, northern, 32
Macedonica (Theagenes), 121
Machapunga, 98–99
MacKenna, 144
Mackenzie (River), 30
Macleay, 126
Macrias, 140
Macrobius, 35
Macushi, 105
Maghā, constellation, 70
magic stick, 100
Mahābhārata, 25, 70, 72, 77, 83, 123
Mahādeva, 119–20
Mahasu, 13
Mahatara, 147
Mahāyāna, 29
Mah Meri, 40
Mair, 84
maize, 96
Majôctsi, 9, 149–50

Major (author), 10, 22, 24
Makiritare, 30
Mako Sicha, 128
Makovskoye, 129
Makunaima, 105
Malay tapir, 126
Malaysia, 40
Malgara, 103
Mali, 18
Malkarra, 92, 106
Mamaravi, 47
Ma'milji, 100
mammals, 1, 123
mammoths, 2–3, 122, 128–29
  carnivorous, 127
Man, Edward Horace, 100
Manabozho, 2
Mandarin, 20, 22, 61
Mándoki, 21, 52
Mandsu-shirin, 29
mane, fiery, 9
Mangamangai, 138
Mangazeya, 129
manikins, 94, 117
Manilius, 68
manioc garden, 118
manitou, great, 26
Manjamei, 147
Mañjuśrī, 29
Manna Hill, 100
Mansi, 72, 74–75
Manu, 119
Māori, 28, 136
Maori College, 137
Mapuche, 144
Mara, Mount, 106
marble, black, 92
Marduk, 23
Mariscal Estigarribia, 6, 14, 114, 151
Mārkaṇḍeya, 77
Mar-lum-bu, 53
Marmora, 141
marriage, sacred, 56
Mars, 21, 59, 61–62, 70–71, 88
marsupials, 13, 124–25, 134
Marumda, 73, 76
Mary, Maid, 91
Masamlu, 12
Mašémikens, 43
Mason, 72, 77, 85
mass deaths, 2, 38, 41, 95, 115
Massola, 143
mastodons, 2, 122, 128
Matangi-reia, 137
Matcito, 36, 40
Matsya Purāṇa, 119
Mattamuskeet, Lake, 96–98
Mawári, 17
Maximilliano, 5, 118
Maya, 10, 12, 68–69, 87, 93–94
Mayor, 121–23, 127
Mayuruberu, 73
Ma'yyan Gannīm, 90
Mazzal, 7
Mbene, 111
Mbuti, 39, 110, 112–14
McBeth, Kate Christine, 37

McBeth, Susan Law, 37–38
McCarthy, 100, 106–8, 124
McCleary, 148
McCrae, Georgiana, 143
McLean, Alexander, 55
medicine men, 79–80
Mediterranean Basin, 121
Mediterranean Sea, 142
Melaka, 40
Melaleuca, 76
Melanesia, 146
Melbourne, 31, 40, 78, 142–43
melting, 31, 41, 44, 49
Melton & Schriever, 95
Memoriales (Motolinía), 130
Mendocino County, 146
Menen, 27
Mercury, 50, 58–59, 61–62, 66, 71
mercy, 4, 45, 78, 98
Mesopotamia, 50
Messina, Strait of, 140
mēsu-tree, 23
metals, 30, 80
Metamorphoses (Ovid), 35, 122
metamorphosis, 148
meteor(ic), 50–52, 61–62, 64, 68–69, 71, 78, 82–83, 95, 98–99
meteor shower, 66, 98
meteorites, 52, 61
Meteorology (Aristotle), 68
methane bubbles, 129
Mexico, Mexican, 48, 62–65, 85
Mictlāntēuctli [Mictlantecuhtli], 85–86
Midraš ha-Gādōl, 90
Midrashic sources, 135
migration, 116
Milbrath, 64, 69–70
Milingimbi, 21, 54–55
military forces, 67
Milky Way, 14
Miller, 35, 40, 120
Mîmbanam, 12
Mimi, 106
minerals, 80
mines, 130
Miniconjou Lakȟóta, 74, 128
Minjiburu, 102
Minnaert, 66–67
Minnesota, 73, 104, 129
Miocene, 123
Mirach, 67
misery, 37, 45, 47, 78
mist, 9, 31
Mitjuna, 53
Miwa, 100
Mixcōātl, 86
Mixe, 148
Moihi Te Matorohanga, 138
molar, 122
molten tar, 28, 82, 112–13, 117
Momostenango, 118
Mongamsea, 129
Monier-Williams, 71

monsters, 1–2, 10, 17, 45, 78, 85, 105, 122, 126–27, 132
  age of, 2, 85
Monterey County, 72, 77, 85
moon, 6, 19–20, 22–26, 33–36, 40–41, 45–47, 57–60, 69–70, 81–83, 91–92, 97–98, 109–12, 120, 148–49, 151–52
  excess, 46
  fallen, 20
  fragmented, 87
Mooney, 4, 39, 93
moonlight, 28, 57
Mora, David, 77
Morichito, 16
morning, 53–54, 57, 64, 69, 84, 86, 101, 105, 138
Morning Glow, 52
morning star, 20–21, 26, 50–55, 65–66, 68, 81–86, 88, 93, 148
  red, 21
  tailed, 51
Mornington (Peninsula), 142–43
Moses, Dick, 133, 144
Most High, the, 84
Mother Earth, 46
Motolinía, 130
Motul, 69
Mound Pig, 10
mountain cat, 4
mountain of Crystal, 47
mountains, 12–13, 22, 24–25, 28, 30–35, 41, 43–44, 47–49, 65, 80–82, 128–30, 132–33, 136, 139, 144
  sky-supporting, 23
  sunset, 140–41
  volcanic, 132, 136
Mountains, Rocky, 30
mountaintops, 28, 42, 48, 82, 112
Mountford, Charles Pearcy & Edwards, 53–54, 101–2, 106–7
mount of congregation, 84
Mowaljarlai, David Bungal & Malnic, 79, 109
Mozley, 140–41
Msimango, 28, 47, 82, 113, 117
Muck, 11
mud, 13, 80
Mûhî, 14
Muir, 119
Mukherji, 85
Mundiga, 106–7
Mungeranie, 31
Munggugnangga, 109
Munkácsi, 74–75
mura mura, 103, 124
Murchison, 123
Murie, 51
Murray, 143
Murray Bridge, 101
Murray Prior Range, 133, 144
Murrumbidgee River, Lower, 126

mūsdē tēbēl, 135
mu-sho-sho-no-no, 82
Mutwa, Vusamazulu Credo, 28, 47-48, 82, 113, 117

N

nahin ocelutl, 130
Nahuatl, 64
Naikala, 21, 54-55
Naiyenesgony, 1-2
Nakotsia-kotchô, 30
Namsky District, 21, 52
Nanabush [Nanaboojoo], 2, 26-27, 80-82
Nānāhuatl [Nānāhuatzin], 148
Nanai, 99
Nansen, 44
Napier, 28, 138
Naples, Dio of, 21
Nappa Merrie, 102, 105
Narahari Achar, 25, 71-72
Natural History (Pliny), 139-40, 142
Navajo, 2
Nawu, 1
near-death experience, 32
near-extinction, 45, 78
Nebraska, 25-26, 51, 127
neck, 9, 140
Neebin, 37, 41
Nelson, 129
Nemean Lion, 122
Neogene, 122
Nepia Te Ika Pohuhu, 28, 138
Nepoko, 111
Neptune, 141
NEqa´umîn Waterfall, 103
neštamaláni, 65
Nestle, 89
Netherlands, central-eastern, 43
netherworld, 25, 27, 88
Neugebauer & Weidner, 57
New Guinea, western, 146
New Mexico, 2, 50, 52
New South Wales, 40, 92, 105, 126, 132
New Spain, 63
New York, 2, 85
New York State, 46
New Zealand, 28, 136
Ngadjuri, 100-101
Ngadyan, 134
Ngaju Dayak, 147
Ngama, 102
Ngamunugarri, Tarpot, 107
Ngarinyin, 79, 108-9
Ngarluma, 76
Ngarrindjeri, 32
Ngāti Hinepare, 28, 138
Ngāti Kahungunu, 28, 138
Ngimun, 135
Ngolngol (Rain Spirit), 109
Ngunaitponi, 32
Ngurulin, 108
Nias, 147
Nickelsburg & VanderKam, 25
Nickerson, 81
Nicola Lake, 103
nights, 6, 37
long, 46
Nihongi, 15
Niimíipu, 37-38
Nimbawah, 106
Nine Gullet, 10
Ninsiana, 57
Nisikni, 13
Nitsch, Twylah Hurd, 47
Nlaka´pamux, 103, 148
Noah, 41, 90, 144
Nock & Festugière, 75
Nohoch Ek', 93
noises, 13, 42
Nommo, 18
Nonomarran, 107
noon, 56-57
Nordenskiöld, Erland, 149
north, the farthest sides of the, 84
North America(n), 2, 26, 30, 75, 77
North Carolina, 2, 85, 93, 95-96, 99
North Island, 28, 138
North Star, 25-26
Northern Arizona University, 5
Northern Districts, 126
Northern Territory, 106-7
Northwest Territories, 3, 29, 44, 146
Npsan, 12
Nullarbor (Plain), 32, 125
Numfor, 148
Nüwa, 24
Nuxaché, 114
Nuxalk, 74, 148-49
Nyamal, 102
Nyiyija, 135

O

Ō no Yasumaro, 15
Oakley, 124
object, long, 78, 88, 117
ocean, 15, 24, 31, 43, 47, 73, 88-89, 125, 140-41, 143
Ochoa, José María, 4, 35
ochre, red, 21
Oenpelli, 106-7
Ogyges [Ogygus], 21
Ohio, 127
Ojeeg, 38-39, 41
Ojibwe, 32, 34, 36-39, 41, 44, 47, 79, 81-82, 99, 129
Oklahoma, 51, 120
Oku´te, 129
Old Bembo, 143
Oldfather, 140, 142
Olympian gods, 73, 121
omens, 25, 70
Ona, 36
Onktehi [Onkteri], 128-29
Ontario, 32-33, 44, 79, 81, 129-30

Opera et Dies (Hesiod), 139
Opler, 52
Oppenheim, 50, 57
Oppenheim & Reiner, 23
Opriiskisku, 52
optical illusion, 65, 68
optical-atmospheric approach, 67
Oqomiut, 43
Oraibi, 36, 40
Oraon, 74, 85
Oregon, 48-49, 103, 119, 127
Orinoco Delta, central, 15, 69
Orion, 140
Orizaba, Pico de, 64-65, 68
Oruendu, 111
Osage, 128
ôtjayuc, 8
otters, 39, 104
outcrop, 92, 107
Ouwehand, 148
Ōuyáng Xiū, 61
overturning, 27-28, 48-49, 112
Ovid, 30, 34-35, 122
Owen, Richard, 124, 126
Ox, 77
Oyahguaharh, 2

P

Pabîjon, 13
Pacajes, 42
Pacha-Camaj, 42
Pacheco, Antonio Lorenzano, 16-18
Pachulia, 120
Pacific northwest, 37, 75
Padang Berimbun [Bĕrambun], 40
pademelon, 133-34
paint, red, 103
paintings, 100, 103-4, 106-9
Paka-Jakes, 42
Palenque, 69
Palléne, 121-22
Palm Island, 144
Palöngawhoya, 49
Pamlico, 97
Panama, eastern, 148-49
Panaramittee (North), 100-101
Pandanus, 21, 53-55
Pandora, 138
Pankenier, 61, 67
Papua, 12
Paraguay, 6, 14, 46, 113, 149
parakeet, 35-36
Parāśara, 71
Pardo, 149
Paris, 63, 86
Parkantji, 92-93
parontomyth, 53, 56, 129
Pasico, 5, 118
Pasikni, 13
Pasin Pass, 12
Pātāla, 119-20

path(way), 14–16, 18–20, 26, 33
spiritual, 79
sun's, 20, 137
patriarchal cultures, 75
Pau, 5, 118
Pausanias, 121
Pawnee, 25–26, 51, 127
peaty soil, 97–98
Pechuël-Loesche, 149
Peck, 133
Pedro, 43
α and β Pegasi, 70–71
Peloponnesus, 121
Peloris, 140
peninsula, 122, 140
Pennsylvania, 96
Pentecost Island, 146
Pentiwa, Otto, 4
Perelko, Island of, 53
Perisoreus canadensis, 78
Persian, 41
Peru, 33, 79, 115
Peruch, Andrés Xiloj, 118
pestilences, 51
Peterson, 92
Petitot, 3, 30, 44, 147
Petosiris, pseudo-, 60
petroglyphs, 81, 99, 101–5, 107, 128
Phaethon, 84, 88
Phanagoria, 122
Phantoms, 30
Pharomachrus, 50
Phelps, Lake, 98
Philadelphia, 96
Philostratus, 121
Phlegra(e), Phlegrean Fields, 121–22
physical deformities, 148
Piasau, Kampong, 14
Pico de Orizaba, 65, 68
Piegan, 148
Pierce, Charlie, 125
Pietersma & Wright, 88
pig, 12–14
Pilbara region, 102
Pilcomayo, 8–9, 46, 150
Piliyam, 12
pillar, jade, 9
pillars, 6, 23–24, 40, 104, 139–40, 146
collapsing world, 23
Pima County, 4, 35
Pimentel, 130
Pimentola, 91
Pine, Fred, 33, 44, 81, 130
pine tree, 93
fast-rising, 119
Pingree, 60
Pipestone National Monument, 104
Pipil, 65–66, 68
Pirá-paraná region, 5, 118
pit, 84, 87–89, 100
Pitahawirata band, 25–26, 127
Pithecussae, 141
Pitta Pitta, 55

Pittingngor, 21
pivot, 24–25, 30
placentas, 18
plains, 31–32, 47
plane, ecliptic, 33, 66
planet, white, 70–71
planetary haloes, 68
planetary motions, irregular, 22
planets, 19–24, 49–52, 55–56, 58–60, 62, 64–67, 70–71, 79, 88, 119
sons of, 71
plants, 4, 32–33, 151
tobacco, 17
plateau, rugged, 106
Platnauer, 122
Plato, 3, 68, 75, 141
Pleiades, 23, 93
Pleistocene, 121, 123–24
Pliny the Elder, 139–42
Pliocene, Lower, 124
poa, 103
Poimandres, 75
Poirier, 84
pole, celestial, 17, 19, 49
pole star comet, 25
poles, geographical north, 41
Politicus (Plato), 3, 75
Polk County, 127
Pomo, East, 73, 76–77
Pond, 128–29
pond, large, 115
pools, 103, 108
Popol Vuh, 45, 69, 94, 118, 132
Pöqánghoya, 49
Port Lincoln, 1
Port Phillip (Bay), 142–43
Portuguese, 116
Poseidon, 140
pot, 118
Potawatomi, 2, 26–27
Potogojecs, 2, 27
Powell, 36–37, 40
Prairie-Falcon, 85
pre-Columbian, 63
prehistoric animals, large, 123
priestess, high, 56
priests, 28, 138, 147
Proboscideans, 123, 129
Proclus, 68
promontories, 140
Prometheus, 138
prophecy, 81, 88
Propontis, 142
Prothero & Schoch, 124
Prussian, 64
Psittacid family, 36
psychopomp, 16–17
Pungo, Lake, 98
Punta del Faro, 140
Purāṇic, 83
Purelko, 53–54
Purli Ngrangkalitji, 92
Purumdal pond, 14

Purús River, 73, 82
Pūrva Bhādra(padā), 70
pus, metamorphosed, 101
Puṣya, constellation, 70
Putnam, Anne Eisner, 112
Pygmies, 39

Q

Qiántáng, 9–10
Qöyawayma, Alfred H., 5
quarrelling, 47
quarry, 104
quartz, white, 101
quebracho
red, 8
white, 8
Quechua, 85
Southern, 79
Queen, S. A., 22
Queensland, 55, 102, 124–25, 133–34, 143–44
Quetzalcōātl, 48, 50–51, 56, 86
Quiché (Maya), 1, 44, 46, 69, 94, 117–19, 130, 132
quincunx glyph, 69
Quiñones Keber, 63–64, 86
Quintana, Juan, 72

R

Rab, 20
rabbits, 63, 104
race
first, 73, 77, 136
legendary, 117, 124
silver, 35
Rackham, 139–40, 142
Rākṣasa's, 123
Rahlfs, 84, 88
Rāhu, 70–71, 83
rain, 8, 10, 31, 33, 36, 48–49, 91–94, 96–98, 105, 107, 112, 115, 117–20, 125, 127
rain gods, 96–98
rain of fire and gravel, 118
rainbow, 14–16, 115
rainbow-serpent, 107, 134
rainstorm, black, 94, 118–19
Rāmāyaṇa, 123
Rangiatea, 137
Rangi-nui, 137
Raymond, Elsie, 107
rays
five, 60, 67
harsh, 119
rebellion, cosmic, 84
receptacles, 118, 136
Red Gorge, 101–2
Red Sea, 144
reeds, 24, 63
refuge, 8, 74, 113, 128
Reggio di Calabria, 140
Regulus, 70
Reguly, Antal, 72, 74
Rehu-tai, 137
Reiner, 23
Reiner & Roth, 23

Reptile Age, 125
reptiles, 11, 45, 56, 78
    giant, 125
resin, rain of, 94, 117–19
retrograde, 70
Revelation of John, 89
revenge, 27, 43
reversed sun, 20, 29
revolution, social, 43, 46
Rhodes, Castor of, 21
rice, 147
Riggs, 105, 129
ring, 102
Ringu Ringu, 55
Río Docamparó, 149
Río Sambú, 149
Río Tarasito, 149
Riordan, 29
ritual, 11, 56, 95, 106, 108, 137
river-banks. *See* banks
rivers, 31, 33, 47, 49, 73–74,
    80, 82, 89, 92, 95, 108, 115,
    118, 129, 142–43
Rivet, 149
Robertson, 69
Robinson, 21, 55
rock, fiery, 88
rock art, 81, 99–109
rocks, 5, 7, 27, 31, 48, 74, 80,
    83, 92–94, 101–9, 127–28,
    143, 150
    converted to, 109, 121
    picture, 104
rockshelter, 108
Rocky Mountains, 30
rodent, 9, 150
Roebourne, 76
Rohiṇī, 70–71
Roman, 30, 34
Romani, 30
Romi Kumu, 5
rope, 15–17, 53, 55, 95–96,
    138, 147
rope-bridge, 17–18
Rosebud Indian Reservation,
    74, 128
Rōš ha-Šānā, 23, 90
Roth, Harold, 22
Round Valley, 146
Royal Asiatic Society of Great
    Britain, 123
Roys, 11–12, 71, 77, 95
Rudra [Rudder], 82–83
Rufus & Tien, 20, 58, 61–62
ruler, 22, 24, 51
Russell, Robert, 143
Russian, 72, 74–75, 120

S

Sabah, 14
Šabbāt, 20, 59
Šabbəta'ī, 59
Sah-kah-odjew-wahg-sahor,
    33–34, 44, 81, 130
Saḥmet, 56
Sahtú, 29, 146
Saint John, 87

Saint Leontius, 21, 52
Śākadvīpa, 24–25
Sakha, 21, 52, 129
Salinan, 72, 77, 85
Salomon & Urioste, 79
Saltlicks, 127
Salvador, 65
Sama, 13
Samoan, 52, 138
Samogitians, 40, 74, 87
Samothrace, 142
Samuel (author), 135
San Antonio Mission, 72, 77,
    85
sand, 47–48, 81, 97
sand-clay pits, 122
Sanggalpunu, 12
Saṅkarṣaṇa, 119–20
San Leonardo de Escalante, 9
Sanskrit, 70
Santal, 85
Santa Teresita mission, 6, 14,
    114, 151
Ṣāpōn, Mount, 84
Sapulpa, 120
Sarapis, 84
Sargon II, 57
Saruk River, 12
Saturn, 34–35, 59, 61, 70–72
Saturnalia Convivia, 35
Sault Ste. Marie, 33, 44, 81,
    130
Savona, 103
Saylor, 127
scars, corporeal, 148
Schafer, 60–62
Schebesta, Paul, 39, 110–11
Schechter, 90
Scheftelowitz, 70
Schinopsis lorentzii, 8
Schinus molle, 7–8
Schmidt, 147
Schoolcraft, 39
Schorr & Malinowitz, 23, 90
Schultze Jena, 65–66
scintillations, planetary, 66,
    68, 71
scoops, wooden, 76
α, σ and τ Scorpionis, 71
scorpions, 89
Scott, 66
Scottish, 31, 93, 106
scrub, open, 134
scrub-turkey, 133
sea, 27, 30, 43, 49, 54, 72–74,
    76, 82, 88, 98, 122, 133, 138–
    44
    frozen, 38
sea-monsters, great, 140
sea of fire, 74
Sea of Marmora, 141–42
season
    luxuriant, 30, 34
    single, 34–35
seasonality, unstable, 22, 37–
    38
seasons, 3, 18, 22, 33–38, 40–
    41, 81

seat, iron, 90
Second World, 46, 49
Ṣedẹq, 20, 59
seeds, 41, 55, 76
    corn, 152
seismic activity, 134
Seler, 148
self-portraits, 106
Selk'nam, 35–36, 145, 149
Semiramis, 56
Seneca (Haudenosaunee), 46–
    47
Sennoi, 122
ša'ōl. *See* Sheol
Sēpar ha-Yašar, 135
Šepišāḻalawayéńčis, 43
Septuagint, 84–85, 88
Serbians, 146
Serekasi, 12
Seroshevskiy, 21, 52
serpent
    feathered, 56
    great horned, 2
    world-supporting, 120
Serpent of Life, 11
serpentine deities, 56
serpents. *See* snakes
Servius Auctus, 60
Śeṣa, 120
settlers, 97, 125
Seven Sisters, 105
Severnaya Sosva River,
    Upper, 74
sexual congress, 44
shaman, 8, 26–27, 32, 36, 79,
    112–13, 117, 127, 129, 138,
    148, 151
shamanic trance, 15
Shānxī, northwest, 124
shark, big, 53
Sharpe, Bill, 97–98
Sharpe & Tunbridge, 126
Shasta, 45
Shastri, 25
Shawnee, 120
sheep, 8, 92
shell fish, 77
shelter, 7, 41
Sheol, 84, 88
Shǐjì, 22, 61, 67
ship, 141, 143
Shooter, 129
shooting, 10, 13, 16, 29, 74, 83,
    99–100, 120, 128
shores, 30, 98, 122, 124, 131,
    145, 149
shoulder, 67
Shuswap, 38, 55, 103
Siberia, 21, 29, 52, 72, 75, 129
Sibylline Oracles, 88–89
Sicily, Sicilian, 140–41
Sicily, Diodorus of, 121–22,
    140, 142
sick man, 32
Siebert, Otto, 124
Sikuani, 75, 148
Siletz reservation, 49
Sīmǎ Qiān, 22, 61, 67

Simms, Maxey, 120
Simon (author), 23, 90
Sing-Bhonga, 36
Sioux, 73, 104–5, 128
Sipsongpanna Dǎi Autonomous Prefecture, 120
šir-namursaǧa, 57
Sirens' Cape, 140
Sirinan, 14
Sirius, 20, 67
Sirrider Swāmi, 83
Śiva, 120
Śiwalīk Hills, 123
Sîyelma, 13
Skeat, Walter William & Blagden, 40
Skidi band, 51–52
skin, 4, 55
Skinner, 78
skins, brown, 80
skulls, 124, 126
sky and earth
  inversion of, 28, 48, 82, 110, 112–13, 117, 151
  separation of, 135, 137, 147
sky dog, 61
Sky-father, 28, 137
sky, low, 147
sky man, 146
Slavitt, 141
sleep, 15, 44, 54, 90
  narcotic, 82
smallpox epidemic, 65
Smith, 28, 125, 138
smith, divine, 25
Smith, Louisa, 49
Smith, William, 49
Smith, William Ramsay, 31–32
smoke-darkened skies, 97
smoke rings, volutes, 63, 66
smoking stars, 63, 68–70
snake
  giant monster, 43
  land, 144
snakes, 11, 17, 43, 45, 52, 64, 78, 92, 104, 129, 144
snow, 10, 38, 40–44, 47–48
Snow God, 41
Sohoburoho band, 16
soil, 31, 80
  lignite, 121
Solinus, 121
solitude walker, 146
Solomon Islands, 30
Somalis, 144
Sombra, Vicente Penna, 33, 115
Sòng Qí, 61
Sòng Shǐ, 61
Songgûwa, 13
songs, 4, 57, 78, 90, 101, 136
Songs of Dzitbalché, 68–69
Soot Heads, 10
sores, 118, 138, 148
Sótuknang, 49, 136
souls, 16–17, 32, 50–51, 53, 69, 115–16
South Africa, 146

South Australia, 1, 30–32, 100–102, 105, 124, 126
South Dakota. *See* Dakota, North and South
South Star, 25–26
South Sudan, 147
Spain, Spanish, 11, 36, 56, 62–64, 86, 93, 130, 139, 145
Spanish-Mexican, 51
spears, 4, 14, 51, 76, 143
species, 2, 27, 36, 42, 75–76, 89, 108, 121, 123–24, 147
  arboreal, 8
  mammal, 126
Speck, Frank G., 96
Spences Bridge, 103
Spica, 70
spirit helpers, 16
spirit, great, 105, 108
Spirit, Great, 26, 96
spirit world, 20, 104
splintering, splinters, 12–13, 49, 87
Spokane (Lower), 131
spring, 89
spring (season), 23, 28–29, 34–35, 42, 52, 61, 138
  eternal, 34
Śrāvaṇa, constellation, 70
staff, 31, 45, 78
Standing Rock Reservation, 129
star
  big, 50, 67, 87
  flaming, 30
  great, 88–89
  mountain of the, 68
  pole, 25, 71
Star, Big or Great, 52, 93
star groups, 70
Star of Death, 26
stars, 18–19, 21–26, 28, 50–55, 57, 60–63, 65–67, 69, 75, 77–79, 81–83, 85–90, 92–94, 96–99, 109
  battling, 68
  blazing, 2, 85
  dislodged, 23
  fallen, 99
  new, 50
  ominous, 61–62
  phantom, 62
  tailed, 96
  terrible, 82
stars of God, 84
starvation, 96–97, 131
Statesman (Plato), 3, 75
Statius, 122
Steiger, 47
Stender, 123
Stepanus, 13
Stephen of Byzantium, 121
Stevenson, 2
stick(s), 94–95
  magic, 100
  throwing, 76, 108
Stieglitz, 20
St. Lawrence, 85

stone(s), 26–27, 48, 73, 80, 94–95, 100–101, 104, 108, 118, 125, 127, 129, 133, 137, 145
  five-colored, 24
  grinding, 103
  hot, 132–33, 144
  kapamari, 133
  sacral, 12, 137
  white, 103
stone capitals, 142
storm, 11, 21, 45, 52, 104
Strabo, 121–22, 140, 142
Strachan, Carolyn, 134
Strait of Gibraltar, 139
straits, 139–40, 144
Strato of Lampsacus, 142
strawberries, 34
Strehlow, 32
Stride (star), 67
string, 20–21, 52–55, 149
substances
  liquid, 120
  oily, 147
  resin-like, 118
  scalding, 74
subterranean creatures, 129
Suen, 57
Śukraḥ, 71
Sumatra, 147
Sumber, mountain, 29
Sumer(ian), 50, 56, 149
Sumeru, 17, 29, 146
summer, 17, 21, 35–37, 40, 41, 52, 61, 65, 120, 131
Summer, 37, 41, 47
summer king, 37
summer solstice, 87
sun, 18–20, 22, 24–26, 28–29, 33–37, 40–41, 45–48, 57–59, 69–70, 73, 81–83, 99–100, 117–20, 148–49, 151–52
  anthropomorphic, 40
  bleeding, 120
  centre of the, 120
  descending, 82
  enclosed, 46
  fallen, 20
  first, 100
  fragmented, 87
  low, 35
  reversed, 20, 29
  strong, 73, 82
  third, 100, 118
  tied, 55
  wounded, 29
sun and moon, 6, 22–23, 33, 36, 46–47, 62, 73, 91, 151
Sun Chief, 51
Sun Rising over the Mountain, 33, 44, 81, 130
sun shooting, 29, 127
sunlight, weak, 73
sunrise, first, 45–46
sunrises, 64, 68
suns, multiple concurrent, 29, 83
sunset, 59, 61, 68, 104
sun's scribe, 58

Sun's son, 70, 72
supaya, 42
Superior, Lake, 80
Supreme White, 67
survival, 34, 44, 75, 80, 82, 96, 113, 115, 125, 151
Sūryaputreṇa, 70, 72
Sûtso, 50
Sūzhōu Astronomical Chart, 20, 58, 62
Svāti, 70–71
Śveta Ketu, 72
śveto grahaḥ, 71
swamps, 79–80, 93, 95, 97, 105
Swimmer, 4, 39
Swimming Mound, 127
sword, fire-steeled, 90
Symplegades, 142
Syria, 140

T

Taeniptera pyrope, 42
Tahchiini clan, 2, 50
Tahitian, 146
Tàibái, 20
tail, 21, 50, 52, 58, 60, 68, 71, 79–80, 82, 89–90, 93
Tàipíng Guǎngjì, 10
Tàipíngyùlǎn, 61
Tàishǐgōng Shū, 22, 61, 67
Talbott, 62, 148
Talmūd, 20, 90
Tamakaka, 137
Taman Peninsula, 122
Tama-tekapua, 137
Tāne, 137–38
Tāne-matua, 138
Tāne-nui-a-rangi, 138
Tāne-te-wānanga, 137–38
Táng, 61
Tangaroa, 138
Tanggusene, 12
Tanté, 46
Tanuuj, 46
Táo Yǒnghuá, 40
Tapirus indicus, 126
Tapuitea, Lady, 52
tar, molten, 28, 82, 112–13, 117
Tarlow, 76
Tasiilaq, 43
Tatars of Daba, 123
T'atsaot'ine, 3, 44
tattoo patterns, ancestral, 148
Tauromenium, Timaeus of, 121
Tä-vi, 37
Tawennaki, 2, 85
Tawhai, 138
Tawhiri-matea [Tawhirimatua], 137–38
Tawhiri-rangi, 137
Taz River, 129
Tcabuinji, 107
tea tree, 76
tears, 120
Tebi, 110

Tedlock, 45, 69, 94, 118, 132
teeth, 13, 122, 128, 150
 mammoth's, 129
Teetonwan, 104–5
Teit, 38, 103
Tempassuk district, 14
temple, 84
Temple of the Cross, 69
Tenenésk, 145
Tenten Vilu [Trentren Vilu], 144–45
Te Pu-motomoto, 137
Terry, 88
Tesakov, Alexey, 122
Tēzcatlepōca [Tezcatlipoca], 86
Tȟáȟča Hušté, 74, 128
Theagenes, 121
thearch, 23–24
Thebaid, 122
theft, 11, 47, 58, 139
Theogony, 73
Theristicus melanopis, 42
Thilo, 60
thirst, 55, 96
Thíthuŋwaŋ, 105
Thompson, David, 128
Thompson Siding, 103
throwing stick, 76, 108
thunder, 9, 22, 43, 56, 91–92, 97, 104–5, 112, 115, 134–35
thunder dragon, 99
thunderbirds, 73–74, 128–29
thunderbolts, 2, 71, 74, 85, 121, 128
Thunders, 39
thunderstones, 121, 124
Thylogale, 134
tiāngǒu, 61
Tiānguān Shū, 61, 67
Tiānwénxué, 61
tidal wave, 72, 90
Tierra del Fuego, 35–36, 42, 145
Tihi-o-manono, 137
Tikitiki-o-rangi, 137
Tilcara, 88
tilting, 114
Timaeus, 68
Timaeus of Tauromenium, 121
Tino taata, 146
Tirawa, 127
Tisnado, Alasco, 52
Titanomachy, 73, 121
Titans, 73
Titicaca, Lake, 42
ti-tree, 103
Tlāhuizcalpantēuctli [Tlahuizcalpantecuhtli], 86
tobacco smoke, 15–18
tobacco snuff, 82
Tobaidischinni, 1–2
Tohono O'odham, 3–4, 35
Toi-hua-rewa, 137
Toi-o-nga-rangi-taupuru, 137
Tokpa, 49
Tokpela, 136

Toltecs, 51
tombs, 88, 122
Tompson, 126
Toneri Shinnō, 15
Tonge, Phyllena Wallace, 4, 35
tongues, 9, 14, 107, 132
topsy-turvy, 27
Toqtogha, 61
torch, 56–57, 89
totemic beings, 106
Tovok Ihavós, 8, 46, 150
toxic effects, 89
trails, 60, 79, 93
Trapezus, 121
tree, 6–8, 10, 12–13, 34–36, 79, 81, 95, 97, 113, 115, 124, 130, 132, 136–38, 150–52
 cabbage, 103
 fast-rising pine, 119
 hard, 9, 113
 hollow sycamore, 39
 milkwood, 21
 molle, 8
 pepper, 7
 pine, 93
 tī, 103
tree kangaroo, 12–13
trees
 bloodwood, 32
 bottle, 108
 deciduous, 35–36
 five, 11
Trenary, 62
Trentren Vilu. *See* Tenten Vilu
Triaster, 67
tropical habitat, 40
troughs, wooden, 143
Trugan, 129
trunks of the sky, two, 14
Tschiffely, 88
Tsiché, 6–7
Tsimshian, 121, 127
Tsuskwǎnûŋ´nǎwa´tǎ, 4
Ttsinnayinén, Julien, 3, 44
tube, 80
Tucci, 33
Tucker, 82
tuco-tuco teeth, 9, 150–51
tuft, 21, 53, 55
Tulen Synty, 90–91
Tu-mata-uenga, 138
Tunbridge, Dorothy, 126
Tungus, 129
Tunis(ia), 122, 140
Tuōtuō, 61
Tupai, 137
Turam, 13
Turkish Straits, 141–42
Turnbull, 112
Turner, 52, 138
turtle, great, 24
Turukhan, 129
Tuscarora, 2, 85, 95, 99
Tvaṣṭṛ, 24–25
Tvveedale, 84, 88
twins, 1–2, 14, 49, 69
Typhoon, 10

Tyrrell, 128
Tzitzimime, 56, 85–86
Tzontemoc, Tzontemocque, 56, 85–87

U

Uddelermeer, 43
Udege, 29
Uepoto, 137
UFOs, 60
Ugni, 95
Ukko, 91
Ukomno'm, 146
Uk'ux kaj, 94
Umpqua, Lower, 48–49
Unaipon, David, 32
underground, 49, 103
underworld, 5, 10–11, 25, 50, 55, 69, 94, 116, 120
Ungarinyin, 108–9
Uŋgud, 108
unidentified flying object, 60
United States, 4, 75
Unktehi, 73, 128–29
Ur, 56
Uralic, 75
Uran Mandsu-shirin, 29
Uru-roa, 137
Uškëšlä́nen, 43
Utah, 37
Ute, 37, 45
Utica, 122
Uttara Bhādra(padā), 70
Uttara Phālgunī, 70
Uttarakhand, 123

V

Vá·as, 114
Väinämöinen, 90
Valerius Flaccus, 140–41
Valladolid, 94
valleys, 31–32, 74, 143, 145
van Beek, 19
van der Geer, 123–24
van Hasselt, 148
Vana Parva, 77, 123
Vanuatu, 146
vara, 41
Varāhamihira, 71–72
Varanus, 45
Varro, 21, 86
Vasu, Minendranatha, 36
Vāyu, 71
Veckenstedt, 40, 74, 87
Vedānta, 83
Vedas, 70
vegetables, 33, 96, 115
vegetation, 30–31, 34
VEI (volcanic explosivity index), 68
Velikovsky, 50, 58–59, 62–64, 66, 70–72, 135
Veluwe, 43
Vendīdād, 41
Venezuela, 15, 17, 69
Ventura, 145

Venus, 21, 50, 52–53, 55–58, 60–64, 66, 68, 70–71, 86
  horned, 52
  sons of, 72
Venus' aureole, 67
Venus generates white comets, 60
Venus' smoking, 62, 64, 68
verdancy, 30, 34–35
vertical cylinder, 14
vessel, 75, 90
Vesuvius, Mount, 121
Vickers-Rich & Archbold, 125
Victoria, 1, 31, 40, 131
Vidale, 41
Vili, 149
villages, 8, 16, 33, 115, 131, 141
vine, long, 138
Virgil, 60
visionary experience, 32
Viśvakarmā, 24–25
Vogt, 75
voice, 4, 135, 146
volcanic field, 132
volcano, volcanism, 1, 64–66, 68, 117, 131–33, 135–36, 144
von Humboldt, baron Friedrich Alexander, 64–66, 68
von Schröter, 91
von Weiher, 148
Vulgate, 84, 88
Vuqub-Kaqix, 132
Vyāsa Muni, 25, 70, 72, 83

W

Wabanung, 81
Wabmaymay, 33–34, 44, 81, 130
Waccamaw(, Lake), 95–96, 99
Wacheeta, 97
Wafford, James D., 4
Wagner, 120
Wäinämöinen. *See* Väinämöinen
Wai-rarapa, 138
Wakinyan (Tanka), 73–74, 128
wall, 107-8, 147
  great rock, 132
Wall Perné, Gustaaf van de, 43
wallaby, 32
  black-nose, 133
  grey, 133–34
Wambilari, 133, 144
Wanalirri, 109
wānanga, 137–38
Wandjinas, 107–9
Wang, 45
Wangkangurru, 30, 34
Waniyok, 12, 14
war, 25, 37, 67, 70, 85–86, 88, 137
Waróna, 108
Warao, 15–16, 18, 69
Warburton, 30–31
Wardaman, 107

Waria, Barney Gunaia Ngadjibuna, 100–101
Warlpiri, 102
Warner, 53
Waruni hill, 101
Washington State, 103, 131
Wassén, 149
Watelbring, 102
water, 4–5, 10–11, 24, 31–32, 42–44, 48–49, 72–76, 82–83, 88–91, 93, 95–96, 112, 127–29, 131–36, 141–46
  boiling, 72–74
  drainage, 98
  fiery, 75
  fresh, 48, 82, 101
  frozen, 31, 39
  sacred, 109
water food, 112
water gardens, 112
water man, 146
water monsters, 73, 128
water snake, 144
Waterfall Creek, 103
Waterfall, NEqa´umîn, 103
waterfalls, big, 103
Waters, Frank, 4–5, 49, 136
Watson, 22
Watson, George, 135
waves, 47, 131, 140, 145
weapon, 45, 73, 78
Webb, Captain William Spencer, 123
Weidner, 57
Weltfish, 51
Wénshān Zhuàng and Miáo Autonomous Prefecture, 40
West Flanders, 27
Western Australia, 76, 102
western sea, great, 30
Whatahoro Jury, Hoani Te, 28, 138
Whatu-kuras, 137
wheat, bearded, 34
Whedbee, Charles Harry, 97
whirlwinds, 48, 133, 137
Whis-tel-po-sum, 131
white circle, 54
White Eyes, 76, 128
White-sea-mist, 137
Widmakara, 100
Wilbert, Johannes, 16–18, 69
Wilbert & Simoneau, 6–9, 14, 46, 113–15, 148, 150–52
Wilcannia, 92, 105
wildflowers, 32
Wiljali, 105
Willamette Valley, 127
Willow, Dick, 93, 106
Wilson, Mount, 132
Winckler, 56
wind
  north, 152
  south, 46
winds, 22, 25, 28, 48, 71, 82, 96–97, 112, 118, 133–34, 137, 152
  catastrophic, 48

cold, 35, 38, 133
wing-feathers, 146
Winikina, 15–17
Winner, 74, 128
winter, 35, 37, 40–41, 44, 49, 73, 77–78, 120, 129
Winter (Ojibwe), 47
winter giants, 43
winter king, 37
Winterreuzen, 43
Wiradjuri, 1, 40
wisdom, 3, 136
Wissler & Duvall, 148
Witdjini, 103
Withnell, 76
Wodoi, 108
Wodongari, 108
Wolaro, 108
wolf, 3, 103
Wolf (person), 51
Wolf Star, 20, 67
Woljamidi, 108
Woma, 124
womb, 55, 136
Wombat-skin, 132
Wongupali, Manuwa, 21, 55
wood(s), 15, 35, 94, 97–98, 118
woodcarvings, 94, 117
woolly rhinoceroses, 121
world axis. *See axis mundi, axes mundi*
world-observing man, 74
worms, 4
Worms, 54
Wormwood, 89
Worn-out-Blanket, 4
.*wòtàem·i-*, 100
Wurundjeri, 31, 40, 45, 78

X

Xacopancalqui, 86
Xbalanque, 1, 69, 132
Xcanul, 132
Xiāo Zǐxiǎn, 61
Xiàojīng Běnjì, 22
xihuitl, 64
Ximiera, 139
Xīn Tángshū, 61
Xolmis pyrope, 42
Xu, 61

Y

Yacatēuctli [Yacatecuhtli], 86
Yahweh, 76
Yájaašága, 43
Yakutsk, 129
Yali, 12–13
Yámana, 42–43, 46
yams, 53, 143
Yamuti, 126
Yandruwandha, 102
Yang dag rgyal po, 33
Yangoor, 20
Yankee Yankee, 143
Yáo, 9–10
Yaolngura, 53

yarkətē ṣāpōn, 84
Yarra River, 143
Yarrabah, 133–34, 144
Yearbearers, 12
Yeli, pig-tree, 12–14
Yellow River Chart, 61
Yellow Road, 20
Yenisei, 129
Yi, 10
Yidindji, 133, 144
Yidyam, 135
Yima, 41
Yingalarri, 107
Yirrkala, 53
Yiwarlarlay, 107
Yìwén Jí, 10
Yocah Ek, Lake, 93–94
Yolngu, 20–21, 53–55
Youn, 37–38
Young Bull, 26, 127
Yucatán, Yucatec, 10, 68–70, 93–94
Yuchi, 120
yuga, 82, 119–20
Yukon River, lower, 129
Yúnnán, 40, 120
Yunta, 100
Yup'ik, 129
Yurugu, 18
Yutana Nire, 2, 85

Z

Żamaites, 87
Zapata, Jaime, 17
Zebbaj, 56
Ẓedek. *See* Ṣedeq
Zēng Zào, 10
zenith, 15–18
zephyrs, gentle, 34
Zeus, 121, 138–39
Zhu Jialu, 120
Zhuānxū, 23–24
Zhúshū Jìnián, 22
Zipacna, 132
zodiacal light, 14, 66
Zöllner, 13–14
Zontemoc, 85–86
Zoroastrians, 30, 41, 74
Zulu, 27–28, 47–48, 82, 112–13, 117
Zuñi, 2, 72, 127

Printed in Great Britain
by Amazon